Muslim Devotions

OTHER BOOKS ON ISLAMIC STUDIES PUBLISHED BY ONEWORLD:

City of Wrong: A Friday in Jerusalem, M. Kamel Hussein (trans. Kenneth Cragg), ISBN 1-85168-072-1

Companion to the Qurán, William Montgomery Watt, ISBN 1-85168-036-5

Defenders of Reason in Islam: Mu'tazilism from Medieval School to Modern Symbol, ISBN 1-85168-147-7

The Event of the Qur'án: Islam in its Scripture, Kenneth Cragg, ISBN 1-85168-067-5

The Faith and Practice of Al-Ghazálí, William Montgomery Watt, ISBN 1-85168-062-4

Islam and the West, Norman Daniel, ISBN 1-85168-129-9

Jesus in the Qur'án, Geoffrey Parrinder, ISBN 1-85168-094-2

Muhammad: A Short Biography, Martin Forward, ISBN 1-85168-131-0

Muslims and Christians Face to Face, Kate Zebiri, ISBN 1-85168-133-7

On Being a Muslim: Finding the Religious Path in the Modern World, Farid Esack, ISBN 1-85168-146-9

The Qur'án and its Exegesis: Selected Texts with Classical and Modern Muslim Interpretations, Helmut Gätje, ISBN 1-85168-118-3

Qur'án, Liberation and Pluralism, Farid Esack, ISBN 1-85168-121-3

Rabi'a: The Life and Work of Rabi'a and Other Women Mystics in Islam, Margaret Smith, ISBN 1-85168-085-3

Rúmi: Poet and Mystic, Reynold A. Nicholson, ISBN 1-85168-096-9

A Short History of Islam, William Montgomery Watt, ISBN 1-85168-109-4

A Short Introduction to Islamic Philosophy, Theology and Mysticism, Majid Fakhry, ISBN 1-85168-134-5

Voices of Islam, John Bowker, ISBN 1-85168-095-0

Muslim

DEVOTIONS

A Study of Prayer-Manuals in Common Use

CONSTANCE E. PADWICK

ONEWORLD
OXFORD

MUSLIM DEVOTIONS: A STUDY OF PRAYER-MANUALS IN COMMON USE

Oneworld Publications
(Sales and Editorial)
185 Banbury Road
Oxford OX2 7AR
England

Oneworld Publications
(U.S. Marketing Office)
PO Box 830, 21 Broadway
Rockport, MA 01966
U.S.A.

Reprinted 1997

A CIP record for this book is available
from the British Library

ISBN 1-85168-115-9

Printed and bound in Finland by WSOY

CONTENTS

PART 4: OUTSIDE THE PRAYER-RITE

ACKNOWLEDGMENTS

Much rich kindness must be left to the thanks of Him who is *Ash-Shākir*. Here I can only offer my gratitude to a few—to Miss E. N. Aidin of Isfahan, for prayers used in her city; to Archdeacon Barakat Ullah, formerly of Lahore, for taking me round the bookshops there; to Dr Dwight M. Donaldson, formerly of Meshed, for his analysis of the relevant parts of the Shī'a traditionists; to Dr Hendrik Kraemer, for reading and criticizing the manuscript; to Dr Howard Read, for modern Turkish booklets; to Miss Freya Stark, for information about the Bā-'alawi leaders in Ḥadramaut; to Miss Katherine Henrey and the Reverend Donald Blackburn for long labour on the transliteration of the Arabic; to the S.P.C.K. for expert care spent on a troublesome manuscript; to Dr W. Montgomery Watt for his kindness in reading the proof; and not least to those under whose roofs the book was put together, the Russian nuns of Ain Karim near Jerusalem and the hostesses of Harlesford, Brighton, and Whitehill Chase, Bordon.

CONSTANCE E. PADWICK

NOTE

In translation the customary honorifics, except after the name of God, have been omitted. The word Muḥammad is sometimes represented by M. The names of well-known places are printed in western spelling.

INTRODUCTION

To anyone who haunts the bookshops of the Muslim world, the sight becomes familiar of a pile of humble little prayer-books. They may lie half buried by school-books and novels in a busy town, or stocked behind all manner of goods in a country grocer's shop, or prominently displayed in a little bookshop by the entrance to some great mosque, or spread on the ground when a pedlar opens his pack. Through all the stresses to-day of nationalist emotion or communist solicitation, these little books still live their quiet life.

It seemed to the present writer that in Islam, as in any other faith, a stranger desiring not to remain a stranger could best feel the pulsing life of religion through a study of the devotions actually in use. A generous gift made it possible to purchase the popular devotional manuals in Arabic, or partly in Arabic, on sale in the cities of Aden, Aleppo, Algiers, Amman, Baghdad, Beyrout, Bombay, Cairo, Damascus, Delhi, Hama, Istanbul, Jerusalem, Lahore, Omdurman, Sidon, Tanta, Tunis, and to undertake the study of them. A few more were kindly sent by friends from Iran, Nigeria, and Bengal.

Many of the little books are common to practically all the above-mentioned cities and travel far beyond them. Dr Hendrik Kraemer writes that in Indonesia the more devout circles have in use such works as *Dalā'il al-khairāt* of al-Jazūlī, introduced by pilgrims from Mecca. The writer has seen in the courtyard of a printing press in Bombay huge bales of Arabic books, Qur'āns, and these small works of devotion, destined for Java. A few of the prayer-manuals are translated into the languages of Asian Muslims for whom Arabic is a sealed tongue, and the Malay students at the Azhar are used by the neighbouring publishing firm of Shaikh Muṣṭafā al-Bābī al-Ḥalabī as translators and proof-readers of these works for Malay readers.

In purchasing the books it was my desire to avoid the more esoteric works for the inner life of the dervish orders, and inquiry was made as to what had a popular sale. Even so, the majority of the books proved to be linked with one or other of the orders that have played, and still in these days of their official submergence play, so great a part in the life of Islam. Indeed it seems almost impossible for a man seeking for instruction in prayer, beyond directions for the daily prayer rite, to avoid works connected with one or other of the orders. Since these became illegal in Turkey there is a dearth of devotional material in Istanbul, once so rich a centre. All that is on public sale consists of little books of Qur'ān *sūras* and instructions in the prayer-rite in the Turkish script. Educated people sometimes use the *Masnavi* of Jalāl-ad-Dīn ar-Rūmī as a bedside devotional book. *Karınca Duası*, "the Ant Prayer", is hawked about the street in Arabic as a charm, and there seems to be a tiny revival of Arabic printing in what may be called the cathedral town of Bursa.

Inquiry among Muslim friends in Arabic lands makes it clear that to possess and use the prayers of one of the orders (except such devotions as are reserved for its inner life and only used with personal authorization) does not necessarily imply membership in the order in question. This is borne out by the existence of books containing famous *awrād* or *aḥzāb* from unconnected orders under one cover, while others contain composite *awrād* claiming to include choice morsels from them all. In this book, prayers from many famous mystics are quoted, but only those found in manuals which the seller claimed to be "popular".

A limitation, for reasons of time and space, had to be imposed, though with reluctance, in the omission of reference to the very numerous volumes of popular religious verse published under the title of *Mawlid*. It is as if in making a study of the popular devotions of Christendom all carols were omitted.

It soon became clear that the publication of these manuals was not publication as known in the West. There is no copyright, no authoritative edition, and generally no distinction between printer and publisher. While a few larger firms in Cairo and Bombay have a regular trade in prayer-manuals for export, for the most part small printings are undertaken here and there. These may be at the cost of a pious benefactor or because the presence of a group of devotees shows a local printer an opportunity for sale. The manuals on which this book is built were purchased over a period of years, and it became a question whether in referring to them page references were of any use. The small, ephemeral edition may be replaced (now that lithography has given way to printing from type) by another with different paging. Page references have been given as a rough guide to the position of an extract within a given book. It is a matter of very great regret that space and expense forbid the publication of the extracts in Arabic.

Friends, both Muslim and Christian, have objected that the study of devotional manuals does not give a true picture of the religious life of the rank and file, but only of the more devout. One who himself held a high position in a dervish order remarked to the writer that for the rank and file the prayers of Islam were "mechanical". To this we reply that while such mechanizing by the masses is a grievous fact, just as the carelessness of the masses in Christendom is a grievous fact, yet none the less we should desire to have worship, Muslim or Christian, judged not by what it means to the lukewarm and the untaught, but by what it gives to those who try to enter fully into its life. This is not only a fairer procedure for the understanding of the life of devotion but it is also probable that in learning what devotions mean when carried to intensity we best learn also to understand the diffused and weakened religious ideas of the masses.

The little books represent the spiritual influence of leaders in many centuries and many countries. There is at one extreme what many Muslims will recognize as a degradation towards sheer magic, a tendency of folk-religion everywhere; at the other extreme are prayers of utter devotion most humbling to our cowardly souls. In this book no attempt has been made to build up an *Idealtypus* of the Muslim worshipper, but rather to show under each heading the types of prayer found, in their range from the naïve and crude to the deeply spiritual.

The sources of the manuals differ widely in date and provenance, and the objection might reasonably be raised that to study these works together must be unscientific. They represent such varied stages in the evolution of theological thought that identical terms may be used by these writers with very varied shades of meaning.

To this we can only reply that this book is not a work of scholarship but a study of religious life to-day, and since all these sources are to-day exerting their influence they must to that extent be treated as contemporary. In trying to describe the ideas found in the manuals the writer has avoided the attempt (far beyond her scholarship) to go outside them and to trace the history in theology of the great terms employed. Fascinating as that might be it could only have blurred a picture which attempts to give some idea of contemporary popular devotion.

Authorship

Nor have we attempted to disentangle the many questions that must arise as to the authenticity of the authorship ascribed to these devotions. It is high time that both Muslim and Western scholars undertook a scientific study not only of what might be called liturgiology, the history of the official devotions of Islam, but of its devotional literature in general. Authorship is often difficult to detect from the fact that the compilers are not interested in it. Among the prayers attributed to a saint will be included, with no indication of their origin, the devotions that he used or recommended from earlier sources. Enough for the compiler that they were the prayers in use by that saint and his circle.

Even with the great saints whose biographies have been carefully studied, and some of whose works have been scientifically edited, much remains to be done in this direction. In the case of 'Abd al-Qādir al-Jīlānī, for instance, even a casual reader is pulled up short by a doubt as to whether that haunting dialogue the *Ghawthiyya*, in its pregnant simplicity of form one of the high-water marks in Muslim spiritual literature, can be from the same pen as many of the sermons and prayers attributed to him and marked by a certain floridity and over-abundance. Where have we the *ipsissima verba* of the saint, and where the re-touching of disciples?

Besides the tendency, common to all religions, to attribute works from the circle he inspired to some great saint himself (we have examples in the cases of St Bernard and St Francis), these Muslim prayers often show obviously legendary attributions—not, however, without religious significance.

When devotions are attributed to dictation by Al-Khiḍr, to a voice heard issuing from the tomb of 'Alī, or to revelation in a vision by the Prophet himself, they come to the ordinary worshipper with the voice of primitive and saintly authority.

A list of the manuals studied appears on page 289. Here we will briefly trace what appear to be the main streams of influence in their compilation.

1. Devotions attributed to Early Saints and Fathers

While such attributions may in part have been a method of protection for new devotions, there would appear to be also a more spiritual connection. When later Jewish books or Christian apocrypha were so attributed, the writers clearly believed in a connection that was more than one of name. And so with Muslim devotions.

It will suffice to take two examples.

(a) *Uwais al-Qaranī* (or *Qarnī*). Although some of the greatest of the third-century traditionists cast doubt on the whole body of the Uwais traditions his legend is undying, perhaps from its spiritual beauty, and it is difficult to think that there was no historical reality behind it. Uwais, who was called in Turkey "the sultan of faithful lovers", is the type of those whose love is not based on physical sight but on spiritual union. He appears as a hermit of the Nejd who never saw the Prophet, but for love of him had the same tooth extracted that Muḥammad had lost at Uḥud. In Turkish legend, so similar to some stories of the desert fathers, Muḥammad left to this unseen friend his woollen mantle the *Burda*[1] long treasured at Istanbul. He died fighting for 'Alī at Ṣiffīn.

In al-Hujwīrī the legend runs as follows:

> The Apostle said to the Companions: "There is a man at Qaran, called Uwais, who at the Resurrection will intercede for a multitude of my people, as many as the sheep of Rabī'a and Muḍar." Then, turning to 'Umar and 'Alī, he said: "You will see him. He is a lowly man, of middle height, and hairy; on his left side there is a white spot, as large as a dirhem, which is not from leprosy, and he has a similar spot on the palm of his hand. When you see him, give him my greeting, and bid him pray for my people."
>
> ... 'Umar and 'Alī set out in quest of him. They found him praying, and waited until he was finished. He saluted them and showed them the marks on his side and the palm of his hand. They asked his blessing and gave him the Apostle's greeting and enjoined him to pray for the Muslim people. After they had stayed for a while, he said, "You have taken trouble (to see me); now return, for the Resurrection is near, when we shall see each other without farewell. At present I am engaged in preparing for the Resurrection."
> *Kashf al-Mahjūb*. Nicholson's translation, p. 83.

The legend points to a life of unseen prayer, and it is not surprising that devotions should be attributed to him or that mystical chains of spiritual descent should sometimes go back to this figure.

(b) *'Alī Zain al-'Ābidīn*. Almost the whole of the great Shī'a Arabic breviary *aṣ-Ṣaḥīfatu 'l-khāmisatu 's-sajjādiyya* in use in Iraq and Syria, as of the sister book in use in India, is attributed to this one figure—a

[1] Which gave its name to the oft-reprinted poem of Al-Būṣīrī.

great mass (some 600 pages) of devotion. To him also is sometimes given the famous *Ḥizbu 's-saifī*.

Here there is no doubt of the historicity of the figure. Great-grandson of the Prophet, grandson of 'Alī and Fāṭima, son of al-Ḥusain, he was a boy and a sick boy when his father was killed at Kerbela in 61/680. He was saved like Joash from the slaughter of his family and brought to Yazīd, who was good to him and allowed him to return to Medina. Although he stands in the list of Shī'a imāms, 'Alī seems to have made no claim to temporal power, never openly rebelling against Yazīd. Tradition shows him as giving his life to piety until his death in 92/710 or 94/712,13. The great body of devotion attributed to him is characterized by a deep humility and sense of sin, and by an intransigent, undying resentment against the foes of his house. The romance woven round this saintly figure is illustrated by the following story of a desert encounter with him.

> We travelled from Zabāla [one of the halting places on the way from Iraq to Mecca] by night, and a black [sand-carrying] wind of darkness met us, and I was cut off from the caravan and wandered in that wilderness till I came to a desert wādī, and in the darkness of the night I repaired to an ancient tree. In the intense darkness, lo a youth came towards me clad in poor white raiment and bearing with him the scent of musk. Then I said to myself, "This is one of the saints of God" . . . and I hid myself as well as I could, and he came to the spot where I was and prepared for the prayer-rite.
>
> Then he began the prayer-rite. And when I saw that the movements of his body ceased and he was still, I approached the spot where he had made ready for prayer and lo there was a spring gushing out with clear water, and I too made ready for the prayer-rite and stood up to pray behind him, and behold I was before a *miḥrāb* as though it were revealed at that moment . . . and I feared lest this personage should pass away from me and I should lose his track, so I went close to him . . . and he said, "If your confidence in God had been real you would not have been lost; but follow me and tread in my footprints", and he came under the tree and took my hand, and it seemed to me as if the earth slipped away from under my feet, and when the day broke he said, "Be of good cheer, this is Mecca." *Ḥammād ibn al-'Aṭṭār* in *aṣ-Ṣaḥifatu 's-sajjādiyya*, pp. 117 ff.

2. The Devotions of Medieval Saints

Of these, two stand out beyond all others in popularity and in the bulk of prayer-material attributed to them and incessantly reprinted and used.

(a) *'Abd al-Qādir al-Jīlānī* d. 561/1166. His devotions, known from Morocco to India, contain much that is strange and difficult for ordinary worshippers. Their popularity is no doubt due to the intense popularity of the figure of the man himself. The story revealed in such books as *Bahjatu 'l-asrār* is undoubtedly that of a kindly saint as well as of one claiming supreme spiritual authority. There are tales of the great preacher, on whom Baghdad hung, bringing with his own hand food to an unknown, weary boy who had wandered into the courtyard of his school, and of his winning the devotion of a circle of friends amongst whom were black servants. It is as the kindly saint that this figure is adored. Women in the pangs of childbirth in Algeria cry, *Yā 'Abda 'l-Qādir!* An officer in the Egyptian Frontiers Administration told the writer that his camel corps men from the borders of the Sudan never started a desert trek without shouting with one voice, *Yā 'Abda 'l-Qādir!* A Sudanese religious leader, Ṣāliḥ ibn Bān an-Nāqa, was converted through a vision of 'Abd al-Qādir sitting Sudanese fashion "on an *angarīb*".

While the very wide extent of the Qādiriyya order to-day partly accounts for the general circulation of his devotions this is also explained by his position as the kindly intercessor.

(b) *Abū 'l-Ḥasan ash-Shādhilī*, d. 656/1258. This saint, who died on the way to Mecca in a desert of Upper Egypt, was born thirty years later than 'Abd al-Qādir, and the Qādiriyya books claim that he urged his children and followers to visit 'Abd al-Qādir's tomb. His devotions show great spiritual depth strangely mingled with magic. To their double attraction, for the spiritual and for the superstitious mind, to the copiousness of the material, and to the fact that his order has an unusual degree of approval from the orthodox authorities at the Azhar, must be attributed their very great popularity to-day, especially in Egypt. A crude and popular modern hymnology is one of the features of this order, from which have sprung, under various names, other orders in West Africa, Algeria, and the Atlas.

3. Eighteenth-century Devotions

Here again two figures stand out in popularity.

(a) *Muṣṭafā al-Bakrī* (b. 1099/1688 at Damascus, died in 1162/1749 at Cairo). With him we pass into another world. His life of Sufism in Damascus, in Jerusalem (which he often visited and where he wrote his first book of prayers), in Cairo, in Istanbul, in Nablus (where he spent eleven months) on its outward side was one of relationship with Turkish authorities, spiritual and governmental.

His devotions, far more than those of earlier days, are preoccupied with the mystical figure of Muḥammad as the centre of the spiritual universe. True to his spirit is the popular belief that groanings are heard from the tomb at Medina when men bless the Prophet.

(b) *Aḥmad at-Tījānī* (or Tījānī or Tajānī) is a figure of the West, with spiritual affiliation to Ash-Shādhilī. Born 1150/1737(38) in a *qaṣar* at the foot of Jabal-Amūr, he studied in Fez and wandered to Tunis, Cairo, and throughout North Africa. It was in a *Zāwiya* built for him by the Sultan Mūlai Sulaimān at Fez that he died in 1231/1815. His order is popular in Tunisia, the Sahara, Timbuctoo, Northern Nigeria, and Kordofan. It was carried into the Sudan largely by travelling Hausas, and has branches to-day as far east as Jerusalem. But his devotions spread even further than his order. Commentaries on his *awrād* have been written in our own day by Shaikh 'Alī al-Makkī deeply devoted to his memory and spirit. These are published in Cairo and popular in Baghdad. His work is dominated by the cult of the mystical figure of the Prophet.

4. Nineteenth- and Twentieth-century Devotions

Here we find two fountain heads of the literature of prayer most popular to-day, the Sanūsī group, and its rival the Mirghaniyya group.

Both had first their spiritual inspiration from the great Shaikh Aḥmad ibn Idrīs, a Moroccan by birth who taught in Cairo for twenty years before settling in Mecca, where he lived 1234/1818 to 1243/1827 till the Meccan 'Ulamā' became jealous of his crowds of pupils. Having begun life in the Shādhiliyya order, he was now leading a reactionary movement in Islam, and the Wahhābīs, to whose territory he fled from Mecca, left him in peace in 'Asīr (then controlled by them), where he died 1253/1837.

He sent missionary pupils to Africa, and both the Sanūsiyya and the Mirghaniyya were affiliated to him and contended for his spiritual heritage. Both incorporate some of his *awrād* with their own.

(a) *The Sanūsī group*. The political and military adventures of this order, of which King Muḥammad Idrīs al-Mahdī al-Sanūsī is the present head, are not the concern of this book. Its *awrād*, simple, straightforward, a conscious throwback to Islam's early simplicity, are widespread in the Sahara, Libya, the Sudan, and sold at Aden to Abyssinians, Somalis, and the Arabs of the East Coast. Some were printed (when in the war of 1914–18 Sīdī Muḥammad Idrīs escaped to Istanbul) in Istanbul and Damascus. They have been published also in Bombay for sale to the Arabs of the Persian Gulf and the East Coast of Arabia and Africa. The following Table shows the principal writers of devotions, names underlined:

Muḥammad Idrīs d. 1253/1837
(Shaikh of the Founder at Mecca spiritual affiliation only)
(Founder of the Order) Sīdī Muḥammad b. 'Alī as-Sanūsī
b. near Mostaganem 1206/1791
d. at Jaghbūb 1276/1859.

(Second leader) Sīdī Muḥammad al Mahdī
b. 1260/1844 at El-Briḍa
d. 1320/1901 at Guro.

Sīdī Muḥammad ash-Sharīf
(Third leader.) Sīdī Aḥmad

(Fourth leader) Sīdī Muḥammad Idrīs
b. 1301/1883 at Jaghbūb

Sīdī ar-Riḍā

(b) *The Mirghaniyya group.* The outstanding figure here is Muḥammad 'Uthmān al-Mirghanī of a Sharīfian family, a pupil of Aḥmad ibn Idrīs at Mecca, and sent by him to Africa. Amongst the Nubians from Aswan to Dongola his work had a resounding success. He married a Dongolawiyya in Kordofan. Although he continued to serve Aḥmad ibn Idrīs until the death of the latter, he later formed the theory of the sanctity of his own family, and he greatly modified the devotional habits of his teacher. He sent his sons to Yemen and Haḍramaut and to Sawākin, Kordofan, Dongola and Nubia, and established his order in the Sudan before he died at aṭ-Ṭā'if in 1270/1853.

This group has a large and warm popular literature of devotion, less puritan, and very strongly permeated by devotion to the Prophet almost amounting to worship. The leading prayer-writers have had many visions of Muḥammad, whose approval granted in visions is claimed for many of their devotions. Their books include much verse of the nature of popular hymns with an easy lilt. An annotator explains that the *sādatu 'l-Mirghaniyya* did not conform to the rules of Arabic verse, but invented something new. Another method of devotion which must lend itself to popular use is a narrative (of the birth or the *mi'rāj* of the Prophet) broken up into short sections divided by a prayer chorus in easy verse. The following table, though not tracing all the ramifications of the family, shows the principal writers of *awrād*:

'Abd Allah al-Mirghanī al-Maḥjūb
b. Mecca, d. 1207/1792. d. Ṭā'if where his tomb is a pilgrimage centre for the order.
|
Muḥammad Abū-Bakr al-Mirghanī
|
Muḥammad 'Uthmān al-Mirghanī
b. 1208/1793 at Ṭā'if. d. there 1270/1853 after travels in Egypt and the Sudan for the spread of the order.
|
Ja'far aṣ-Ṣādiq | Al-Ḥasan Muḥammad | 'Abd Allah | Muḥammad Sirr al-Khatm

These devotions, to-day of very great popularity, spread during the last century through Western and Southern Arabia, from Suakin through the Sudan and Abyssinia and all Nubia. They have penetrated Ethiopia and are the beloved companions of Nubian servants and Sudanese doorkeepers in Cairo.

The Mirghaniyya family seat is now at Kasala in the Sudan. The heads of the family combine the spiritual leadership of the order with life as wealthy squires and political leaders.

(c) *The Ḥaddādiyya group*. A note must be appended concerning a group of little books of the Ḥaddādiyya order, because they represent a less-known but truly Arabian religious activity to-day.

The widespread family of the Bā-'Alawī (going back to Ja'far aṣ-Ṣādiq and so to 'Alī) produced many learned *ṣūfīs* in South Arabia in the seventeenth century. This family group, of which al-Aidarūs, the famous saint of Aden was a member, now leads an order (its books stressing the importance of having *Arabian* shaikhs of the true descent) with very popular straightforward *awrād*, Ṭarīm a city of sacred tombs, and Sai'un with a family mosque being centres.

The order is called Ḥaddādiyya from the family name of the founder As-Sayyid 'Abd Allah al-Ḥaddād al-'Alawī al-Ḥusainī. His son 'Umar 'Abd ar-Raḥmān al-'Aṭṭās who died at Huraidha 1074/1663–4 is the author of one of the manuals, while a pupil of the latter, 'Abd Allah ibn 'Alawī al-Ḥaddād (unrelated) from a small village, Al-Hāwī, near Ṭarīm, is the author of a second. A grandson of the founder 'Ali ibn Ḥasan al-'Aṭṭās, buried at Meshed 1172/1758–9, is the writer of a third manual. The leadership of the order is in the hands of this family and the leaders have the title Al-Ḥabīb. Their books are printed in Cairo or in Aden for circulation in Arabia and are also sold at Aden to Arabs from the East Coast of Africa. Their *awrād* are not deeply mystical and their advice to youth is marked by common sense and kindliness. The little books might be unnoticed in a crowd of rivals in Cairo, but have their own interest as representing a spiritual movement to-day in Ḥaḍramaut and Yemen.

Use of Ḥadīth

The collection of popular manuals was found to contain three tradition books,[1] two of them long established and well known, one almost contemporary. These are not universal in their scope but are limited to traditions concerning words and acts of devotion. That their purpose is edification rather than codification is shown by their omission of references. Traditions, usually without any attempt at *isnād* or reference, are also scattered liberally through the manuals.

Sometimes no doubt for the sake of escaping criticism, but more often through the force of sheer devotion to that figure, a supporting tradition, linking it with Muḥammad, has to justify each of the most outstanding phrases and usages of worship. Other traditions quoted for edification are not Prophetic but tell of the words or deeds of

[1] (a) *Adhkār*. Muḥyī ad-Dīn Yaḥyā an-Nawawī. Ed. Cairo 1348. (b) *Al-Kalimu 'ṭ-ṭayyib*. Taqī ad-Dīn ibn Taimiyya ad-Dimishqī 728/1328. Ed. Cairo 1349. (c) *Riyāḍu 'l-Janna*. Yūsuf an-Nabhānī (a judge in Beirut). Ed. Cairo 1348.

outstanding saints. In this book, as in the manuals themselves, scientific critical study of these traditions would be out of place, even were the writer capable of it. The question here is not the factual reliability or the historical source of the tradition, but its action to-day in the moulding of devotional life. The traditions of the saints in such a work as the *Risāla Qushairiyya*, like the tiny legends and apothegms (which they often strongly resemble) of the desert fathers in the Lausiac Chronicle of Palladius or in the writings of Cassian, have a historical value beyond factual accuracy. They are spiritual *genre* pictures in which an attitude of mind, a mood of soul, the ideals of a group and an age can be seen as vividly as we see the round mirror and the red and white tiles in some Dutch picture. In this book, then, traditions that have found their way into popular manuals will be quoted uncritically as to historical source and accuracy, for the value of what they may mean to the devout souls for whom the manuals are spiritual guides.

The traditional prayers attributed to the Prophet form a large block of the material of these devotions, sometimes printed together as a group, sometimes inserted here and there into the fabric of a *wird*. Muḥammad is held up as the type and model of the man at prayer:

> No praiseworthy trait or blessed quality but he made request for it; no disfiguring carelessness or slackening in religion but he sought for protection from it, generally and in each particular. *al-Wirdu'l-a'ẓam*, 'Alī Muḥammad al-Qārī.

Use of the Qur'ān

The Qur'ān is the psalter as well as the lectionary of Muslim worship, and its style dominates the whole. Muslim devotions are as full of Qur'ānic texts and echoes as are Christian devotions of biblical. It is a difficult exercise, but one necessary for true understanding, to try to hear some of the overtones of spiritual and emotional association which such phrases carry with them.

Some of the *aḥzāb* are nothing more nor less than collections of separate verses, arranged, with more or less connection of subject, for devotional use. Mysterious virtue and guarding power are often attributed to these. One bearing the name of al-Ghazālī occurs in several of the manuals and the story attached to it illustrates this protective use:

(By Shaikh Muḥammad 'Uqaila al-Makkī.) When I was living in Mecca at the beginning of Shawwāl in the year 1013/1604[1] the Sharīf Sa'd ibn Zaid came there as governor. After a few days he began to degrade all the religious officials who had been in leading positions under the rule of his cousin the Sharīf 'Abd al-Karīm. And he treated many of the leading men and worthies of Mecca with the greatest arrogance till his tyrannous oppression even reached Shaikh 'Abd al-Laṭīf ibn 'Abd as-Sulṭān az-Zamzamī, then the mosque Time-Keeper at Mecca. Him he confined in his house, so cutting him off from the Sanctuary at all the hours of prayer. And another who was confined to his house was the Door-Keeper of the Sanctuary, Shaikh Muḥammad of the Banī Shaiba. Now one of those against whom the said Sharīf Sa'd was hostile was the distinguished scholar Sayyid Muḥammad As'ad, Mufti of Medina, so that it was expedient for him to fly from Medina in the company of the pilgrims returning to Syria and elsewhere. But after the pilgrims had left Medina, instead of continuing with them he went to Mecca to the house of the Banī Shaiba, and moved about everywhere openly without fear, so that everyone was astonished at him and people knew that he could only reach that degree of daring if he relied on some inviolable protection against the Sharīf and his armies.

I met him one day and he gave me a little manuscript entitled "The Secret of Secrets and the Treasure of the Righteous . . . beneficial whether recited or carried, all difficulties by its blessed power (*baraka*) being made easy etc." I was consumed with curiosity as to the arrangement of verses and began to make enquiries about it from every learned man I met, but without result till I happened—in a manuscript in the possession of 'Alī al-Qārī the Ḥanafī—on the very information I sought, which was that the verses were put together by Ḥujjatu 'l-Islām the Imām al-Ghazālī, and I treasured it (the *ḥizb*) extremely and applied it to my own concerns. *al-Fuyūḍāti 'r-rabbāniyya* Ismā'īl Muḥammad al-Jīlānī.

The Qur'ān texts quoted in this book are not set out as giving the full Qur'ānic teaching on the subjects in hand, nor has an attempt been made to state the interpretation placed on them by the great commentators. They are here simply because in the prayer-manuals they are treated as basic for various types of devotion, and any explanations offered are those of the manuals themselves.

[1] There appears to be some confusion as to dates. Sa'd ibn Zaid did not succeed until 1666. The story is, however, highly characteristic of the confused period after the death of the Sharīf Ḥasan in 1601 and of the Meccan resentment at what Snouck Hurgronje calls the "reforming work" of these Sharīfs in reducing the residents to order. (Snouck Hurgronje. *Mecca* I, 112–23.)

Style

A very small proportion of these prayer-manuals are by men famous as writers of Arabic; for the most part the writers are more famous in religion than in literature. Rhymed prose is more common than unrhymed. There are passages with a careless naïveté that is almost colloquial, and sometimes verse only to be compared with hymns in use in popular evangelistic meetings in Christendom. Occasionally we meet a style of rumbling assonances, rhyming words strung together in such phrases as *bi 'ajībi gharībi makhzūni makhnūni* . . . etc., almost intolerable to read. But it is to be remembered that these works were not written for reading in the ordinary sense, and just as Péguy's hammered repetitions are tedious to the eye, but have a cumulative effect when read aloud, these rumbling sentences may have a strange power when murmured by a group of worshippers.

The Sacramental Tendency

> As in all mental apprehension and conviction there is always somewhere, the element of the stimulation of the senses, so also does the spirit awaken to its own life and powers on occasion of contact with material things. (F. von Hügel, *Eternal Life*, p. 359.)

Here is the human need—the need of creatures living at once in a material and a spiritual world for the sacramental.

Islam, which in its doctrine of *tawḥīd* exhibits an effort of the human mind at austere conation, and in its mystical life (in part conditioned by that doctrine) exhibits the effort of the human spirit to escape not only beyond the sensory but beyond conation, yet exemplifies the human need for sacramentals—for the outward and visible sign of the inward and spiritual grace. Curiously enough these are most fully developed in those very dervish orders whose effort has been not to subsume but to cut off (*fanā'*) one by one all sensory and mental helps towards the vision of God.

The initiation to these orders, the clothing with the *Khirqa* or other vestment, the sprinkling of the novice at his clothing, the handing of a book (transmission of the *awrād* of the order) or of a chalice (*Qādiriyya*) are strongly sacramental. This is most marked in the use of the Hand-clasp so close to the laying on of hands in Christian confirmation and ordination. The Qur'ān verse basic for all these forms is 48.10. "Those who swear allegiance[1] to thee do but swear allegiance to God. The Hand of God is over their hands."

The following account by Muḥammad al-Mahdī (d. 1320/1901) of the transmission of spiritual authority to him as a young lad, from his father Muḥammad as-Sanūsī gives a glowing sense of the sacramental nature of the Handclasp (*muṣāfaḥa*):

> The Master used to say to the brethren "There is only this hand between you and the Prophet." Even clearer than this is what he said to me during his last illness. For I entered his room one day and found him exultant, spiritual radiance streaming from him as he said, "This is the hand of the Prophet." And he extended his noble hand which I took and saluted, my whole soul accompanying the action; and that was as it were the moment of my glorification in union, the union of two spirits in one essential personality.
> *ad-Durratu 'l-fardiyyatu fī bayāni mabnī 't-ṭarīqati 's-Sanūsiyya*, p. 14.

But these sacraments of ordination belong only to the inner circles. For the great mass of worshippers there are no sacraments in the technical sense of the word, but yet many sacramentals, things and actions and especially words, which are outward signs of inward grace. We shall try to show that the *qibla*, the *miḥrāb*, most of the gestures and words of the prayer-rite, the *basmala*, the *tahlīl*, and especially the calling down of blessing on the Prophet have, for those with eyes to see, the quality of sacramentals. In his calling down of blessing on the Prophet the worshipper believes that he is, by the utterance of a few words, not only entering into communion with an activity of heaven but is *setting in motion* a correspondent heavenly activity.

Islam, then, for all its simplification of ritual acts and of the surroundings of worship, has not escaped the universal human need for the sacramental; but, as we shall try to show, it has attached this value to words, to *adhkār*, the well-known several phrases of devotion.

Baraka

With the sense of the semi-sacramental value of certain phrases (*adhkār*) must be connected the idea pervading the prayer manuals of the peculiar *baraka*, blessedness, attached to many a prayer, to many a single phrase.

Because the Muslim use of *baraka* differs from that in Christian Arabic devotions we must pause over this word. It constantly

[1] The verb seems to have the meaning of ratifying a transaction by a handclasp.

stands in the manuals for a kind of power, a spark of divine power attached to *personalities*[1] and pre-eminently to the personality of the Prophet:

> And forgive us by his *baraka*. *Qiṣṣatu 'l-mi'rāj*, M. 'Uthmān al-Mirghanī and constantly.
>
> O God call down blessing on our Lord Muḥammad and by his *baraka* deliver us from the bane of the Arabs and the non-Arabs and the bane of all Thy creatures.
>
> O God call down blessing on our Lord Muḥammad and by his *baraka* deliver us from the bane of heat and cold, of rain and wind, of serpents and scorpions and beasts of prey. . . . *Ad'iyatun mamzūjatun bi ṣalawātin 'alā'n-nabī*, M. 'Uthmān al-Mirghanī, p. 82.

Such phrases pervade the prayer-books and take us behind the definitions of divines to common human experience.

> In all religions the man who has intercourse with the mysterious superhuman powers is thereby accredited with his own atmosphere of mystical sanctity, which enables him to walk in perilous neighbourhood with the supernatural sources of power. This "sanctity" has in itself no ethical sense, it is a power capable of employment for good or evil, as it may be severally used. Islam also knows the blessing, *baraka*, of the holy man, which in general does not imply what we understand by spiritual blessedness. *Die Person Muhammeds in Lehre und Glauben seiner Gemeinde*, Tor Andrae, p. 166.
>
> The point is that the "holy man" or the "prophet" is from the outset, as regards the experience of the circle of his devotees, something more than a "mere man" (*psilos anthrōpos*). He is the being of wonder and mystery who somehow or other is felt to belong to the higher order of things, to the side of the numen itself. It is not that he himself teaches that he is such but that he is experienced as such. *The Idea of the Holy*, Otto, p. 162.

In folk-religion everywhere the mysterious *baraka* of the holy man is felt to pass into objects with which he has had contact, and inside or outside Islam there are folk cults, many of them no doubt primitive, of kissing, touching, or stroking holy objects. In Old Cairo, for instance, Muslim women of the neighbourhood go on Sunday mornings to a room under the Greek Orthodox Church, where there is a chain, once reputed to have had some connection with the legend of St George, but no longer kept in the Church or much regarded by its officials. The women ask the Church doorkeeper to pass this chain

[1] Pedersen's account of the Hebrew *baraka* in his *Israel* is very suggestive for its use in the Muslim prayer-books.

round them or their children, and in answer to inquiries as to what they are doing, they say *nistabrik*—we seek the *baraka*.

In the prayer manuals we find the idea of *baraka* passing over to holy books. (Compare the extract about al-Ghazālī's *Ḥizb* above.) Thus Shams ad-Dīn ibn al-Jazarī tells of his experience when Timur Lengh besieged Damascus in 791/1389, just as al-Jazarī had finished a book of the Prophet's sayings in regard to prayer, which he named *The Impregnable Fortress* (*al-Ḥiṣnu 'l-Ḥaṣīn*):

> And when I had finished the arrangement of it an enemy sought me against whom none but God Most High could defend me. And I fled from him to concealment and took refuge in this *Impregnable Fortress*. Then I saw the Prince of the Apostles who said "What is your desire?" And I said, "O Apostle of God, pray for me and for the Muslims." So he raised his noble hands as I watched, and he prayed and then passed them over his noble face. And this happened on the eve of Thursday, and on the eve of Sunday the enemy fled, and God gave relief to me and to the Muslims by the *baraka* of what is in this book. (Quoted in preface to *al-Wirdu 'sh-shāfī*, an-Nabhānī.)

These instances from of old are quoted for the encouragement of those who use the same devotions to-day. But the manuals show a strong development of the idea that each of the great holy phrases, the *adhkār* of prayer, has its own *baraka*, by virtue of which each of them can severally be wielded as a weapon or used for a shield of defence, or presented as an acceptable offering. This sense of their practically independent holy power ranges from the spiritual to the semi-magical. It is at its strongest, of course, with any word from the Qur'ān and with the blessing on the Prophet (*Ṣalli 'alā 'n-Nabī*), in which the *ṣalāt* of God himself is joined with that of the worshipper.

> A calling down of blessing on the Prophet, by the *baraka* of which our sicknesses and diseases will be healed. *Fatḥu'r-rasūl*, M. 'Uthmān al-Mirghanī, p. 80.
>
> [In a prayer, half of which is a charm.] Be quiet oh headache and pain by the greatness of God. . . . Be quiet by "There is no might nor power save with God." (Urdu-Arabic manual, Delhi.)

THE MOSAIC

As compared with Christian prayers, as known in the West, many Muslim devotions have the character of a mosaic of tiny distinct fragments. The packed and balanced sentence of the Latin "collect", which passes so nobly into the English tongue, is an almost impossible form to translate happily into Arabic.

While the prayers of some of the saints show a spiritual individuality, the great mass of these devotions is built up of well-tried small items arranged in ever new patterns—traditional prayers of the Prophet, Qur'ān verses, blessings of the Prophet, forgiveness-seekings, refuge-seekings, cries of praise, all on known and authorized forms. A group of these *disjuncta membra* is bound together in the following prayer:

> O God I have ready for every dread which I encounter in this world or the next *lā ilāha illā 'llāh*, and for every care and anxiety *mā shā'a 'llāh*, and for every grace *al-ḥamdu lillāh*, and for every ease and hardship *ash-shukru lillāh* and for every wonder *subḥāna 'llāh*, and for every sin *astaghfiru 'llāh*, and for every pressure of circumstance *ḥasbī allāh*, and for every calamity *innā lillāhi wa innā ilaihi rāji'ūn*, and for every destiny and decree *tawakkaltu 'alā 'llāh*, and for every obedience and transgression *lā ḥawla wa lā quwwata illā billāh*. (*Ḥizbu 'l-kalimāti 'l-'ashara*, 'Alī Wafā.)

> (The last sentence is explained by the fact that certain groups have used *lā ḥawla wa lā quwwata illā billāh*, as part of their public confession after failure to fulfil one of the *ṭā'āt*, legal observances, an expression of their own powerlessness to do right.)

Of such well-worn items (that in the wear have acquired those dear associations and spiritual overtones familiar to all who use liturgical prayer) the *awrād* are very largely built up. In some cases there is fear of originality, especially if it come by way of the flash of inspiration (*ilhām* or *hatafa hātifun*, not unlike the Hebrew *bath qol*). The Muslim saint, like Saint Teresa of Avila, must learn to scrutinize this with rigour:

> If there occurs to thee in thine acquaintance with God the whisper of what appears to be information by way of inspiration and revelation, perhaps tending to fancy, do not accept it, but return to the sharply delineated truth of the Book of God and the *Sunna* of His Apostle, that thou mayest not be at fault in the matter. For thou wilt say that God has guaranteed thee freedom from error on the part of His Book and the *Sunna*, but He has not guaranteed freedom from error on the part of thy personal revelation and inspiration. And if thou dost accept any truth by way of inspiration, it must only be after exposing it to the Book and the *Sunna*. *al-Mafākhiru 'l-'aliyya fī 'l-ma'āthiri 'sh-shadhiliyya*, Aḥmad ibn Muḥammad ibn 'Ibād, p. 50.

For the most part the longer devotions are built up of small and well-known single utterances woven together in ever new patterns. The attempt to analyse some of the longer *awrād* has left the impression that many of them are best left unanalysed. The quotations in this book, isolating and grouping *adhkār* to illustrate one subject, fail to give the impression of the whole complicated mosaic. To read many of these *awrād* is to be reminded of that Muslim theory of a creation composed of discrete atoms, incapable of fusion, but given ever renewed and varied juxtaposition in the forms of the physical universe, by an ever-renewed divine fiat. But to read the *awrād* is not the same thing as to use them as a mode of worship. Then the mind and heart may be borne along in a gentle undulation. There is often no sense of climax, and the final *taṣliya* is reached with no very strong conviction as to why it should occur just then. Some Arabic Christian devotions (not, of course, those with the clear march of the great liturgies) show something of this undulating quality, as does the Compline service of the West. But in these the single items marking off different moods or phases of worship are more massive. The man who allows himself to be slowly borne along these winding streams will enter upon a different experience from the single effort of mental and spiritual concentration called out by a brief climaxial prayer, whether in Christianity or Islam.

The predominant part which great single phrases play in Muslim devotion, whether of the masses or of the saints, led the writer to feel that a study of the popular devotions in these manuals should be based on these recurring notes, and among them those of the daily prayer-rite have been given the primary place.

This book has grown from a deep sense of the need for better understanding of Islam by Christians as of Christianity by Muslims. It is an attempt to provide for other beginners information that the writer would most gladly have had at her disposal on arriving in Arabic lands. The manuals themselves have been its "universe of discourse", and the writer has tried to let them speak for themselves, believing that in every religion the *lex orandi* is in a very real sense the *lex credendi*, and that such a study is perhaps a truer way to some knowledge of the working beliefs of religious folk than one based on more formal theological treatises.

Part 1

TYPE-NAMES FOR DEVOTIONS

TYPE-NAMES FOR DEVOTIONS

(a) ʿIbāda

The root *ʿbd* gives us both the widest and the most fundamental Arabic words for the approach of man to God. From dim antiquity Semitic names of God had pointed to His despotic lordship, His ownership of His worshippers—Baʿal, Melekh, Rabbat, Adōn, and Jewish thought had passed into the Christian use of *mar*, *rabb*, *kurios*. The Arabic *rabb*[1] and *mawlā* carry on the ancient tradition.

The root *ʿbd*, which may possibly have had a primary meaning of "make" or "do" (still given to it in Syriac), passing into the sense of service, has in half a dozen Semitic languages provided the correlative to these words of despotic lordship, the name of the *ʿabd* or slave.

The Hebrews rendered a service to religion when the word *ʿabōdā*, bondservice, passed from the sense of literal service to a god (as in sacrificing at an altar) to a spiritual meaning, both analogous to the English use of "divine service" and more inward in the phrase "the *ʿabōdā* of the heart". (See Heiler, *Das Gebet*, p. 483; Midrash on *Sifr Lev*, 80 on *Sifr Dt*, 41, 80a; Elbogen, *Der jüdische Gottesdienst*, p. 4.)

In Arabic the root gives us words for all these meanings. *ʿibāda* can be the relationship of slave to lord (or, when that Lord is the Creator, the relationship of creatureliness), and also devotion, cult, canonical rite.

It is for this that men were created:

> God created His servants (or worshippers, *al-ʿibād*) for the purpose of worshipping Him. (Preface to *Wirdu's-saḥr*, Muṣṭafā al-Bakrī.)
>
> God Most High has said, "I only created the jinn and mankind that they should worship. I do not desire from them sustenance or livelihood." Thus it is clear that they were created for worship and it is their duty to concern themselves with that for which they were created. *Riyāḍu 'ṣ-ṣāliḥīn*; an-Nawawī, p. 2.

[1] A few of the Arab prayer-manuals prefer to see in *rabb* a connection with the verb *rabbā*, to foster, bring up. "My Lord (*rabb*) is God who fostered (*rabbā*) me and all the universe through His grace." (*Shurūṭu 'ṣ-ṣalāt*, M. ʿAbd al-Wahhāb, p. 5.) This meaning has been adopted in all the modern literature of the Aḥmadiyya Movement.

Thou hast created them to worship Thee and sustained them to praise Thee and guided them to Thy unity that they may affirm it. *al-Munājātu 'l-injīliyyatu 'l-kubrā*, 'Alī Zain al-'Ābidīn.

An English child who learns his Church Catechism is taught that at his baptism he was made "the child of God". A Muslim child (if we may judge by a fairly wide collection of first lesson books intended for use in primary schools) learns first that he is the '*abd* (slave, creature, worshipper) of his Creator. The word is endeared by its long religious use on the part of those who have filled it with spiritual meaning.

Truly spoke he who said that word "slave", for all of us are slaves to Thee. None can withhold when Thou givest or give when Thou withholdest. *al-Ḥizbu 'l-a'ẓam*, 'Alī M. al-Qārī.

I come to Thee this evening, Thy humble bondservant unable to control for myself good or ill or to defend myself from evil. *Du'ā'un fī layyāli shahri Ramaḍān*, 'Alī Zain al-'Ābidīn.

No name more sums up what the believer should be than that of servitude. For God, ever to be praised and exalted, said in the description of the Prophet on the night of the *Mi'rāj*, at this moment of greatest honour in this life, "Most high praise to Him who carried His servant ('*abd*) by night from the Mosque of Mecca to the Mosque al Aqṣā," (*Qur.* 17.1); and that other word: "And He revealed to His servant ('*abd*) what He revealed" (*Qur.* 53.10). Had there been a nobler title than that of servitude, He would have given it to the Prophet. *Risāla Qushairiyya. Bābu 'l-'ubūdiyya.*

In a religion in which the tenderer couplet father-child is excluded from worship, the relationship *Rabb* (or the more intimate *Mawlā*)—'*abd* has to be packed all the more fully with spiritual emotion. We find in it a sense of mutuality in which the voice of religious experience accords strangely with the remoteness of the doctrine of *tanzīh*.

Then he shall return to his prostration and say: "If I am the worst of bondservants, Thou art the best of lords, pardon! pardon!" (a hundred times). *Du'ā'u Shahri Rajab.*

Nor do I see a generous Lord who would be more patient with a wretched slave than Thou with me. *Du'ā'un fī ṭalabi 'l-ḥawā'ij, aṣ-Ṣaḥīfatu 's-sajjādiyya*, p. 116.

One of the pious stood on 'Arafat and said, "My God and my Master, if one of us has a slave who grows old in his service and in his house, he does not sell that slave nor beat him. And I have grown old in Thy household, then of Thy generosity free me."[1] *Ṭahāratu 'l-qulūb*, Ad-Dīrīnī, p. 144.

More than this, we find the worshipper glorying in the relationship with something of that passion of devotion with which St Paul declared himself the slave of Christ (indeed *'abd* comes very near to the New Testament *doulos*), and Muslim prayers close in spirit to that pre-Islamic phrase in Christian devotion "whom to serve is to reign".

> For God Most High requires of you to be a bondservant to Him, and you delight that He shall be a Master to you. If you are such a bondservant as contents Him, He will be to you such a Master as contents you. (ash-Shādhilī quoted in *al-Mafākhiru 'l-'aliyya*, p. 51.)
>
> Enough of splendour for me to be Thy slave. Enough of glory for me that Thou art my Lord. My God I have found Thee the God that I desire, make me then to be the creature that Thou desirest. *Lawāmi'u 'l-bayyināt*, Fakhr ad-Dīn ar-Rāzī, p. 39.

An almost similar sentence is found in a *ḥizb* based on the *tahlīl* and attributed to 'Abd al-Qadir al-Jīlānī. (*Majmū'u awrādin wa aḥzāb*, 'Abd al-Qādir al-Jīlānī, p. 47.)

All this relationship of the *'abd* to his Master and Lord refuses to be packed into the word *'ibāda*, which indeed has come to mean those outward observances by which the relation is expressed in cult or rite.[2] (Its synomyn is *ṭā'a*, obedience, which, generally used in the plural, expresses the carrying out of prescribed rites.) *Al-'ibāda ṣūra ṣawwarahā 'sh-sharī'a*, says al-Ghazālī, "Canonical rites are an outward form traced by the sacred law."

[1] The meaning of "free me" here may be either that of the traditional phrase "God's freemen from the Fire" or the more spiritual one indicated by Al-Qushairī, and approaching the thought of St Augustine, that one fully and willingly obedient becomes free.

[2] Here our analogy between *'abd* and *doulos* breaks down, for *douleia* in the New Testament never expresses more than bondage and slavery. (Cf. Rom. 8.15,21; Heb. 2.5, etc.) We have to turn to *leitourgia* for a similar sense of religious service or ministry (Luke 1.23; Heb. 8.6 and 9.21), the LXX translation for *'abōdā* in the later O.T. Books. But in order to correspond with the meaning *'ibāda*, leitourgia must be stripped of that sense of free or voluntary service which it carried over from its Athenian use for the discharge of a public office at a man's own expense. *'Ibāda* in Islam, however readily the saint may offer it from his heart, is yet the obligatory service of slave or creature.

Dear as these outward forms may be, and the following prayer shows their preciousness to worshippers,

> As Thou hast solaced the people of this world through their world, so solace me through Thy worship (*'ibāda*). *al-Wirdu l-a'ẓam*, 'Alī M. al-Qārī, (sentence said to be Prophetic)

it has been found necessary to call into service two more words from the same root to express the more inner meaning of the relationship of the *'abd* to his Lord—*'ubūdiyya* and *'ubūda*.

> *'Ubūdiyya* is nearer perfection than *'ibāda*. First comes *'ibāda*, then *'ubūdiyya*, then *'ubūda*. *'Ibāda* is for all believers, *'ubūdiyya* for the inner circle, *'ubūda* for the innermost circle. I have heard Abū 'Alī ad-Daqqāq say *'ibāda* is for those who possess the certainty of intellectual proof, *'ubūdiyya* is for those who possess the certitude of immediate knowledge, *'ubūda* is for those who are possessed by certitude.[1] I have heard him say *'ibāda* is for him who fights the good fight; *'ubūdiyya* is for those who endure hardness, and *'ubūda* is a quality of the people of vision. *Risāla Qushairiyya*, p. 98.

So our prayer-books describe Muslim saints as:

> Those who don the raiment of the glory of servitude (*'ubūdiyya*). *Majmū-'atu 'l-wirdi 'l-'āmm*, p. 66.

(b) Ṣalāt

If *'ibāda* is, as we have seen, the general name for the rites by which the *'abd* expresses his creatureliness, by far the most esteemed part of this activity is that for which the word *ṣalāt*[2] is used.

> The most excellent of the ways of worship is the *ṣalāt*, since it is a pillar of the faith, and includes within itself the invocation of God Most High and the declaration of His transcendence, and thanks to Him; and *ṣalāt* is the negation of immorality and of blameworthy or insolent conduct, and purifies and strengthens the body.[2] *Durūsu 'd-dīni wa 'l-akhlāq*, I.12. (Primary School Course, Damascus.)

[1] The three phrases, *'ilmu 'l-yaqīn*, *'ainu 'l-yaqīn*, *ḥaqqu 'l-yaqīn*, are taken from *Qur.* 102.5,7 and 56.95, and employed (with no reference to their Qur'ānic context) by the people of the inner life, to denote three stages of religious certitude.

[2] The usual Qur'ānic phrase is *aqāma 'ṣ-ṣalāt*. To-day *qāma bi 'ṣ-ṣalāt* or *qāma ilā 'ṣ-ṣalāt* or *aqāma ilaihā* he rose up to pray, is more often used, just as in Judaism the saying thrice daily of the Eighteen Benedictions (obligatory since shortly after the Fall of Jerusalem) is called the '*amīda* or "standing". Other phrases in the manuals are *Atā bi 'ṣ-ṣalāt, Adda 'ṣ-ṣalāt, qaḍā 'ṣ-ṣalāt, shahida 'l-'ishā', dakhala fī ṣalātihi, bāshara ṣalātahu*. For finishing the prayers the manuals have *kharaja min ṣalātihi, intahā min ṣalātihi, faragha min ṣalātihi, faraqa ṣalātahu*.

The word, when Islam adopted it, had a long history. The Aramaic verbal noun *sᵉlōtā*, which at first meant bowing, bending, had passed into several dialects with the meaning of prayer, and, as Mittwoch pointed out, was used by Aramaic-speaking Jews for the obligatory recital of the Eighteen Benedictions thrice daily. (*Zur Entstehungsgeschichte des islamischen Gebets*, Abh. Pr. Ak. Wiss. 1913.) Similarly the word *namāz* used by Iranian and Indian and Turkish Muslims for the prayer-rite had an original sense of bowing oneself. The word *ṣalāt* has not so far been found in pre-Islamic Arabic and would seem to have been adopted from Aramaic, or less probably from Syriac, for the worship of the new religion. It has passed into Christian Arabic also, and here we have to note an important variance between Muslim and Christian use.

Islam limits the word almost, though not quite, exclusively to two meanings: first the official prayer-rite of the five hours, and of Friday, with its variants for special occasions; and secondly the calling down of blessing on the Prophet (dealt with in Chapter XI). Our manuals show no example of its use in a wider sense. It is possible that in the course of centuries the Christian Arabic world has extended the meaning of the word *ṣalāt*, just as the Muslim world has limited it. Certainly its meaning in modern Christian books is as wide as that of the English word "prayer", and like that word it can also be restricted to a single Godward utterance, "a prayer". This variance in the use of so well known a word, as between Muslim and Christian, is enough to give Christian devotional books a strange sound in Muslim ears.

If Western scholars believe that, as with the liturgies of other religions, the full development of the five prayer-periods and their ritual was a gradual one, the writers of our manuals have no doubt that the prayer-rite, as they experience it, is both primitive and fundamental, a dictation of the Prophet himself.

Muḥammad who taught us the phrases we should say at the standing, the bowing, the prostration. *Awrād Aḥmad at-Tījānī*, p. 51.

Your Lord, Mighty and Majestic, says: He who performs the prayer-rite at its due time and observes it carefully, not slighting it by admixture of anything else, has a pact with Me that I shall make him enter Paradise. And Muḥammad said: Best of all works in the sight of God is the prayer-rite at its due time—that is to say, beginning with punctuality. *al-Fatḥu 'r-rabbānī*, M. 'Abd Allah b. Ḥasanain, p. 43.

(Both traditions are quoted in the *Iḥyā'* 4.1. To the second al-Ghazālī adds (as most of our manuals would agree) that the prayer-rite is next in value among good works to *tawḥīd* and that, had there been any better rite of worship, God would have taught it to His angels, whom, however, we see engaged in the *ṣalāt*, bowing, prostrating themselves, and standing (*Qur.* 48.29).)

So our manuals constantly repeat the Abrahamic prayer of the Qur'ān:

> My Lord make me one who performs the prayers[1]—and my descendants. *Qur.* 14.40.

It is hard for those trained in another school to realize the universal and inescapable character of *ṣalāt* for a practising Muslim. A little Christian can be taught to pray at his mother's knee and can know in his home something of the reality and fellowship of Christian worship, while he has little or no knowledge of the official service books of his Church. Such a state of affairs is unthinkable in Islam. A little Muslim is taught *first* the practice of the set prayers. The primers provided for teaching religion in the primary schools of any Muslim country contain nothing recondite, hardly anything interior, but always begin with careful and kindly instruction in the exact ritual and wording of the prayers of the five hours.

An Indian Muslim, enquiring of *The Light*, Lahore, as to the value of the external movements which he described as "tedious mechanical drill" received the following explanation:

> It is not a mechanical drill, but the various postures of humility in *ṣalāt* indicate complete external or bodily submission to God which conforms with the spiritual submission, and this is a necessity since man has a body as well as a soul which exercise great influence on each other through their movements. The submissive movements of the body in this prayer produce equivalent submissive movements in the soul.

Ṣalāt, then, is the dominant note in the music of Muslim devotions. The rubrics in our manuals commonly enjoin that the various devotions shall be said after the prayers of one of the canonical hours, partaking in the cleanness of its ablution. Or they may give directions for extra and voluntary performances of the *ṣalāt* with special intention and with inserted petitions for forgiveness or protection. In spite of

[1] muqīma 'ṣ-salāt: see footnote (2), page 6.

their richness and fullness, these devotional manuals claim only the position of a glorious appendix to the prayers of the five hours. To draw a comparison from Christendom, it is as though the whole laity of the Anglican Church had to say the services of Morning and Evening Prayer daily throughout the year before it was permissible for them to say any other prayers.

Our manuals show fully that for the saints the rite may be deeply spiritualized (see below, *sujūd, munājāt*).

> One of his prayer-phrases when he rose up for the daily prayers was: "Make this prayer-rite a link between me and Thee, let it not be a commercial transaction of mine with Thee. Make it a performance free from all that is unseemly or disapproved and teach me in it to invoke Thee with the greatest of invocations." *al-Mafākhiru 'l-'aliyya*, ash-Shādhilī, p. 191.

They also show the sense of all inward worshippers that the outward rite, if it may not, for legal as for spiritual discipline, be dispensed with, may sometimes be left behind and transcended in the experience of immediate Presence:

> Then I said: "O Lord what performance of the prayers is nearest to Thee?" And He said: "The prayer-rite in which there is none but Me and the performer of it is absent from the rite he performs." *al-Ghawthiyya*, 'Abd al-Qādir al-Jīlānī.

This had been of old a counsel of the desert fathers. Cassian gives the words to St Anthony:

> There is no perfect prayer so long as the monk is conscious of himself and the business of his praying. (Cassian, *Coll.* 9.31.)

(c) SUJŪD

We have seen (note 2 under *ṣalāt*) that the standing position is typical of the whole prayer-rite, which is a "standing up to pray". The word used for the bowing position, *rukū'* (often used in *ḥadīth* for the prostration), has also become typical of the rite, *rak'a* being used elliptically for the whole cycle of acts and words surrounding a prostration.[1] But the word and the act which has been most filled with

[1] *rukū'* corresponds to the Hebrew *kerī'ōth*, which, originally meaning "falling on the knees", is now represented by a bending of the knees. Mittwoch sees in the curious fact that Islamic prayer mostly used two or multiples of two *rak'as*, never one alone, an echo of the double saying of the Jewish *tefilla* by leader and

spiritual meaning is the prostration, *sujūd, sajda.*[1] This is extended from the set prayers to Qur'ānic reading of the fourteen "verses of prostration". The act is so perfect an expression of the worship of humiliation, of abandon and surrender, that the word is sometimes used to express this without implying the physical act and so comes to be a general term for worship, though the thought of prostration is never far away. How can it be for any man who has had as part of his religious inheritance from childhood the sight of those rows of prostrate figures in the mosque?

> I beseech Thee with the beseeching of the abased sinner, the petition of one whose neck is bowed before Thee—whose face is in the dust before Thee. *Du'ā' for the 23rd day of Ramaḍān*, 'Alī Zain al-'Ābidīn.

> Lord, wilt Thou blacken faces that fall prostrate before Thy greatness? *Munājātun 'aẓīma, Majmū'atu 'l-aḥzāb*, Aḥmad Ḍiyā' ad-Dīn.

But prostration is the attitude not only of penitent humiliation but of adoration. The whole creation is thus said to adore God.

> Thou art He before whom the blackness of night, the light of day, the rays of the sun, the rustling of the trees, the voice of the waters make their prostration. *Fatḥu 'r-rasūl*, M. 'Uthmān al-Mirghanī.

And it is the mark of the saints, very literally their mark, for the Qur'ān says of them that they bear the traces of it in their faces (*48.29*) as the blessed in the Book of the Revelation have their Lord's name in their foreheads. (*22.4.*)

> It is said that the worshipper is at his nearest to God Most High during his prostration, therefore be abundant (at that time) in petition. (Based on *Qur. 96.19. al-Kalimu 't-ṭayyib*, p. 40. (al-Bukhārī, Abū Dāwūd, an-Nasā'ī.)

Of Muḥammad our manuals tell us:

> When he prostrated himself he used to say in his prostration, "Before Thee I prostrate myself, in Thee I believe, to Thee I am surrendered. My face is prostrate before Him who created it and moulded it and pierced for it (the openings of) hearing and sight. Blessed be God the Best of Creators." Ibid., p. 37.

people (loc. cit., p. 19). The devotional explanation of the two prostrations given by ash-Sha'rānī is, that the first is an act of obedience directly contrary to Satan's disobedience in refusing to prostrate himself, while the second is an act of thanks for having been allowed that grace of obedience. (*Laṭā'ifu 'l-Minan*, p. 227.)

[1] The Shī'a breviary is *aṣ-Ṣaḥīfatu's-sajjādiyya* and a prayer carpet is often called a *sajjāda*.

The Shī'a books order a still fuller form, and say that it was used by 'Alī Zain al-'Ābidīn "when he made his prostration in the mosque at Kufa":

> My worn mortal face is prostrate before Thine everlasting, ever abiding Face. My face is prostrate, dust-soiled, before its Creator, and meet and right is this prostration. My face is prostrate before Him who created and formed it and pierced for it (the openings of) hearing and sight. Blessed be God, the Best of Creators. My miserable and lowly face is prostrate before the Mighty, the Glorious. *aṣ-Ṣaḥīfatu 's-sajjādīyya*, p. 349.

It is to be regretted that some, though not all, of the Christian communities in Muslim lands are becoming like the pew-bound West, and as they tend to lose their freedom of expression in worship lose with it the help of prostration so eloquent of lowly adoration.

(d) Munājāt

A tradition in three of the great collections makes the Prophet say that when a man is at his prayer-rite he is in intimate converse with (*yunājī*) his Lord. (al-Bukhārī, *Ṣalāt* 39, *Mawāqit* 8; Muslim, *Masājid* 54; Aḥmad II.34.) The prayer-rite then is *munājāt*, confidential converse, like the "entretien et conversation de l'âme avec Dieu" of St François de Sales. So great a word could not fail to be fruitful in devotion. Our prayer-manuals give us *munājāt* attributed to many saintly authors, to Moses, to 'Īsā, to 'Abd al-Qādir al-Jīlānī. To 'Alī Zain al-'Ābidīn many are attributed in the Shī'a books, including three with the title "evangelical", said to be so called "because their sayings on poverty, on denudation, are like most of the sayings on poverty in the exhortations of the Gospel which descended on 'Īsā, not the Gospel which circulates amongst Christians to-day".[1]

The word *munājāt* is used not only as a title for devotions but in many a prayer of spiritual longing:

> My yearning for Thee is not solaced except by communion (*munājāt*) with Thee. *Munājātun 'aẓīma* in *Majmū'atu 'l-aḥzāb*, p. 455.

[1] *aṣ-Ṣaḥīfatu 's-sajjādiyya*, p. 162. The portrait of Jesus given by Muslim tradition is strongly ascetic, and recalls many of the ideals and sayings of the hermits of the Syrian and Nitrian deserts. These particular *munājāt* are, however, not remarkable in this respect.

Direct the tongue of my knowledge, through Thyself, in the presence-chamber of Thy converse (*munājātika*), to fitting behaviour towards Thee and to receptiveness towards Thee. *Ḥizbu 's-sayyid 'Alī Wafā.*

Intervene between me and any who would preoccupy me from my occupation of converse with Thee. *Wirdu 's-saḥr*, Muṣṭafā al-Bakrī, *Awrād*, p. 55.

O Transcendent in Praise and in Holiness, make me to taste the bliss of the converse of "Approach and fear not, thou art of those who are secure." *Ḥizbu 'l-waqāyā*, Ibn 'Arabī.

This prayer refers to the *munājāt* between Moses and his Lord at the Burning Bush. *Qur.* 28.31.

(e) Du'ā', Su'l, Taḍarru'

Du'ā', sometimes *da'wā*, *ad'iya'*. A cry or call (the same root-meaning lies behind the Hebrew *tefilla*), hence the offering of supplication in general; or in particular a single supplication, "*a* prayer", is *du'ā'*. This use is practically universal in Muslim Arabic. It is found in Christian Arabic (the Collects in the Liturgy, for instance, being so described), but modern Christian Arabic shows a tendency to give the word *ṣalāt* to a single petition. Possibly this could be justified by the history of the word, but in view of the strongly marked Muslim practice it is regrettable.

Da'ā li is to pray in favour of someone, to make vows on his behalf (as *da'ā 'alā* is to pray against, to curse) and is the common word for intercession, except that of prophets for lesser mortals. Modern Christian usage tends to substitute *ṣallā li'ajli* for *da'ā li*.

When a believer prays for his brother, the unseen world is revealed and the angel says "Amen" to his intercession. Al-Kulīnī, *al-Kāfī*, *Kitābu 'd-du'ā'*.

Synonyms of Du'ā'[1]

1. *Su'l* and the related verb, to ask (as in English the same verb is used of asking in the sense of questioning), used identically with *du'ā'*.

[1] *Ṭalab* (and the related verb) the thing sought, the *request*, though a much used synonym, is not included in this list because it does not occur as a title for devotions, but only in the course of them.

2. *Taḍarru'* (and the related verb). This is a "prayer of humble access" carrying a greater sense of abasement and humility than *du'ā'* and *su'l*. Thus in the Qur'ān text *Ud'ū rabbakum taḍarru'an*—"Make petition to your Lord with humble supplication" (7.53) the latter word is explained as meaning "with abasement and self-humiliation". (*Majmū'atu 'l-wirdi 'l-'āmm*, p. 99.)

3. *Tawassul* (see chapter 2 below).

The word *du'ā'* and its synonyms are often associated with spreading out the hands, and the proper position for petition is with outspread hands, palms upwards, as though to receive blessing, an ancient and natural gesture used in Babylonia and Egypt and Israel of old, and common to all Arab lands. The hands may be wiped over the face at the end of the petition in token of the application to the worshipper of the blessing received.

Traditions tell us that the Prophet sometimes used this gesture.

Some women dervishes (Darqawiyya) who invited Miss E. T. Ridley to their *dhikr* at Tlemcen held their heads *cupped* before them when their shaikha offered petitions. The outspread hands may be seen in some of the Eastern Churches at the recitation of the Lord's Prayer. Conversely, in a beautiful phrase constant in Muslim prayer, the Lord is said to be "opening His hands with good things" (*Al-bāsiṭu 'l-yadaini bi 'l-khair*). (Cf. Ps. 104.28; 145.16.)

(f) Dhikr

"But we will make mention of the Name of the Lord our God" (Ps. 20.7). The Hebrew *Zākār b^eshem* and the Aramaic *dukrānā* have flowered in the Arabic *dhikr* into a great system of devotion through the mention or invocation of the Name.

The verb in Arabic means to *remember*, *recollect*, and sometimes carries this sense in our manuals.

> My God, how sweet are the inner impulses inspiring our hearts to remembrance of Thee! *Munājātun 'aẓīma* in *Majmū'atu 'l-aḥzāb*, p. 457.
>
> Muḥammad, remembrance of whom is the spirit of our personality. *al-Qaṣīdatu 'l-Muḥammadiyya*, Al-Būsīrī.

At the same time, remembrance being a kind of inner mentioning, the word is identified with outward mentioning by the tongue.

> The spirits of lovers ever incline to moaning, nay weeping and wailing befits them, since they cannot be content with the less as a substitute for the

great. But the raising of the voice in the mention (*dhikr*) of the Beloved is more necessary and desirable than weeping over the distance of the Goal. *as-Silsilatu 'dh-dhahabiyya*, M. Aḥmad al-Madanī, p. 32.

The Qur'ānic use of the word is sometimes like the Hebrew "making mention of the Name of the Lord" (*87*.15). It is several times associated with *ṣalāt* (*87*.15; *33*.41; *4*.142; *5*.91), and once, in *62*.9, to "make mention of God" would seem to be a synonym for joining in the Friday prayer rite. Our manuals sometimes follow the Qur'ān in treating the word as a general term for worship. In the following passage Christian Arabic would probably have substituted *'ibāda* for *dhikr* without any change of meaning.

The worship (*dhikr*) of the eyes is weeping; the worship of the ears is listening; the worship of the tongue is praise and laud; the worship of the hands is distribution and giving; the worship of the body is effort and accomplishment; the worship of the heart is fear and hope, and the worship of the spirit is surrender and satisfaction in God. *Lawāmi'u 'l-bayyināt*, Fakhr ad-Dīn ar-Rāzī, p. 39.

When used in the plural (*adhkār*), the word has a special sense. It is the technical term for the phrases to be said in the prayer-rite as against the actions (*af'āl*) to be performed, and has come to mean any of the individual phrases of worship.

Everyone who becomes the disciple of one of the Shaikhs of the order, the erudite in inner reality, must know the formulae (*adhkār*) of his Shaikh's worship, and his litanies (*awrād*, in which the *adhkār* are strung together)—and must use the formulae imparted to him or such of them as are within his scope and capacity. *al-Mafākhiru 'l-'aliyya* (Shādhiliyya), p. 2.

We have then in *dhikr* a very rich word, combining the ideas of recollection, even, as we shall see, of recollectedness, of making mention, of invocation and of worship, especially under its aspect of invocation of the Name of God.

But there has been a further development highly characteristic of the spiritual life of Islam. This worship of invocation, found in rudiment wherever a religious soul calls upon the name of God, has grown in Islam into a system, the discipline and the solace of the devout. The word has come to stand for recitations of certain fixed phrases (usually based on the Name or Names of God, though other sacred phrases are used) in a given order. This outward recitation is undertaken to induce a state of inward recollectedness, of spiritual concentration on the One who is named. It is usually performed in common, and into the building up of these services the various religious orders have poured the treasures of their psychological and spiritual experience. They are planned with careful gradation of exercises, with the help of group suggestion, of rhythmical speech and breathing and of rhythmical movement, so as by a kind of self-hypnotism to banish any external sight or sound or thought.

The fascination of this semi-hypnotic experience, as well as religious ardour, draws to the *dhikr* circles some whose lives are poor and starved of rich sensation. Such village *dhikr* circles as those of the Mirghaniyya Order, so common among Berber servants or in the Sudan, of the Shādhilī Order, so common in the Egyptian Delta, of the little Khalīlī Order, once so common in Southern Palestine, or the *dhikr* circles of the Baiyūmī Order in some Cairo slum, consist of lesser bourgeoisie, peasants or workmen living in the world, led by one adept who knows the *dhikr* of an order. The only connection of this group with the order may be attendance at these meetings, when, hypnotized by rhythm of sound and action, they may escape from the immediate pressure of hard lives.

The *dhikr* gathering, however, is not only the village prayer meeting of Islam, nor does it attract only the illiterate and lowly. The writer knows men of education and position who have sought in this way food for spiritual hunger. The man who enters the *dhikr* seriously and with instruction has, in the suspense of all sensation, save that of the rhythmic beat of the uttered Name, a goal of the spirit. The suspension of all other consciousness is to be in favour of the flooding and interpenetration of his whole being by the influence, the Divine Reality, behind one of the Divine Names. So his being is to be transfused and unified through the Living Reality.

Our manuals are busy with the *dhikr*.

Dhikr may be that of the heart and that of the tongue, and best of all is that of both at once, but if he cannot accomplish both, that of the heart is to be preferred. *Adhkāru 'n-Nawawī*, p. 4.

The description of the *dhikr* is that thou art making mention with thy tongue and gazing with thy heart. ash-Shādhilī in *Al-Mafākhiru 'l-'aliyya*, p. 48.

The required *dhikr* is that of the heart, the tongue is only a way to that. He who perseveres with sincerity of purpose in the mention of God Most High finds that the blessing of that *dhikr* reaches his heart, and his heart lives through the *dhikr* of God Most High. . . . And Dhū 'n-Nūn said: He who really makes mention of God forgets all else beside that mentioning, and God keeps everything from him and is his recompense for everything else. *Ṭahāratu 'l-qulūb*, Ad-Dīrīnī, pp. 20, 22.

O God the recollection (*dhikr*) of the heart is the recollection of (Thine) actions; and the recollection of the inmost being (subconscious, *sirr*) is the recollection of (Thine) attributes; and the recollection of the spirit is the recollection of (Thine) Essential Being. *Ḥizbu 's-sirri 'l-maṣūn*, 'Abd al-Qādir al-Jīlānī.

Qur'ānic Support

So great a development of devotional activity outside the prescribed rites of Islam, one which still to-day is suspect amongst some orthodox theologians, and illegal in Turkey, stood in great need of a justifying basis in Qur'ān and Tradition. Our manuals quote at large in its support. The Qur'ānic texts most used in this way are *2.200*; *3.41*; *7.204*; *72.25*, and especially the command with promise, the verse of *adh-dhikru bi 'dh-dhikr*, remembrance for remembrance, mention for mention, *2.152*, *Udhkurūnī adhkurkum* "Remember Me and I will remember you." In all the devotional comments and prayers based on the promise, the meaning hovers between "remembrance" and "mention":

How can I forget Thee when Thou dost ever remember me? *Munājātun 'aẓīma* in *Majmū'atu 'l-aḥzāb*, p. 447.

Remember me O God and cause me to remember.

Turn to me and forgive me with a forgiveness that shall make me forget all else but Thee. *Ḥizbu 'n-nūr*, ash-Shādhilī.

O God, Thou art for ever the Remembered and the Rememberer. *Majmū'atu 'l-wirdi 'l-'āmm*, p. 62.

Thou hast said, and Thy word is truth, "Make mention of Me and I will make mention of you." (*Qur.* 2.152.) Thou hast, then, commanded us to make mention of Thee, and hast promised that for this Thou wilt make mention of us, an honour and a glory and a dignity to us.

Lo! here are we making mention of Thee as Thou hast commanded, then bring to pass for us what Thou hast promised, Thou Mentioner of them that make mention. *Munājātun 'aẓīma* in *Majmū'atu 'l-aḥzāb*, p. 447.

Remember Me through grace, I will remember you through mercy. Remember Me in petition, I will remember you in bestowal. Remember Me in this world, I will remember you in its sequel. Remember Me in solitude, I will remember you openly. Remember Me with repentance, I will remember you with forgiveness. *Lawāmi'u 'l-bayyināt*, Fakhr ad-Dīn ar-Rāzī, p. 30.

Traditional Support

The traditional support adduced in our manuals for *dhikr*, is of two kinds, those traditions which connect the *dhikr* with the Prophet's practice and approval, and those traditions (*ḥadīth qudsī*) in which a saint expresses the spiritual illumination that God has given him as an utterance of God Himself.

From numerous examples we can only quote a few:

I. PROPHETIC TRADITIONS

A man said, "O Messenger of Allāh, the legislation of the faith has become too complicated for me, tell me then of some one thing to which I can apply myself." He said, "Let thy tongue be for ever moistened with the mention of God Most High." *al-Kalimu 'ṭ-ṭayyib*, Taqī ad-Dīn ad-Dimishqī, p. 6.

He (M.) said, if he were to smite the unbelievers and polytheists with his sword till it was broken and blood-stained, yet those who make mention of God would be better than he. *Adhkār an-Nawawī*, p. 20.

The following is interesting as a justification of the ecstatic condition of the *dhikr*:

Muḥammad who said, "Be abundant in the mention of God Most High to such a degree that men call you demented." *ad-Durru 'l-fā'iq*, Muṣṭafā al-Bakrī, p. 34.

And the following would make Muḥammad the precursor of all the many *dhikr* gatherings that use the *tahlīl* as their formula:

And it has come down to us that he (the Prophet) taught 'Alī ibn 'Abī Ṭālib. The Shaikh Yūsuf al-Kūrānī narrated, with a sound *isnād*, that 'Alī asked the Prophet saying, "O Apostle of God guide me to the nearest way to God and the easiest for His worshippers." Then the Prophet said, "The best is (to say) what I and the Prophets before me said *Lā ilāha illā 'llāh*." Then 'Alī said, "How shall I make mention, O Apostle of God?" And he said, "Close your eyes and listen to it from me three times, then you say it three times while I listen." And the Prophet said *Lā ilāha illā 'llāh* three times with closed eyes and raised voice while 'Alī listened. Then 'Alī. . . .

It is narrated of Shaddād ibn Uwais that he said, We were with the Apostle of God, and he said, "Have you among you any?"—meaning any people of the book.[1] We said, "No." So he said, "Raise your hands and say *Lā ilāha illā 'llāh.*" And we raised our hands for an hour saying *Lā ilāha illā 'llāh.* (*as-Silsilatu 'dh-dhahabiyya*, M. Aḥmad al-Madanī, p. 26.)

2. ḤADĪTH QUDSĪ

Of these, round which the meditation of worshippers has played, we give only two examples.

(a) God Most High said, I am the Companion[2] of him who recollects Me and I am with My servant when he makes mention of Me and his lips move with the mention of My Name. *Jāmi'u 'l-uṣūli fī 'l-awliyā'*, Aḥmad al-Kamshakhānī.

(The tradition is in the *Usūlu 'l-Kāfī* of *al-Kulīnī* (Kitābu 'd-du'ā') but is constantly quoted in Sunnī as well as Shi'a devotions. Massignon traces it to Ka'b al-Aḥbār on the authority of *Ḥilyat al-awliyā'*.)

(b) The Prophet said, God Most High has said, When my worshipper's thought turns to Me, there am I with him. And when he makes mention of Me within himself, I make mention of him within Myself: and when he makes mention of Me in company, I make mention of him in a better company. And if he draw nigh to Me a handbreadth, I draw nigh to him an arm's length. And if he draw nigh to Me an arm's length, I draw nigh to him the length of both arms outstretched. And if he come to Me walking, I come to him running.

The meaning of this session of God with His servant is that His mercy and His care and His provision and generosity, and the light of His Names and attributes are so near to a servant who is sincere in the mentioning of His Name, that the worshipper's heart is indwelt and filled with those lights. *Lawāmi'u 'l-bayyināt*, Fakhr ad-Dīn ar-Rāzī, p. 34, and *Ṭahāratu 'l-qulūb*, Ad-Dīrīnī, p. 20. Cf. Aḥmad ibn Ḥanbal, *3*.430.

CEASELESS DHIKR

In the idea of the ceaseless *dhikr* of the heart we come very near to the New Testament ideal of "prayer without ceasing".

It has been said, "Satan never ceases for one instant to busy himself with a human being"; then it behoves thee unceasingly to busy thyself with Him

[1] Apparently, literate persons, or persons acquainted with the Qur'ān (?) who might lead the prayers of the group.
[2] Literally "the one who sits with".

who holds thy forelock in His hand, that He may save thee from Satan's troubling; and the only method for so busying thyself is by abundance of *adkhār*. *Majmū'atu 'l-wirdi 'l-'āmm*, p. 103.

One of the verifiers[1] said that every religious observance prescribed by God Most High was prescribed with its limit and termination, after which the worshipper was free to enter upon other occupations, with the sole exception of the *dhikr* to which no limit and termination is known, and which none is free to depart from unless he be of unsound mind. For indeed it (the *dhikr*) is an unqualified and general duty, commanded at all times, in all places and under all conditions. *Durru 'n-nufūs*, Muṣṭafā al-Bakrī, p. 103.

So 'Abd al-Qādir al-Jīlānī could say his famous word:

Dhikruka shi'ārī wa thanā'uka dithārī—"The mention of Thee is my badge, and Thy praise my robe." *Du'ā'u 't-tawassul*. Cf. Isa. 61.3.

This method of prayer through the repetition of the Name has never taken root in the West, but is not foreign to Eastern Christianity. To show the close kinship of method we quote from the story of a Russian *staretz* who may be compared to a wandering dervish. His instructor said to him:

Sit down alone and in silence. Lower your head, shut your eyes, breathe out gently and imagine yourself looking into your own heart. Carry your mind (i.e. your thoughts) from your head to your heart. As you breathe out, say, "Lord Jesus Christ, have mercy upon me." Say it moving your lips gently, or simply say it in your mind. Try to put all other thoughts aside. Be calm, be patient, and repeat the process very frequently.

Here is a rosary. Take it, and to start with say the Prayer three thousand times a day. Whether you are standing or sitting, walking or lying down, continually repeat, "Lord Jesus Christ, have mercy upon me." Say it quietly and without hurry, but without fail exactly three thousand times a day, without deliberately increasing or diminishing the number. God will help you, and by this means you will reach also the unceasing activity of the heart.

(Later on the number of recitations was increased.)

In my lonely hut I said the Prayer of Jesus six thousand times a day for a whole week. I felt no anxiety. Taking no notice of any other thoughts, however much they assailed me, I had but one object—to carry out my staretz's bidding exactly.

At times I do as much as forty-three or forty-four miles a day, and do not feel that I am walking at all, I am aware only of the fact that I am saying my

[1] The people of first-hand religious experience.

Prayer. When the bitter cold pierces me I begin to say my prayer more earnestly and I quickly get warm all over. When hunger begins to overcome me, I call more often on the Name of Jesus, and I forget my wish for food. When I fall ill and have rheumatism in my back and legs, I fix my thought on the Prayer and do not notice the pain. If anyone harms me, I have only to think, "How sweet is the Prayer of Jesus" and the injury and anger alike pass away and I forget it all.

After no great lapse of time I had the feeling that the Prayer had, so to speak, by its own action passed from my lips to my heart. That is to say, it seemed as though my heart in its ordinary beating began to say the words of the Prayer within, at each beat. Thus, for example, *one* "Lord", *two* "Jesus", *three* "Christ" and so on. I simply listened carefully to what my heart was saying. From *The Way of a Pilgrim*, trs. R. M. French, pp. 22–32.

For Muslim and Christian alike the *dhikr* is no end in itself. When it has worked its perfect work it is superseded.

In the *Mawāqif* of Shaikh Muḥammad an-Niffarī (24.1) it is written: He who is the Truth, Blessed and Exalted, caused me to stand before Him in a dream and said to me, "If Thou dost not see Me, then persevere with My Name." Now He, Blessed and Exalted, only commanded him to be busy with the recitation of His Name when he did not see Him, for the presence-chamber of Open Vision is the presence-chamber of speechless wonder and dumbness where voices are hushed in their awe of the Merciful. *Laṭā'ifu 'l-minan*, Ash-Sha'rānī, p. 125.

(g) Wird

It may be that the traveller's arrival at a watering-place, his descent to drink, has given to religion this name for litanies of approach compiled to facilitate the soul's arrival at her goal. This explanation would seem to be in the mind of the writer who composed the following sentence:

Praise be to God because those whom He would (*arāda*) He caused to reach (*awrada*) the place of watering (*mawrūd*) and among all His worshippers singled out the people of the *awrād* by special wafts of His generosity, granting them the grace of divine inspirations (*wāridāt*). *Majmū'u ṣalawāti wa awrādi Sīdī Muṣṭafā al-Bakrī*, p. 51.

A less picturesque, but very possible source of the name lies in the fact that the word *wird* was used for divisions of the Qur'ān and also for divisions of the day or night. Al-Ghazālī so used it, the twenty-four hours being cut into seven *awrād*, to each of which was to be allotted its devotional exercises. It is possible, then, that *awrād* were divisions of the Qur'ān allotted for recitation, or offices of the hours (Christian Arabic *siwā'iyya* from *sī'ā'* a portion, an "hour" of the night), before they were litanies or devotions in a more general sense.

Our writers with their love of play on words enjoy connecting the *wird* with *ward*, a rose, a flower, so making it a kind of rosary.

> O aspirant, diligent in plucking the flowers of the *awrād*. *Wirdu 's-saḥr*, Muṣṭafā al-Bakrī, preface.

Another favourite play on words is a combination of *awrād* with *wāridāt*. The latter are divine effusions that suddenly flush the soul, inrushes of grace or inspiration.

> *Wāridāt* come by way of *awrād* and he who has no *wird* as part of his outward life has no effusion of grace (*wārid*) on his inward life. *Rabī'u 'l-fu'ādi fī ādābi 't-ṭarīqa*, 'Abd Allah ash-Sharqāwī, p. 104.

In the composition of these litanies of approach, or these rosaries of strung-together *adhkār*, devotional freedom and variety of personal taste has been great. Each order cherishes a bunch of such litanies compiled or adopted by its spiritual leaders. The most famous *awrād* are all known by name. The verb *laqqan*, to teach by dictation, by word of mouth, plays a great part in the story of the *awrād*. Though they are written down, this is often still the method of their impartation, and many of them claim to have been received in that way from the greatest spiritual personages of old, or even from the Prophet.

> We have been informed that he (Aḥmad at-Tījānī) saw the Prophet (not in a dream but) waking and received from him, face to face, the *wird* of his order. *al-Fatḥu 'r-rabbānī*, M. ibn 'Abd Allah ash-Sharqāwī, p. 104.

Of Muṣṭafā al-Bakrī it is said:

> He ordained for his children *awrād* that he had himself learnt at the beginning of his religious life and others that he had composed towards the end of it. Some of them came to him through the oral teaching of prophets, others through that of saints. And he arranged for their recitation after the prayer-rite and urged perseverance in this recitation at other times also. Preface to *Majmū'u ṣalawātin wa awrād*.

If the *awrād* have their home in the dervish orders, only a few, to be said with special authorization, have remained their exclusive property. The general community of the faithful stood in need of such devotional help and the use of *awrād* has passed far beyond the membership of the orders.

The following recommendation occurs in a general book which does not contemplate attachment to any of the orders:

> It is incumbent on one who believes in God and the Last Day not to forsake his *wird*, which comes from the *Sunna* of the Prophet . . . for carefulness to recite his *wird* leads a worshipper out of the merely animal life and helps him to experience a perfect humanity. *Majmū'u 'l-wirdi 'l-'āmm*, p. 101.

(h) Waẓīfa, Rātib

Waẓīfa is first of all a duty, an office. In devotion it is a daily office usually prescribed to an individual by his director.

> Praise be to Him who facilitated him in the performance of his religious duties (*waẓā'if*) and the *awrād* of worship. *Majmū'u 'l-wirdi 'l-'āmm*, p. 2.

> As a man increases his daily offices (*waẓā'if*) so God Most High increases for him the delicate touches of His grace. *Risāla Qushairiyya*, p. 7.

In the word *rātib*, also used for a daily or fixed office, we have primarily the idea of something set or established. The word is used for the extra prostrations from the *sunna* of the Prophet enjoined after the five daily prayers, and in practice a fixed part of these. So also it is used of any regular daily office.

Of those who compiled *awrād* it is written:

> He arranged or ordered (*rattab*) their recitation after the five prayers. (Said of As-Sanūsī, *Al-Fuyūḍāti 'r-rabbāniyya fī ijāzati 'ṭ-ṭarīqati 's-Sanūsiyya*, and of Muṣṭafā al-Bakrī, *Majmū'u ṣalawātin wa awrād*, preface.)

Those who follow such a devotional rule may be called *ahlu 'r-rātib*. Of one *rātib* the composer says:

> Its excellences are many, among them that one of our brethren saw the Prophet urging him to sit with him on a prayer-mat, and he refrained saying, "I will not sit till you assure me of the safety, on the Resurrection Day, of every one of the people of the *rātib*." And the Prophet said, "I assure you of their safety."
>
> One of our brethren in his sleep heard a crier call from the direction of the Lotus Tree of Finality, who pointed out to him a paradise higher than any other. "That," said he, "is for the people of the *rātib*." *Sharḥu 'r-rātibi 'l-musammā bi 'l-anwāri 'l-mutarādifa*, M. 'Uthmān al-Mirghanī, p. 4.

(i) Ḥizb

The name, used for a party or division, is a technical term for a division (one-sixtieth) of the Qur'ān. It has probably passed from being a part of the Qur'ān allotted for recitation to being any single form of devotion. Many devotions are called *wird* in one collection and *ḥizb* in another, and no Muslim friend has yet been able to explain to the writer any difference in the use of the two words.

> Know that the real meaning of *ḥizb* is the *wird* received and used in worship, and such like. And idiomatically it is a collection of *adhkār* and petitions and approaches of the heart, arranged for recital and memorizing, and for refuge-seeking from evil and request for good and for resultant knowledge, spiritual and intellectual, with the gathering up of the whole heart towards God. *al-Mafākhiru 'l-'aliyya fī 'l-ma'āthiri 'sh-shādhiliyya*, p. 148:

There is, however, an unacknowledged tendency of the word (more than in the case of *wird*) towards semi-magical protection. The first notion which the phrase *ḥizbun 'aẓīm* gives to the ordinary reader is that of guardianship. Thus, of a prayer called *du'ā'u 'l-faraj*, the petition of relief:

> Ibn 'Asākir traced from Ja'far ibn Muḥammad from his father, from his grandfather 'Alī Zain al-Ābidīn, from his father al-Ḥusain, from his father 'Alī that the Prophet, when he was troubled by something (*aḥzabahu amr*) used to pray this petition, and used to say that it is the "petition of relief" and it is a great protective prayer (*ḥizbun 'aẓīmun*) famous for its blessed power (*baraka*). *Riyāḍu 'l-janna*, Yūsuf an-Nabhānī, p. 102.

Many famous *aḥzāb* have directions for use in order to quell or subdue (*taskhīr*) hostile forces of men or nature, some being what we should recognize as real devotions with this virtue attributed to them, and others apparently constructed as magical formulae.

Ibrāhīm ad-Dasūqī gives us examples of the latter.

> I have lifted off from the bearer of this writing and shielded him against, and fended off from him and barred him from the evils of. . . . (*Ḥizbu Ibrāhīm ad-Dasūqī, Majmū'atu 'l-aḥzāb*, p. 195.)

The famous *aḥzāb* of ash-Shādhilī, though true devotions, have, and it seems were intended by the saint to have this use. Of the universally known *ḥizbu 'l-baḥr* the following account is given:

The shaikh was travelling on his way to the Mecca pilgrimage in the sea of al-Qulzum with a Christian, and they were becalmed for days. Then he saw the Prophet in a vision of encouragement who taught him this *ḥizb*. And ash-Shādhilī recited it and ordered the Christian to set sail. "But where is the wind?" he answered; and the shaikh said, "Do as I say, for the wind is coming to you now." And as he said, so it happened, and the Christian accepted Islam. *al-Mafākhiru 'l-'aliyya*, p. 152.

When dying in the desert ash-Shādhilī is said to have gathered his disciples round him:

And gave them as a legacy *ḥizbu 'l-baḥr*, saying to them, "Make your children commit it to memory, for it contains the Greatest Name of God." Ibid., p. 39.

This semi-magical use of devotions is very prevalent in the prayer-manuals and has a far more respectable place in Islam than in Christianity, where the surrender of magical books was (Acts 19,13–20) and still is required of converts. That this white magic has been questioned in pious circles and again defended is shown by an interesting discussion concerning another *ḥizb* of ash-Shādhilī. "The *Ḥizb* of the Circlet"—*ḥizbu 'd-dā'ira*, said to have been compiled by him at the request of al-Mu'izz and given by the saint special *baraka* as an amulet:

The Shaikh (ash-Shādhilī) . . . said, "He who has this circlet on his head will not die." One of the shaikhs says that ash-Shādhilī's meaning in this was that such a man would be, through the *baraka* of the *ḥizb*, continually in the keeping and preservation of God against the oncoming of death so long as it (the *ḥizb*) was on his head, to such an extent that when God desired to take his spirit at the end of his ordained term of life, He would decree the removal of the *ḥizb* from his head by whatever means He chose. And this is proved by the fact that after ash-Shādhilī had written it for the King al-Mu'izz, saying to him, "So long as this circlet is on your head you will not die," when God wished to put into execution His decree (for the death of al-Mu'īzz) He disposed him to enter the bath, and in stripping for the bath he removed the "circlet", and in that bath he was killed.

If you say, "Since God had decreed his death it must of course take place at the end of his allotted term, and when that term was reached nothing could defend him or prevent his death, where then is the benefit of carrying the *ḥizb* and of the virtue which the shaikh assigned to it, since he knew that everyone must die at his decreed term, he who carries the *ḥizb* just as much as he who does not carry it?"—the answer is that a great benefit is to be noted from the assignation of this virtue to the *ḥizb* since he who carries it has his mind at rest. So long as it is on his head he is untroubled by the ambushes of foes, the stratagems of schemers, the treachery of traitors and by robbers and plotters who may assault him. So the *ḥizb* will be for him like a conquering army and an impregnable fortress. He said, "The proof of this is that the Lawgiver (Muḥammad) while he asserted for us that there is no bar to God's will and no defence against His decrees, yet at the same time set us the example of the use of protective and guarding formulae, and promised to those who say them God's protection and guardianship by their means. He commanded us also to protect ourselves against the foes of God by the use of fortresses and armies and breastplates." *al-Mafākhiru 'l-'aliyya*, p. 200.

(j) Ḥirz

The word means a stronghold and as such it is often applied to God, with its synonym *ḥiṣn*, in prayers like many of those in the Psalms, where God is addressed as my Rock, my Fortress, my Stronghold.

> O God set me and them in Thy refuge, Thy protection, Thy security, Thine inviolable sanctuary, Thy stronghold (*ḥirz*), Thy fold, safe from evil of every sultan and satan and jinn. *Ḥizbun usbū'ī*, Ḥasan al-'Ashshāq.

> And be to me a fortress (*ḥiṣnan*) and a stronghold (*ḥirzan*) O Cave of them that seek refuge. *Mukhtaṣaru ad'iyati Ramaḍān*, p. 30.

> He is an inaccessible stronghold (*ḥirzun manī'un*) against that which I fear and dread. His creation has no power comparable with the power of the Creator. *al-Ḥizbu 'ṣ-ṣaghīr*, Ibrāhīm ad-Dasūqī.

In the titles of devotions, however, the word has fallen from grace and indicates their use as talismans or amulets. It is the name given to extracts from the Qur'ān, written cabbalistically and sewn up in leather for carrying on the body as protection. As a title for prayers it is sometimes synonymous with *ḥizb*. The famous *ḥizbu 's-saifī* is also called *al-ḥirz al-yamānī*. *Ḥirz* has a less respectable synonym in *ḥijāb* used of some talismanic prayers, and which has not like *ḥirz* also a nobler use.

Part 2

ON THE THRESHOLD OF THE PRAYER-RITE

I

THE CALL TO PRAYER

Ādhān, Iqāma, Takbīr

The first phrase that pierces the twilight of the dawn from the minaret is *Allāhu akbar*, God is greater. Whether in the prayer-rite or in our little manuals it punctuates Muslim worship like a minute gun. Short and sharp as a battle-cry (and indeed *Allāhu akbar* has been one of the most terrible of the world's battle-cries, compelling as the *Deus le vult* of the Crusaders) it is the shout that turned virile desert men into the ironsides of Allāh, and even to-day in any moment of fierce excitement, in city riots, or in a discussion when tolerance comes to an end and the opponent's voice is to be drowned, *Allāhu akbar* still rattles out of hoarse throats. It is a cry both of the single-hearted adoration and of the sterner side of Islam's early days of struggle, as when in the spring of A.H.3 the murderers of Ka'b ibn al-Ashraf (whose satirical poems had incited the Quraish to revenge after the battle of Badr) cast his bloody head at Muḥammad's feet with the cry *Allāhu akbar*.

The most moving *takbīra* of a Muslim's life must be that which he utters at the climax of his Mecca pilgrimage. Muḥammad, returning to Mecca as a conqueror, entered the *Ḥaram*, the sanctuary of his fathers, and touching the sacred Black Stone with his staff broke out into an *Allāhu akbar* that spread in a rolling wave of sound through the host that followed him. That was the dedication of the heathen sanctuary to God who was greater, and to-day the pilgrim's guide-book tells him when he reaches the Black Stone to kiss it (or to touch it with his staff and kiss that), "and a *takbīr* with every kiss".[1]

The *Takbīr* is a *Stossgebet*, an ejaculation. Voices may be raised for it (though not those of women), while the rest of the prayer-rite should be said in an undertone. No one who has heard the low thunder of it as it used to roll from thousands of throats in St Sophia on the Night of Power can forget the sound. It is so short and so simple that it has almost no place in devotional commentaries. Without explication it

[1] *Dalīlu 'l-ḥajj*, Muḥammad Ḥasanain Makhlūf, p. 10.

stands woven into the whole body of Muslim devotion, a recurring point in the rich design, one of those things which, most taken for granted, have the most influence on human life.

The Qur'ānic basis for the *takbīr* is the command in *17.111*, "And proclaim his greatness by magnifying." *Takbīr*, the magnifying of the Lord, had of course its firm place before the rise of Islam in the worship of Jew and Christian, whether in the Psalms (e.g. 40.16; 70.4; 96.4; 145.3), in the *Magnificat*, or in the *yigdol elohīm* of Hebrew prayer, in which last, indeed, some have seen the origin of the Arabic *Allāhu akbar*.

Others have seen in the reiterated *takbīr* of the Call to Prayer a shout of defiance, a word of power, against the dethroned heathen gods believed (as so often also in primitive Christianity) to be living demonic forces, ousted by the new worship of Allāh but resentful. "God is greater" may have meant "greater than all the gods of the heathen".[1] Such an explanation would account for a whole range of traditions about the fear felt by evil forces at the recitation of the Call to Prayer. We have examples in the manuals.

(From Abū Huraira.) The Apostle of God said: When the Call to Prayer is sounded Satan retires. He has a break-wind so that the sound of the *ādhān* may not reach him. When the *ta'dhīn* is finished he comes forward again. Then when the second call within the mosque is given he once more retires. When that is over he approaches again to introduce ideas into the mind of the worshipper ("between the man and his soul") and he says, "Say this (utterance of the prayer-rite); say that," suggesting *adhkār* that the man was not then about to say (i.e. out of their proper course) till the worshipper in a state of confusion does not know the point he had reached. *al-Kalimu 'ṭ-ṭayyib*, Taqī ad-Dīn ad-Dimishqī, p. 53.

Suhail ibn Abī Ṣāliḥ said: My father sent me to the Banū Ḥārītha, a servant or friend of ours being with me. And a voice called to him by name from a wall, but when my companion advanced to the wall he saw nothing. I mentioned this to my father who said, "If I had realized that you would encounter this, I would not have sent you. But if you should again hear a voice, recite the Call to Prayer, for I heard Abū Huraira recount that the Prophet said, 'Satan retires when the Call to Prayer is given.'" Ibid., p. 54. (Tradition from al-Bukhārī, *10.4*.)

Zaid ibn Abī Aslam reported that he was put in charge of some mines and was informed that *jinn* were numerous in them. So he ordered them

[1] See Goldziher, *Zauberelemente im Islamischen Gebet*. Z.D.M.G. Vol. 49.

(the miners) to recite the *ādhān* at all hours of prayer, and to multiply their recitation of it, after which nothing more was seen. *al-Kalimu 'ṭ-ṭayyib*, p. 53.

The belief in the potency of the Call against evil still lives in popular religion. Thus a correspondent of the Aḥmadiyya paper, *The Light*, Lahore, inquires:

Is it on the authority of Qur'ān or any authentic *Ḥadīth* that during epidemics some people give *Ādhāns* at the top of their voice at dead of night in the affected locality, to drive away the disease, disturbing sleep and causing annoyance to the Muslims as well as non-Muslims residing in the same locality?

To which the modernist editor replies:

Nothing of the kind is mentioned either in the Qur'ān or the *Ḥadīth*.

It is probably this protective value of *Allāhu akbar* which has led to its being the first religious word heard by many a Muslim babe, for the custom is still common of sounding the Call to Prayer in the ear of a new-born baby. Snouck Hurgronje found it to be a regular part of the eighth day naming ceremony of the babes of Mecca.[1]

Abū Rāfi' said: I saw the Apostle of God give the Call to Prayer in the ear of al-Ḥasan ibn 'Alī when Fāṭima gave him birth. *al-Kalimu 'ṭ-ṭayyib*, p. 85. (Abū Dawūd *40*.106, Aḥmad VI. *9*.391,392.)

The following form of the tradition shows clearly that the practice is protective against demon powers:

He (M.) said: If a man, when a child is born to him gives the call to prayer in its left ear, Ummu 'ṣ-ṣubyān (a well-known female demon, snatcher of boy babies) will not hurt him. *al-Kalimu 'ṭ-ṭayyib*, p. 85, "from Ḥusain ibn 'Alī." (Ibn as-Sunā, al-Buhaiqī, *Adhkār an-Nawawī*.)[2]

The need for protection against the dangers that surround the spilling of "the blood that is the life thereof" when a beast is slain for food or sacrifice, may underlie the saying of *takbīr* at such a moment. A modern and edifying explanation of this is given by the editor of *The Light* in reply to a puzzled reader:

Question: What is the necessity of reciting *takbīr* at the time of *dhabaḥ*.

[1] Snouck Hurgronje, *Mecca*, p. 111.

[2] Compare the story in *Risāla Qushairiyya* of Ibrāhīm al-Khawwāṣ who ordered the Call to be sounded in the ear of a man afflicted with an evil spirit.

What difference would it make if we recite nothing at that time? Please discuss scientifically.

Answer: *Takbīr* makes no difference so far as meat is concerned. The effect is psychological. We take the life of a lower animal and the only justification for it is that it promotes the welfare of the higher species, man. When we do so, we must remember that there is a Being higher to man—in fact, above all else (*akbar*), and so at a higher call from Him we must likewise be ready to lay down our life.

Response to the Call to Prayer

Although the actual call from the minaret is a *sunna kifāya* (a usage fulfilled if some perform it on behalf of the rest) yet each individual has his part to play. It is a summons to preparation of heart.

> Cause us when we hear the Call to Prayer to turn ourselves exclusively to Thy mercy. *Majmū' tabāraka dhū 'l-'ulā*, anon., p. 4.

But it has its ritual requirement in the responsive echoing (*tarjī'*, a word used also of the assonances in rhymed prose or of a refrain in verse) of the Call, with certain variations.

> From 'Abd Allah ibn 'Umar (it is related) that a man said, "O Apostle of God, the *mu'adhdhins* are superior to us." And the Apostle of God replied, "Say the same as they, and when you have finished, make petition, and it will be granted you." *al-Kalimu 'ṭ-ṭayyib*, p. 32. (Al-Bukhārī, An-Nasā'ī, Ibn Ḥabbān.)

A charming variation on this which reads like a direction for a sort of angelus prayer at home on the part of a woman who is not going to the public prayers is quoted but has not passed into general use:

> (From Umm Salmā.) She said: The Apostle of God taught me to say at the sunset Call to Prayer, "O God, this is the time of the oncoming of Thy night and the passing away of Thy day, and the time of the voices of Thy *mu'adhdhins*, and the presence of Thy prayer-rite, then forgive me." *al-Kalimu 'ṭ-ṭayyib*, p. 35. (Abu Dawūd, At-Tirmidhī, Al-Ḥākim, Al-Buhaiqī, *Kitāb ad-da'wati 'l-kabīr*.)

The method of the *tarjī'* is as follows:

The words "God is most great (twice), I bear witness that there is no god save God. I bear witness that Muḥammad is the Apostle of God," are to be repeated by the listener. Then when the words "Come to prayer" are reached, the listener is to respond, "There is no might nor power save with God." And a similar response is to be made to the words "Come to prosperity",[1] while the final *takbīr* and *shahāda* is to be again echoed.

A deeply interesting suggestion was made by C. H. Becker that this little responsive dialogue and still more that which follows in the *iqāma* had its original place not in the call to prayer but as a preliminary part of the service itself ("*ursprünglich ein stück Liturgie*") corresponding to the preparatory prayers of all the Eastern Christian liturgies, which are in great part a dialogue between the priest and the deacon who represents the congregation.[2]

The Takbīr in the Prayer-Rite

As has been said, the whole Muslim prayer ritual is punctuated with the *takbīr*:

> Know that in the set prayer of two prostrations eleven *takbīrāt* have been appointed; and in that of three prostrations, seventeen *takbīrāt*, and in that of four prostrations twenty-two *takbīrāt*. *Adhkār an-Nawawī*, p. 21.

In the prayers of the great feasts twelve more *takbīrāt* are added (*takbīrātu 'z-zawā'id*).

Takbīratu 'l-iḥrām

The *takbīrāt* of the set prayers have various parts to play in the rite, some of them at its heart, and some of them during the change of

[1] This is the usual translation of *Hayya 'alā 'l-falāḥ*. Mittwoch, however, made the very interesting suggestion that *falāḥ* is, like *ṣalāt*, a foreign loan word. He points out that in Aramaic the root *flḥ* means first to till the soil (the general sense in which the root is used in Arabic also) and thence to serve God. (Cf. Latin *cultus*.) The phrases of the Call to Prayer may therefore probably be translated "Come to Prayer, Come to divine service." (See E. Mittwoch, *Zur Entstehungsgeschichte des Islamischen Gebets und Kultus*. Abh. Pr. Akad. Wiss. 1913. No. 2, p. 10 ff.) The Shī'a substitute for the phrase is *Hayya 'alā khairi 'l-'amal*—Come to the best work, the *opus Dei*. R. Strothmann, *Kultus der Zaiditen*, p. 51, gives a tradition from MS. Berlin 4947, fol. 78b that this was the original form for all Muslims and "It was 'Umar who commanded that it should be dropped for fear that men would not go out on the *jihād* but would stand praying."

[2] C. H. Becker, *Zur Geschichte des islamischen Kultus* (*Der Islam* 3.386). But there is also in Jewish prayer an introductory element before the Shema', for which in some synagogues the Vorbeter does not stand out, and of which Elbogen says, "Der erste Abschnitt wurde überhaupt nicht in der Synagoga, sondern im Hause gesprochen und diente als Vorbereitung für den öffentlichen Gottesdienst." *Der Jüdische Gottesdienst*, p. 15.

position which marks off one phase of the prayers from the next. The first *takbīra* is honoured with a special name, for it forms the barrier between the moment when a man preparing to pray has yet not entered upon the rite itself, and the moment when he is at his prayers, cut off from all else, in "the consecrated state".

This first *Allāhu akbar* is called *takbīratu 'l-iḥrām* or more shortly the *taḥarrum* or the *taḥrīma*—the prohibition or taboo—because it shuts off the prayer-time as sacred, and makes unlawful all ordinarily right acts, only the acts and words of the set prayer being permitted.[1]

> "When you have made your intention", the lesson books tell the primary schoolboy, "raise your hands till the two thumbs are at the level of the lobes of the ear and say *Allāhu akbar*.
>
> And this *takbīr* is called the *takbīr of prohibition*, or the opening *takbīr*, and it is also called the *prohibiting*, because the saying of it makes illegal what was permissible before entering upon the set prayer. One of the conditions of the validity of the Prohibition is that it should follow immediately upon the pronouncing of the Intention, and that the position should be that of standing upright, or as near to that as possible. . . . It is permissible that the Prohibition shall be made with other forms than 'God is most great', taken from right mentionings of Him such as 'God is most reverend'—but these must be said in a spirit of prohibitive aversion (from all that is not legal during the set prayers)." *Durūsu 'd-dīni 'l-islāmī*, 5, p. 103.

The saints after their manner pour spiritual meaning into the outward rite:

> Abū 'Amr az-Zajjājī was asked, "Why do you change colour at the first *takbīra* in the set prayers?" And he said, "Because I dread opening my duty of prayer with anything of untruth. For he who says *allāhu akbar* while in his heart something else is greater than God, or who has even in the passage of time magnified anything beside God, is in his heart giving the lie to his tongue. *Risāla Qushairiyya* (Malījī's edition, Cairo 1319), p. 30.

The Funeral Takbīr

The Muslim who has lived with the sound of the *takbīr* in his ears is laid to rest with it. It is in full accord with the noble God-consciousness of Islam that this note should be so dominant in the burial service that "to pronounce the *takbīr*" over anything is a synonym for declaring it dead to the speaker—for burying it out of mind.

[1] For a similar reason the special garment of the Mecca pilgrimage is the *iḥrām*, and the sanctuaries at Mecca and Jerusalem the *ḥaram*.

In an Urdu-Arabic primer the man who is about to say the funeral prayers over a fellow Muslim is taught to make this intention:

> I intend to perform four[1] *takbīrāt*, the funeral prayer-rite—praise to God Most High, calling down blessing on the Prophet, and prayer for this dead man (this I have resolved to do), facing the direction of the noble Ka'ba. *Majmū'u suwar wa ad'iya*, Anon. Bombay.

These *takbīrāt* (which are separate from the committal prayers at the tomb) are said in some countries in the mosque, in others in front of the dead man's house, sometimes in an enclosure. The imām standing at the head of the bier in the case of a man, at its foot in the case of a woman, pronounces them with hands raised. After the first he says the *Fātiḥa*, after the second the *ṣalātu 'alā 'n-nabī*, after the third a *du'ā'* for the dead, and after the fourth a *du'ā'* for those who take part in the prayers.

This most solemn *takbīr* of farewell has been used metaphorically by the saints. Abū Yazīd al-Bisṭāmī said that he had pronounced four *takbīrāt* over the creation—it was dead to him. Abū Sulaimān Dawūd ibn Nuṣair aṭ-Ṭā'ī said to one of his disciples, "If thou desirest welfare bid farewell to this world, and if thou desirest grace (*karāmat*) pronounce the *takbīr* over the next world."[2] (Even the next world may be a veil to hide the immediate vision of God.)

In Private Devotion

The prayer manuals abound in directions for the recitation of *takbīrāt*, literally by the hundred. The forms are sometimes slightly varied, as with a haunting repetition—*Allāhu akbar, akbar, akbar*; or with some intensification, *Allāhu akbar kathīran*, God is far greater, or *Allāhu akbaru 'l-akbar*, God is greater than the greatest.

The deeper souls are drawn out by the bare affirmation towards the mystery of the adorable Godhead:

> Praise be to the great God—and God is most great—magnifying Thy majesty. O our God this majesty is Thine in the soleness of Thy Unity. *Ḥizbu 'l-fatḥiyya*, 'Abd al-Qādir al-Jīlānī.

> Thou hast magnified Thyself before other magnifiers magnify Thee. *Du'ā'* of ash-Shādhilī.

[1] Shī'as say five.
[2] From Nicholson's translation of Al-Ḥujwīrī, *Kashf al-Maḥjūb*, p. 109.

But for the most part the fruit of *takbīr* in the life of Islam seems to be that quiet and dignity which grows out of the recognition of greatness. "Thy very greatness is a rest to weaklings as we are."

Aṭ-Ṭabarānī and others traced with a trustworthy *isnād* to Ibn 'Abbās that the Prophet said: If you are going before some dreaded potentate and fear that he will treat you harshly, say "*Allāhu akbar*, *Allāhu akbar*, mightier than all His created beings. God is mightier than him whom I fear, than him I dread." *Riyāḍu 'l-janna*, Yūsuf an-Nabhānī, p. 80.

2

THE PRAYER OF MEDIATION

Wasīla, Shafā'a

He who recites the Call to Prayer and the *Iqāma* and he who hears them should at once join in the Prayer of Mediation (*du'ā'u 'l-wasīla*):

> O God, the Lord of this completed call and of the prayer-rite now inaugurated, give to our Lord Muḥammad mediation and merit and a high rank, and that praiseworthy station which Thou has promised to him. *Dalā'ilu 'l-khairāt, al-Kalimu 'ṭ-ṭayyib, Fatḥu 'r-Rasūl* (from al-Bukhārī).

The utterance of this traditional prayer at this moment in the ritual is commonly supported by another tradition:

> (From 'Abd Allah ibn 'Amr ibn al-'Āṣ.) He heard the Apostle of God say: When you hear the *mu'adhdhin*, repeat what he says, then call down blessing on me, for he who calls down blessing on me, on him will God call down ten blessings. Then ask God to bless me with mediation, for that is an office in Paradise reserved for one only of the servants of God, and I hope to be he. And whoever asks for me the power of mediation shall have the right to my intercession. (*al-Ḥirzu 'l-manī'*, p. 102, *Adhkār*, an-Nawawī, 19. as-Suyūṭī explains *ḥallat lahu 'sh-shafā'atu* as *wajibat lahu*, it became his due.)

These two traditions have been the fruitful mothers of an immense tribe of prayers; but before considering their great influence on Muslim devotional life we should ask the meaning of the two crucial nouns in them, *wasīla* and *shafā'a*.

The Meaning of Wasīla

Wasīla is a noun used only twice in the Qur'ān (*5.34* and *17.57*—of seeking means of access to God). It means recommendation, means of access, favourable influence. The cognate noun *wāsila* is familiar to all who know the daily talk of Arabic lands; the man desirous of approaching an official or seeking to obtain a post says, "I want a *wāsila*," a go-between, a favourable introduction.

This is the general use of *wasīla* in the prayer-manuals:

(Of a set of blessings of the Prophet interlarded with Qur'ān verses.) When the possessor of them (these devotions) is concerned about some affair, every blessing of the Prophet in them will be a means of access (*wasīla*) for him to the Prophet and every Qur'ān verse in them a pleader for him with the great Lord. *Bashā'iru 'l-khairāt*, 'Abd al-Qādir al-Jīlānī.

My God I have no favourable recommendation (*wasīla*) to Thee save Thy compassionate pity and the intercession of Thy Prophet, the Prophet of Mercy. Then let these two recommendations secure me Thy forgiveness. *Munājātun 'aẓīma* (anon) in *Majmū'atu 'l-aḥzāb* of Aḥmad Ḍiyā' ad-Dīn, p. 454.

Wasīla is a noun of the court, and as Tor Andrae remarks on *du'ā'u 'l-wasīla*, the kind of nearness to God envisaged by that prayer is not the mystic union but the honourable position next the monarch. The nearer a man's position to the King the more effective his recommendation. That of the *wazīr* sitting on the King's right hand is the most potent of all, and this is the position envisaged for Muḥammad in *du'ā'u 'l-wasīla*. (See *Muḥammad in Lehre und Glauben seiner Gemeinde*, p. 260.)

Wasīla we learn from philologists is that with which we approach a king or a great man. One says *tawassalt* meaning "I approached." And it (*wasīla*) only refers to the highest position, as is explained by his phrase "for it is a position in Paradise". *al-Ḥirzu 'l-manī'*, As-Suyūṭī, p. 103.

The Meaning of Shafā'a

Shafā'a is intercession, but Christian readers need to note that whereas in the New Testament the same Greek verb is used of the heavenly intercession of Christ on behalf of His people, and of the earthly intercession of little Church groups on behalf of their rulers and of "all men" (Heb. 7.25; 1 Tim. 2.1), *Shafā'a* could only be used in the first case. It is the intercession of a mediator with the right to intercede, of the greater or more worthy on behalf of the lesser or less worthy. Its Muslim use is like the use of "blessing" in the Epistle to the Hebrews. "Without any dispute the less is blessed of the better." (Heb. 7.7.)

So our manuals explain:

Our *ṣalāt* for the Prophet is not intercession (*shafā'a*) from us on his behalf, for such as we do not intercede for such as he. *al-Ḥirzu 'l-manī'*, As-Suyūṭī, p. 23.

This general limitation of *shafā'a*[1] has left Arabic, Muslim or Christian, poor in expressions for the normal intercession of human beings for one another. *Da'ā li* (pray for) is a hard-worked substitute. It is to be remarked that no branch of prayer is so thin and scanty in the Muslim prayer-manuals as this of intercession for fellow-men

Qur'ānic Basis

The Qur'ānic use of *shafā'a* and the cognate verb as employed for intercession is interesting, the texts falling into three groups.

One group pictures sinful men after death unable to find any intercessor, all those on whom they trusted for this office failing them (*2*.48,123,254; *7*.53; *26*.10; *74*.48).

The second group asserts that *shafā'a*, mediation, is reserved by God as His own prerogative: *lillāhi 'sh-shafā'atu jamī'an* (*6*.51,70; *10*.18; *32*.3; *33*.45). This family of texts is behind a group of prayers in our manuals to be noted later.

The third group of texts is behind the overwhelming majority of Muslim prayers concerned with *shafā'a*. In this group there is no absolute prohibition of mediation, but because it is God's prerogative He gives the right to it to whom He will. No one can intercede *illā bi idhnihi*—except with His permission (the throne verse), *illā limani 'artaḍā*, except him who is approved (*21*.28). (See *2*.255; *10*.3; *20*.109; *21*.28; *34*.23; *43*.86.) Nowhere is any person named as having this privilege, but one verse is of outstanding importance as the basis for the claim that this right is exclusively Muḥammad's. This is *43*.86—"And those on whom they call beside Him have not the authority for intercession, except him who bears witness to the truth, as they are aware."

[1] There are a very few traces of a more general use in the manuals. Thus in *Ḥizbu 'l-fatḥīyya* attributed to 'Abd al-Qādir al-Jīlānī occur the words *Shafī'ī dumū'ī* (my tears are my intercessor) and *lā shafī' siwā 'l-amal* (hope is my only intercessor), while in an Algerian folk-poem very close to the spoken Algerian Arabic (*qaṣīda fī faḍli 'l-Qur'ān*, anonymous) it is said that he who carries the Qur'ān with him will in the Resurrection *yashfa'u fī 'l-qurbā wa'l jīrān*—will (have the right to) intercede for his relatives and neighbours. (*Majmū'u 'l-qaṣā'idi wa 'l-ad'iya*.) A Nubian fellaḥ told the writer of a belief that the souls of babes who died in their innocence will ask and be allowed to intercede for their parents at the Judgment. They will say, "This is my father, this is my mother, *shaffa'nī fīhim*."

Worshippers' Questionings Concerning Shafā'a

The magnitude of the claims put forward for the mediation of Muḥammad has roused questionings in two directions. The first is the question as to whether the Qur'ānic data justify the enormous weight laid upon Muḥammad's intercession in the devotional practice of Islam.

An Indian Muslim writes to *The Light* of Lahore:

> What is your idea of *Shafā'at* (intercession)? Does the Holy Book confirm the Shafā'at of our Prophet? *Shafā'at*, as I have read in the *'Aqā'id-al-Islam* seems to me like another form of atonement. If *Shafā'at* popularly held is possible, then certainly atonement of Christ is also right.

The question is answered by Dr Bashārat Aḥmad Shah of Jhelum. His remarks on the Christian doctrine of the Atonement do not concern us here. His explanation of *Shafā'a* is as follows:

> Sometimes we feel moved at the plight of some one and wish to forgive him. But as a mark of respect to some one dear to us, we invite his recommendation on behalf of this offender. This form of prayer for forgiveness is known as *Shafā'at*, i.e. intercession. In Islam such intercession is always *with* Divine permission. Unless God should Himself invite it, there can be no *Shafā'at*.

In the prayer manuals ash-Shādhilī is credited with words that raise the whole question:

> I asked: What is the sin of association of anyone or anything with God? He (ash-Shādhilī) said: The taking of helpers or mediators (*Shufa'ā'*) other than God. "Ye shall have no helper and no mediator other than Him." (*Qur.* 6.51.) I asked: and what is lack of confidence in God? He said: He who hoped in others than God and sought the succour of others than God, out of despair that God Himself would help him. *al-Mafākhiru 'l-'aliyya fī 'l-ma'āthir 'sh-Shādhiliyya*, Aḥmad ibn Muḥammad ibn 'Ibād, p. 27.

The other questioning is at the opposite pole. From a full acceptance of the position of Muḥammad as the privileged Mediator and Intercessor, the questioner inquires why the worshipper should be directed to ask at every prayer-rite in *du'ā'u 'l-wasīla* that the Prophet should have a position which all know to be already his.

> If it is asked, "What is the good of requesting *wasīla* for him when he said 'I hope that I may be he', and his hope is realized without fail?"—the answer is that our asking this for him is a matter of obedience to what he

commanded in regard to his noble person, and this applies to our *ṣalāt* for him and greeting him with peace, although his former and his latter sins were all forgiven, as has come down to us in the *Muqaddima*. God knows best. *al-Ḥirzu 'l-manī'*, As-Suyūṭī, p. 103.

(The writer apparently holds the old view that God's *ṣalāt*, asked for the Prophet, means His forgiveness.)

A third question arose as to whether a righteous and law-keeping Muslim stood in need of the Prophet's intercession. Was it not only for the sinful? This was disposed of as follows:

It has been said, "Do not say, 'O God, provide us with the intercession of the Prophet,' for only those who deserve the fire are interceded for." But I say that this was sheer ignorance, for how many a tradition in the *Ṣaḥīḥ* shows us the longing desire of Muslims who were perfect keepers of their covenant for the intercession of the Prophet offered in his own word, "He who repeats after the *Mu'adhdhin* his words has obtained my intercession." . . . The traditions in the *Ṣaḥīḥ* of Muslim and other collections firmly establish the fact of intercession being made for some groups that they may enter Paradise without judgment, and for another group that their position in Paradise may be a higher one. *Adhkār*, an-Nawawī, p. 169.

The Prayer of Assurance

Although in *du'ā'u 'l-wasīla* the form is gone through of asking this position of central influence for the Prophet, the majority of the devotions concerning *shafā'a* show no manner of doubt that he has obtained it. The hope is supported by *Qur.* 93.5. As his figure looms ever larger and larger before his people, and as they consider what they feel to be his supreme and universal mission on earth, how can they doubt that his will be a supreme and universal mission in the other world also?

O Lord, as his was the work of setting forth Thy message, and as he delivered the creation from its ignorance and strove against infidelity and error, and called men to affirm Thy Unity, and gave right measure of orthodoxy for the guidance of Thy worshippers, even so grant him what he asks, let him attain his desires, and give him mediation and favour. *Dalā'ilu 'l-khairāt*, p. 160.

O God, I ask Thee by his position with Thee, and his confidence in Thee, and his yearning for Thee, to appoint him a Mediator to whom is given the task of intercession for me and for my parents and for all who believe in Thee. *Ikhtitām 'Ashshāqiyya.*

We approach Thee through him, and make him our Mediator with Thee, him the lord of the Great Intercession, and of the august influence. *Wirdu 'ṣ-ṣalāti 'l-kubrā*, 'Abd al-Qādir al-Jīlānī.

Thou hast selected me for the grace of belonging to the Prophet whose call is the greatest, whose intercession is the highest, whose station is the nearest to Thyself. *al-Ḥizbu 's-saifī.*

He is the friend of God: his intercession it is
On which alone our every hope is based;
And in him alone our defence is to be sought
Against the most appalling dangers
O thou most excellent of created beings!
To whom but thee can I fly for refuge
In that moment so terrible to every mortal?

(Contributed in English by M. U. Aḥmad to *The Epiphany* of Calcutta.)

As the Christian worshipper makes his petition "through Jesus Christ our Lord", so the Muslim worshipper expects the acceptance of his petitions through the *wasīla* of Muḥammad:

I proffer Thee all this for acceptance through the August Influence. *Ḥirzu 'l-azal*, Muḥammad ash-Shādhilī.

Who are included in Muḥammad's "Shafā'a"?

He is "*shāfi'u man fī 'd-dārain*", intercessor for those in both worlds, and as we have seen, for saints as well as sinners. The overwhelming majority of the prayers imply however that his intercession will be reserved for those of his own people, his *umma*, his community:

O God, appoint our lord Muḥammad as the most trusted of speakers and the most prevailing of requesters and the first of intercessors, and the most favoured of those whose intercession is acceptable, and cause him to intercede acceptably for his nation and his people, with an intercession in which the first and the last are included. *Dalā 'ilu 'l-khairāt*, p. 105.

One Shī'a prayer stands out alone in the manuals, in regarding his ministry as for other communities:

Accept his intercession for his community and for other communities. *Du'ā'* for the 30th Day of Ramaḍān attributed to 'Alī Zain al-'Ābidīn.

The Relation of Muḥammad's "shafā'a" and "wasīla" to that of other Prophets

One of the petitions in *Dalā'ilu 'l-khairāt* (echoed elsewhere in the manuals) runs:

> O God, accept the Great Intercession of our lord Muḥammad. Grant him his request in this world and the next, as Thou didst grant the requests of our lord Ibrāhīm and our lord Mūsā.

This does not, however, imply an equal standing for those prophets in the ministry of *shafā'a*.

A Shī'a prayer asks that all the prophets may have the power of petition in the next world:

> And give them utterance in petition when mouths are dumb before Thee. *Du'ā'un fī 'ṣ-ṣalāti 'alā 'n-nabī* attributed to 'Alī Zain al-'Ābidīn.

Although one or two of the manuals quote al-Ghazālī's *'aqīda*:

> And that he should believe in the intercession of the prophets, next of the learned, next of the martyrs, next of the rest of the believers—each according to his dignity and rank with God Most High (*Iḥyā'*, II, pp. 17–44)

on the whole they indicate a belief that *shafā'a* is the ministry of Muḥammad alone and that other prophets are indebted to his *wasīla*[1]:

> And by that name (of Muḥammad) Adam named him and through him interceded, and blessings were called down upon him (M.) in the nuptials of Eve . . . and by that name 'Īsā will name him in the other world when he indicates him for mediation; and by that name Gabriel addressed him in the tradition of the *Mi'rāj* and in others; and by that name Abraham also called him in the tradition of the *Mi'raj*. And the Angel of the Mountains addressed him by that name, and with that name the Angel of Death ascended weeping when he bore his soul away, crying: "Oh me! Muḥammad, Ah!" And by that name he called himself to the Guardian of Paradise, when he asked for its opening and it was opened to him. *Fatḥu 'l-Karīmi 'l-Khāliq*, 'Alī al-Makkī.

> Call down blessing on Muḥammad—who was the *wasīla* of Adam and of Abraham, the means of access of Moses and of Noah the illustrious, the succourer of 'Īsā and of David thy *Khalīfa*. *Fatḥu 'r-rasūl*. M. 'Uthmān al-Mirghanī.

[1] The manuals do not necessarily represent the considered opinions of theologians. al-Baiḍāwī and az-Zamakhsharī, for instance, in their comments on *Qur.* 3.45 attribute *shafā'a* in the next world to 'Īsā. Devotions are an index of the beliefs of the heart rather than a handbook of official theology.

Address to Muḥammad

As his figure grows ever more august, more numinous, in his people's eyes, it is but a short step from asking God for Muḥammad's mediation to asking the Prophet himself for it. So in the religion whose mission has been the great witness to the unity, whose dread and abomination has been the sin of *shirk*, we find the phenomenon of what can hardly be otherwise described than as prayer to the Prophet. It is to be noted that these prayers make their appearance in *modern* works of popular devotion, the fruit of long centuries of seeing in Muḥammad something more than mere man.

My God I make my petition to Thee, approaching Thee through thy Prophet our Lord Muḥammad, the Prophet of Mercy.

Our Lord Muḥammad, I have approached my Lord through thee in this my need that is to be met (here he is to name his needs). *Riyāḍu 'l-janna*, Yūsuf an-Nabhānī, p. 91.

My God I have transgressed at morn and at evening. My heart from its perpetual remembrance is in hardship.

Then, O Aḥmad, be to me an Intercessor for my distress; since between me and the Lord stands the fear of one who has sinned. *Fatḥu 'l-karīmi 'l-khāliq*, 'Alī al-Makkī.

Thou art the Beloved whose mediation is hoped for at the great assize to which all mankind will throng.

Thou art the Intercessor whose mediation is hoped for on the narrow path when footsteps slide.

Then be my Intercessor when I am in the tomb, and have become thy guest, for a guest is respected. *Majmū'u tabāraka dhū 'l-'ulā'*, Anon., p. 5.

(Sometimes Muḥammad himself is approached through the *wasīla* of other saints. Thus of 'Uthmān, Ḥamza, 'Abbās, Ḥasan, Ḥusain:)

I have come pleading through them O Best of Mankind and far be it from them that having come I should fail. . . . Here am I offering, O generous one, their honours as my introduction. And far be it from them that I should meet with refusal. *Aḥzāb Aḥmad at-Tījānī*, pp. 150, 151.

When thou dost rise on the Resurrection Day going direct to God with petition such as no other prophet makes, then be my Intercessor. Lo I come to thee with this plea, and by God, I am a sinner that comes to thee, and thou art the cave to which all may flee for shelter. *Majmū'u tabāraka dhū 'l-'ulā'*, p. 30.

Messenger of God, my heart is powerless. Beloved of God heal the sickness of my heart.

Messenger of God, give me from thyself succour and from thyself security for my family and my community.

Messenger of God, give me from thyself an overflowing[1] of thine abundance and any degree of nearness to thine honour. *Riyāḍu 'l-madḥ*, Ja'far as-Ṣādiq al-Mirghanī.

But whose is this figure, the Beloved, the Chosen, this healer of the soul's sickness, this cave of shelter for sinful humanity, this one mediator between God and man, this one who ever liveth to make intercession for his people?

Strange irony, that a development of devotion so precariously based on the Qur'ān, so different from its general trend, should have found a home within Islam; and yet what more pathetically natural than that sinful human nature confronted with the Godhead should feel its need of a mediator.

God's "Shafā'a"

Finally we turn to the prayers based on the group of Qur'ān texts which claim *shafā'a* as God's own prerogative. These are hard to reconcile with the development of the strictest doctrine of *tawḥīd*, but there may be penetrations of spirit where reason has not learnt to follow, and these prayers point to the mystery of the Divine life. To the Christian they are suggestive of the truth by which he lives, of an act of mediation that took place in history, proffered by God and accepted by God for the bankrupt soul of man.

If I remain silent no one will speak on my behalf and if I intercede for myself I am not worthy to be an intercessor. O God, call down blessing on Muḥammad and his family, and make Thy generosity the intercessor on behalf of my errors.

O God I have no escort to Thee, therefore let Thy pardon be my escort. I have no mediator with Thee, therefore let Thy generosity be my mediator. *Du'ā'un fī 't-tawba*, 'Alī Zain al-'Ābidīn.

O God, as Thou wast my guide to Thyself so be my Mediator with Thyself. *Ḥizbu 't-tawassul*, ash-Shādhilī.

And Thyself plead for us with Thyself. *Du'ā'un munawwirun abṣāra 'l-'ārifīn*, 'Abd al-Qādir al-Jīlānī.

[1] The word *faiḍ* (above translated "overflowing") is a remarkable one to employ in addressing the Prophet because of its constant use for a Divine effusion on the soul, a Divine motivation of the life.

My God I have sought Thy mediation with Thyself for me, and have asked Thy protection for me from Thyself. *Munājātun 'aẓīma. Majmū'atu 'l-aḥzāb.*

Note on Shī'a Use

The great majority of the manuals studied being of Sunni origin it is necessary to remark that the preoccupation with the *wasīla* and *shafā'a* of Muḥammad is not so dominant in Shī'a devotion because the same honourable office is shared by the Shī'a *Imāms*. Thus in visiting the tomb of the Imām Riḍā the worshipper says:

The peace of God to thee from me, my lord, the son of my lord. Be my mediator and the mediator of my parents, in thine own right and in the right of thy grandfather and thy virtuous pure forefathers. *Ziyārat Nameh.* (Kindly supplied by Dr Donaldson from Meshed.)

At the tomb of 'Alī

My lord, to thee is my mission, and through thee I seek mediation with my Lord for the attainment of my purpose. And I bear witness that he who seeks thy mediation does not fail, and he who makes request through thee is known never to be turned away with his need unmet. *Miftāḥu 'l-janān,* p. 233.

The Intercession of all the Imāms

O Muḥammad, O Abū 'l-Qāsim thou art my father and my mother. I beg God for thine intercession and that of the Imāms born from thee (prayer repeated, replacing the name of Muḥammad by that of each of the twelve Imāms in turn.) Ibid., loc. cit.

Al-Kulīnī reports a tradition in which the souls of believers are said to ask for the office of intercession on behalf of other believing souls.

The Prophet said, "If a believer pray for his fellow believers, men and women, God will return to him (as a greeting is returned) a prayer equivalent to what he asked for them from every believer, male or female, of all past time since the beginning of the age, and of all time to come until the Resurrection Day. And (on that day) the believers, men and women, will say, 'O Lord, this is the man who used to pray for us, allow us then to intercede for him (*shaffa 'nā fīh*).' And God will give them the office of intercessors for him and he will be saved." *Usūlu 'l-Kāfī. Kitābu 'd-du'ā'.*

This belief is borne out in the following prayer:

Let Thy heavens and the dwellers therein, let Thine earth and the dwellers thereon hear the regret for sin that I have laid before Thee, and it may be that one of them through Thy mercy will show me mercy in my evil case, or be moved to compassion at my hard condition and grant me the boon of a prayer from him more acceptable with Thee than my prayer, or an intercession more certain than my own, through which I may be saved from Thy wrath. *aṣ-Ṣaḥīfatu 's-sajjādiyya*, p. 373.

3

THE INTENTION

Niyya, Ḥuḍūru'l-qalb, Ikhlāṣ

Ritual Use

The little boy at school learning to say his prayers is taught:

> If you desire to make your ablution, say: "I make the intention of legal purification," then wash. . . . *Durūsu 'd-dīni 'l-islāmī*, Book I, p. 29.

When he stands up to pray he again has a form of "intention" to learn:

> I stand facing the *qibla*, and raising my hands to the level of my ears, I say: "I make my intention to perform the two prostrations of the prescribed prayer-rite of the morning hour." *Durūsu 'd-dīni 'l-islāmī*, Book I, p. 52.

So far the children are taught in school. As they grow older they find that not only the daily performance of the prayer-rite, but many another formal act of worship is prefaced by its "intention", *niyya*—(compare the Jewish *kawwana*).

> (Prayer for solace in the grave.) Then he shall perform two prostrations (i.e. two *rak'as* of the prayer-rite) making the intention of companionship in the grave. *Rabī'u 'l-fu'ād*, 'Abd Allah ash-Sharqāwī, p. 113.

> (For seeking refuge with God.) He shall say, "I make the intention of performing them (two prostrations) for God Most High," and he shall recite the two refuge-taking *sūras*, his intention being the recitation of these two and the seeking of refuge with God from the evil of that day and that night. Ibid., p. 110.

> (Before reading the *ṣalawāt* in *Dalā'ilu 'l-khairāt*.) O God I make the intention of calling down blessing on the Prophet, in obedience to Thy command and as an act of trust in Thy Prophet Muḥammad and of love to him and yearning for him and glorifying of his rank. *Dalā'ilu 'l-khairāt ma'a 'l-aḥzāb*, p. 12.

> (Before a complete reading of the Qur'ān at one session.) He shall say, "I intend the prostration of the recitation. God is Most Great." And he shall bow prostrating himself. Then he shall say during his prostration, "O God write for me by this recitation a reward, and remove from me an entail of

sin. And make this recitation a treasure stored up with Thee for me, and accept it from me as Thou didst accept it from Thy servant David." Then he shall raise his head and give the greeting of peace to right and to left, after which he shall procede with the complete reading of the Qur'ān. *Majmū'u ṣalawāti wa awrādi Muṣṭafā al-Bakrī.*

Here then is a universal custom of worship in Islam. Among the prayers to be used by those initiated as members of various crafts, found in a Persian manuscript at Lahore, was even a *niyya* for a soldier to make on drawing his sword, with the words *Ya Fattāḥa 'l-bāb fī kulli ḥāl,* Thou opener of the door under all circumstances.[1]

Extension of the Niyya beyond Ritual Use

A tradition (apparently envisaging the ablution as made outside the mosque) carries the blessedness of *niyya* beyond the single formula to the worshipper's intention of heart as he walks to the mosque. (Compare the Jewish sense of the sacredness of hurrying to the house of prayer.)

The Apostle of God said: "The prayer-rite of the man who joins the congregation is more than twenty degrees better than that of him who prays in his place of merchandise or in his house. And this is because if one of you after making a full legal ablution walks to the mosque with no desire in his heart save the prayer-rite, nothing but the prayer-rite impelling him, not a step does he take on his way to the mosque which does not raise him a degree and wipe out for him a sin." *Riyāḍu 'ṣ-ṣāliḥīn*, an-Nawawī, p. 5.

So the idea is extended. The *iḥrām*, the sacred garment donned by the Mecca pilgrims and involving chastity is described as a sort of *niyya*. (See *Dalīlu 'l-Ḥajj*, M. Ḥasanain Makhlūf, p. 35.)

This wider use indicates a more inward view of the meaning of *niyya* and the Ḥanafites hold that the act should be an inward one only.

The ninth condition (for a valid prayer-rite) is the intention and its place in the heart. The outward saying of it is an illegal innovation. *Shurūṭu 'ṣ-ṣalāt*, M. 'Abd al-Wahhāb.

While as a rule the little schoolboy's lesson books teach him only the phrases to be said to ensure the validity of his prayer-rite, and while it is clear that for the majority of worshippers, "*nuwait*" expresses no more than the intention "to do as the Church does", the thoughts of

[1] *Sipahi Nameh* in Revue des Études Islamiques, 1927, p. 261.

the devout have been busy on a phrase so capable of deeper interpretation, and our manuals show traces of its use as a spiritual discipline.

Mental Concentration

Al-Ghazālī in a passage which finds its echoes in the manuals is clear and emphatic on the necessity of holding the "intention" in mind and spirit at the very least until the *taḥrīma* is said, if the prayer-rite is to be not only legally but spiritually valid:

> Recollectedness of heart is the spirit of the set prayers. The very least that will keep that spirit just gaspingly alive is that the heart shall be present at the moment of *takbīr*. Less than that is fatal. According as there is increase in that recollectedness of heart, the quickening spirit spreads through more parts of the worship. How many living beings are yet without movement, all but dead! Just so the prayer-performance of one who is inattentive beyond the *takbīr* is like one alive but lacking movement. *Iḥyā'*, 4.3.

One method of training in concentration was to try to make the intellectual act of the "intention" so inclusive that nothing in the prayer-rite should be excluded from it. A friend trained in the Tījāniyya Order told the writer that he was required, on making his intention, by an act of intense concentration, to see every word and movement of the prayer-rite "set before him like coffee cups on a tray". Concerning this ash-Sha'rānī wrote:

> He who said that it is incumbent on the man who performs his prayer-rite to recall to his consciousness all the actions of the rite at the time of the (opening) *takbīr*, said this because the true worshipper enters the presence of God Mighty and Majestic, rather in spirit than in body. And that recollection is easy to such as he, for it is the special work of the advanced. As for him who said that this recollection is not necessary because of its difficulty, he is in the position of one whose bodily nature dominates his spiritual as is the case with most people. He is unable to picture a thing in his mind unless he sees it before him. *Laṭā'ifu 'l-minan*, p. 125.

Some of the prayers bear evidence, in their form, of an earnest striving for concentration on the spiritual act, as:

> I do, I do, I do refer all my affair to Thee. *Ḥizbun usbū'ī fī 'ṭ-ṭarīqati 'l-'ashshāqiyya* in *Majmū'atu 'l-aḥzāb*, p. 315,

like the moving, "I believe, I believe, I believe", in the Coptic liturgy.

Supporting Traditions

The classical text for the importance of intention often quoted in our manuals is the famous tradition *Innamā 'l-a'mālu bi 'n-niyya*, Deeds are only of value through the intention behind them; and a second is like unto it *Man ḥasunat niyyatuhu ṣaluḥa 'amaluhu*, His rightness of intention makes a man's action right (quoted frequently in the manuals). al-Makkī has a still stronger sentence, *an-Niyyatu ablaghu mina 'l-'amal*, the intention is more important than the performance. (*Qur.* 2.152.)

(From 'Umar ibn al-Khaṭṭāb.) I heard the Apostle of God say, Deeds are measured by intentions. Every act is worth only what was intended in it. He whose emigration (*hijra*) was to God and His Apostle, to God and His Apostle he came. He whose emigration was for worldly ends or in order to marry a woman, emigrated for that reason only. *Riyāḍu 'ṣ-ṣāliḥīn*, an-Nawawī, p. 4, *muttafaq 'alaihi*.

(One of the manuals says that this tradition was often in former days written at the beginning of a Qur'ān volume as a message to readers.)

Ash-Shādhilī said (concerning the word of the Prophet, "His rightness of intention makes a man's action right"): Rightness of intention as between you and God is the direction of your heart to the giving of due weight and glory to God and to God's commands and to that which God has commanded to be done. As between you and fellow-servants of God, rightness of intention is the direction of heart with sincerity towards them, performing your dues towards them, not seeking for special favours, and meeting opposition with patience towards God and submissive trust in Him. *al-Mafākhiru 'l-'aliyya fī'l ma'āthiri 'sh-Shādhiliyya*, p. 63.

An anecdote in *Kashf al-Maḥjūb* shows that the spiritual value of intention has even been felt to outweigh the Muslim's desire for the perfect performance of the prayer-rite that is to him so sacred:

(Of Ḥabīb al-'Ajamī.) One evening Ḥasan of Baṣra passed by the door of his cell. Ḥabīb had uttered the call to prayer and was standing engaged in devotion. Ḥasan came in but would not pray under his leadership, because Ḥabīb was unable to speak Arabic fluently, or recite the Koran correctly. The same night, Ḥasan dreamed that he saw God and said to Him: "O Lord, wherein does Thy good pleasure consist?" and that God answered, "O Ḥasan you found my good pleasure but did not know its value; if yesternight you had said your prayers after Ḥabīb and if the rightness of his intention had restrained you from taking offence at his pronunciation, I should have been well pleased with you." al-Hujwīrī, *Kashf al-Maḥjūb*, Nicholson's translation, p. 88.

As a Spiritual Discipline

The spiritual teaching about the "intention" found in the manuals takes two directions, positive and negative. The positive is summed up in the phrase *ḥuḍūru 'l-qalb*, the negative in the phrase *ikhlāṣu 'n-niyya*.

Ḥuḍūru 'l-Qalb

In its lighter use this means little more than "presence of mind" in the sense of attention. But its meaning deepens into heart-presence with the One who is worshipped. *Allāh qiblatu 'n-niyya* said Sahl at-Tustarī, and a tradition, echoing I Sam. 16.17, tells us, "God looks neither to your bodies nor your outward appearance. He looks only to your heart," (Muslim, from Abu Huraira).

Outward means may be used as a help to inward attention:

> The closing of his eyes so that the path of outward sensations may be barred, and the way opened to the inward sensations of the heart. *Rabī 'u 'l-fu'ād*, p. 117.

There should be a harmony between the inward and the outward action:

> Sincerity in the (outward) repetition together with heart-presence so that there may be a symmetry of the inner and the outer man. Ibid., loc. cit.
>
> Seeking to enter into the inward sense of the invocation, and if another thought than that invocation flashes into his mind, let him return to the meaning of the invocation and so cast out the intruding thought. (Directions for a Qādirī *Khalwa*.)

The meaning of *ḥuḍūru 'l-qalb* like that of *niyya* passes beyond the technical acts of devotion:

> He said to me, O Thou Help from the Almighty neither eat nor drink nor sleep except with presence of heart and a seeing eye. *al-Ghawthiyya*, 'Abd al-Qādir al-Jīlānī.

Ikhlāṣu 'n-Niyya

The negative extension of the teaching about the "intention" is summed up in this phrase, which in its common use may not mean anything more than bare sincerity of intention. It forms part of the rubric before many prayers:

> (Of *Ad-Durru 'l-a'lā* of Muḥyī ad-Dīn Ibn al-'Arabī.) He who carries (this prayer) is secured against both earthly and heavenly calamities and protected against all satanic and human calamities and injuries. It is efficacious against malice and pestilence and the red wind and magic and difficult child-birth. But at the time of its recital, heart-presence and sincerity of intention are necessary, and also perseverance in the recitation.
>
> (Of the *Basmala* of 'Abd al-Qādir al-Jīlānī.) It is to be recited with a whole heart and a sincere intention and entire concentration of his powers.

But for the deeper souls the meaning of *ikhlāṣu 'n-niyya* becomes one of searching discipline. The verb *akhlaṣa* in the Qur'ān is used to describe the sincerity of monotheistic faith in people who *akhlaṣū dīnahum lillāh* (4.145), a very practical question in the days of the struggle with polytheism, when Muḥammad's heart was often sore because he knew of the hypocrisy of those who joined him for reasons of policy rather than of faith. This Qur'ānic idea has had a deep development in devotion, as men have come to see that to have none other gods than God involves devotion to Him of every power of mind and spirit.

Ikhlāṣu 'n-niyya, then, at its highest, means the purification of the intention, not only by mental concentration, shutting out all other thought than that of the devotion in hand, but by spiritual purging from all other desires than the desire for God. In this connection the word *riyā'*, hypocrisy, means the implicit hypocrisy in any sort of vain-glory or "human respect".

So Muḥammad is described as *man 'alā 'n-niyya mu'min*, faithful in his intention; and the worshipper says:

> Unite us to the "intention" and with it to sincerity and singleness of heart. *Ḥizbu 'l-fatḥiyya*, Qādiriyya.
>
> I ask Thee not to reject me because of the corruptness of my intention. Shī'a *du'ā'* for the 29th day of Ramaḍān.
>
> Cleanse my heart from hypocrisy, my work from ulterior motives, my tongue from lying, my eye from deceitfulness, for Thou knowest the deceitfulness of the eye and that which the breast conceals. *Mukhtaṣaru ad'iyati Ramaḍān*, p. 6.

Such searching sincerity towards God is as necessary, and as difficult, in study as in devotion.

Let one of his rules of conduct in acquiring knowledge be purity of intention in his quest for God and for the other world, with no ulterior purpose of using his knowledge among men as a means of government (employment or favour). For that is the great danger. *al-'Aṭiyyatu 'l-haniyya*, 'Alī ibn Ḥasan al-'Aṭṭās.

Know that there are three degrees of single-heartedness, of which the highest is the worship of God for Himself, not for desire of His Paradise or fear of His Fire. The second is to worship Him out of desire for His Paradise and flight from his Fire. The third is to worship Him for the improvement of life on earth so that it may be made easier for you and so forth, and this is implicit hypocrisy or the sin of association. *Uṣūlu 'l-Kāfī,* Bāb 5.

This demanding *ikhlāṣu 'n-niyya*, with all that it involves of self-stripping, may be compared with the "single eye" of the Gospels, the reward for which is the flooding of the being with light; or with their "poverty of spirit", the reward for which is the Kingdom of heaven. *Ikhlāṣu 'n-niyya* may perhaps best be translated "singleness of heart" and al-Kulīnī quotes a saying that it will lead to salvation *Bi 'l-ikhlāṣ yakūnu 'l-khalāṣ.*

The "intention" involves place and time and method and ideal. We ask Thee for the purity of those places, the observance of those times, for faultlessness in that method, and for full realization of that ideal. We ask Thee for due fulfilment of the obligation and for right purpose, and for a desire for the Countenance of God Most High.

Now the place of the "intention" is the heart; its time is at the beginning of the actions of the prayer-rite, its method is a binding control of the heart and of the members. It is built up of four elements, purpose, determination, desire, an act of will, all of these united in one idea. And the "intention" has two aspects, first the direction of the heart in the rite with full awareness, and secondly single-heartedness towards God out of longing for the reward that He has to give and desire for His Countenance. *al-Mafākhiru 'l-'aliyya fī 'l-ma'āthiri 'sh-shādhiliyya*, p. 63.

And purify them (our hearts) from the rivalries of other things, through a single-hearted affirmation of Thy Unity, till we shall not behold anything but Thy doings, Thine attributes and the radiant glory of the augustness of Thine essential Being. *Ḥizbu 'r-rajā'*, 'Abd al-Qādir al Jīlānī.

The true nature of "intention" is that on entering upon it anything other than the one thing intended shall be absent from your mind. Its perfection is the fullest companionship. *Aḥzābu wa awrādu Aḥmad at-Tījānī*, p. 29.

4

THE PRAYER OF CONFRONTATION

Qibla, Miḥrāb, Istiqbāl, Tawajjuh

Qibla

The little schoolboy learning how to say his prayers is instructed as follows:

> Then you are to stand facing the *qibla*, that is turning your face towards the revered Ka'ba. Now if the worshipper is actually present, beholding the Ka'ba, he may turn towards any corner of it that he chooses. But if he is not at the Ka'ba he will perform his prayers directed towards it. *Durūsu 'd-Dīni 'l-Islāmī*. Book 3, p. 28. Muḥammad Zuhdi 'l-Khamāsh, course approved by Ministry of Education in Damascus. (But the sentence can be matched almost word for word in numerous religious instruction books for primary schools throughout the Middle East.)

So the whole Muslim world at prayer is ringed round one tiny centre. Even the traveller saying his prayers on a camel, should turn his face to the *qibla* at least when he makes his intention, if it is not possible to maintain the right direction. Often no other thought than the unitive power of this inward turning of the whole worshipping world of Islam is offered to the schoolboy, but the ever-present picture of the *qibla* (the direction point), the *miḥrāb* (the niche in the mosque wall marking the *qibla*) and the worshipper's facing of it (*istiqbāl, tawajjuh*) has provided some of the vocabulary of worshipping minds.

Both *qibla* and *miḥrāb* are Qur'ānic words, and from their use there, would seem to have been recognized as part of the heritage from earlier prophets: Moses and Aaron are ordered to make their houses a *qibla* in Egypt, *10*.87, and Zachariah is said to have been praying "in the *miḥrāb*" when the angel appeared to him (*3*.38).

One of the manuals also connects the word *miḥrāb* with David:

> It is related that David said: O Lord, I find in the *Zabūr* light streaming forth. Every time I recite it, my *miḥrāb* is shaken, my heart rejoices and my mosque (or place of prostration) is lighted up. Then a voice cried, "That is

the Light of Muḥammad for whose sake I created this world and the other." *Al-Majmūʿatu 'l-mubāraka fī 'ṣ-ṣalawāti 'l-ma'thūra*, p. 40.

The manuals show no consciousness that the earliest *qibla* of Islam was that of Israel, the Temple at Jerusalem. For them it is enough that they pray towards Muḥammad's *qibla*. Thus, in a prayer after visiting the tomb of Muḥammad, the worshipper should say:

I lean back on the support of the Tomb of the Prophet and I face the *qibla* which Thou didst prefer for Muḥammad.[1] *Duʿā'un baʿda ziyārati qabri'n-nabī*. Attributed to ʿAlī Zain al-ʿĀbidīn.

Muslims are *ahlu 'l-qibla* and one of the signs of joining the community is to face the same *qibla*:

I am commanded to make war on mankind till they say *Lā ilāha illā 'llāh*. And if they say this and perform our prayer-rite and face our *qibla* and sacrifice our sacrifice then their blood is forbidden to us and we have no right to their property. *Kitābu 'ṣ-ṣalāt*, al-Bukhārī, 34.

The sacredness of the *qibla* is reinforced by popular tradition:

The Prophet said: "Does not the man who turns away his face during his prayer-rite (i.e. in another direction than that of the *qibla*) fear that God will turn his face into that of a donkey?" al-Ghazālī, *Iḥyā'*, 4.1.

One of the Companions related that the Apostle of God saw spittle in the *qibla* and became violently incensed. Then he scraped it with a dried palm branch that was in his hand and said, "Bring me some aromatic scent." So he smeared over the trace of the spittle with saffron. Then turning to us, he said, "Which of you would like to be spāt upon in his face?" We said, "Not one of us." He replied, "Well, any one of you when he enters on the performance of his prayers has God between him and the *qibla*, so let no one of you spit before him or on his right side[2] but rather on his left side and on to his left foot." A variant reads: "When one of you performs the prayer-rite in the mosque he is in intimate converse with his Lord turning his face towards Him."[2] al-Bukhārī, *Ṣalāt*, 33,39,74,79. *Mawākib*, 8. Muslim, *Masājid*, 54. Aḥmad, II.34 sq.

[1] The reference in *raḍaita li Muḥammadin* is to the command to change the *qibla* in *Qur.* 2.144, where Muḥammad is told, "We have appointed for thee a *qibla* that will please thee (*tarḍāka*)."

[2] The prohibition of spitting to the right is explained in another tradition by the words, "for on his right is an angel". (al-Bukhārī, *Ṣalāt, 38.*) That there was a demon on the left was a prevalent idea. In the letter of consolation written by Jacob of Sarūg near Edessa to the Himyarite Christians of South Arabia at the

This sacredness of the *qibla*, then, is not its own. It is one of Islam's sacramentals, a direction point towards Mecca, and (as indicated by the root *qbl*) towards a spiritual reception place.

Muḥammad is often described in the manuals as the heavenly *imām* of his people's worship, and they may be said to face the *qibla* under his leadership and thus more sure of acceptance. From this approach led by Muḥammad, it is but a short step to regard him as himself the *qibla*, the direction point by which men approach God. Al-Baiḍāwī explained the refusal of Iblīs (*Qur.* 2.32 and 7.10–13) to prostrate himself before the pre-creation "form" of Adam as a refusal to prostrate himself before God, with Adam as *qibla*. So in the prayer-manuals Muḥammad is his people's *qibla*.

> Thou hast appointed him to be a *qibla* and an alighting place for the needs of all thy creatures. *Fatḥu 'r-rasūl*, M. 'Uthmān al-Mirghanī, p. 69.

He is

> The *qibla* of the people of access (those saints in bliss closest to the divine Presence) (*Ṣalawāt*, Muḥammad aṣ-Ṣiddīqī),

the focal-point for human worshippers and also the focal-point for divine illuminations:

> The *qibla* of the irradiation of the divine Selfhood, (*Fatḥu 'r-rasūl*, p. 68).

But not all thoughts of the spiritual *qibla* and *miḥrāb* are Prophet-centred. The fifth year primary schoolboy in Syria is taught (in the lesson course quoted at the beginning of this chapter) to make some voluntary devotions at the end of his prayer-rite. "They shall make petition with awe and silence, for themselves and the Muslims, raising their hands to heaven, *for heaven is the qibla of petition.*" So the boy learns to spiritualize the word.

Miḥrāb

Here is a word which seems to have wandered far in the history of speech, and perhaps has further to go in the history of spiritual thought.

Becker pointed out that, like *qibla*, *miḥrāb* was a noun of the royal

beginning of the sixth century, Judas is called "The Demon, the son of the left hand", and in the Targums and later Hebrew writings Satan is called "The Left". (*Trostschreiben Jakob's von Sarug an die himyaritischen Christen.* R. Schröter—*Z.D.M.G.* 31, p. 360 ff.)

reception room. He saw it as "a *nomen loci* connected with the lances (*ḥarb*) which were carried before chiefs (as also before the Prophet and his Caliphs) in the South-Arabian–Ethiopic culture-cycle, perhaps also in the Persian. The name of this niche, then, is a term taken from the palace."[1]

Rhodokanakis noted,[2] however, that at the rise of Islam the word had already several shades of meaning in connection with building. It could be the castle (apparently) of a South Arabian chief, and it could be a balcony or upper room. It could also be a raised seat where a ruler was isolated. The work of Strzygowsky and others on pre-Islamic architecture in the East led the word-hunters to seek also for the evidence of stone, and in the palace of Tak-i-Kisra an example of the probable original of the *miḥrāb* was found. Over against the entrance arches (like the great entrances to medieval Persian mosques) was an apsidal niche, raised from the ground, where the Emperor gave audience. There he sat facing the people "on a small semi-circular altar inlaid with mosaic".[3]

Becker, summing all this up in a later article,[4] considered that the meaning which passed into Muslim religious use was exactly this of the throne niche, and that when the word in general literature was also given to a whole audience chamber or possibly a whole castle, this was the type of extension that European languages know when they speak of "the Holy See" (*sedes*, seat) or that is common in English when we speak of a nobleman's "country seat".

If *qibla* enshrines the basic idea of reception, *miḥrāb*, then, enshrines that of presence and of confrontation—of the monarch face to face with his people. The spiritual use of the word in the prayer-manuals accords well enough with this, for while, as we have seen, *qibla* has the spiritual sense of a direction point which is also a focal point for divine manifestation, *miḥrāb* as spiritualized in the manuals is above all the place of presence, the sanctuary (probably its meaning in *Qur. 3*.38).

[1] C. H. Becker, *Zur Geschichte des islamischen Kultus. Der Islam* III, p. 392. There was till lately in Amman a man who had carried the ceremonial lance of Ibn Sa'ūd.

[2] *Zur Semitischen Sprachwissenschaft*, W.Z.K.M. 25, pp. 74 ff.

[3] We have to remember the Ethiopic use of *Mekuerrāb* as apse or sanctuary in a church. (Jeffery, *Foreign Vocabulary of the Qur'ān.*)

[4] C. H. Becker, *Die Kanzel im Kultus des alten Islam*, Nöldeke-Festschrift, p. 331.

Give us entrance through his rank and virtue to the heart of the *miḥrāb*.
al-Munājātu 'l-injīliyyatu 'l-wuṣtā, 'Alī Zain al-'Ābidīn.

Here *miḥrāb* is the place of meeting with the divine presence. The word "sanctuary" has for Christians a similar story. Used for the holiest part of a building, it had a symbolic use also. In a sermon (*circa* A.D. 502) of Narsai of Nisibin we find:

> The sanctuary also forms a symbol of the Garden of Joseph, whence flowed life for men. In another order it is a type of the Kingdom which our Lord entered and into which He will bring with Him all His friends. The adorable Altar thereof is a symbol of that Throne of the Great and Glorious, upon which He will be seen of watchers and men in the day of His revelation.

In common Christian parlance the word is spiritualized as in such phrases as "the sanctuary of His presence".

There is for some worshippers a *miḥrāb* of the heart, an inner sanctuary like St Teresa's "little cell".

> Make us those in whose hearts is written the record of the awe of Thee, till the secret tongues of those hearts whisper to Thee with the long-drawn-out *miserere* of their solitude in the *miḥrābs* of the holy fear of the lowly-hearted. *Fatḥu 'r-rasūl*, M. 'Uthmān al-Mirghanī, p. 102.

But there is also, by a play of words perhaps, but it seems with deeper meaning than mere word-trickery, a *miḥrāb* within the divine Nature, where takes place the Divine *Ṣalāt* for the Prophet.

> The pure blessings called down in the *miḥrāb* of the very *hā'* of the *huwiyya* (the Divine Ipseity Itself). *Aḥzāb Aḥmad at-Tījānī*, p. 10.

Here the spiritual and glorified Muḥammad is believed to have the unique privilege of worship. He can therefore be described as:

> The worshipper in the *miḥrāb* of the *hā'* of *huwiyya*. He who is illumined in the *miḥrāb* of Thy transcendent holiness and Thine intimacy. *al-Ḥizbu's-saifī*.

The honour, here ascribed to Muḥammad, of supreme entry into the Divine Holy of Holies is strangely reminiscent, for Christian readers, of the teaching, given so long before Muḥammad's day, in the Epistle to the Hebrews (9.24) where Christ is revealed in the heavenly sanctuary, there "to appear (His *tawajjuh*) before the Face of God for us".

ISTIQBĀL, TAWAJJUH

The outward act of turning towards the *qibla* (*istiqbāl*) and confronting it (*tawajjuh*) is also extended, as might be expected, from physical direction to spiritual. The outward and inward acts are to go together. Thus, when a man is about to put himself under the direction of a Shādhilī shaikh, he is told that at the service of reception he should place himself:

facing the *qibla*, intensely present in heart with God.

Here the *qibla* is the direction of Mecca. But at the same service his *tawajjuh*, the direction in which his whole being faces, is to be his new director:

> Let him sit before his master with humility and all courtesy, reverencing him with a heart void of uncertainty and doubt, confronting him (*mutawajjihan*) with his whole heart and his whole being. *as-Silsilatu 'dh-dhahabiyya fī 't-tawassuli bi's-sādāti 'sh-shādhiliyya*, pp. 9, 10.

A Turkish (Naqshabandī) worshipper about to recite his *silsila* of connection with the Prophet is given the following directions:

> First the faithful seeker must free his heart as much as in him lies from all evil thoughts, must face the *qibla* and sit in the proper posture for prayer, must close his eyes, and direct all his senses to the side of the fir-cone (*sanābar*. stone-pine) shaped heart. Then he must confront (*mutawajjih*) God as present in all His greatness and love. (Manuscript prayer bought from a street hawker in Istanbul.)

Tawajjuh has a very rich history in devotion. The words to be said by the worshipper in the prayer-rite immediately after his first *tasbīḥa* are known as *du'ā'u 't-tawajjuh* (the prayer of confrontation) which has its source in a prayer attributed to Abraham in the Qur'ān (*6.79*):

> I have turned my face towards Him who created the heavens and the earth, a sincere monotheist and no polytheist, verily my prayer and my devotion and my lifetime and my death time belong to God the Lord of the worlds, to Him who has no fellow. And thus I am commanded, I being one of the Muslimīn.

The manuals refer these words to the Prophet's own usage through a tradition traced to 'Alī by Muslim.

Other forms than this universal one are recommended (outside the prayer-rite) for the purpose of *tawajjuh*. Thus of the *taṣliya* known as *al-fātiḥiyya* (beloved of the Tījāniyya order) it is said:

Nor does any confronter confront God Most High with words more well-liked than these. *al-Futūḥātu 'r-rabbāniyya*, p. 3.

The word *tawajjuh* is also often used for an introduction (sometimes in verse) prefaced to a *wird* to induce the right spiritual attitude for its recitation.

The high doctrine of Muḥammad's person which our manuals display has led to many directions for spiritual *tawajjuh*, not directly to God, but to Him through the person of the Prophet. Shī'a worshippers, with their devotion to the Prophet's family, love to associate the whole family in such a *tawajjuh*:

> He who says this will be with Muḥammad and the family of Muḥammad if he says before opening the prayer-rite: O God, I turn towards Thee (*atawajjahu ilaika*) through Muḥammad and the family of Muḥammad and present them (on my behalf) at my prayer-rite, and approach Thee through them. *Usūlu 'l-Kāfī, Kitābu 'd-du'ā'*.
>
> Then let him begin the *dhikr* and at the beginning of it he must turn towards (*yatawajjah ilā*) the Apostle of God in his heart and ask his permission to enter into the presence of God Most High, for he is the door. And (the worshipper) will say, "Permission (*dustūr*), O Apostle of God!" And likewise he will turn to (*yatawajjah ilā*) God Most High and say, "Permission (*dustūr*), O God!" And likewise will he turn to (*yatawajjah ilā*) his shaikh and so begin his *dhikr*. *Rabī'u 'l-fu'ād*, 'Abd Allah ash-Sharqāwī, p. 109. (*Bakriyya.*)
>
> O our lord, O Muḥammad, lo I turn through thee to confront my Lord in my need. *al-Wirdu 'sh-shāfī*, Yūsuf an-Nabhānī, p. 48.
>
> Make thine approach (confrontation) to God through him, the best approach. *Dīwān fī madḥi 'n-nabī*. (Ḥarfu 'd-ḍaḍ) Abū Zaid al-Fāzāzī.

This seems a recognized approach in modern prayers. In 1941 in national emergency in Egypt, a *Shar'ī* lawyer, Shaikh Aḥmad 'Abd al-Majīd, led the worshippers in the mosque at Bacos, Alexandria, in a prayer for the country, saying:

> O Muḥammad we turn (*natawajjah*) through thee unto thy Lord. *al-Wafdu 'l-Miṣrī*, 3 May 1941.

Such is common usage to-day, but in earlier prayers, as in *Du'ā'u 't-tawajjuh* above, worshippers seek a more immediate confrontation. For there may be, for Islam, a Confrontation. The Qur'ān rings with the great phrase "the Face of Allah", "They desire the Face of Allah". "All things perish save the Face of Allah" (*28*.88). "The Face of thy Lord remaineth, majestic, glorious" (*55*.28), renewing that earlier cadence of Hebrew prayer "The Lord lift up His countenance upon thee" (Num. 6.26).

Glory to Him who fills with the Light of His Countenance the bases of His Throne. *Majmū'atu 'l-wirdi 'l-'āmm*, p. 32 (frequent).

I take refuge in the Light of Thy glorious Countenance which illuminates the heavens and dispels the darkness and by which the affairs of heaven and earth are ordered. *al-Wirdu 'l-a'ẓam*, 'Alī Muḥammad al-Qārī, p. 113.

I ask Thee for the rays of the confrontations of shining, flashing, transfiguring graces from the Light of Thy glorious Countenance. *al-Ḥizbu 'l-kabīr* (Rifā'ī).

Grant us to look upon Thy glorious Face. *Majmū'u tabāraka dhū 'l-'ulā'*, p. 8.

But such confrontation has its searching discipline; it involves a turning away from all else. From the earliest days to do something *li wajhi 'llāh* has meant to do it for His sake only, with no ulterior motive; it is used conversationally of any disinterested act. *Ibtighā'an li wajhika* is the Qur'ānic phrase often echoed in the manuals.

The *dhikr* is a great grace of God. It is required that in it you shall have no other aim than the Face of God Most High. One of the great ones has said, if a man in the *dhikr* aims at becoming a saint, an idolater is better than he, for the idolater says, according to the account of the Qur'ān concerning them, "We only worship them that they may bring us a closer approach to God." And this man in his *dhikr* and his worship seeks his own benefit, not obedience to his Lord's command and a longing to give Him satisfaction. *Rabī'u 'l-fu'ād*, p. 103.

Here are we, turning to Thee with our whole selves, then turn us not away. *Aḥzābu Aḥmad at-Tījānī*, p. 54.

O God! O God! O God! And (we ask) that Thou wilt turn away our faces from any other goal than Thyself and grant us to gaze towards Thy noble countenance till we see Thee in everything. *Majmū'u 'l-wirdi 'l-kabīr*, M. 'Uthmān al-Mirghanī, p. 98.

Part 3

WITHIN THE PRAYER-RITE

Analysis of Two Rak'as

	Chapter of this book
1. (Stand, hands raised to ears) *Takbīratu 'l-iḥrām*	1
2. (Stand, right hand on breast)	
Du'ā'u 't-tawajjuh	4
Thanā, Tasbīḥ	5a
Ta'wīz	6
al-Qirā'a: *Basmala*	7
al-Qirā'a: *Fātiḥa*	8
al-Qirā'a: *Ta'mīn*	8
al-Qirā'a: *Sūra*	8
3. *Takbīr* (while bending for *rukū'*, hands on knees)	
4. (During *rukū'*) Second *Tasbīḥ* (3 times)	
5. (Rise while saying) *Tasmī'*	5b
6. *Takbīr* (while descending for first prostration, *sujūd*)	
7. (During prostration) Third *Tasbīḥ* (3 times)	
8. *Takbīr* (while changing to sitting position)	
9. Pause (while sitting) *julūs, sakta*	9
10. *Takbīr* (while returning to prostration)	
11. (During second prostration) Fourth *tasbīḥ*	
12. *Takbīr* while rising to stand for second *rak'a* (Second *rak'a* repeat 1–11 without *Du'ā'u 't-tawajjuh*)	
13. Return to sitting position *qa'da*	
14. While sitting say the *Tashahhud*:	
(a) Greetings	14
(b) *Shahāda*	10 a and b
(c) *Taṣliya* and Abrahamic *Taṣliya*	10 a and b
(d) *Istighfār*	12 a, b, c
(e) *Du'ā'*	13 a and b
15. Turn head to right and left and give the greeting of peace, *Salām*	14

5 a

THE WORSHIP OF PRAISE: PRAISE OF TRANSCENDENCE

Tasbīḥ, Taqdīs

The saying of the great phrase *subḥāna 'llāhi*, "(I proclaim) the glory of God," is known as *tasbīḥ*. As with all the great recurring phrases of Muslim worship a Qur'ānic basis is sought for it, and in this case is not far to find, the noun *subḥān* occurring twenty-six times in the Qur'ān. In *20*.130 and *24*.41 the verb *sabbiḥ* is used in close connection with references to *ṣalāt*, and it is probable that we have in *tasbīḥ* one of the most primitive elements of the Muslim prayer-rite.

Arabic-speaking Christians use the same praise verb, and in Arabic (as generally but not quite always in Syriac), it is reserved for the praise of God alone.

Tasbīḥ is for both religions the praise of God supernal and transcendent, as against *taḥmīd*, praise of the God of providence, Donor of gifts and graces. For both religions *tasbīḥ* soars into the heavenlies, carrying worship into realms where *omnia exeunt in mysterium.*

> The meaning of *subḥānaka allāhumma* is "I declare Thy transcendence with such a declaration of it as befits Thy majesty." *Shurūṭu 'ṣ-ṣalāt*, M. 'Abd al-Wahhāb, p. 22.

Playing with the fact that the root *sbḥ* means to glide or swim[1] Arabic writers describe this type of praise as swimming in a shoreless sea:

> He praises (*yusabbiḥ*) in a shoreless sea, in the rich vestment of the mystery beyond, and its obscurity. *Qaṣīdatu safīnati 'l-'arsh*, Ibn al-'Arabī, included in *Majmū'atu 'l-aḥzāb*, p. 563.

In his daily prayers the Muslim worshipper, having by his *takbīratu 'l-iḥrām* fenced off the moments and the acts of worship, utters as his

[1] This is probably its original meaning in Arabic. In Aramaic it had long meant "to praise" and Dr Jeffery thinks that it was through Aramaic that this sense came to it in Arabic. (*Foreign Vocabulary of the Qur'ān*, p. 161.)

first word the *tasbīḥa*, true to the spirit of the whole ritual which is one of adoring praise. The root *sbḥ* is a constantly recurring one in Syriac worship and Mittwoch[1] suggested that the reiterated *tasbīḥ* of the Qur'ān and of the Muslim prayer-ritual might be an echo of the constantly recurring "Glorias" of the Christian Liturgies. In their Arabic form these are usually rendered not by the root *sbḥ*, but by *mjd*, a root sparingly used in its verbal form in the Muslim prayer-manuals though the word *majd* is found for God's glory. It is used in response to the *tasmiya* in the Ḥanafite prayer-rite "*Rabbanā laka 'l-majd*".

Tasbīḥ and Taqdīs

In both religions *tasbīḥ* is closely associated with *taqdīs* the uttering of God's holiness, another recurring note in the Eastern Liturgies as well as in the frequent *Kaddesh* of Hebrew prayer.

The great three-fold *taqdīs*, Holy God, Holy Strong One, Holy Immortal One, rings through all the services of the Eastern Church. In Egypt it is chanted by Coptic Christians as they carry a body to the grave.

The common Muslim form is:

Subbūḥ, quddūs, rabbu 'l-malā'ikati wa 'r-rūḥ,[2] Most glorious, most transcendent, Lord of the Angels and the Spirit.

The last two nouns are a Qur'ānic couplet, and *quddūs* is one of the Ninety-Nine Names, but no one has traced the origin of this constantly recurring and haunting phrase.

The Heavenly Worship

For both religions the *tasbīḥ* and *taqdīs* of the earthly worshipper are an entering upon the employment of the heavenly places. The *trisagion* of every Christian liturgy (*quddūs, quddūs, quddūs*) is offered "with angels and archangels and all the company of heaven". In the Arabic translation of the Greek Orthodox Liturgy the *trisagion* is called the *taqdīs*.

[1] *Zur Entstehungsgeschichte des Islamischen Gebets und Kultus.* (Preuss. Akad. Wiss., 1913.)

[2] "The Spirit is Gabriel (says al-Baiḍāwī in *Qur.* 70.4) thus singled out because of his greater excellence or greater character than that of the angels." Some of our manuals hold that the *Spirit* is Muḥammad.

Muslim prayer-manuals show that for the Muslim worshipper too, his act of praise is a sharing in the worship of "angels and men in a wonderful order". *Tasbīḥ* is often described as the occupation of all the angels, as in the Qur'ānic text: Those who are in thy Lord's abode do not think themselves too great to worship Him. They offer praise (*yusabbiḥūna*) to Him and prostrate themselves before Him (7.205).

So the manuals echo:

> O God, call down blessings on Thine angels and Thy heavenly courtiers who praise Thy glory day and night unceasingly. *Dalā'ilu 'l-khairāt,* al-Jazūlī, and frequently in the manuals.

Some of the descriptions in the prayer-manuals would seem to suggest a special order in the heavenly hierarchy known as the *musabbiḥūn*, the glorifiers:

> O God, call down blessings on our lord Muḥammad, and our lords Jibrīl and Mīkhā'īl and Asrāfīl and 'Azra'īl and the Bearers of the Throne, and Riḍwān and Mālik and the noble Guardians and Recording Angels, and Munkir and Nakīr and the Dwellers in the Splendour, and the Guards of heaven and earth and their Abode, and the Angels of Access and the Encompassing Angels, and the Angels of the Ranks (of the heavenly host) and the Glorifiers (*al-musabbiḥūn*) and those who call down blessing on the Prophet and the Gazing Angels and the Visitants of the Ḥaram, and the Cherubim, and the Angels of the Wind, and the Spirit and the Greatest Spirit. (Vigil *wird* of Maḥmūd b. as-Sayyid Aḥmad al-Mar'ashī.)

This angelic *tasbīḥ* and *taqdīs* is so holy and powerful that a man will beseech God by the virtue of it:

> I beseech Thee O Lord, by the supernal praises and the glorias of the Bearers of the Throne and the Angels of Access. *Ḥizbu 'l-ḥiṣnu 'l-ḥaṣīn,* attributed to al-Ghazālī.
>
> I beseech Thee by the *sanctus* (*taqdīs*) of the Cherubim and the murmur of the heavenly host and the supernal praise (*tasbīḥ*) of the Angels of Access. *Sharḥu 'smi 'llāhi 'l-a'ẓam,* Aḥmad al-Būnī.

Tasbīḥ is also described in the prayer-manuals as the activity of Paradise; the Garden itself seems to utter its praise:

> Glory to Him whose high lauds are uttered by the angels with their varied tongues! Glory to Him whose supernal praise is uttered by Paradise with wondrous *tasbīḥ*. *Ḥizbu Uwais al-Qaranī,* cf., Ps. 29.9.

The human worshipper's praise, then, may be a communion in the great worship of the heavenly places, as the writer of one of our manuals clearly indicates in his chapter on *tasbīḥ*:

> I have set in it a collection of the praises of the dwellers in the world above as these have been delivered to us by the saints, so that the reader may be a sharer in the worship of the angels, honour enough for him! *Majmū'atu 'l-wirdi 'l-'āmm*, M. al-Fatḥi al-Marrākushī.

Sometimes a worshipper may not only know that from afar he is bearing his little earthly part in the total chorus, but may be rapt into conscious participation in the heavenly doings. So in one of our manuals 'Alī Zain al-'Ābidīn speaks as follows:

> Those from whose sight Thou hast withdrawn the veil of blindness, so that their spirits soar on angels' wings and they are called visitors of the supernal Kingdom, sojourners[1] in the realm celestial, and they make answer in the ranks of the Glorifiers. *al-Munājātu 'l-injīliyyatu 'l-wuṣtā.*

Christian and Muslim Tasbīḥ

The two faiths are at one in seeing in *tasbīḥ* and *taqdīs* a sharing in the heavenly worship. But the central note of the Christian's *tasbīḥ* is abhorrent to that of his Muslim brother.

> I heard a voice of many angels round about the throne and the living creatures and the elders, and the number of them was ten thousand times ten thousand and thousands of thousands; saying with a great voice, Worthy is the Lamb that was slain to receive the power and riches and wisdom and might and honour and glory and blessing. Rev. 5.11,12.

For the Christian, then, *tasbīḥ* is the praise of the Transcendent, but of the Transcendent who has also descended to his rescue. For him, "in the midst of the throne", is "a Lamb as it had been slain", slain on a Friday in Palestine, but also "slain from the beginning of the world", because sacrificial Love is no parvenu on the eternal throne, but the Eternal Nature itself.

The Christian worshipper shares with his Muslim brothers in the experience described in the famous *Ḥizbu 's-saifī*.

> He who plunges deep into meditation on thy Creative Activity and thy high praise finds that his glance returns to him blinded and exhausted, his intellect stunned, and his thought bewildered and paralysed.

[1] The word, *'ummār*, is one used for those who make a spiritual retreat at Mecca.

The Christian experiences this, and then comes home to a revelation of the Divine Nature that no longer leaves him a lost child in the midst of vast eternities. "Jesus we know, and He is on the Throne."

His Muslim brother sees the Throne and the serried ranks of angels, but the Lamb that has been slain is absent from his vision.[1]

The Muslim *tasbīḥ*, as against the more personal warmth of *ḥamd* (thankful praise of a benefactor), is a courageous, lonely praise of One separated from his worshipper by a fathomless *tanazzuh*, by the *balkafiyya*, the incomparability of his revealed attributes with anything in our human experience, even be it called by the same name. *Tasbīḥ* then is a high and rarefied praise of the infinitely Other.

One of the commonest forms in Muslim prayer (derived from *Qur. 23.96*) is

> *Subḥāna 'llāhi 'ammā yaṣifūna*—Glorified be God with a glory remote from all representations of Him.

We give the approach of two Muslim worshippers to this high task of *tasbīḥ*:

> O Thou who art described though no description reaches thy True Being, nor does any deliminator draw limits for Thee. Thou who art absent from us in mystery yet not lost, Thou Seer who art not seen, Thou who art sought and found, for neither the heavens nor the earth nor the intervening space is void of Thee for the flicker of an eyelid. Thou art not liable to modality nor susceptible of spatiality or localization. Thou art the Light of Light and Lord of Lords encompassing all things. Glory (*Subḥān*) to Him whom nothing resembles, the All-Hearer, the All-Seer. Glory to Him who is thus and no other is thus. (Attributed to 'Alī Zain al-'Ābidīn in *aṣ-Ṣaḥīfatu 's-sajjādiyya.*)

and this:

> My God, were it not incumbent on me to obey Thy commands, I should have considered Thy transcendence too great for me to direct my invocation to Thee. My invocation is only according to my power, not according to

[1] But a very curious and touching heavenly scene with a central lamb was described by M. Galal (*Les rites funéraires en Egypte actuel*. J.E.I. 1937. Cahier III, p. 252) as a popular belief in Egypt. "When (after the final Judgment) all are satisfactorily classed in their new abodes, the inhabitants of Paradise and of Hell will wonder whether they will have to live and die a second time. They will put the question to God, who will affirm that their condition is now finally determined, and as proof of this He will slay before their eyes a sheep representing death with the words, "Death no longer exists. You have everlasting life."

Thy power. Perhaps my power may even attain to finding a place for the declaration of Thy transcendent holiness (*taqdīs*), since one of Thy greatest blessings to us is that Thou hast set our tongues to the invocation of Thyself, and that Thou dost permit us to call on Thee and to declare Thy transcendence (*tanzīh*) and thy glory (*tasbīḥ*). *Munājātu Abī Sa'ūd* in *Majmū'atu 'l-aḥzāb* of Aḥmad Ḍiyā' ad-Dīn.

Christian and Muslim Taqdīs

Such praise is intimately connected, we have seen, with *taqdīs*.

In Christian thought holiness always contains within itself a double movement, a movement first of separation away from everything that is "common" or "profane", and a movement secondly of inclusion, whereby the separate holy goes forth again to draw into itself everything from which its separation has removed it. This duplicity of movement is exactly represented in the difference between the holiness of Jehovah in the Old Testament and the holiness of the Father of Jesus Christ in the New. *The Christian Sacraments*, O. C. Quick, p. 107.

In Muslim Arabic its meaning is the dissociation of the thought of God from any attribute, a negative and ascetic meaning.

Examples from the prayer-manuals, turning the definitions of theologians into the food of worship[1]:

There is no God but Thee who art transcendent of embodiment or division or appellation.

There is no God but Thee who art exalted beyond kind or similitude or locality or direction.

Who art not perceived by imagination or supposition of the mind, nor grasped by thought or sight—

Thou art the One, the Permanent, Transcendent of mate or offspring or partnership or companion or localization or modality. *Majmū'atu 'l-wirdi 'l-'āmm*, M. al-Fatḥi al-Marrākushī.

Thou whose Essential Being is separated in transcendence from resemblance and likeness, whose qualities are transcendent of resemblance to any similitude. *Wirdu 's-sattār*, Muṣṭafā al-Bakrī.

Traditional Blessedness

Like all the other great phrases of Muslim devotion, the *tasbīḥa* is referred in the manuals not only to the Qur'ān but to the usage of the

[1] Compare the beginning of the "Creed" of thirteen articles by Maimonides which is half worship of the Transcendent, half doctrine of transcendence.

beloved Prophet. The ritual use of *Subḥāna rabbī 'l-'aẓīm* at the beginning of the set prayers (three times in public prayer, seven or ten times when performing the ritual alone) is reported by a group of traditions as his habit. And many are the traditions of the blessedness of this word. They take us into the realm of popular religion where holy words have an objective blessedness, and the utterance of them brings its allotted reward which may be heightened by due attention to the favoured number of recitations:

> The Apostle of God said: "Two words are light upon the tongue but heavy in the scales of judgment (when good works are weighed against evil ones) beloved by ar-Raḥmān—laud supernal (*tasbīḥ*) to God and thankful praise (*ḥamd*)—Glory (*subḥāna*) to the great God." (Tradition frequently quoted in the prayer-manuals. In the *Saḥīḥain* from Abū Huraira. Also Aḥmad, at-Tirmidhī, Ibn Mājah, Ibn Habbān.)

A similar Shī'a tradition of the merit-weight of *tasbīḥ* is referred by al-Kulīnī to 'Ali Zain al-'Ābidīn:

> *Tasbīḥ* fills half the scale and *al-ḥamdu lillāhi* completely fills it, while *allāhu akbar* fills the space between heaven and earth. *al-Kāfī, Kitābu 'd-du'ā'*. A sunnī version is given in *Adhkāru 'n-Nawāwī*, p. 9.

Yet another tradition of the weight of *tasbīḥ* is quoted:

> Muslim traces the tradition from Juwairiya, Mother of the Faithful, that the Prophet went out from her early to the morning prayers, leaving her in her place of prostration. When the morning was well advanced he returned to find her still in her prayer-place. He said: "Have you been there ever since I left you?" "Yes," she replied. Then the Prophet told her, "I for my part have said just four words, three times which if weighed against all that you have said to-day would outweigh it. *Subḥān* and thankful praise (*ḥamd*) to God to the measure of the number of His creations, of His own good pleasure, of the weight of His throne and of the extent of His words." *Riyāḍu 'l-Janna*, p. 37, Yūsuf an-Nabhānī. (Muslim, Aṣḥāb as-Sunan.)

The form thus blessed by Prophetic tradition is used incessantly in the manuals and very often with directions for a threefold recitation in accordance with the tradition. Other traditions attach special blessedness to hundredfold and thirty-threefold repetitions of *tasbīḥ* and these are consequently often found in the manuals. The tradition blessing thirty-three repetitions is as follows:

> It is recorded from Abu Huraira that the poor *muhājirūn* came to the

Apostle of God and said, "The wealthy[1] have attained the same high rank and blessed performances as ourselves. They perform the prayers as we do, they fast as we do, and they exceed us in wealth with which they make the pilgrimage and perform the ceremonies at Mecca and offer sacrifices and give alms." Then (the Prophet) said, "Shall I not tell you something in which you can equal those who were ahead of you and in which none shall be more meritorious than you unless he follow the same practice?" They said, "Most certainly tell us, O Apostle of God." And he said, "Say *Subḥāna 'llāhi* and *Al-Ḥamdu lillāhi* and *Allāhu akbar* thirty-three times at the end of every prayer-rite." (Bukhārī gives the number of recitations as ten. Muslim increases it to thirty-three, "*wa hiya maqbūla*", says Taqī ad-Dīn ad-Dimishqī. It is probably due to this form of the tradition that the Khatmiyya *wird* after the prayer-rite opens with a thirty-threefold *tasbīḥ*.)

Although in such traditions the numbers may only be a Semitic way of indicating the blessedness of abundance in such sacred acts, they are often followed very literally by the rubrics in the prayer-manuals.

Against numberings of recitations we have to put other passages in the manuals where the worshippers see their praise as an unnumbered, everlasting, many-voiced chorus:

> And my praise of Thee shall be unbroken, continual, enduring from age to age, with every shade of *tasbīḥ* and *taqdīs* and all the variations of praising tongues. *al-Ḥizbu 's-saifī.*

Values of Tasbīḥ

The values of *Tasbīḥ* held out by the manuals vary from semi-magic to what is inward and spiritual.

One not far from magic is set out in the following tradition:

> Aṭ-Ṭabarānī traced a tradition to Ibn 'Amr that Sa'd called down a curse on Kal'āb which brought God's destruction on him. And the Prophet said to Sa'd, "What was the formula of your curse?" He answered, "I said *subḥānaka*, there is no God but Thee to whom belong Majesty and Honour; destroy this dog." Then the Prophet said, "O Sa'd you prayed on a day and at an hour and with a formula that would have brought God's answer had you used it against anyone in heaven or earth. Good news, Sa'd!" Quoted in *Riyāḍu 'l-Janna*, Yūsuf an-Nabhānī, p. 16.

[1] Those who suffered loss of wealth in the Prophet's cause when they left Mecca for his sake complain of later believers who had suffered no such loss.

Because the words of the *tasbīḥa* are dear to God (*aḥabbu 'l-kalāmi ilā 'llāhi*) they are to be used by the man who needs the boon of forgiveness:

> Muḥammad said: He who says a hundred times *Subḥāna 'llāhi wa bi ḥamdihi* has the load of his sins lifted off him, be they like the foam of the sea in quantity. an-Nawawī, *Adhkār*, p. 9. (In the Saḥīḥain, also Aḥmad, etc.)

A Shādhilī manual directs the use of *tasbīḥ* to ward off the assaults of evil thoughts:

> Let him put his right hand on his breast and say seven times, "Glory to God, high in His holiness, the Creator, the Doer." Then let him say, "If He wills He will remove them [the evil suggestions] and replace them by a new creation; that is a small thing to his creative power." (*Qur. 14.19.*) *al-Mafākhiru 'l-'aliyya*, Aḥmad b. Abādir, p. 197.

The Psalm-like quality of self-forgetful God-consciousness in the best of Muslim worship is nowhere better seen than in *tasbīḥ*. We close with some noble examples from a rich store in the manuals:

> Most high praise to Him who is robed in power and in power has spoken.
> Most high praise to Him who clothed Himself with glory, and in glory is generous.
> Most high praise to Him to whom praise is due as to no other.
>
> *Du'ā'u 'l-iḍṭijā'*, M. 'Uthmān al-Mirghanī.

> Glory to Him who girds Himself with might!
> Glory to Him who wraps Himself in greatness!
> Glory to Him who is unique in his soleness!
> Glory to Him who is veiled in light!
> Glory to Him who quells his servants with death!
>
> *Aḥzābu Aḥmad at-Tījānī.*

> All laud to the Lord of greatness and magnitude, Lord of the great throne.
> All laud to the Lord of power and abidingness, Lord of the noble throne.
> All laud to Him whom all things praise, the Exalted, the August.
> All laud to Him whose knowledge contains all things, the Everlasting, the Eternal.
> All laud to Him to whose glorious Face such praise alone is due.
> All laud to Him who alone knoweth the mode of his Being, the Powerful, the All-Wise.
> All laud to Him the depth of whose eternal greatness is unthinkable by the minds of men.
>
> *Ḥizbu 'ṭ-ṭarīqati 'l-'ashshāqiyya.*

To Thee be most high praise! In worshipping Thee we have not attained the fulness of worship
O worshipped One!
To Thee be most high praise! In invoking Thy name we have not attained the fulness of invocation
O Thou who art invoked!
To Thee be most high praise! In thanking Thee we have not attained the fulness of thanksgiving
O Thou who art thanked.
To Thee be most high praise! In seeking Thee we have not attained the fulness of seeking
O Thou who art the goal.
To Thee be most high praise! In describing Thee we have not attained the fulness of description
O Thou who art described.

Khatmu 'ṣ-Ṣalawāti 'l-khams. Muṣṭafā 'l-Bakrī.

5b

THE WORSHIP OF PRAISE: THANKFUL PRAISE

Taḥmīd, Tasmīʻ, Shukr

His name is Muḥammad and Aḥmad, his people are the people of praise (*ḥamd*)—and his prayer-rite and the prayer-rite of his people is opened with praise. In the Preserved Tablet in God's abode it was written that his Caliphs and his Companions, in writing The Sacred Volume, should open it with praise (*Qur. 1.2*). And in his hand on the Resurrection Day will be the banner of praise. And when he then prostrates himself before God in intercession on our behalf and it is accepted he will praise his Lord with a new song that shall then be revealed to him, for his is the heavenly Station of Praise—and when he rises up in that Station all the assembly shall praise him, Muslims and misbelievers alike, the first and the last, and all meanings and modes of thankful praise shall be gathered up and offered to him. (Preface to *Al-Ḥirzu 'l-manīʻ*, Jalāl ad-Dīn as-Suyūṭī.)

Such is the picture painted by as-Suyūṭī, 911/1505, of *ḥamd* in the Muslim community, quoting, however, from a work written nearly seven centuries earlier, the preface to the famous tradition book of ad-Dārimī 255/861.

The Meaning of Ḥamd. Its Use in the Set Prayers

The opening phrase of the prayer-ritual runs *Subḥāna 'llāhi wa bi ḥamdihi*. With the word *ḥamd* we pass to a warmer climate, from the praise of the God of Transcendence to the praise of the God of Providence. *Ḥamd* (a word not confined like *tasbīḥ* to the praise of the Divine Being), when used of praise to God is the praise of the God of human experience. One of the manuals thus defines it:

Ḥamd in ordinary language means beautiful and voluntary praise, a recounting of the beauty of kindness received, drawn out by that kindness, and tending to the honour and magnifying of its bestower, whether this praise be for special favours, peculiar graces, or for wide-spread favours, customary gifts of grace. Idiomatically, *ḥamd* is the showing forth of the greatness of His goodness to the one who praises. *Fatḥu 'l-karīmi 'l-khāliq*, 'Alī al-Makkī.

However high and remote his ideas of transcendence, his *lex orandi* keeps safe for the Muslim the sense of some sort of connection or response. The worshipper may affirm with conviction:

> Thou art neither benefited by the religious obedience of the good, nor harmed by the transgression of the evil, *Ḥizbu 'ṭ-ṭarīqati 'l-'ashshāqiyya*. (The idea is constantly expressed in the manuals.)

But whenever he enters upon his prayer-rite, a few seconds after his *tasbīḥa* he will be saying *sami'a 'llāhu li man ḥamidahu*, God hearkens to one who utters his praise.

With that affirmation (known as the *tasmī'a*) constantly on his lips, the highest transcendentalist need not lose his sense of personal touch.

> No servant of God on waking from his sleep says, "Thankful praise to God who created sleep and waking"—without God saying, "My servant has spoken a true word!" *al-Kalimu 't-ṭayyib*, Taqī ad-Dīn ad-Dimishqī (Ibn as-Sunā and an-Nawawī, without isnād).

> The Prophet said: If when God grants a grace to one of his servants, he says *al-ḥamdu lillāh*, God Most High says, "Behold my servant to whom I gave an immeasurable gift has given me a priceless return for it. *Majmū'atu 'l-wirdi 'l-'āmm*, p. 97. (From Ibn 'Abbās.)

In popular religion the mere fact of saying *al-ḥamdu lillāh* is regarded as an acceptable offering and may be turned to self-interest.

> If one of you is asking for something that he needs, let him laud and praise God. For if a man wants to obtain something from a sultan, he prepares for him the finest speeches that he can make. Then if you want to ask something from God, you should glorify God the Mighty, the All-Powerful, and laud and praise Him. al-Kulīnī, *al-Kāfī* (*Kitāb ad-du'ā'*).

The *tasmī'a* like the rest of the set prayers is directly attributed to the Prophet's usage. It is said as the head is raised from prostration. Then, when the upright sitting position is reached, the clause *Rabbanā laka 'l-ḥamd* (To Thee O Lord be praise) is added, often with the addition (equally attributed to the Prophet),[1] Thine is the praise O Lord, to the

[1] (Muslim, Aṣḥāb as-Sunan, Aḥmad.) Already in Muḥammad's days the Jews were responding to the *Shmōneh 'Esreh* with, "Praise be to Thee, O Lord." In the Muslim prayer-rite the fact of a variance in traditions as to the words said after *laka 'l-ḥamd* might suggest that a primitive form had ended there. One such

fulness of heaven and earth, and to the fulness of whatever else Thou wilt.

Ḥamd and Shukr

The word *shukr* (thanks, thanksgiving) is not found in the prayer-ritual, but it is clear that for Muslim worshippers its meaning is covered by that of *ḥamd*. In Aramaic the root *ḥmd* bore the meaning of thanksgiving. *Ḥamd*, then, is thankful praise. The manuals are rich in phrases that show the kinship of the two words:

> He who says *al-ḥamdu lillāh* has given thanks for every grace of God Mighty and Majestic. *aṣ-Ṣaḥīfatu 's-sajjādiyya (qism fī tamjīdi 'llāhi ta'ālā).*

> The meaning of thy name *Ḥamīd* is that Thou art for ever by continual acts of grace doing that for which thankful praise is due. *al-Ḥirzu 'l-manī'*, as-Suyūṭī, p. 26.

> *al-ḥamdu lillāh* is a word of thanks, and when a worshipper says *al-ḥamdu lillāh*, God Most High says, "My servant has thanked me." *Majmū'atu 'l-wirdi 'l-'āmm* (quoting from a tradition of Ibn 'Abbās).

Shukr like *ḥamd* carries for the Muslim worshipper a sense of God's recognition, nay His appreciation. Its basic Qur'ān text is *16*.114. "Thank the grace of God if you are his worshippers."

> Thou hast given me from Thy Providence widely, abundantly, of Thy free will and Thy good pleasure. And Thou hast asked from me in return the easy task of thanking Thee. *al-Ḥizbu 's-saifī.*

His Muslim worshippers are very conscious of the obligation upon them.

> I take refuge with Thee from my failure to thank Thee (*Du'ā'u 't-tawassul*, Qādiriyya).

says 'Abd al-Qādir al-Jīlānī in a prayer used by his followers, and he asks for the joyous, thankful heart,

tradition is traced by al-Bukhārī to Rifā'ah ibn Rāfī' who said: We were one day saying the prayers behind the Prophet, and as he raised his head from the prostration he said, "God hearkens to him who praises Him." And a man behind him said, "Thine is the praise O Lord, abundant, good and blessed praise." As he left after the prayers the Prophet said, "Who was it who said that?" The speaker said, "I." And the Prophet replied, "I saw more than thirty angels vying with one another as to who should record it first." (*al-Kalimu 'ṭ-ṭayyib*, 6. an-Nawawī, *Adhkār*, 26.)

The bulbul of its rejoicing singing like the song of the bulbul in the branches, giving thanks, invoking Thee. *Ḥizbu 'l-ḥamd* 'Abd al-Qādir al-Jīlānī.

The followers of ash-Shādhilī are taught:

If as you sit meditating on your past you think of the good knowledge that you accumulated, then give thanks and ask forgiveness. If on the other hand as you sit meditating you think of your past faults, then ask forgiveness and give thanks. *al-Mafākhiru 'l-'aliyya*, p. 51.

'Alā Kulli Ḥāl. Shukr and Ṣabr

If *tasbīḥ* calls out the courage of the soul baffled by mystery and transcendence, *ḥamd* has its own courage, one of the great notes of the Muslim soul, expressed in the common phrase *Al-ḥamdu lillāhi 'alā kulli ḥāl*, Praise be to God under all conditions.

Even though in the small coin of talk the phrase has become a way of telling an inquirer that the speaker is not in good health or that all is not well with him, this is only a sign of the deep-rootedness of the idea in the Muslim soul. It is attributed, like all the great sayings of worship, to the Prophet himself:

If he saw what pleased him he said: Praise be to God whose grace brings all goodness to perfection. If he saw what he disliked he said, Praise be to God under all conditions. *al-Kalimu 't-ṭayyib*, p. 27 (traced by Ibn Mājah to 'A'isha).

It has passed fully into the life of prayer, in Christian Arabic as well as Muslim:

We thank Thee under all conditions and for all conditions and in all conditions. (From a MS. Christian prayer to be used before the "*Hours*" of the Greek Orthodox Church.)

The word *ḥāl* in the phrase *al-ḥamdu lillāhi 'alā kulli ḥāl* is that used by the mystics for successive states of soul through which they pass on their road to God, and the following prayer has made use of the popular phrase in reference to these soul-states.

Praise be to God, abundant praise, in this present state.
Praise be to God in all states.
Praise be to God before all states.
Praise be to God when all states shall be cut off (in the ultimate union with the changeless reality).

Ḥizb attributed to Uwais al-Qaranī in *Majmū'atu 'l-Aḥzāb*, p. 319.

This courageous praise under all conditions is closely connected with the great virtue of *ṣabr*, strong endurance, often a twin word with *shukr*:

Thou who hast made endurance our help under Thy trials and hast made thanksgiving a means to still more benefits, I ask Thee for endurance under Thy testing and for Thy help in thanksgiving for Thy graces. *Taḥmīdu 'l-Bārī*, ash-Shādhilī (*Qur. 14.7*).

How many a grace hast Thou given me for which my thanksgiving was small? With how many a trial hast Thou tested me under which my patience towards Thee was small? Thou who didst not deprive me of Thy grace because of my little thanksgiving, Thou who didst not forsake me for the smallness of my patience under trial—defend me—

(From a prayer attributed to 'Alī Zain al-'Ābidīn when he was in fear because of the expected entry of the conquering general Muslim ibn 'Uqbā into Medina 68/682. This sense of the inadequacy of our thankfulness is very strong in Shī'a devotions. The prayer has passed into general use, Sunnī as well as Shī'a. Thus in modern times it was introduced by M. 'Uthmān al-Mirghanī into his *Fatḥū 'r-rasūl*.)

aṣ-Ṣabr ya rabb! is the prayer of all the oppressed poor in Arab lands, and very greatly do their lives exemplify this virtue. But some worshippers have held that as an attitude towards God it is only a second best:

Shaqīq al-Balkhī asked Ja'far ibn Muḥammad al-Bāqir about generosity. And Ja'far said, "What do you think it is?" He replied, "Generosity is to give thanks when we receive gifts and to endure patiently the withholding of them." Ja'far replied, "Our dogs in Medina do as much as that." Then Shaqīq said, "O son of the daughter of the Prophet of God, what is generous behaviour with you?" He said, "If gifts are bestowed on us we accept them and if they are withheld from us we give thanks." *as-Silsilatu 'dh-dhahabiyya*, M. ibn Ḥasan Ẓāfir al-Madanī.

The Prophet said: If the child of one of his servants dies, God says to His angels (the angels of death), "Have you seized the child of my servant?" And they say, "Yes." Then He says, "You seized the child of his heart?" And they say, "He praised Thee repeatedly." Then God Most High says, "Build for my servant a house in Paradise and call it The House of Praise." *Adhkār*, an-Nawawī, p. 42. (al-Bukhārī, *Imān* 19, Aḥmad 4.410.)

Values of Ḥamd and Shukr

The Qur'ān points to an unspecified reward for gratitude: "If you give thanks, I will give you increase." (*14.7.*) And the manuals vary as to their interpretation of this promise.

A tradition says that the first who will be summoned to Paradise on the Resurrection Day are the praiseful who give grateful praise to God in prosperity and adversity. *Majmūʿatu 'l-wirdi 'l-ʿāmm*, p. 99 (Ibn Ḥanbal 4.434).

Gratitude is the virtue of generous hearts and in *taḥmīd* and *shukr* we find little of the popular tendency to look upon their recital as a rather mercantile insurance. Sometimes, however, they are regarded (and with some spiritual truth) as insurance against loss of grace:

He who neglects grateful praise and thanks to God Most High even for an hour is like the dumb cattle, and the result may be the departure of grace, and the hardening of the hearts of mankind towards him, and such difficulties in attaining all his aims that he may even desire death and find it denied him. . . .

Gratitude is the chain retaining what we have and the hunter chasing what we have lost. Ibid., p. 98.

If you are in a state of grace, cultivate it: stretch out your hand while the branches bend low.
Secure its continuance by thanks to God. For transgressions also have their fruitage. Ibid., p. 99.

On the whole, however, there is a more positive sense that gratitude brings its own spiritual joy and reward, "the garment of praise for the spirit of heaviness", a light and blessing now and hereafter:

Thankful praise to God! Praise that shall be to me chastity and sufficiency and such riches that, possessing them, I shall not be in need of any created being. Thankful praise to God! Praise that shall be to me power and authority by which I shall repulse the assaults of all who oppress me and bear a grudge against me. Ibid., p. 53.

O my God to Thee be grateful praise: praise that shall illuminate my heart.
O my God to Thee be grateful praise: praise that shall illuminate my grave.
O my God to Thee be grateful praise: praise that shall illuminate my hearing.
O my God to Thee be grateful praise: praise that shall illuminate my seeing.
O my God to Thee be grateful praise: praise that shall illuminate my flesh.
O my God to Thee be grateful praise: praise that shall illuminate my bones.
Ibid., p. 65 (used frequently in the manuals).

Praise be to the Lord of the Worlds: praise surpassing, higher and more excellent than the praise of all praisers of the Lord, first and last: praise that shall be to Him well-pleasing and to us safe keeping and a treasure laid in store with the Lord of the Worlds. *Ḥizbu fawātiḥi 'l-baṣā'ir*, ʿAbd al-Qādir al-Jīlānī.

I praise Him with the praise of the grateful ones: a praise that accords with and surpasses the best, the most beautiful and the most perfect of acts of praise: a praise in which I shall find satisfaction and knowledge of the divine laws, and requital and approach to Him and a safe-guard and safe-keeping with my creator. *Khawāṣṣu 'l-Fātiḥa*, Al-Ghazālī.

With the word *riḍā*, mutual satisfaction, well-pleasing, we reach the noblest thought of the reward of praise, a looking away from self to the Lord who is praised:

Thankful praise to God: a praise which brings to the praiser only the reward of pleasing Him. *Du'ā'u 'l-iftitāḥ li ad'iyati Ramaḍān* (anon.) and frequently.

Typical Examples of Ḥamd

Muslim *taḥmīd* is most moving when it is praise of His clemency and generosity to frail and erring servants. Three common forms are:

Thy generosity is not lessened by the meagreness of thanksgiving for Thy grace, any more than Thy treasury is exhausted by Thy wide-spread gifts. *Du'ā'u 'l-iftitāḥ li ad-'iyati Ramaḍān* (anon.) and frequently.

Praise be to God for His clemency in spite of His knowledge (of shortcomings) and praise be to God for His pardon in spite of His power (to punish) and praise be to God for His long-suffering in His anger. *Shī'a* prayer for the beginning of Ramaḍān, and frequently.

Perfect was thy light and Thou didst guide us:
Praise be to Thee!
Great was thy clemency and Thou didst pardon us:
Praise be to Thee!
Thou didst extend Thy hand and give to us:
Praise be to Thee!

(Referred to the Prophet by a tradition from Ibn 'Umar—a very frequent form in the manuals.)

Or this, perhaps the most beautiful of all Muslim thanksgivings:

Praise be to Him who when I call on Him answers me, slow though I am when He calls me.
Praise be to Him who gives to me when I ask Him, miserly though I am when He asks a loan of me.
Praise be to Him to whom I confide my needs whensoever I will and He satisfies them.
My Lord I praise, for He is of my praise most worthy.
Du'ā' for the 24th of Ramaḍān. 'Alī Zain al-'Ābidīn.

The greater part of Muslim praise and thanksgiving is solitary. Except in the *Fātiḥa* the speaker in the prayer-rite is a single individual, even at the communal prayers on Friday. This is true also of the greater part of the Psalms and of the New Testament canticles and does not hinder common use. But the note of *Te Deum laudamus* or "Now thank we all our God" is missing in Muslim praise, and perhaps such all-inclusive forms as the following (they are very common) are an unconscious compensation:

> (Such a praise) that from me alone there shall come to Thee in every twinkling of an eye or less than that, praise equal to the praise of all praisers; the affirmations of all affirmers of thy Unity and of all the single-hearted; and the declaration of thy transcendence by all and sundry who have attained to the mystic knowledge of Thee; and the praise of all who say the *shahāda* or call down blessing on the Prophet or say *subḥāna 'llāh*.
>
> *al-Ḥizbu 's-saifī.*

6

REFUGE-TAKING

Ta'awwudh, Isti'ādha

"I take refuge with God from Satan the accursed!" This cry of fear breaks into the praise and adoration of the prayer rite shortly after the *taḥrīma* (the exact position varying with the different *madhāhib*). It is there, Muslim worshippers tell us, in obedience to a Qur'ānic command, for the central feature of the first part of the prayer-ritual is a Qur'ān recitation and this comes under the command in *Qur.* 16.98. "When thou recitest the Qur'ān take refuge from Satan, the accursed."[1]

The same cry of frightened humanity "I take refuge with God" should have been the worshipper's first utterance after stepping into the mosque and on entering on his ablution. (*Adhkār an-Nawawī*, p. 16. *Durūsu 'd-dīni 'l-islāmī*, Book I, p. 29.)

Here we have a prayer-pattern that recurs constantly in the manuals, and one that is undoubtedly primitive, its roots going back long before Islam—the prayer of the man in a demon-haunted world, in a world, too, where the evil eye is to be feared as well as the attacks of less uncanny human enemies.

Use of the Root 'Ādh

The verb here used, *'ādha* (synonym *lādha*) appears to have the root meaning of clinging, as of flesh to bones, and hence expresses clinging to someone for refuge from some person or some cause of fear.

The first form of the verb is the one constantly used in phrases like *a'ūdhu bi'llāh* and its *maṣdar*, *'iyādh* is also used with the meaning of shelter:

[1] Literally "the stoned". For the many simple worshippers who use the popular books of the Khatmiyya order M. 'Uthmān al-Mirghanī explains: *The stoned* means the one who was driven away by stoning, cast out from the mercy of God. (*Sharḥu 'r-rātibi 'l-musammā bi'l-asrāri 'l-mutarādifa.*) To the folklore of the Near East, meteors mean that the angels are stoning down *shayāṭīn* from the ramparts of heaven.

O God Thou art my refuge (*'iyādhī*) in Thee I take shelter. *Ḥizbu yawmi 'l-khamīs*, 'Alī Ḥasan al-'Aṭṭās.

Muḥammad who is the shelter (*'iyādh*) of the worthless. *ad-Durru 'l-fā'iq*, Muṣṭafā 'l-Bakrī, p. 15.

The fourth form of the verb is used for giving refuge and so also for invoking shelter for another, putting him under protection:

(Giving protection.) Make secure for us our activity and give us protection (*a'idhnā*) from failure and sloth. *al-Munājātu 'l-injīliyyatu 'l-kubrā*, 'Alī Zain al-'Ābidīn.

The root is closely enmeshed with the thought of charms and amulets (for which the words *'ūdha, ta'wīdh, ma'ūdh, ma'āwidh* are all used) and that is perhaps why it is consistently avoided in the Beirut American translation of the Bible into Arabic, though its essential thought is one that belongs in a marked way to the Psalms. The following refuge-taking, for instance (although both the words for refuge are also associated with the use of charms), is strongly reminiscent of the Psalms:

Set me O God in an inaccessible refuge (*'iyādh manī'*) of thine appointment and a fortress-shelter from all thy creation. (Cf. Ps. 21.2,20.) *al-Ḥuṣūnu 's-sab'a*, M. al-Fatḥī al-Marrākushī.

Qur'ānic Uses

All the modes of Muslim devotional life have to find however slight a basis in the Qur'ān. In the case of *ta'awwudh* there is no need to juggle with texts for justification: the idea is well embedded in the very stuff of the Qu'rān. The root *'ādh* occurs in some ten passages, three of which have been formative in Muslim devotion. These three are:

(1) *16*.98. The verse quoted in the opening paragraph of this chapter, which by relating *ta'awwudh* to every recital of the Qur'ān has made of what might have been an occasional cry one of the main utterances of the Muslim soul, a part of its habit of life. The form of refuge-taking in this verse is the most general of all, the first taught to a child in the primary school, and to be said at all performances of the prayer-rite including the funeral prayers.

(2) and (3) The two short psalm-like *sūras* that end the Qur'ān, *The Daybreak* and *Mankind*, are original examples and patterns in

Islam of *ta'awwudh* and are known as "The two Refuge-seekings", *al-Mu'awwidhatān*.

Modern scholarship holds that they have always had this nature of amulet-prayers and are liturgical additions to the Qur'ān rather than part of its original structure; this is supported by the tradition that they were revealed to heal Muḥammad of a disease brought on him by Labīd the Medinan Jew. (See Nöldeke-Schwally, *Geschichte des Qur'ans*, I, pp. 108, 109.)

They are so short that they have lent themselves not only to use as inspired cries for help, but also as script for amulets, and are constantly carried about the person.

Sūratu 'l-falaq, one of the earliest taught to children provides a cry for protection against night dangers and against the envious eye. It forms part of the famous and widespread devotion found in many of our manuals and known as *al-Musabba'ātu 'l-'ashar*, the Ten Sevenfold Cries.

Sūratu 'n-nās can be used as a cry for refuge from men and devils, from temptation and from spooks, and is the most acceptable cry in such cases. Al-Ghazālī recommends its use before the performance of *ṣalāt*—a safeguarding of the rite.

Prophetic Usage

All the great type-forms of Muslim devotion are connected by traditions with the Prophet's use or words, and *ta'awwudh* is particularly rich in these. One of those quoted in the manuals describes his use of the *mu'awwidhatān*.

> (From 'Ā'isha.) When he went to bed he would put his two hands together and recite *al-Ikhlāṣ* and the *mu'awwidhatān* then blow into his hands and pass them over as much of his body as he could reach, beginning with his head and his face and the nearer parts. And this he would do three times. To copy him in this is approved.[1] *Adhkār an-Nawawī*, p. 44.

[1] The action is a well understood one in folk-religion for applying to one's body the *baraka* of some holy object touched by the hands (in this case the breath used for uttering the safety-bringing *sūras*). Anyone who has stood beside some holy object in the Near East (as for instance the Bābu 'z-Zuwaila at Cairo sometimes consecrated by the presence of a Quṭb) must have seen it again and again. The writer has watched the worshippers in the great mosque at Aleppo touching the reputed footprint of the Prophet with their hands and then passing them over their bodies as described in this tradition.

Another tradition quoted in the manuals is basic for one of the commonest forms of *ta'awwudh*. In its rhyming form it may go far back into desert life. Muḥammad is made to say to Ḥasan and Ḥusain:

> I put you both under the protection of the perfect words of God, against all demons and noxious reptiles and against every evil eye, and he further adds, and it is said that your father Abraham used to seek refuge through these words for Ishmael and Isaac. *al-Kalimu 'ṭ-ṭayyib*, p. 61. (Bukhārī.)

The form "I take refuge with the perfect words of God" is a recurring note in the prayer-manuals. M. 'Uthmān al-Mirghanī explains the "perfect words" for his numerous followers, as meaning the Qur'ān (*Sharḥu 'r-rātib*, p. 17), but a much earlier *ḥizb* (attributed to Aḥmad al-Būnī, who died *circa* 91–3/709–11) would seem to understand them not only of the limited number of "words" in the Qur'ān but of all God's words:

> Thy perfect words which, if all the trees of the world were pens and the seven seas their inkpot, they would not exhaust the perfect words of God. *Ḥizbu 'd-du'ā'* (in *Majmū'atu 'l-aḥzāb*, p. 366).

This explanation agrees better with the tradition which attributes the phrase to Abraham. Refuge-taking is so natural, so primitive an instinct that one wonders whether the little lilt in this tradition may enshrine some scrap of the ancient religious life of the desert.

The traditions of the Prophet's *ta'awwudh* are numerous and in this type of prayer his people feel that they are treading in his footsteps so that they will often summarize their own refuge-seekings by placing at the end of a long series of them the words:

> O Lord we ask Thee those good things that our lord Muḥammad Thy Prophet and Apostle asked Thee, and we take refuge with Thee from those evil things from which our lord Muḥammad Thy Prophet and Apostle took refuge. *al-Ḥizbu 'l-kabīr* (Qādirī), and very frequently in the manuals.

Against Demonic Powers

The innumerable forms of *ta'awwudh* and the directions for their use take us into a demon-haunted world. Such prayers are often called in Persian–Urdu manuals, *Haikal*, sanctuary. *Isti'ādha* is the natural instinct of a man frightened by the uncanny. A Qur'ānic text gives special sanction to this use: And say, My Lord I take refuge with Thee against the suggestions of the satans. My Lord I take refuge with

Thee that they (the satans) may gain no access to me. (*23*.97, 98. Cf. also 5.199.)

So we find the resulting prayer form, recommended for saying when one feels lonely on going to bed:

> I take refuge with the perfect words of God against his wrath and his punishment and against the evil of his servants and against the suggestions of the satans that they may gain no access to me. *Adhkār*, an-Nawawī, p. 57. *al-Kalimu 'ṭ-ṭayyib*, p. 23. (Traced to Prophet by Abu Dāwūd, at-Tirmidhī, Ibn as-Sīna, etc.)

The explanation is appended that the "suggestions" of the devils are the ideas that they flash into the minds of men.

Refuge-taking is enjoined for those occasions or actions which are most exposed to demonic assault, and of course among these is the time of worship, execrated by evil powers. The formula quoted above has been widely used:

> Ibn 'Amr used to teach these words to all his children who were capable of learning them, and for a child not yet able to learn them he used to write them and hang them on the child's person. *al-Kalimu 'ṭ-ṭayyib*, p. 23.
>
> The Prophet said: Iblīs the enemy of God came with fiery darts to cast them into my face. And I said three times, "I take refuge with God from thee." Then three times, "I curse thee with the utter curse of God from which there is no refuge." Then I was about to seize him, and by God had not our brother Sulaimān pleaded for him, I would have tamed him so that the children of the people of Medīna could safely play with him. *al-Kalimu 'ṭ-ṭayyib*, p. 54 (Muslim).
>
> 'Uthmān ibn Abī 'l-'Āṣ said, O Apostle of God, Satan hovered between me and my prayers and between me and my Qur'ān recitation, confusing them. Then the Prophet said, "That Satan is called Khanzab. If you feel his presence take refuge with God from him and spit three times on your left side."
>
> And so I did, and God sent him away from me. Ibid., p. 55 (Muslim).

Other occasions felt to be specially liable to demonic attack are the marriage night (as the story of Tobias shows), entrance to a bath, or a privy, and the sudden rising of the wind. Desert winds carry whirling dust-clouds, the home of roving demons, as is well known to those who listen to folk-stories. Examples:

> *On the marriage night when the bride is given to her husband*, or when a new slave or beast has been bought. The Prophet is reported to have said: "When

one of you marries a bride or buys a slave, let him say, O God, I ask Thee for the good of her and the good of the disposition Thou hast given her, and I take refuge with Thee from the evil of her and the evil of the disposition Thou hast given her. And when he buys a camel, let him put his hand on the summit of its hump and say likewise." *Adhkār*, an-Nawawī, p. 124.

On the rising of the wind. We ask Thee, O God, for the good of this wind and the good of what is in it and the good that Thou hast ordained through it, and we take refuge with Thee from the evil of this wind and the evil of what is in it and the evil that Thou hast ordained through it. Ibid., p. 80.

Against Danger from Human Beings

The greatest of these is ill-will and the envious evil-eye with the mysterious power attributed to it. This is one of the haunting fears of the Near East which even to-day makes it unwise, for instance, to praise a baby to its mother, in uneducated circles, unless adding *mā shā'a 'llāh* or some other protective word, without which she will fear the speaker's possible envy and its dreadful consequences.

A general and characteristic *isti'ādha* against the evil eye is the following included in numerous manuals:

I take refuge with Thee from the tyranny of every tyrant and the cunning of every deceiver and the oppression of every oppressor and the magic of every magician and the envy of every envier and the defection of every traitor and the snare of every ensnarer and the hostility of every enemy and the calumny of every calumniator and the backbiting of every backbiter and the ruse of every trickster and the malice of every malicious one and the secret rancour of every grudge-bearer. *al-Ḥizbu 's-saifī.*

Before travel

He who wishes not to see anything objectionable on a journey should say what the Prophet of God used to say: O God I take refuge with Thee from the hardships of travel and from collision and overturning, and from the evil eye upon property or family or child. *Khalāṣatu 'l-maghnam*, 'Alī b. Ḥasan al-'Aṭṭās, p. 19.

Another and most unusual traveller's *ta'awwudh* is a prayer before entering a village, which, with its plural form, almost makes one see a group of dervishes on one of those missionary journeys that have played so great a part in the spread and in the revivification of Islam:

O God, Lord of the seven heavens and what they overshadow, Lord of the seven earths and what they uphold, Lord of the demons and what they mislead, Lord of the winds and what they drive before them, we ask Thee for the good of this village and the good of its people and we take refuge with Thee from the evil of this village and the evil of its people and the evil of what is in it. O God bless us in it, support us on its fruits. Make us love its people and make the righteous among them love us. *al-Wirdu 'sh-shāfī*, Yūsuf an-Nabhānī.

The Dual Aspect of Created Things

A very remarkable feature of the prayers of refuge-taking is an apparently ingrained idea that every created thing, however "neuter", is far from neutral in respect of man, but has in it an active principle of good and an active principle of evil. The common form of *isti'ādha* in regard to this is "I ask Thee for the good of it and I take refuge with Thee from the evil of it." The more theologically balanced prayers of Islam never equalize the good and evil powers of created things as do these *isti'ādhāt* giving voice to an idea that is who knows how old?

When putting on a new garment

O God to Thee be praise who hast clothed me with this. I ask Thee for the good of it and the good for which it was created, and I take refuge with Thee from the evil of it and the evil for which it was created. *Adhkār*, an-Nawawī, p. 11.

On entering the Market

O God, I ask Thee for the good of this market and the good of what is in it, and I take refuge with Thee from the evil of it and the evil of what is in it. I take refuge with Thee lest I let fall a false oath or conclude a wrongful bargain. Ibid., p. 133.

At nightfall

I take refuge with Thee from the evil of this night and the evil of what is in it, and the evil of what was before it and the evil of what follows it. *Wirdu 'l-ghurūb*, Muṣṭafā al-Bakrī.

A more truly Muslim form is the following:

Abū Huraira said I heard the Apostle of God say: The wind is one of the blasts of God, coming with mercy and with chastisement. If you see that there is a wind do not revile it. Ask of God the good of it and take refuge with Him from the evil of it. *al-Kalimu 'ṭ-ṭayyib*, p. 64 (Abu Dāwūd, Ibn Mājah).

Against Spiritual Dangers

The worshipper has also to take refuge from the evil that is in himself, in his *nafs*, his lower self urgent to evil. *Isti'ādha* is the prayer of human nature under the warnings of conscience and the fear of the Last Things.

I take refuge with Thee from the evil of my lower self and from the evil of every beast whose forelock Thou dost grasp. (Referred to the Prophet.) Ibid., p. 17 (an echo of *Qur. 11.56*).

I take refuge with Thee that Satan may not injure me at my death. *Ṣalāt* of M. 'Uthmān al-Mirghanī (in *Fatḥu 'r-rasūl*, p. 59).

O God I take refuge with Thee from miserliness and I take refuge with Thee from cowardliness and I take refuge with Thee from being sent back to degradation and I take refuge with Thee from the seductions of Anti-Christ and I take refuge with Thee from the pains of the tomb. *Majmū 'atu 'l-wirdi 'l-'āmm*, M. 'Abd Allāh al-Fatḥi, p. 89.

I take refuge with Thee from the evil of my hearing and the evil of my seeing; from the evil of my tongue and from the evil of my heart and from the evil of my sexual life.

I take refuge with Thee O God from unprofitable knowledge and from a heart without reverence, and from an ever-demanding self, and from unheard petition. From these four I take refuge with Thee.

I take refuge with Thee from hunger, the worst of bedfellows, and from treachery that ruins friendship, and I take refuge with Thee from the evil suggestions of the breast and from the frustration of affairs and the temptation of the grave.

O God with Thee do I take refuge from Thy torments on the day when Thou shalt raise Thy servants, from a speedy torment and a harsh judgment, for Thou art swift in punishment. *Majmū'atu 'l-wirdi 'l-'āmm*, M. al-Fatḥī al-Marrākushi, p. 87 ff. (The first paragraph is, in *Riyāḍu 'l-janna*, attributed to the Prophet.)

"With Thee from Thyself"

So the timorous mortal turns to find refuge from his sin and from the Divine Judgment.

But to whom shall he fly for refuge from the Judge save to the Judge Himself? And the great and significant phrase appears—one of the greatest in Islamic prayer—"I take refuge with Thee from Thyself."

Like all the great recurring phrases of Muslim worship it is given a Prophetic setting:

In a tradition attributed to 'Ā'isha:

I missed the Prophet one night and felt for him, and my hand lighted on the soles of his feet, for he was prostrating himself and his feet were in a vertical position. And he was saying: O God, behold I take refuge with Thy good pleasure (*riḍā* satisfaction, the exact sense of *eudokēsa* in Mark 1.11) from Thy wrath and with Thy pardon from Thy punishment, and I take refuge with Thee from Thyself. It is beyond me to express Thy praise. Thine own praise of Thyself alone can express what Thou art. *Riyāḍu 'l-janna*, Yūsuf an-Nabhānī, p. 96. *Majmū'atu 'l-wirdi 'l-'āmm*, p. 87 (an-Nasā'ī).

In the above form the prayer is constantly found, its sacredness increased by a tradition that it was first uttered during the Night of the *Mi'rāj* round which the mystical thought of Islam has ever played. In the sequence of its sentences an ascent of the spirit has been traced:

It has been said that the Prophet only pronounced these words on the Night of the Ascension, between Paradise and the Fire, when he said, "I will not turn to Paradise, for had Paradise any virtue in itself Adam would not have made his slip there. And I will not turn to the Fire, for had it possessed any burning power in itself Abraham would not have been cool and peaceful in it. But I will forsake Thy Paradise and lay hold on Thy pardon, I will forsake Thy Fire for the fear of Thy punishment."

... And when he remembered that Paradise only existed through the good pleasure of the Lord and that the Fire only existed through the wrath of the Lord, he turned away from both Paradise and the Fire to the attributes of the All-Powerful King. And it came into his heart that, just as the existence of Paradise depends on God's good pleasure, and the existence of the Fire depends on His wrath, so good pleasure and wrath are themselves two of His attributes, and the attribute only has existence through the one to whom it is attributed.

He turned away, therefore, from the attribute of the Owner to the Owner of the attribute, saying, "I take refuge with Thee from Thee. . . . Had there been any other than Thee, I should have fled for refuge to him, out of fear of Thee. But since none but Thee exists I can only take refuge from Thyself with Thee."

And the *bā'* (of *bika*—"with Thee") is a conjunctive particle. It is therefore as though the Prophet had said, "I seek refuge from separation in conjunction"; the prayer amounts to, "If Thou tormentest me, torment me not with the degradation of separation from Thee." . . .

"I fly for refuge with Thee from Thyself" is outwardly a cry of distress and inwardly a thanksgiving, for the meaning of the cry is, "Thou art a necessity to me. To whom but Thee shall I go?"

The three first sentences of this prayer are praise mingled with petition. Now when a man is making a petition he is concerned with himself; so he put himself aside and turned his eye away from self, saying, "I cannot express Thy praise." Then when his consciousness had died to all save God and dwelt in God, he said, "Thou art as Thou hast praised Thyself." *Lawāmi'u 'l-bayyināt*, Fakhru 'd-Dīn ar-Rāzī, p. 36 ff.

Deep and humbling, for less consecrated souls, as is the experience behind these comments of the saintly theologian, they still leave us faced with the unresolved discord so frankly stated in this prayer and the many for which it is the norm.

> I take refuge with Thy good pleasure from Thy wrath, and with Thy pardon from Thy punishment, and I take refuge with Thee from Thyself.
>
> O God we take refuge with Thy friendship from Thy aversion, with Thy nearness from Thy distance, and we take refuge with Thee from Thee. *Du'ā'* of 'Abd al-Qādir al-Jīlānī in *al-Fuyūḍātu 'r-rabbāniyya*, p. 76.

Still the antitheses remain

good pleasure	wrath
pardon	punishment
friendship	aversion
nearness	distance

summed up by the Christian writer as "the goodness and severity of God" (Rom. 11.22).

Is there in these prayers of antithesis a real solution of discord or only a verbal juxtaposition? "Good pleasure and wrath are themselves two of his attributes" says ar-Rāzī in the passage just quoted, and some, though not all, of the prayers built on this pattern give the impression of so playing off one attribute against another (since the sinner's only hope is that "good pleasure" will in relation to himself prevail over "wrath") as to endanger the formal doctrine of the Unity. But what if these worshippers with their "I-thou" relationship to living Reality are penetrating further than formal definition with its treatment of that living Reality as a subject of discourse? What if "the insistent paradoxes of experience" are closer to Divine Reality than any conceptual scheme? Within the mystery of the Divine Nature must be the reconciliation of incompatible attributes and perhaps it may be too tremendous in its reality to be expressed in syllogisms.

> It is only in Him that two attributes are united simultaneously without His experiencing discordance; for when He appears He remains latent, and when He veils Himself He remains patent. He, the Apparent, the Hidden, the Near, the Distant. *Akhbār al-Ḥallāj*, Massignon and Kraus, p. 20.

The Christian worshipper also takes refuge "with Him from Him". "What way have I but to fly from Thee to Thee?" (St Augustine on Ps. 33.) He has as strong a sense of the antithesis in these prayers as his Muslim brother. The two arms of a cross can never be parallel; they can only meet at a point of intersection. Before that point of intersection, of the clash of incompatibles, the Christian says: "Behold brethren, the goodness and the severity of God, reconciled not in a syllogism but in one Body . . . on the Cross. God was in Christ, reconciling . . .". And on his awestruck lips he takes the prayer of his Muslim brethren, "I seek refuge with Thee from Thyself."

7

THE NAME IN WORSHIP

Basmala, al-Asmā'u 'l-Ḥusnā

The central part of the section of the prayer-rite known as *al-qirā'a*, "the recital", is a brief Qur'ān recitation. This must be introduced, however, by the *basmala*, the saying of the opening phrase attached to every *sūra* of the Qur'ān, much as the *Gloria* is attached in Christian worship to the end of every Psalm.[1]

This phrase, *Bismi 'llāhi 'r-raḥmāni 'r-rahīm*, usually translated into English by "In the Name of God the Merciful the Compassionate", is for ever on Muslim lips and pens. While the Jewish people honoured the Name by refusal to pronounce it, Muslims choose to honour it by constant use. All the events of life and the little fears of the heart are to be tamed, as it were, and made innocuous and set at rest by coming under the control of the Name.

This constant naming of the Name may be an act of simple confidence, or a light superstitious nothing; a conjuration charged with magical power; or, in saintly lives, a bringing of all things into relation with God, a signing of all life with his Name. Like the use of the sign of the Cross, the *basmala* may mean everything or nothing.

Popular Use of the Basmala

The late Mr A. T. Theobald of Algeria kindly communicated the following observations of popular usage there which might be duplicated or added to from many another land:

> You must say the *basmala* on entering a room or a house, or on opening a book. Never tread on a piece of paper, the Name of God may be written upon it.
>
> Often in market places, when we are selling portions of the Bible, the books

[1] Although in their analyses of the prayer-rite Muslim and especially Ḥanafite writers set the *basmala* as a separate item from the recitation which it precedes, it is quite definitely regarded by them as an intrinsic part, the first verse, of each *sūra*.

are brought back to us by purchasers because on the title page the *basmala* does not appear. Our bookseller points out that the name of Allāh occurs in the first verse of Genesis, but is told, "No, we are forbidden to read anything which does not begin *bismi 'llāhi 'r-raḥmāni 'r raḥīm.*"

Always put your hand before your mouth when you yawn, lest the devil enter in. Should you forget to do this, repeat the *basmala* and then spit three times.

If you do not utter the Name of God before you drink, the demons get the first drink. If you do not repeat the Name before you eat, the demons get the first mouthful.

Should you forget to say the *basmala* before entering your bed, the evil ones will be there before you, and you will pass a restless night.

Once upon a time two malicious spirits met together; one was extremely stout and well-favoured and the other miserably thin and weak. The stout one addressed his friend and said, "How is it, brother, you are so thin?" "Ah, I live in a very holy place: they all repeat the Name of God so faithfully that I can find but little to eat and drink, neither can I rest day nor night." The well-favoured one said, "I am glad that I live in a wicked town where no one remembers the Name of God. I have all I need because of their forgetfulness."

The popular saying about eating without the *basmala* is supported by a tradition quoted in our manuals:

(From Umayya ibn Makhshī.) The Apostle of God was sitting with a man who was eating and did not name the Name of God Most High till he reached the last mouthful of his food. Then as he raised that to his mouth he said, "In the Name of God, the first of it and the last of it." And the Prophet laughed and said, "A *shaiṭān* had been eating with him all the while, and when he made mention of the name of God the food in that *shayṭān's* belly turned to poison." *al-Kalimu 'ṭ-ṭayyib,* p. 78 (Aḥmad I, 208).

A similar idea in pre-Islamic times of the necessity of "saining" food is found among the fathers of the Egyptian desert.

Because the blessed fathers knew the wiles of Satan, and that they would certainly bring upon them that which would do them harm by means of such things as are employed as food, they signed what they ate with the holy sign of the great Cross, so that they might slay all the craftiness of the Calumniator. *Questions and Answers on the Ascetic Rule* in *The Paradise of the Fathers,* translated from Syriac by Wallis Budge, II, 269.

The story of the happy and the unhappy devil, a cliché in popular preaching, and coming in this instance from Algeria, is much older than Islam in the Near East and also had its counterpart in the third and fourth century life of the Egyptian desert:

> Abba Pachomius heard one of them (the devils) saying, "I have (strife) with a man who constantly (defieth) me, for whensoever I approach to sow thoughts in his mind, immediately he turneth to prayer, and I depart from him consumed with fire." And another devil said, "I have (strife) with a man who is easy to persuade and he doeth whatsoever I counsel him to do and I love him dearly." It is right, then O my brethren that we should keep ourselves awake always, and that, making ourselves mighty men in the Name of the Lord, we should strive against the devils, and then they will never be able to overcome us. (Wallis Budge, *op. cit.*, I, 359.)

Traditions support the use of the *basmala* on all kinds of occasions, on entering the market or the house, on paying the *zakāt*, or on putting the right foot over the threshold of the mosque.

The formula in writing should stand at the beginning of every book, and though sometimes omitted from modern works in the European style, it does generally so stand, not only in religious books but even in pornographic books and grubby little crime stories. *Shī'a* books sometimes use the form *bismi 'llāhi 'l-mu'izzi 'l-muta'āl*. The *basmala* has of course its part to play in the writing of charms; it stands at the beginning of each *ḥizb* or *wird* in our prayer-manuals, and often over the entrance to houses or shops. It is the preface to the ablution before the prayers, some holding that the validity of the rite depends on it.

> He has made no ablution who has not invoked the Name of God upon it. *Adhkār*, an-Nawawī p. 34.

Another ritual use is on slaying the victim at the Feast of Sacrifice.

> It is not approved that a man shall say, "I do so and so over the Name of God", for his Name, glory be to Him, is over everything. The Qāḍī 'Iyād and others say that this statement is an error. For sound traditions have confirmed that at the Feast of Sacrifice the Prophet said to his companions, "Sacrifice over the Name of God, which means saying, 'In the Name of God'." Ibid., p. 169.

"Saining"

What is the feeling behind all this popular usage? Sometimes an essentially irreligious one. Here in the *basmala* is something with *baraka* in it. A tiny coin of supernatural value that may be spent for one's own profit. Often from the sense that weak and sin-stained man in a jinn-haunted dangerous world needs at every turn the protection of something strong and pure and holy. The closest usage to this in Christendom is represented by the old word "sained", and the use of the sign of the Cross to control or purify what is suspect of evil influence, and to bless and sanctify the common acts of life. In the Near East the Christian peasant puts the sign of the Cross over his house door, and the Muslim peasant says his *basmala* as he enters his. Both practices, by their very simplicity, may easily become mechanical and meaningless. No one can claim that they are not often so. Yet both have been and may be acts of conquering faith in the Holy Strong One.

The *basmala* is much used in the morning to "sain", to place in safety, the acts of the forthcoming day. Thus our manuals order repetitions of it after the dawn prayer-rite. Or the form:

> The Name of God over my religious practice, over myself and my child and my family and my property. (*Majmū'u 'l-'awrādi 'l-kabīr*, M. 'Uthmān al-Mirghanī, and frequently in the manuals.)

is included in morning devotions, and is also expanded after the fashion of these prayers into

> I say over myself and over my religious practice and over my kinsfolk and over my children and over my property and over my friends and over their religious practices and over their property a thousand thousand basmalas. *Ḥizbu 'n-Nawawī* in *Dalā'ilu 'l-khairāt ma'a 'l-awrād*, p. 220.

or still more generously:

> The name of God on my religious practice and on myself and my children.
> The Name of God on my property and my kinsfolk.
> The Name of God on all things that my Lord has bestowed on me.
> With the Name of God, Lord of the seven heavens and the seven earths and of the Great Throne.
> With the Name of God, with whose Name nothing in earth or heaven is harmful.
> With the Name of God, best of all names in earth and heaven.
> With the Name of God I begin and with that Name I conclude. Allāh! Allāh! Allāh! Allāh! Ibid., p. 227. (Such sainings can be matched in many devotions.)

Similarly the *basmala* may be used as a committal prayer on going to bed, a saining against the dangers of the night, a kind of holy insurance:

And say when going to sleep, "In the Name of God the Merciful the Compassionate," twenty-one times, for it is a safeguard against theft and fire and flood. *al-'Aṭiyyatu 'l-haniyya*, 'Alī ibn Ḥasan al-'Aṭṭās, p. 116.

The first two of the morning forms given above are also employed for bedtime. Another evening form of self-committal and one claiming Prophetic usage is:

In thy Name I die and live (Sleep being a little death). *Wirdu 'l-ghurūb*, Muṣṭafa 'l-Bakrī.

(From Abū Huraira.) The Prophet said, "If one of you gets up from his bed at night, then returns to it, let him dust it three times with the fringe of his head-cloth, for he cannot tell what may have taken his place on the bed when he left it. And when he lies down let him say, 'In thy Name my Lord I lay me down and in Thee I raise me up.'" *al-Kalimu 'ṭ-ṭayyib*, p. 18 (agreed tradition).

A Word of Power

It is clear that the *basmala* formula is above all things a word of power. We have here the Semitic belief in the power and mystery of a name, reminding us of the Hebrew *Ba'al Shem*. And we have in some prayers the tendency to pass from simple confidence in Him who is named, to confidence in the power of the formula, which is sometimes wielded like a weapon against foes, or handed up to God, as a coin of proved value.

O God, by the excellence of "In the Name of God the Merciful the Compassionate" let us enter into thy inviolate fortress. O God, by the excellence of "In the Name of God the Merciful the Compassionate" cause us to dwell in Thy inviolate fortress. (*Basmala* for driving away fatigue and for wandering over the earth. *Ḥizbu 'l-baḥr*, ash-Shādhilī.)

"In the Name of God" upon my heart that its thirst may be quenched.
"In the Name of God" upon my knees that they may be strengthened.
"In the Name of God" upon the earth that it may be traversed.
al-Fuyūḍātu 'r-rabbāniyya, 'Abd al-Qādir al Jīlānī, p. 196.

(Against foes or the evils of mankind.) I set forth as a barrier before me and before them "In the Name of God the Merciful the Compassionate" and likewise on my right and their right and likewise on my left and their left and likewise in front of me and in front of them, and likewise above me and above them and likewise below me and below them, and likewise enclosing me and enclosing them. *Ḥizbu 'n-Nawawī*, also in *Ḥīzbu 'n-naṣr* of 'Abd al-Qādir al-Jīlānī and in a *Ḥizb* attributed to the Imām al-Ghazālī in *Majmū'atu 'l-Aḥzāb* of Aḥmad Ḍiyā'u 'd-Dīn.

Al-Nawawī's whole *Ḥizb* is in reality an enlargement and application of the *basmala*. Later, passing from the thought of foes to friends, he again applies his safeguard in all directions:

> Then breathe out without spitting, three times on your right and three times on your left, three times in front of you and three times behind. Then say, "I have hidden myself and them in the treasures of 'In the Name of God the Merciful the Compassionate.'" *Ḥizbu 'n-Nawawī* in *Majmū'u 'l-awrād li-Muṣṭafā al-Bakrī.*

The Letters of the Basmala

There is clearly for these worshippers a mysterious power in the very formula itself.

> I beseech Thee by virtue of every mystery which Thou hast set in "In the Name of God the Merciful, the Compassionate." *Du'ā'u Yā Sīn, Majmū'atu 'l-aḥzāb*, Aḥmad Ḍiyā'u 'd-Dīn, p. 395.

Many worshippers feel that the mystery is latent in the very letters of which the formula is composed. For Arab minds have seen "signs" of God not only in the verses (*āyāt*) of the Qur'ān but in the very Arabic letters in which the revelation was embodied. Some have held them to have been created before the worlds.

There is a science of letters (*'ilmu 'l-ḥurūf*) and of their inner meaning and philosophical value (*'ilmu 'l-jafr*), connected with their numerical values, and not confined to mystical circles. Goldziher gives reasons for thinking that the legends underlying this passed from rabbinical circles to Islam, though there was probably also a return current flowing from Islam to Jewish *haggada*.[1] This science of letters partly lies behind the cabbalistic use of them in charms, but it also has a nobler and more truly religious life of its own. In the devotions based on the *basmala* it often comes to the fore, for here, the writers feel, we are near the heart of all mysteries. The very letters become numinous.

We give some examples from the manuals, of this way of thinking and of worshipping:

[1] See Goldziher *Linguistisches aus der Litteratur der muhammadanischen Mystik*. Z.D.M.G. 26, p. 764 seq. The rabbinical legend of the strife between *alif* and *bā'* since the Qur'ān like the Torah begins with *bā'*, has found its way into Muslim religious circles.

O God I ask Thee by virtue of the *bā'* of Thy name, the letter of "with-ness", the conjunction with the greatest Object of Desire, and the finding of all that was lost.

And by the point beneath the *bā'* guiding to the secrets of Thy ever-lastingness and Thy pre-eternal and sole Being, and by the attractive power (like the inflective power of the preposition) to its lovers, and its supreme disposal of all, particularly and universally and by the *sīn* initiating that authoritative disposal, the mystery of supremacy transcendent of place or time, the only source of relief from cares and affairs of this world or the next.

And by the *mīm* of life-giving and death-dealing (*muḥyī* and *mumīt*, two of the Names of God) to all creation, knowing no "before" and "after", transcendent of modality, and by its authoritative disposals and its Muḥam-madic meanings.

And by *alif al-waṣl* (i.e. not cut off from the previous letter by a *hamza* above it) by which Thou hast set up all things that are. And it is an unin-flected letter, commanding all the other letters, whether of the fiery or earthly or airy or watery elements, the recognition of it perceived as the splendour of the sun; Thy authority which penetrates to non-existence giving it existence, and subduing every existence to it. And by virtue of Thine attributes of quelling I quell our enemies and Thy enemies.

And by the *lām* of *Allah*, the letter of transcendence alike of fellowship or opposition, which stands for the object of worship. By virtue of its assigning to every soul that which it has brought on itself of good or evil, and by virtue of its knowledge of hearts and thoughts, give us of its bestowals of grace. Open to us by its knowledge and give us realization of truth through the secret of its efficient, penetrating mysteries. Entrust us with its mysteries as pleaseth Thee, and seemeth good to Thee.

And by the *hā'* of the Ipseity (of Allāh) self-existent, worthy of all praises, exalted with the *basmala* in the majesty of its declaration of the Unity. Thou didst send down the books that were from eternity, which bear witness of its affirmation of Unity. And the people of its blessedness bear witness and affirm and the people of its vision are absorbed in the secret of its mysteries.

And by the mystery of *ar-Raḥmān*, giver of the glories of grace showing mercy to the aged and to the babe and to the embryo in the womb. The Merciful One of this world and the next. . . .

And by the mystery of *ar-Raḥīm* with its delicacy of mercy, giver of the glories of grace and its fine touches, the adored of heart after heart, drawing each by the sympathy of the spiritual content of that Name of Thine, *ar-Raḥīm*. *Du'ā'u 'l-Basmala*, 'Abd al-Qādir al-Jīlānī.

The following discussion in another manual, a commentary on the devotions known as *ad-Durru 'l-fā'iq* of Muṣṭafā al-Bakrī, deals with the meaning of the *bā'* of the *Basmala* in a rather more homely way:

> The *bā'* of the *basmala* is either a sign of companionship by way of blessing, or it stands for the seeking of help, and there is no objection to seeking help through His Name as we seek help from Himself. Of the two it is preferable to hold that it stands for companionship, for the meaning "the seeking of help" would be less seemly, since seeking of help involves God, and that would mean that we were writing the name of God with a purpose of our own other than Himself.
>
> The *shaikh al-akbar* (Ibn al-'Arabī) said that the noun and its preposition were dependent on a (suppressed verb of) praising God, for God Most High is only praised through his Names, and the meaning of *bismi 'llāhi* is thus, "By the Name of God I praise Him." And He opened His Book with the letter *bā'* and selected it to have precedence over all the letters especially the *alif* because in the (upright) *alif* is exaltation and magnifying and in the *bā'* is depression and lowliness. And when the *alif* exalted itself, God humbled it, and when the *bā'* humbled itself God exalted it, as says the tradition, "He who humbles himself before God is exalted by God." And Abū Madyān used to say, "I see nothing without seeing the *bā'* written on it," as who should say, "Everything exists by Him." *Fatḥu 'l-karīmi 'l-khāliq*, 'Alī al-Makkī.

The *basmala* formula as used in the manuals would seem more often to have the sense of "with the Name of God" than "in the Name of God" as understood by Christians. Indeed the form attributed to the Prophet, and second only in popularity to that of the Qur'ān, would seem to point to this:

> In the name of God who injures nothing in heaven or earth with his Name (i.e. nothing that is linked with His Name). *Majmū'u 'l-awrād*, Muṣṭafā al-Bakrī.

AR-RAḤMĀN AR-RAḤĪM

ar-Raḥmān ar-Raḥīm comes in for similar exegesis, letter by letter. The four rivers of Paradise flow out from the four radicals contained in these names, and they are words of authority over the world above and the world below. Writers find it necessary to rebut the idea that the word *raḥmān*,[1] Syriac in form, is of foreign origin. Did not God Most High announce the sending down of an Arabic Qur'ān? How

[1] Although an Arabic adjective is built on this form (*na'sān*, sleepy; *kaslān*, idle) it is in all other cases from intransitive verbs.

then should part of its opening phrase be non-Arabic? It is necessary, the commentators say, that *raḥīm* shall be a more intensive form than *raḥmān*, for one does not say, "he is a man of deep learning, a learned man", but rather, "he is a learned man, a man of deep learning", with increase of emphasis.

With the vast mass of comment in Arabic theology we are not here concerned. The general tendency of what the manuals have to say may be summed up as follows. The word *raḥmān* paints for us the Lord whose mercy is over all his works while *raḥīm* describes the Lord whose mercy is over them that fear Him (cf. *Qur.* 33.43).

> His being *ar-Raḥmān* involves the inclusion in His mercy of everything in this world and the next, and thus of the righteous man and the evil doer. As for *raḥīm*, that is concerned with His mercy to believers.
>
> *ar-Rahmān* is He who gives when he is asked, *ar-raḥīm* is He who is vexed when He is not asked to give—*ar-Raḥmān* is concerned with deliverance from the Fire, *ar-Raḥīm* with entry into Paradise. *Lawāmiʿu 'l-bayyināt*, Fakhru 'd-dīn ar-Razī, p. 130.[1]

Many prayers are built on these two glorious names. One which is very widely spread, appearing even in Urdu-Arabic manuals, is traditional (Ibn Māja):

> O God the Merciful One for this world and the next, the Shower of Mercy to them both, have mercy on me in this my need, a mercy that shall put me beyond the need of mercy from any other than Thee. *Riyāḍu 'l-janna*, Yūsuf an-Nabhānī, p. 90.

The Basmala and Christian Worship

There are many examples in pre-Islamic Christianity of a similar sense of the power of the Name. The Life of St Anthony, attributed to St Athanasius, is rich in them:

> The Blessed Anthony . . . encouraged the brethren who were with him not to be terrified or to tremble at such visions as these. For, said he to them,

[1] Know that *ar-raḥīm* is more specialized than His Name *ar-raḥmān* and *ar-raḥmān* more general than the other. The mercy which includes everything is an effusion of His Name *ar-raḥmān*, and the mercy written down "for the God-fearing who pay their tithes" is an effusion from the Name *ar-raḥīm*. (*Insān Kāmil*, p. 84.)

they are only empty phantoms which perish as if they had never existed at the Name of the Cross. . . .

He looked at them boldly and said unto them, "If ye have received power over me (from the Lord), draw nigh and delay not, for I am ready for you; but if ye have made ready and come at (the command of) Satan, get ye back to your places and tarry not, for I am a servant of Jesus the Conqueror." And when the blessed man had spoken these words, Satan was straightway driven away by the mention of the Name of Christ like a sparrow before a hawk. . . .

There appeared unto me a devil of an exceeding haughty and insolent appearance, and he stood up before me with the tumultuous noise of many people, and he dared to say unto me, "I, even I, am the power of God", and "I, even I, am the Lord of the worlds." And he said unto me, "What dost thou wish me to give thee? Ask and thou shalt receive." Then I blew a puff of wind at him and I rebuked him in the Name of Christ, and I made ready to smite him, and when, as I thought, I did smite him, at that very moment all his strength and all his hosts, at the Name of Christ, came to an end. *The Paradise of the Fathers*. Wallis Budge's trans., I.16,44,73.

The hymn, attributed to St Patrick, of the Irish missionaries of the fifth century, is another example (which may be compared with the *basmala* of all directions quoted above) of this claiming of protection in a demon-haunted world. It is saved from superstition through the fact that trust is put in a living Person rather than in a word or formula:

Christ be with me, Christ within me,
Christ behind me, Christ before me,
Christ beside me, Christ to win me,
Christ to comfort and restore me;
Christ beneath me, Christ above me,
Christ in quiet, Christ in danger,
Christ in hearts of all that love me,
Christ in mouth of friend and stranger.

(Translation by Mrs Alexander, *English Hymnal* No. 212.)

Christian Arabic books of the Middle Ages often begin with the *basmala* in its Qur'ānic form. In the wording of the formula, as in most of its Muslim expositions, there is nothing that a Christian cannot take upon his lips. It contains thoughts of God enshrined in the Psalms and used in Christian worship. *ar-Raḥīm* is constantly found in the Eastern Christian liturgies. Yet on the whole, and especially in modern times, Christian Arabic shows a tacit avoidance of the formula and the writer has known an eastern Christian congregation take strong exception to the introduction of a sermon by these words, to them identified with a faith that is not Christian.

The Christian *basmala* has not been free, with shame be it confessed, from the degradation, so commonly imposed on the Qur'ānic *basmala*, of use as a word of power in charms.

Thus in a "Christian" Chaldaean manuscript written in 1802/3 among the mountains of Turkish Kurdestan we find various charms against headache, etc., introduced by the Triune *basmala* and containing such "words of power" as:

> By the Name of the Word of the Lord, in whose dominion are the heaven and the earth, and at whom the rebellious demons tremble: By the Name I am that I am, Almighty God, Adonai, Lord of Hosts. *The Book of Protection*, Syriac Charms, Herman Gollancz.

These charms are intended to be carried about and we have therefore a kind of fetishism, a trust in the written word all too dimly combined with a trust in the Living Lord.

The true Christian equivalent of the *basmala* is probably the phrase "in the Name of Jesus Christ our Lord", appended to prayer. It has never become common coin in daily speech for it involves too much.

A Christian is baptized not only "in the Name", but "into the Name", a distinction which the Arabic of the baptismal formula no more than the English has been able to mark. When in the New Testament we are told that a Christian is to "do all in the Name of the Lord Jesus" (Col. iii, 17), we find that, though the Arabic phrase is similar, the difference between this and the ordinary use of the *basmala* carries us into another world. "In the Name of", as used in the New Testament, means "in full accord with and surrender to His character and purpose". It is a costly word.

The Use of the Names of God

God has many names. The "Ninety-Nine Names of Moral Beauty" (*al-Asmā'u 'l-ḥusnā*) grew, at what date is uncertain, out of the effort to codify the statement in Qur'ān 7.180, in order the better to fulfil the command coupled with it. Lists of these names are frequent in prayer-manuals, together with the prayers based on them—prayers in prose, of which one of the noblest is the Shī'a *Du'ā' Nūr*, or in verse with a line for every name. The manuals also give lists of all the names found in the Qur'ān, and sometimes of those in the *Ḥadīth*. These are to be learnt by heart. The commonest rosary (*ṣubḥa*) has a bead for each of the Ninety-Nine Names.

"He who counts them enters Paradise," and the meaning of "counts" is "commits to memory". *al-Wirdu 'sh-shāfī*, Yūsuf an-Nabhānī, p. 75.

Fakhr ar-Rāzī said at the beginning of his commentary:

I saw in some of the tradition books that God Most High has four thousand Names, a thousand of them in the Qur'ān and the sound Traditions, a thousand in the Tōrah, a thousand in the Injīl, and a thousand in the Zabūr, and it is said a thousand others in the Preserved Tablet, and that thousand has not been made known to the world of men. . . .

aṣ-Ṣāwī said in the margin of the *Jalālain*; His Names, may He be exalted, are many. It is said three hundred and it is said a thousand and one, and it is said a hundred and twenty-four thousand, the number of the prophets, for every prophet is endowed with the inward reality of a special Name. *al-Istighāthatu 'l-Kubrā*, Yūsuf an-Nabhānī, p. 141.

It is clear, then, that the Ninety-Nine Names do not exhaust all His Names of Beauty, and the commonest formulae of prayer through the Names are:

O God, I beseech Thee by every Name of Thine by which Thou hast named Thyself or which Thou hast sent down in Thy book or taught to any of Thy creatures or made Thine own in the unseen world. . . . *Lawāmi'u 'l-bayyināt*, p. 50 attributed to the Prophet (frequent in the manuals).

I beseech Thee by Thy Names of Moral Beauty, those of them which I know and those which I do not know. *Riyāḍu 'l-janna*, p. 95, attributed to the Prophet (frequent in the manuals).

The prayer-manuals show equal preoccupation with the mysterious "Great Name". Theories are put forward as to which it may be, and prayers are cited with traditions assuring the user that they contain this Name of power. An example of the latter may be quoted from a Shī'a manual where a great-grandson of 'Ālī had for twenty years besought God to teach him "The Greatest Name":

And one night as he stood at prayer his eyes closed (in sleep) and he saw the Prophet coming towards him, and he (the Prophet) approached and kissed him between the eyes saying, "What have you asked of God?" He said, "My grandfather, I asked Him to teach me His Greatest Name." Then the Prophet said, "My little son, write with your finger on your palm. . . ." (A prayer follows presumably containing the Name.) *aṣ-Ṣahīfatu 's-sajjādiyya*, p. 288.

A book as long again as this would be needed to describe all the uses of the Names in worship. Here the briefest notes must suffice.

Magical Application

As with the *basmala*, the Semitic thought of power through the wielding of a name is very prominent, not only with the cabbalistic Al-Būnī, but with men whose prayers show a deep sanctity.

God Most High has appointed to every one of His Names a secret not to be found in the others. Through some rain is brought; some still the winds and the sea; some are used for walking on the water, some for flying through the air; through others the blind and lepers are healed, and so forth. *al-Istighāthatu 'l-Kubrā*, Yūsuf an-Nabhānī, p. 148.

The Name is "laid upon" (*wuḍi'a 'alā*) whatever is to come under its authority. (Compare Numbers 6.27 for a similar phrase, but used in blessing.)

Thy Names of Moral Beauty to which all things upon which they are laid are subdued. *Khalāṣatu 'l-Maghnam*, 'Alī Ḥasan al-'Aṭṭās.

Or the Names "fall upon" (*waqa'a 'alā*) it:

All Thy Names of Moral Beauty which, falling upon anything cause its body to be subdued. *Ḥizbu Aḥmad al-Būnī, Majmū'atu 'l-aḥzāb*, p. 365.

Personal Appropriation

The use in worship of special Names is recommended for each of the holy months of the Church's year—Rajab, Sha'bān, Ramaḍān, Murḥarram. (*Majmū'u 'l-wirdi 'l-kabīr*. M. 'Uthmān al-Mirghanī.) But there is also a personal appropriation, based on the numerical value of the letters in the worshipper's name and in the Names of God.

He who takes the total numerical value of the letters in his name and looks to see which Name of the Names of Moral Beauty agrees with it in value, and perhaps he may find it in one Name, if not in two or three or four taken together . . . (Directions are then given for a *wird* using these particular Names, which are to be his spiritual exercise.) *al-Istighāthatu 'l-Kubrā*, p. 127 (quoting Ibn al-'Arabī and Muṣṭafā al-Bakrī).

A less haphazard appropriation was described to the writer by a friend who had had some training in the Shādhilī Order, and who said that his shaikh would study his group of novices and allot to each a Name to be used in his *wird*, which he thought would prove the corrective to some defect in his character or training.

The Rifā'ī Order prays:

> Grant me a Name from the Names of Thy Light. *al-Ḥizbu 'l-kabīr*, Rifā'ī.

ash-Shādhilī is reported to have prayed:

> Grant me a particle of Thy Name The Keeper (Al-Ḥāfiẓ) by which Thou dost keep the order of the universe. *al-Mafākhiru 'l-'aliyya fī 'l-ma'āthiri 'sh-Shādhiliyya*, p. 187.

At other moments the saints have ceased to wish to wield the Names for their own ends, however spiritual, and see in them only the revelation to man of the Divine Nature:

> Thou hast made them paths for Thy descents and manifestations of Thine irradiations. *Du'ā'* of ash-Shādhilī, *Majmū'atu 'l-aḥzāb*, p. 102.

8

THE RECITATION

Qirā'a, Fātiḥa, Ta'mīn, Sūra

Here we have the very heart of the prayer-rite, and possibly that round which the rest was built. In the monotheistic worship which had entered Arabia before the rise of Islam, that of the Jews and Christians, the reading of Scripture in other tongues than Arabic played a great part. In fact the technical name for the invariable and central portion of the synagogue worship and of the daily private prayers of Jewish worshippers—the recitation of "Hear O Israel" was "the reading" *qārā'*, *qĕrī'āh* (Mishna Berakhoth 1,2,3). Muḥammad's revelation came to him as "an Arabic *qur'ān* (*12.2*), a reading or recital in the tongue of his people. The Qur'ān speaks of the dawn prayers of Islam as *qur'ān al-fajr*—the dawn reading. (*17.78*.)

It is the invariable duty of the worshipper in the Muslim prayer-rite to recite "The Opening of the Book" *Fātiḥatu'l-kitāb*, beginning as we have seen, with the *basmala*, and following it with *Amen*. After this he should recite a short *sūra*, or a long verse, or three short verses of a long *sūra*. But the *Fātiḥa* is the essential:

> The recitation (*qirā'a*) is obligatory both on the *imām* and on those whom he leads in all the set prayers; for the Apostle of God said, "He who has not recited *Fātiḥatu 'l-kitāb* has not performed the prayer-rite. (Bukhārī, *al-Ādhān*, 97.)

Islam's liturgical rule that *Āmīn* is to follow the *Fātiḥa* makes part of her universal utterance that great affirmation of Jewish and Christian worship, so characteristic of the speech of Jesus Himself in moments of emphasis that the Greek narratives of His life leave it there in its Semitic form, *Amēn legō humin*, Verily I say unto you. Just as in Judaism and Christianity, *Āmīn* in Islam is to be the utterance of all the community of the faithful with one voice (Deut. 27.15–26; Ps. 106.48; 1 Cor. 14.16) and as in Christianity it follows the Matthaean account of the Lord's Prayer and is inseparably linked with that Prayer in the Church's worship, so it is inseparably linked with the prayer that in Islam holds the place of the *Paternoster*.

And it is an approved custom that the *Āmīn* of those led in the worship shall be said with that of the *imām*, neither before nor after. And this is the only place in the prayer-rite where the word of the worshipper is united with that of the *imām*, for in the other utterances he shall follow after the *imām*. *Adhkār an-Nawawī*, p. 25.

The Place of the Fātiḥa in Muslim Devotions

It is, as we have said, the *Paternoster* of Islam, the universal prayer, and to it is given a position of supremacy.

It has come down to us that it is equal to two thirds of the Qur'ān. *Sharḥu 'r-rātib*, M. 'Uthmān al-Mirghanī, p. 4.

Were the *Fātiḥa* to be put in one balance of the scales and the Qur'ān in the other, the *Fātiḥa* would outweigh the rest seven times. Ibid., p. 5.

This is more spiritually expressed by ash-Sha'rānī, who says,

"All the meanings of the Qur'ān are gathered together in the *Fātiḥa*. It is as though in every *rak'a* they prayed the whole Qur'ān." *Laṭā'ifu 'l-minan*, p. 126.

As an Adjuration

Its virtue and *baraka* are so great that the *Fātiḥa* can be used as an adjuration, and is so used especially in the prayers attributed to 'Abd al-Qādir al-Jīlānī. These build various devotions on the *Fātiḥa*, the *Ḥizbu fawātiḥi 'l-baṣā'ir* being simply an interlarded *Fātiḥa*, the verses recited with pious interpolations. In his prayer of the hundred recitations of the *Fātiḥa* we find:

O God by virtue of this Opener (*Fātiḥa*) open to us a victory near at hand. (*Qur.* 48,18, 61.13.)
O God by virtue of this Healer, heal us from every infirmity and scourge in this world and the next.
O God by virtue of this Sufficient, suffice us in all our concerns of this world and the next.

Du'ā'u 'l-fātiḥati 'aqaba 'ṣ-ṣalawāti 'l-khamas.

Or in one of the prayers for authority so characteristic of him:

I ask Thee by virtue of *Fātiḥatu 'l-kitāb* to subjugate all things to me. *Ḥizbu fawātiḥi 'l-baṣā'ir.*

This use as an adjuration suffers a degradation towards magic. Thus in a sort of charm attributed to 'Alī b. Abī Ṭālib the various clauses of the *Fātiḥa* are mingled with some of the Divine Names and calls on the archangels to help in subjugating the person named:

> Reply O Michael, attentive and obedient, by virtue of "Thee do we worship and of Thee we seek help." *Khawāṣṣu 'l-fātiḥa* in *Majmū'atu 'l-aḥzāb*, p. 496.

An Acceptable Offering, rendering Petition acceptable

It is very characteristic of the widely spread popular prayer-books of the Mirghanīyya Order (but not of these alone) to present the recitation of the *Fātiḥa* and sometimes of other Qur'ān texts, as an acceptable offering to God.

And so great is the sense of the virtue and mystery of this offering that it is felt that petitions accompanied by it will be the more acceptable. Is there not for the encouragement of the faithful a story of the Prophet's own use of the words?

> (From Abū Mūsā al-Ash'ārī.) Concerning the Prophet, that he was on a raid and he said, "O King of the Day of Doom, Thee do we worship and of Thee we seek help." And Anas said, "and I saw the men falling, smitten by angels from before and behind". *al-Kalimu 'ṭ-ṭayyib*, Taqī ad-Dīn ad-Dimishqī, p. 32.

> And I offer to Thee in the presence of all this, the *Fātiḥa*. O God divert from us calamities and temptations. *Majmū'u 'l-awrādi 'l-kabīr*, M. 'Uthmān al-Mirghanī, p. 127 (frequent).

> O God hear our prayer and accept us by the mystery of the *Fātiḥa* (and the worshipper shall recite it, then raise his hands on high and say) I ask forgiveness of God. . . . (Devotions after the prayer-rite. *Awrād Muṣṭafā al-Bakrī*, p. 171.)

> Accept us by the secret and the sacredness of the *Fātiḥa*. *Rabī'u 'l-fu'ād*, 'Abd Allāh ash-Sharqāwī, p. 107.

> When thou art seeking sustenance and the achievement of thy purpose from slaves and free men and the speedy possession of what thou desirest, then be at rest from fears and complaints. For in *Fātiḥatu 'l-kitāb* lies the secret of secrets for obtaining what is hoped for. Persevere, then, in the study of it at all times; and in the morning, at noon, afternoon, and the sunset prayer, daily recite it ninety times completed by ten more. And thou shalt gain

what thou wilt of respect and might, of awe-inspiring greatness and exalted power. (Verses attributed to al-Ghazālī in *Majmū'atu 'l-aḥzāb.*)

Of the *Fātiḥa* as acceptable petition Fakhr ad-Dīn ar-Rāzī says that it sets a pattern in opening with pure praise. He points out a gradation from pure praise to pure petition.

> This *sūra* is a spiritual ascension (*mi'rāj*) for the worshippers. So He said, "Praise be to God, Lord of the Universe, King of the Day of Doom." This is all pure praise. Then He said, "Thee do we worship and to Thee we turn for help." This is all praise mingled with petition. Then He said, "Guide us in the straight path"—and so on to the end. This is pure petition. *Lawāmi'u 'l-bayyināt*, p. 36.

As Spiritual Alms-Giving

The manuals show a clear sense that the recitation of the *Fātiḥa* carries with it an assured reward. This may be due to the belief in *shafā'atu 'l-Qur'ān*, the intercession at the Last Day of the Qur'ān for its readers:

> (From Abū Umāma.) He said: I heard the Apostle of God say, "Recite the Qur'ān, for on the Resurrection Day it will come as an intercessor for its companions." *Riyāḍu 'l-janna*, an-Nawawī, p. 172.

And here is a great means of spiritual almsgiving; this reward may be donated to other souls. In view of the fact that these devotions contain very little of intercession for others, this outlet for unselfish care for them should be noted. It appears that the *Fātiḥa* is the only act of devotion generally employed in this way. It is constantly used "with intention" for (*li* or sometimes *ilā*) other souls in this world or the next. A letter from the late Lyman MacCallum of Istanbul written shortly after the death of C. F. Andrews in India gives an example of such use:

> Recently I brought word of the death of Mr C. F. Andrews to X, who was sitting with other four or five middle-aged Turks. X knew C. F. Andrews well, and spoke of him to the others. Then he said, "Let us pray for him, not that such a saint stands in need of our prayers but to satisfy our human need of doing something." We had had a moment of silence when X interrupted, "Let me make my ablutions and have it a real prayer." When he returned he began to pray aloud, impromptu, but when he mentioned those who were striving to heal the ills of humanity, he suddenly broke down, and covering his face with his hands, gave way to grief. It was an

affecting scene—the five men sitting silent in that little room filled with evening twilight, striving to give their leader the comfort and support of their spirits in this hour of weakness. After a few minutes he managed to say brokenly, "*Al-Fātiḥa, Āmīn,*" and I saw the lips of his friends moving to the unheard music of the *Fātiḥa*, recited for the dead Christian Saint.

The author or compiler of a *wird* often asks for this donation, as the authors or scribes of Christian Arabic manuscripts in the Middle Ages always asked the prayers of the readers for their forgiveness. The inscriptions on the older Turkish tombstones often asked the boon of a *Fātiḥa* from passers-by, and to-day it is the custom to engrave the one word "*Fātiḥa*" at the end of tomb-inscriptions. Some of the dervish orders teach regular "bidding prayers"[1] ending with the *Fātiḥa* just as the "bidding prayers" still in use in English University Churches end with the Lord's Prayer.

(For the compiler of a *wird.*) Convey to his spirit the reward of this *Fātiḥa. al-Wirdu 'sh-shāfī*, Yūsuf an-Nabhānī.

Let the reader of his generosity give to the compiler the reward of *Fātiḥatu 'l-kitāb* and of one of the *ṣalawāt 'alā'n-nabī* (contained in the book). *Majmū'atu 'l-wirdi 'l-'āmm*, M. al-Fatḥi al-Marrākushī.

(For all believers.) For all and every the people of the House of the Apostle of God and for the whole company of the believers and the righteous. *al-Anwāru 'l-mutarākama*, M. 'Uthmān al-Mirghanī, p. 1.

The *Fātiḥa* on behalf of all the saints of God in the east and the west of the earth, alike the living and the dead. *Awrād* (after the prayer-rite), Muṣṭafā al-Bakrī, p. 19.

Keep us O God and have the travellers in Thy keeping and heal the sick, and relieve the distressed and give security to the fearful of the nation of our Lord Muḥammad. (Then recite the *Fātiḥa* silently.) And I offer to Thee, in the presence of all, this, the *Fātiḥa. Majmū'atu 'l-wirdi 'l-kabīr*, M. 'Uthmān al-Mirghanī, p. 16.

The "bidding prayer" of a very small Order which had its headquarters at Hebron (Khalīliyya) may be given as an example of this type:

Then the Shaikh who is present, or the novice authorized to take his place, will say with all the other novices: On behalf of his honour the

[1] Dr Kraemer doubts whether these bidding prayers, generally for the founders, former leaders, present shaikhs, and brethren of the Orders, are to be regarded as intercessional prayers. He feels that they are more in the nature of homage.

Prophet; and on behalf of his honour Abraham the Friend and his noble descendants and their pure wives and all whom the Cave (of Machpelah under the mosque at Hebron) encloses; then on behalf of their honours our Father Adam and our Mother Eve and all the prophets and apostles descended from them; and on behalf of all the Family of the Prophet, and his good and pure Companions; then on behalf of the diligent Imāms and the laborious divines and the rightly-guided Caliphs and the Pole-Saints and the Noble-Saints and the Stake-Saints and the Substitute-Saints, and on behalf of all and every the righteous men of God; then on behalf of the spirit of his honour my lord and teacher the Sayyid Shaikh 'Abd ar-Raḥmān ash-Sharīf, and for his Mother and his Father; then on behalf of his son the Sayyid Ḥusain, and for all the people of their spiritual descendance, and for all our lords the people of the religious orders generally; and on behalf of our dead and of all the Muslim dead, the Fātiḥa. *Wirdu 'd-durrati 'l-yatīmiyya*, p. 6, Shaikh 'Abd ar-Raḥmān ash-Sharīf al-Ḥusainī. A similar (Khatmiyya) bidding occurs in *Majmū'atu 'l-awrādi 'l-kabīr*, M. 'Uthmān al-Mirghanī.

(For Muḥammad.) Then read the Fātiḥa for the spirit of the Prophet. *al-Āsāsu 'lladhī yusta'mal 'aqiba 'ṣ-ṣalawāt*. M. 'Uthmān al-Mirghanī.

But this brings us back to the question of the legitimacy of such bestowals on such a one as the Prophet. The *awrād* of Musṭafā al-Bakrī (†1162/1749) seem to be the earliest in our selection of manuals that include these donations of the *Fātiḥa*. And apparently its appropriateness as regards the Prophet has been called in question as late as the nineteenth century. A Khatmiyya leader thus deals with it:

> There are some who say that the *Fātiḥa* for the Prophet is objectionable. But others reply to them that it is akin to the calling down of blessing on the Prophet. They say that the cause of the objection is his state of perfection, since perfection calls for no increase. But others say, why then was the calling down of blessing on him permitted and enjoined in spite of the fact that it does imply increase? Does he benefit from the prayers of his people for him and their blessings on him? And the right answer is that the prophets do benefit from the prayers of their people for them, for as regards God (even) they are needy. *al-Asrāru 'l-mutarākama* (*Sharḥu 'r-rātib*), M. 'Uthmān al-Mirghanī, p. 19.

Protective Use

What has been said is sufficient to make clear the overwhelming sense in Muslim devotions of the holy power of the Qur'ān, a power which is felt to be a spiritual protection. Such a sense may easily degenerate into magical beliefs, and hence the innumerable uses of

Qur'ānic texts in charms, and the output of separate *sūras* printed in minute form to be carried on the person for protection.

> O Lord make the Qur'ān to us a companion in the darkness of night, a guardian against the depredations of Satan and the evil ideas that he suggests to us . . . till our hearts are penetrated with the understanding of its wonders and the expulsive power (against foes) of its maxims, which the towering mountains in their solidity will be too weak to remove. *Du'ā'un 'inda Khatmi 'l-Qur'ān*, 'Alī Zain al-'Ābidīn.

The Whole Qur'ān

The whole Qur'ān, like the Psalter in Judaism and Christianity lives in the devotional life of its people. Those who spread the knowledge of Islam in the Eastern Sudan were said to "light the fire of the Qur'ān" (*awqadū nāra 'l-Qur'ān*), a phrase literal as well as metaphorical, since they read it and taught it by the light of a bonfire, and one of the tasks of their disciples was to collect the firewood for this purpose.[1] The Qur'ān school is as blessed in pious eyes as *Beit ha-Midrash* in Jewish piety. And probably more than any other sacred book, unless the Psalter, the Qur'ān has been and still is committed to memory from cover to cover.

In the description of the community of Muḥammad in *Munājātu Mūsā* occur the words:

> Their gospels are in their hearts while others read them from the sacred volumes.

The devotional manuals include prayers for help in such memorizing:

> I ask Thee O God by Thy Majesty and the Light of Thy Countenance to bind to my heart the memorizing of Thy Book as Thou hast taught me, and to endow me with the (power of) reciting it with the grammatical inflection that shall win me Thy approval. And I ask Thee to illuminate my heart and my vision through Thy Book, and to grant my tongue fluency in it, and to relieve my heart and dilate my breast, and wash away my sins by its means, and (I ask) that Thou wilt strengthen me for this and help me in it, for none can help me and aid me to the truth but Thyself. (Recite this prayer for three weeks or five or seven, and you will memorize it with God's permission.) *al-Ḥirzu 'l-manī*. 'Aṣ-Ṣuyūṭī, p. 125.

[1] Hillelson. *Aspects of Muhammedanism in the Eastern Sudan*. J.R.A.S. 1937.

A complete reading at one session is called a *Khatma* (sealing) and instances are quoted in the manuals, of saints who thus recited the whole book every night. Such a *Khatma* is a special opportunity for petition.

For traditions have come down to us that this place is the place for petition, and that at the sealing of the Qur'ān there is a descent of mercy. Ibid., p. 124.

The wide-spread Sanūsī order have a united Qur'ān recital, "with one voice", as their only common *wird*, the others being said individually. The brothers in any one neighbourhood meet monthly for this and it is known as *al-ḥizbu 'sh-shahrī*.

Individual Verses

But each Qur'ān verse (and not only such famous texts as the Light Verse and the Throne Verse) has for its people an almost independent sacredness, each verse for them a rounded bead perfect in itself, in the glorious necklace of the whole. The manuals abound in directions for the suitable use of individual verses.

It has come down to us that if a man persevere in the recitation of it (The Throne Verse) after every prayer-rite, God will take upon Himself the holding of his spirit enclosed in His Hand. *al-Anwāru 'l-mutarākama*, M. 'Uthmān al-Mirghanī, p. 5.

If you want to make a journey, short or long, conceal the fact, and start early. If you decide upon a Monday or a Tuesday, those are the best days, but if not, all God's days are blessed. Recite, before you start from the house, the Throne Verse, and the well-known "prayer of anxiety". Then write the letters which are the beginning of every *sūra* (the basmala and the mysterious combinations of letters with which some *sūras* open) and carry the writing with you, for it contains a great secret of repelling and defence.

If you want to embark on the sea, then write it on a piece of earthenware and throw it into the sea just before embarkation, and you will experience a wonder of facilitation. *Khalāṣatu 'l-maghnam*, 'Alī al-Aṭṭās, p. 86.

Ibn as-Sunā traced a tradition from 'Alī that he said: The Apostle of God said that *Fātiḥatu 'l-kitāb* and the Throne verse and verses 17 and 18a and 25 and 26 of *sūratu Āl 'Imrān* are hung upon the Throne; between them and God there is no veil. . . . And God Most High said, "I have sworn that none of my servants shall recite you after every prayer-rite without my making Paradise his place of repair on account of what he has done; and without my placing him in the enclosure of holiness; and without my glancing at him with my eye of mystery, seventy glances every day; and without my supplying for him daily, seventy needs, the least of them the need of forgiveness; and without my sheltering him from every enemy and giving him victory. *Riyāḍu 'l-janna*, Yūsuf an-Nabhānī, p. 12.

Special Uses of Sūras

Amid all the multitudinous uses of the Qur'ān in devotion, three passages stand out in our manuals as most used of all. They are *Sūratu 'l-ikhlāṣ* (112), the last three verses of *Sūratu 'l-baqara* (2), and *Sūratu Yā Sīn* (36).

Sūratu 'l-ikhlāṣ

This tiny *sūra*, one of the first taught to children, finds its way into almost every *wird*, sometimes woven into the text of it and sometimes with a rubric for its recitation a given number of times. It is felt to be both essential and sufficing, and it was a true instinct that made it thus central in the devotions of Islam, for in its brief negative sentences may be seen the germ of the great negative developments of the doctrines of *tawḥīd* and *tanazzuh*.

(A ritual for applying the blessing of it to the worshipper's own life.) Then he shall put his hand on his eyes and recite *sūratu 'l-ikhlāṣ* once. Then he shall put his hand on his breast and recite it again. Aḥmad at-Tījānī, *Awrād*, p. 89.

(From 'Ā'isha.) The Apostle of God sent a man into Syria. And he always recited *qul hūwa 'llāhu aḥad* for his companions at their prayer-rite. When they returned they told this to the Apostle of God who said: "Ask him why he does this." So they asked him and he said, "Because it is the description of *Ar-Raḥmān*, therefore I love to recite it." Then the Apostle of God said, "Tell him that God Most High loves him." *Riyāḍu 's-ṣāliḥīn*, An-Nawawī, p. 81. (Bukharī, Muslim.)

The Prophet said, Whoever recites *qul hūwa 'llāhu aḥad* a hundred times has bought his soul from God and a voice cries from before God Most High throughout His heavens and His earth, "Is not so-and-so God's freed man? Therefore anyone who has a claim against him shall receive it (not from him but) from God Most High." *al-Kalimu 'ṭ-ṭayyib*, Yūsuf an-Nabhānī, p. 30.

The Last Two (or the Last Three) Verses of Sūratu 'l-baqara

These verses are the penitential psalm of Islam. Hardly a passage of forgiveness-seeking in the devotions but makes use of them. They are recommended as the last words to be said before sleep.

If a man read the last two verses of *sūratu 'l-baqara* at night they will be repellant. It is said that they will repel anything objectionable from him that night. *Riyāḍu 'ṣ-ṣāliḥīn*, An-Nawawī, p. 175.

(From Ibn 'Abbās.) He said: While Gabriel was sitting with the Prophet he heard a voice from above, and raised his head. Then he said, "That is the door of heaven, opened to-day, which was never opened before." And an angel descended from it, and he said, "That is an angel come down to earth who never came down before." And he gave a greeting and said, "Receive good news of two lights brought to you which were never before brought to a Prophet, *Fātiḥatu 'l-kitāb* and the last verses (*Khawātim*) of *sūratu 'l-baqara*; of these thou shalt never recite a single letter without being granted thy request." Ibid., p. 174.

Sūrat Yā Sīn

The request for "popular prayers" in a Muslim bookshop will probably produce among the larger volumes one of the tiny booklets of this *sūra*, sold by the thousand, and, like peanuts, celluloid toys, and stale biscuits, hawked on the Cairo tramways before the Muslim All Souls' Night, the night of Mid-Sha'bān.

It was on the fifteenth day of Sha'bān that Muḥammad, returning as conqueror, re-entered the shrine of his fathers at Mecca, which had replaced Jerusalem as the *qibla* of his people's prayers. A day so decisive in triumph and in renewal was bound to be remembered; but how and when did the night preceding it become identified with the mysterious night of divine decision, of which a thousand popular preachers speak in the terms of one of our manuals?

(On that night) God Most High metes out the term of life to His servants and orders their end near or far. And it is said that God writes on the midmost night of Sha'bān the name of him who in that year shall be born, and him who shall die, and him who shall stand on 'Arafat. And Abū Huraira said, "When the night of Mid-Sha'bān comes round, the doors of the seven heavens are opened and angels stand at every door asking forgiveness for the Muslims, and every Muslim shall be forgiven except him who was enticed to a mortal sin." *Ṭahāratu 'l-qulūb*, Ad-Dīrīnī, p. 125.

It is All Souls' Night, a watch-night, and a moment for popular religion. The multitude is concerned more with the chances of physical life and death than with the life and death of the spirit. Yet a breath of eternity blows over it. The little prayer-books sold by the thousand at this season contain the *du'ā'* for the night, and also its special *sūra*, *Yā sīn*, with its grave warnings of death and resurrection to judgment.

This is the *du'ā'* of Mid-Sha'bān. Begin after the sunset prayers by reciting *Yā sīn* three times, the first with the intention of length of life, the second with the intention of warding off calamity, and the third with the intention of averting dependence on men.

Three pictures by a young Scandinavian traveller in the Sanūsī country of Libya, whose wanderings landed him in prison at Derna on suspicion of espionage, show the place of the *sūra* in the life of its people:

(1) On their shoulders they carried the bier. . . . In about half an hour we arrived at a small mosque, evidently built over the tomb of a marabout. Round about in the yellow sand were graves, on which had been placed rifles, ploughs, and all kinds of implements which the dead had used during their lifetime.

The bier was put down outside the door of the mosque in the sand, and we entered the small room the floor of which was covered with dry grass.

The man with whom I had spoken last night and who was evidently the leader of the little community turned towards Mecca and said a prayer in a loud voice. When that was over and he had finished the two *rak'as* with *as-salām 'alaikum wa raḥmatu 'llāh*, he came up to me and said: "*Ya Shaikh*, your boy said that you knew the Qur'ān. I only know the prayer. Will you read the Death *Sūra*?" Luckily I knew the Death *Sūra*. We went outside where the first tiny streak of daylight just began to tint the eastern sky and the sickle of the moon grew fainter and fainter, and while all present covered their faces, I read the Death *Sūra*: *Wa'l qur'āni 'l-ḥakīm*.

(2) We banged at the door. There was no answer. We banged again. Still silence reigned. Then we pushed the door open and slipped inside. Foul air met us. It was half dark in the room, and, dazzled as we were from the strong sunlight, we could at first see nothing. Then we became aware of a figure lying on the stone couch at the far end of the room. It was an old man with a long grey beard. We drew nearer and saw that he was dead. He had been dead so long that he was almost mummified. One hand hung down towards the floor where stood an empty stone jar. On the table lay a Qur'ān, open at *Yā Sīn*, the Death *Sūra*. The Arabs said: "He must have been a marabout. He has not wished to leave the tombs of the dead, and as the wells were blocked up, he died of thirst."

(3) (In prison at Derna.) Suddenly I heard a voice singing verses from the

Qur'ān. "Who is that?" I said. "Come with me and you can see for yourself." He led me to the end of the courtyard, to the cell from which the song came. I looked in. On the floor were seated six Arabs. They were in rags and their feet were bare, but they were unusually handsome and vigorous, appearing to be in the prime of life. One of them was singing. Their faces shone with a sublime calm as if they hardly knew that they were in prison, and their eyes were set in a fixed gaze as if they hung on every word that was formed on the lips of the singer.

"They are condemned to death," said the pock-marked Arab, "and they will probably be shot to-morrow, in the back like the others because they are rebels." They continued listening to the heart of the Qur'ān, the death *sūra*, *Yā Sīn*. (*Desert Encounter*, Knud Holmboe.)

The Awe of the Qur'ān

So the book lives on among its people, stuff of their daily lives, taking for them the place of a sacrament. For to them these are not mere letters or mere words. They are the twigs of the burning bush, aflame with God.

> The Qur'ān is His word for eternity and it is uncreate (*Ṭahāratu 'l-qulūb*, Ad-Dīrīnī)

says a popular book, using words about which the storms of theology have raged. Then in the next breath the booklet continues:

> It is recited by tongues, written in volumes, memorized in breasts. Ibid.

Is not this essentially sacramental?—the written word a sacrament of the unwritten word.

If orthodoxy condemns as an admission of *ḥulūl* the practice of listening for God's Voice as the Utterer of the words in which His eternal Word is expressed, a homely little manual for Ramaḍān comes very near to that. It is part, says the little book, of the *ādāb* of Qur'ān reading—.

> That the reader shall be filled with the greatness of the Speaker, Mighty and Majestic, lowly before His Majesty, his heart filled with awe, his members as though, through his ascription of greatness and his awe, he were indeed standing in the presence of God to read before Him His own book containing His commands and prohibitions.
>
> For this is fitting in one acquainted with the Qur'ān and with Him who speaks through it. *al-Mukhtārātu 'l-ḥuṣān fī faḍli wa aḥkāmi Ramaḍān*, Ḥasan 'Alī Sharīf.

Qur'ān Readers' Prayers

O Thou who art great, none gives what is great save the Great, and none save Thee makes great the destitute, giving to Him abundance. I then, a destitute one, beseech of Thy great goodness that Thou wilt generously grant me the secrets of Thine august Book and wilt not allot as my portion a tongue-reading like that of customary careless readers.

Give me the joy of right listening to Thy Word and send down into my heart those gifts of Thine which in that Word Thou hast granted to Thy purified ones and the honoured ones brought near to Thee. *Rāṭibu 'l-Mahdī* (one of the most popular devotions in the Sudan).

Increase our longing for it; multiply our delight in it, to the number of the raindrops and the leaves on the trees. Through it, perfect our confidence in the guidance of the good and the glad tidings of men of spiritual experience. Bring to our minds what we have forgotten of it. Teach us what we do not know of its radiant truths and secret touches of meaning. Make it for us an *imām* and light and guidance and mercy in the abode below and the abode everlasting. And grant us the reading of it in the hours of night and the seasons of the day. *Ḥizb jamā'ahu Ismā'īl Muḥammad al-Khalwatī mina 'l-'ulamā'i 'l-ḥunafā'*, also in *al-Wirdu 'l-ā'ẓam*. 'Alī ibn Sulṭān Muḥammad al-Qārī.

9

THE WORSHIP OF STILLNESS

Ṭuma'nīna, Iṭmi'nān, Sakīna

Ritual Use

The daily prayer-rite is often described in the children's lesson-books as a drill. It is saved from being a breathless drill by slight pauses which are an essential part of it, as rests are an essential part of some musical passage. In each of the positions of the prayer there is an obligatory pause and brief moment of physical balance, of composure, this is called the *ṭuma'nīna* or *iṭmi'nān*.

And the *iṭmi'nān*—that is a slowing down in the work of the essential acts of the prayer-rite. *Majmū'u waṣiyyati 'l-muṣṭafā.*

Then I raise my head till I am sitting upright and I pause in that position (*Aṭma'innu*). *Durūsu 'd-dīni 'l-islāmī*, vol. 1.

And a pause of stillness (*ṭuma'nīna*) in all the postures. *Shurūṭu 'ṣ-ṣalāt*, M. 'Abd al-Wahhāb.

Ṭuma'nīna is the pause, balance, composure of the body, but there is also the pause of silence for the voice (*sakta, sakna*). This is part of the duty of the *mu'adhdhin* whose song has its rests.

He shall divide sentence from sentence by a silence (*sakna*). *Durūsu 'd-dīni 'l-islamī*, vol. 5.

The imām's pause after saying the *Fātiḥa* so that the worshippers behind him may make their recitation is also called a *sakna*.

The use of ritual stillness has passed out beyond the daily prayer-rite. Thus at the Pilgrimage during the ascent of 'Arafat part of the ritual is:

a pause of rest (*ṭuma'nīna*) at the halting place, equal to the sitting between two prostrations in the prayer-rite. This may be standing, sitting, or riding. *Dalīlu 'l-ḥajj*, M. Ḥasanain Makhlūf, p. 14.

Slight though the use of stillness is in the Islāmic ritual, it is enough to secure the principle which may be extended as men praying together learn the deep value of united silence. That it is, in the prayer-rite, regarded as an opportunity for devotion that may be prolonged according to the ability of the worshipper is shown by the following sentence:

> The worshipper when he is weak is urged to prolong the *ṭuma'nīna* in the sitting position; as he grows stronger he is urged to prolong the *ṭuma'nīna* in the prostrate position more and more. Ash-Sha'rānī, *Laṭā'ifu 'l-minan*, p. 127.

And in non-canonical prayer brief stillnesses have found a place. Thus, 'Abd al-Qādir al-Jīlānī, before beginning the sermons on which so many hung, would make his opening ascription "Praise be to God, Lord of the Worlds" and then pause in silence, a silence which must have steadied and composed the crowd. (*Majmū'u 'l-aḥzābi wa 'l-awrād* . . . li 'Abd al-Qādir al-Jīlānī.)

Bakriyya groups also know the use of united silence:

> Then they shall recite the *Fātiḥa* and each one shall make petition as he needs. Then they shall lay their hands on their breasts, inclined towards the left, and pray the petition of silence. *Rabī'u 'l-fu'ād*, 'Abd Allāh ash-Sharqāwī, p. 109.

This vital minimum of stillness in the heart of the daily ritual has brought into the vocabulary of every schoolboy who learns his prayers two words, different yet closely akin. *Ṭuma'nīna* and *sakna* are words taught with the bare meaning of physical stillness, but full of spiritual over-tones for those with hearts to understand.

IṬMI'NĀN

This word is eight times used in the Qur'ān, but one verse is quoted again and again in our manuals, whether as a Qur'ānic basis for the *dhikr*, or in prayers for inward peace.

> They who believe and whose hearts are stayed (*taṭma'innu*) in the recollection (or mention, *dhikr*) of God: is there not serenity of heart in the recollection (*dhikr*) of God? (*13*.28).

Of these words the late Professor D. B. Macdonald wrote:

> "I have no question that for Muḥammad the meaning was that anyone who gave himself to the thought of God would receive from God rest, calm, and strength." *Aspects of Islam*, p. 189.

This much-loved verse is the basis for hundreds of petitions for the quiet mind:

Trembling hearts are quieted by the recollection of Him. *Ḥizbu Kāmil Sa'diyya, Majmū'atu 'l-Aḥzāb*, p. 338.

Send down O God, O Gentle, O Compassionate, into my heart faith and tranquillity and stillness, that I may be of those whose "hearts are tranquillized by the mention of God". *Ḥizbu'l-waqāya*, Ibn al-'Arabī.

My God, in Thee depressed hearts find rest, and in the knowledge of Thee divided hearts are made whole. Nor are hearts tranquillized save by the invocation of Thyself, nor souls quieted till they meet with Thee. *Munājātun 'aẓīma* (no author given) in *Majmū'atu 'l-aḥzāb*, p. 458.

Bestow on me tranquillity. That is, let me realize in my heart peaceful stillness till I do not turn to any of the movements of created things. Bring this about by the recollection of Thyself granted to hearts, whence comes their tranquillization. "Are not hearts tranquillized by the recollection of God." *Sharḥu 'r-rātibi 'l-musammā bi 'l-asrāri 'l-mutarādifa*, M. 'Uthmān al-Mirghanī.

The tranquillity thus longed for is a recognized "stage" of the mystic way, but here we consider the more general use of the word. It has been compared to the Christian phrase "a state of grace" (Massignon, *Lexique Technique*, p. 121) and the explanations offered in the prayer-manuals accord well with this. For *ṭuma'nīna* has to be reached by way of repentance.

And their souls found the grace of peace through their return to the Lord of Lords. *Munajātun 'aẓīma* in *Majmū'atu 'l-aḥzāb*.

It must thus have left behind what hinders personal knowledge (*ma'rifa*) of God, which hindrance Muslim writers often describe as ignorance.

I ask of Him a heart tranquillized from the constriction of ignorance *Sharḥu 'smi 'llāhi 'l-a'ẓam*, Al-Būnī, p. 8,

and it must have that *riḍā* which is the fruit of faith.

O Lord I ask Thee for a soul tranquillized by Thee, believing that it will meet Thee, well satisfied with Thy decrees, sufficed by Thy gifts. *al-Wirdu 'l-a'ẓam*, M. 'Abdallāh b. Sulṭān al-Qārī.

Ṭuma'nīna, then, for all its stillness, *tranquillus tranquillans*, is no drowsy peace, but a gift of grace that can only come to hearts ready to make the response of faith and costly discipline. In worship it may result in "the prayer of quiet":

Requests break off in presence of His bounty, and needs fade away as the soul finds her support in Himself. The need of the creature is not satisfied by the whole of created things, rather is it necessary for his infinite need to be met by infinite generosity and power, that is to say, by none other than the Truth Himself, praised and exalted be He. *Lawāmi'u 'l-Bayyināt*, Fakhr ad-dīn ar-Rāzī, p. 10.

Sakīna

The Qur'ānic use of *sakīna*, the sister word to *ṭuma'nīna*, which the manuals would relate to *sakna*, has caused some trouble to commentators. While in *Qur.* 2.249 it is a mysterious sign in the ark of Israel by which Saul may be recognized as King, in other cases it is some kind of help sent down from heaven. From the fact that in a day of stress, the Day of the Trench (*Khandaq*), in A.H. 5, Muḥammad is said to have prayed:

Send down *sakīna* upon us,

some Muslim commentators would see in *sakīna* succour in the form of victory. But the fact remains that the word is from the root *sakan*, to be quiet, to rest, and is used of calm dignity; while in prayer it often means the quieting and steadying of the soul.

(Abū Huraira from the Prophet.) He said: When you hear the *iqāma*, go to the prayers and you should go with calm (*sakīna*) and sedateness. Do not hurry. If you are not in time, pray (afterwards) the part that you missed and so complete the rite. al-Bukhārī. *al-Ādhān, 32. Muwaṭṭa'*, I.126.

For Thou dost calm (*tusakkin*) the fears of the trembling. Shī'a *Du'ā'* for Monday, *aṣ-Ṣaḥīfatu's-sajjādiyya*, p. 317.

O Thou, except in whose nearness and irradiations the heart cannot be at rest (*yaskun*). *al-Ḥizbu 'l-kabīr*, Qādiriyya.

But the use of the word in prayer is strongly influenced by a body of traditions which Goldziher believes to have been a later development (see *Abhandlungen* I, 177 ff.), in which the meaning of *sakīna* is aligned (possibly through the Syriac) with that of the Hebrew noun from the same root, for the Cloud of Glory, the *Shekina*, manifesting the presence of the Lord. In prayer then, *sakīna* has a rich double sense of stillness and of irradiation, the sign of the *Numen praesens*. This is parallel to its use in Syriac Christian mysticism:

When the solitary reaches the divine cloud and enters the harbour of all service, and sees with his mind, face to face, the glory of the Lord, and is made radiating by it, and is transformed into His likeness—then his mercy is poured out over all, like that of God. (Bar Hebraeus, quoting from an unknown author in *Ethnikon*. Translated in Wensinck, *Book of the Dove*, p. 305.)

As examples of the "Shekina" traditions found in the manuals we may quote:

(From al-Barā' b. 'Āzib.) He said that he was reciting *sūratu 'l-kahf*, and beside him was his horse tethered with two ropes. And a cloud came over him and descended upon him, and his horse began to fly from it. Next morning the Prophet came and (al-Barā') told him of this. Then the Prophet said, "That Shekina descended because of the Qur'ān." *Riyāḍu 'l-janna*, Yūsuf an-Nabhānī, p. 173.

Never does a company meet in one of the houses of God to read the Book of God and study it together without *as-sakīna* descending upon them and mercy covering them and the angels hovering over them. Muslim V.297. (Cf. *Pirkē Ābhōth*, *3.7*. When ten sit together and occupy themselves with the Tora the Shekina lowers Itself amongst them.)

So the great word stands ready for the worshipper's use:

I ask Thee to cause some of Thy *sakīna* to descend on us and to cover our faces with the irradiations of Thy love. *Munājātun 'aẓīma* (no author given) in *Majmū'atu 'l-aḥzāb*.

10a

THE WITNESS OF ISLAM (SHAHĀDA): TO THE UNITY

Lā ilāha illa 'llāh

I bear witness that there is no god but God and I bear witness that Muḥammad is the Apostle of God.

This, the witness of Islam (*ash-shahāda*) which floated down from the minaret at the Call to Prayer, was said by the worshipper at his ablution; and now in the prayer-rite after the greeting of the Prophet and his fellow-worshippers (see Chapter 14), the duty must be fulfilled, a duty to God and the world, of setting his seal to the essential beliefs of his religion.

When the Egyptian woman visiting the cemetery of her people says "Peace be to you, people of *lā ilāha illā 'llāh*"[1] she sums up in that word the mission of the people of Islam. For them the crying of a babe during its first four months of life is an utterance of the *shahāda* (*Al-Ḥirzu 'l-munī'*, p. 27), and as they have lived with this word on their lips, so the people of Islam seek to die pronouncing it. Over against the polytheism of Arabia, Islam took up the great affirmation of Judaism in her *Shema'* (its recitation a daily duty for every Jew since the time of the exile), "Hear O Israel, the Lord our God is One Lord." She took up the great affirmation of Christianity in its creeds, "I believe in One God,"[2] and she has made the affirmation of that Unity her essential life and witness.

The formula is called the *shahāda*, the witness (the saying of it *tashahhud*, witness-bearing) or, in portmanteau fashion, the *tahlīl*. It is

[1] She is using a phrase from a tradition of the Prophet thus quoted by al-Ghazālī (*Iḥyā', kitābu 'l-adhkār*, 3): Muḥammad said: For the people of *lā ilāha illā 'llāh* there is no loneliness in their graves or at their resurrection. It is as if I see them raising their heads from the dust and saying, "Praise be to God who has driven sadness away from us. Verily God is forgiving and thankworthy."

[2] Dr Merrill connected the two-limbed *shahāda* of Islam with John 17.3, "That they should know Thee the only true God, and Him whom Thou hast sent, even Jesus Christ." (Macdonald Presentation Volume, p. 295.)

also *al-Kalima*, the word, par excellence, or *Kalimatu 't-tawḥīd*, the word of the affirmation of the Unity. Little boys at school are taught:

> You must know, my boys, that the two witness-bearings (in the set prayers) are the *word of salvation* by which a man is saved from fatal unbelief and becomes one of the number of the Muslims whom God loves.
>
> And the two witness-bearings contain *the word of affirmation of the Unity*, which is *lā ilāha illā 'llāh*, and this word of Unity is the best of all utterances of worship. When you make mention of God Most High, mention Him with this word that He may be pleased with you and grant you bliss. *Durūsu 'd-dīni 'l-islāmī*, vol 2, p. 17.
>
> In the *Kalima* of *single-hearted* sincerity, said by no worshipper without God delivering him from the Fire, except such as are magnifying themselves and full of pride. *aṣ-Ṣaḥīfatu 's-sajjādiyya*, Mukhsin al-Ḥusainī, p. 28.

FORMS OF "TAHLĪL" USED IN WORSHIP

Although the *shahāda* is deeply true to the spirit of the Qur'ān it is not a Qur'ānic word. The nearest form to it is found in the Throne Verse and in *27*.26 and *28*.88, *la ilāha illā hūwa*, a phrase constantly used in worship.

There are no variants for the *tahlīl* (a sign that it was accepted and universal from primitive times) but there are non-official additions to it and embroiderings to it on the tongue of worshippers ever busy with it. It is often placed in the second person and sometimes God is addressed by it as though it were one of His Names.[1]

> By virtue of "There is no god but Thee" endue them with Thy succour, Thou "There is no god but Thee". *Mukhtaṣaru ad'iyati Ramaḍān*, p. 89.

Or the words *waḥdahu, waḥdahu* (He alone) are added, in accordance with the *Ḥadīth qudsī*:

> Blessed is the man of thy community who says, There is no god but God, He alone! He alone! He alone! al-Kulīnī. *al-Kāfī. Kitābu 'd-du'ā'*.

Thus a striking form to be said after the Shī'a *namāz* is:

> There is no god but God, and we are his surrendered ones (*Muslimīn lahu*).
> There is no god but God, and none but Him will we worship.
> There is no god but God, our Lord and the Lord of our first fathers.
> There is no god but God, He alone, He alone! *Majmū'u Miftāḥi 'l-janān* makes this form obligatory after every prayer-rite.

[1] Not unlike the use of, "I am that I am", as a Name in the Old Testament.

Or again, as in the Qur'ānic form above-mentioned, the word "He" is substituted for *Allāh* in the formula, and this, the great pronoun of the Divine Ipseity is played upon in a way that defies translation.

> God is my sufficiency, there is no god but He. Thou "He", Thou "He who art He", Thou than whom "there is no He but He". *Majmū'atu 'l-wirdi 'l-'āmm*, p. 21.

The Khatmiyya-Mirghaniyya circle of worshippers add to the *tahlīl* in their recitations their particular formula, taught, they say, by the Prophet to Aḥmad b. Idrīs in 1232/1827.

> "There is no god but God and Muḥammad is the Apostle of God", in every glance and every breath, to the number that only God's knowledge can comprehend. *Majmū'atu jamī'ati awrādi Aḥmadi b. Idrīs*, p. 174, and frequently in the literature of these orders.

Other variations lay stress on the word "I bear witness", to make the *tashahhud* a strongly personal act. It is changed into the very emphatic *Anā shahīd*, and sometimes the sign manual of the appropriation of holy words is used, the passing of the hand over one's own face or body in saying them:

> Then he shall pass his hand over his face and say the *tahlīl* three times, and all the brethren shall say it with him. *Rabī'u 'l-Fu'ād*, 'Abd Allāh ash-Sharqāwī (Bakriyya).

Or emphasis may be given by long-drawn-out enunciation, especially of the final *Allāh*:

> He prolongs his vocalization from veneration of it. *Majmū'atu 'l-wirdi 'l-'āmm*, p. 95 (so in the *Mishna Berachoth* 19.a it is ordered that the final *Echād* of the *Shema'* shall be emphasized by long-drawn-out enunciation).

A constantly used form changes "I bear witness" into "I call to witness X. that I bear witness . . ." or "I call to witness X. that there is no god but . . ." Thus called to witness are God Himself, the angels, the prophets, mankind, and the whole creation.

There are two much used classical forms for this cosmic witness-bearing:

> (a) (From Anas.) The Prophet of God said: "Whoever says at morning or at evening, 'O God, this morning I call Thee to witness, and I call to witness the Bearers of Thy Throne, and Thy angels and Thy books, and Thy

apostles, and all Thy creatures, that Thou art God. There is no god but Thee alone, Thou hast no partner. And Muḥammad is Thy servant and Thine Apostle.'—God frees a quarter of the man who says it from the Fire; and whoever says it twice, God frees half of him from the Fire; and whoever says it three times, God frees three-quarters of him from the Fire; and whoever says it four times, God frees him from the Fire." *al-Kalimu 'ṭ-ṭayyib*, Taqī ad-Dīn ad-Dimishqī, p. 15. (at-Tirmidhī. Abū Dāwūd. an-Nasā'ī. aṭ-Ṭabarānī.)

To the same family belongs:

> Lo I make a covenant with Thee in this life of the world below, and I call Thee to witness, and Thou as a witness art sufficient, that I bear witness that there is no god but Thee. *al-Wirdu 'sh-shāfī*, Yūsuf an-Nabhānī, p. 16 (frequent).

(b) The other classical form, also frequently used, especially by the Qādiriyya, is:

> God and His angels bear witness that there is no god but He, and I too bear witness to that to which God and His angels bear witness. *Du'ā'u 't-tawassul* of the Qadiriyya Order.

The cosmic as well as the heavenly *shahāda* is a favourite Qādiriyya theme:

> O God there is never a passing breeze nor a drop in the clouds nor a lightning flash nor a thunder roll, nor aught in the Throne and the Seat, nor a sign in the Kingdom of our Universe or of the angelic world, that is not saying its *tahlīl* and bearing witness that Thou art God, there is no god but Thee. *Ḥizbu 's-suryānī*, 'Abd al-Qādir al-Jīlānī (frequent).
>
> Thou hast unveiled to whom Thou wouldst the secret of Thine affirmation of the Unity, for to this, existence and creation and created things bear witness. *Ḥizbu 'r-rajā'*, 'Abd al-Qādir al-Jīlānī.

Uses of the Shahāda

A Covenant

In one of the forms quoted above the worshipper called his *tahlīl* a covenant with God, made in the life of the world below. This thought often recurs; the *shahāda* is a covenant in which God's part will be to give salvation in the next life, or it is a deposit, laid up with God, to be repaid with the interest of a reward in the next life.

It (the *shahāda*) will accompany its utterer on the Resurrection Day, and God most High will say, "I have a covenant with this servant of Mine, and I am true to the fulfilment of covenants. Let My servant enter Paradise." *Sharḥu 'r-rātibi 'l-musammā bi 'l-asrāri 'l-mutarādifa*, M. 'Uthmān al-Mirghanī, p. 7.

I deposit this witness-bearing with God. This witness is for me a deposit laid up with God, who will pay it back to me on the Day of Resurrection. *Du'ā'u 't-tawassul*, Qādiriyya.

Protective

Muḥammad said: God Most High says: *Lā ilāha illā 'llāh* is My fortress, and he who enters my fortress is safe from My chastisement. *Majmū'atu 'l-wirdi 'l-'āmm*, p. 95.

One of the righteous saw 'Īsā son of Maryam in a dream, and he (the dreamer) said to him, "I want to make a signet-ring. What shall I engrave on it?" And 'Īsā said, "Engrave on it 'There is no god but God, the Manifest Truth'—for that will drive away cares and anxieties." *Ṭahāratu 'l-qulūb*, Ad-Dīrīnī, p. 11.

I have hidden myself from the thoughts of enviers by means of *lā ilāha illā 'llāh, Muḥammadun rasūlu 'llāh.*

I have veiled myself from the eye of the possessors of the evil eye by means of *lā ilāha illā 'llāh, Muḥammadun rasūlu 'llāh.*

Thou hast driven off Satan from me when I carry *lā ilāha illā 'llāh, Muḥammadun rasūlu 'llāh.*

Thou hast banished from me the evil of the Wanderers of night and day by means of *lā ilāha illā 'llāh.*

I am protected from haunting spirits and demons and magic and (demonic) mates of evil and all the hosts of Iblīs, by means of *lā ilāha illā 'llāh.*

I have taken shelter from everything noxious, in the fortress of *lā ilāha illā 'llāh, Muḥammadun rasūlu 'llāh.*

I cling to the hem of *lā ilāha illā 'llāh Muḥammadun rasūlu 'llāh.*
I grasp the handle of *lā ilāha illā 'llāh Muḥammadun rasūlu 'llāh.*
I am wrapped in the mantle of *lā ilāha illā 'llāh.*
I am girt with the sword of *lā ilāha illā 'llāh.*

Majmū'atu 'l-wirdi 'l'āmm, pp. 28, 30.

The Mark of Entry into Islam

As in Christianity a witness to belief by a baptismal creed has from primitive times been part of the service of admission to the Church, so in Islam has the *shahāda* been used from very early times as the formula for embracing the faith.[1]

Although to-day the witness to the Prophet as well as to the Unity is required of converts, this does not appear to be primitive; as one of our manuals remarks, in the course of defending the use of the first half only of the *shahāda* in the utterances of the *dhikr*:

> As in the tradition (Muḥammad says), "I am commanded to wage war with men till they say *lā ilāha illā 'llāh*," and he does not say *wa Muḥammadun rasūlu 'llāh*. And since *Muḥammadun rasūlu 'llāh* is a confession of his apostleship which it suffices to say once in a life-time, while *lā ilāha illā 'llāh* is the fountain head of the *dhikr*, most beneficial in its healing and reformation of the heart, and in the making of it acceptable to Him who is therein mentioned, the *Ṣūfis* chose the latter for the training of their novices. *as-Silsilatu 'dh-dhahabiyya*, M. Aḥmad al-Madanī.

As a Means to Forgiveness

The detailed embroidery of the following is like the preoccupation of the arabesque designer with the curves of the letters of the *shahāda* that he weaves into patterns on page or metal-work or stucco or stone:

> Know that *lā ilāha illā 'llāh, Muḥammadun rasūlu 'llāh* is made up of twenty-four letters. . . . And there is not amongst them a single dotted letter, but all of them are free of dots, a sign that he who pronounces them must be free from all save the Most High. And they are twenty-four letters, for a night and a day are twenty-four hours, and every letter atones for the sins of an hour. And they are seven words, as Fakhr ar-Rāzī said, because transgression is always through one of the seven members—the ears or the eyes or the hands or the feet or the tongue or the belly or the pudenda. And every word atones for the transgression of one of the members. There is a reference also in this to the fact that, by the generosity and mercy of God, the seven doors of Hell are locked against him who says the *shahāda*. *al-Mukhtārātu 'l-ḥusān fī faḍli wa aḥkāmi Ramaḍān*, Ḥasan 'Alī Sharīf, p. 36.
>
> And the tradition tells us that when a worshipper says *lā ilāha illā 'llāh* a pillar of light goes up from his mouth and stands before God Most High. And God Most High says to that light, "Go to My Throne"; and it says, "Nay, by Thy Might I will not go till Thou hast forgiven the one who uttered me." Then God says, "By My Might and Majesty, it was I who

[1] No sign of this in the diplomatic correspondence of Muḥammad on the terms on which tribes may enter Islam, but customary by the second half of the seventh century A.D. See Wensinck, *Muslim Creed*, p. 33.

moved his tongue to say thee, have I not already forgiven his sins?" *Majmū'atu 'l-wirdi 'l-'āmm*, p. 96.

Since Islam has so earnestly taught that every man has to bear his own burden of sin and none can atone for another it is of very great interest to find that the *shahāda* is occasionally regarded as a spiritual donation, an acceptable offering for other souls.

This form is used:

O God I call Thee to witness to that to which Thou hast borne witness concerning Thyself, and to which Thine angels and Thy prophets and Thy men of learning have borne witness. And whosoever has not borne witness to that to which Thou hast borne witness, do Thou write my witness-bearing in the place of his. *Al-Ḥizbu 'l-a'ẓam*. 'Alī Muḥammad al-Qārī (also in a prayer written in 1232/1817 by M. 'Uthman al-Mirghanī in the sanctuary of the Mosque at Medina).

In the Hour of Death

The *shahāda* is to be the last utterance, the passport of the soul. So it was and is with the Jews; with their last breath they make confession of the Unity in the *Shema'*. The *shahāda* of the Jewish Church is used by the friends of the dying as their commendatory prayer:

(When the end is approaching.)
The Lord reigneth. The Lord hath reigned.
The Lord shall reign for ever and ever (three times).
Blessed be His Name whose glorious Kingdom is for ever and ever (three times).
The Lord He is God (seven times).
Hear O Israel, the Lord our God is One.

Berachoth 15.b.

So too in Islam. The upright stones at either end of a Muslim grave represents the two limbs of the *shahāda*. From her deep intimacy with her Muslim neighbours Lilias Trotter of Algiers wrote of many a heart-rending scene in which the families of the dying assisted by a *ṭālib*, struggled, in their love and anxiety, to win this confession from the lips of one in the death agony. In Egypt, among the fellaḥīn, the passing prayer of the friends of the dying is the *shahāda* interspersed with the pathetic jingle in the Egyptian colloquial *Kullinā amwāt, wilād amwāt. Nabī 'l-hudā garā luh kida*, "We are all dead children of the dead. Even so it befell the Prophet of Guidance."

The manuals abound in prayers for strength and faith to say the all-availing formula at the moment of departure.[1]

> Enlighten my heart with the light of faith at the end of my life when my agony is upon me, that I may say, "I bear witness that there is no god but God and Muḥammad is the Prophet of God. *Ḥizbu 'sh-shaikhi Abī 's-Sa'ūd.* (*Majmū'atu 'l-Aḥzāb*, p. 305.)

A recital of the *shahāda* is used as a commendatory service, their mass for the dead, by followers of Muṣṭafā al-Bakrī:

> When one of them has been gathered to the mercy of God, they meet and perform a *tahlīla* for him, that is to say, seventy thousand *lā ilāha illā 'llāh* after the *wird* of the twilight prayer. And the Shaikh holds the rosary, or orders a trusty person to hold it, for the exact counting of the number recited. And it is necessary to exceed the number a little, to cover the possible temporary absence of any of the brethren or his silence in the course of the *dhikr*. *Rabī'u 'l-fu'ād*, 'Abd Allāh ash-Sharqāwī, p. 115.

The Shahāda as Spiritual Training

Practically every Order uses it for the training of beginners in the spiritual life; almost every prayer-manual gives directions for its recital as a spiritual exercise:

> A hundred times, fifty with the tongue and fifty with the heart, with closed eyes and swaying and concentration of spirit. (*Khatmiyya–Mirghaniyya*) *Majmū'u 'l-awrādi 'l-kabīr*, p. 76.

It should be remembered that many a devout soul enters on the first stage of one or other of the Orders, though perhaps with no intention of proceeding further. Those entering on the first stage of the Qādiriyya Way are to say:

> My God, cause the authority of *lā ilāha illā 'llāh* to appear in my outward life, and by the realities of *lā ilāha illā 'llāh* make real my inward life. Absorb my outward life in Thee through the enclosing of it by *lā ilāha illā 'llāh*. *al-Fuyūḍātu 'r-rabbāniyya fī 'l-ma'āthiri 'l-qādiriyya*, Ismā'īl b. M. Sa'īd al-Jīlānī, p. 15.

As a purifying discipline the beginner has before him a recitation of

[1] For Muslim authority for the *shahāda* as passport for the dying see Aḥmad ibn Ḥanbal V. 247, with the warning note of al-Bukhārī's introduction to his *Bābu 'l-Janā'iz*.

70,000 *tahlīlāt*, and as he begins it, after the *salām* at the end of the set prayers, he says:

> O God I buy from Thee my evil-urging self, by this seventy thousand. Ibid., p. 33.

The *Shādhilī* beginner has a similar training:

> (On the direction of the soul to *lā ilāha illā 'llāh.*) Know, O earnest novice, that, if thou desirest to direct thy soul to this the revered "Greatest Name", the sword of Islam, the convincing argument of mankind, thy confrontation of it should be after sunrise and after the purifying of thy clothing and body from all defilement, and thine inward being from all evil suggestions and prejudices and unseemliness. For everyone who makes his confrontation while his heart is occupied with other than God has placed walls between himself and God. And everyone who makes mention of God while his heart is with other than Him of whom he makes mention, is veiled with a thousand veils. When thou hast purified thyself, then, outwardly and inwardly, say *lā ilāha illā 'llāh* twelve thousand times. And take heed lest in such a numbered *dhikr* you treat the number of recitations as though you were counting out jewels and pearls and such property; for the root of the *dhikr* is pleasure and sweetness. And if awe and tears and burning overcome you, that is a sign of divine help. *al-Mafākhiru 'l-'aliyya fi 'l-ma'āthiri 'sh-shādhiliyya*, Aḥmad b. M. al-'Ibād, p. 137.

This recital of the *shahāda*, which by one method or another is urged by every spiritual director in Islam, is an ascesis of mind, heart, and spirit. Fakhr ar-Rāzī says that though there was but one *Mi'rāj* (night ascent to heaven) of the Prophet, this recital has become the *mi'rāj* of all who know God.

The two limbs of the sentence, negative and positive, have their part to play:

> This matter is only perfected through negation and affirmation. That negation he expresses in the word *lā*, and that affirmation in the word *illā*, and they are united in *lā ilāha illā 'llāh*. (*Lawāmi'u 'l-bayyināt*, p. 38.)

The negative side of this way to God is a purging of the mind from every pre-conceived idea of God, from all human images and comparisons, a *via remotionis* of the intellect not unlike that of St Thomas Aquinas, but not only of the intellect:

> If I regard myself, my heart fails to gaze on Thee. If I regard Thee, I cannot abide with Thine abiding. My intellect is occupied with Thy transcendence, and my heart with its "yes" to Thy truth; my soul serves Thee,

my spirit loves Thee, and my inmost being beholds Thee. But my God, Thou art nearer to me than my mind's declaration of Thy transcendence, or my heart's affirmation, or the converse of my soul, or the love of my spirit, or the vision of my inmost being. I take refuge with Thee from the veiling of Thee by my own nature. My God, I yearn for Thy nearness, as Thou art; let not my being as I am veil Thee from me. ash-Shādhilī, *Al-Mafākhiru 'l-'aliyya fi 'l-ma'āthiri 'sh-shādhiliyya*, p. 192.

Make the "between" fall from me, that there may be no "between" between Thee and me. Ibid., p. 158.

As for the second limb, the positive confrontation, the rules here cease. The worshipper can attain by his *via negativa* the moment of *fanā*, of emptiness, of nakedness, of suspense. He cannot attain by rule the lifting up of the Countenance upon him, for that is a thing not earned but given. The unbearable, longed-for moment of Confrontation is not his to command.

When the Confrontation is granted, and granted it is by the testimony of many a Muslim saint, as it was not his to command, so it is not his to describe "the blazing mystery of bared eternity".

Prayers of the Soul asking for God Alone

We are here in the world of the mystics, very far, perhaps, from the daily experience of the great commonalty of Islam. Yet these prayers stand in books that are popularly used. They stand there as invitations to sanctity that he who will may follow.

My God, if I ask Thee for succour, I have asked something beside Thee. If I ask for what Thou hast guaranteed to me I show suspicion of Thee. If my heart rests in aught else but Thee I have been guilty of the sin of association (*shirk*). Thine attributes in their majesty are above contingency, how then can I be with Thee? They are transcendent of causes, how then can I be near to Thee? They are exalted above the dust of earth, how then can my stay be other than Thee? *Du'ā'* of ash-Shādhilī in *Majmū'atu 'l-Aḥzāb*, p. 124.

O God Thy riches are absolute and ours are limited. We ask Thee then by Thy limitless riches to enrich us with riches that leave no room for poverty save our continued need of Thee. *Wirdu 's-saḥr*, ash-Shādhilī.

Thou Who art compensation for all else, and for Whom nothing else is a compensation. *al-Munājātu 'l-injīliyyatu 'l-wuṣṭa*, attributed to 'Alī Zain al-'Ābidīn.

Make me Thine own, till there is no lordship in my life but Thine. M. 'Uthmān al-Mirghanī, *Majmū'u 'l-awrādi 'l-kabīr*, p. 56.

Thou art the First, before all things, and the Last, after all things, and all that is contingent perishes and is lost. There is no existence but in Thy existence, and no life for spirits but in the vision of Thee.

Thou makest a sign to spirits and they respond to Thee. Thou drawest back the veil from hearts and they are healed. *Ḥizbu 'r-rajā'*, 'Abd al-Qādir al-Jīlānī.

O God, some sought from Thee this world and Thou gavest it to them. And others sought from Thee the next world and Thou didst satisfy them. But I ask Thee neither for this world nor the next, but only for the increase of love to Thee in my heart. *Ḥizbu 'l-Ḥifẓ*, 'Abd al-Qādir al-Jīlānī.

10 b

THE WITNESS OF ISLAM (SHAHĀDA): TO THE PROPHET

Muḥammadu rasūlu 'llāh

In that moment, so tremendous to him, when the Muslim pilgrim stands before the Tomb of the Prophet at Medina he says:

> I bear witness that thou art the Apostle of God. Thou hast conveyed the message. Thou hast fulfilled the trust. Thou hast counselled the community, and enlightened the gloom, and shed glory on the darkness, and uttered words of wisdom. *Dalīlu 'l-ḥajj.* (Four Sunnī rites), M. Ḥasanain Makhlūf, p. 88.

Or, if he is a Shī'a, he gives an even fuller picture of the Prophet's mission:

> I bear witness that thou hast conveyed the Lord's messages and declared His command and hast borne hardship in His cause, and hast summoned men with wisdom and fair exhortation to His way, and hast fulfilled that which was entrusted to thee, and hast been compassionate to believers and harsh to stubborn unbelievers, and hast worshipped in single-heartedness which brought thee utter certitude. Thou art to me as father, as mother, as self, as family, as property, as child. *Miftāḥu 'l-janān*, Part 2, p. 80.

This is an affectionate enlargement in the moment of emotion, of the affirmation made from infancy to death at every prayer-rite and at how many another time, when the worshipper says:

> I bear witness that there is no god but God and I bear witness that Muḥammad is the Apostle of God. (An alternative form, "His servant and His apostle" (Aḥmad b. Ḥanbal, 4, 2) is occasionally used in private devotions.)
>
> O what a lord is he whose name is coupled with Thy name! *al-Jawāhiru 'l-mustaẓhira*, M. 'Uthmān al-Mirghanī.

So breaks out a worshipper pondering on the twofold witness.

Those hostile to Islam have not failed to remark on the conjunction, as is shown in the following question addressed by an Indian Muslim to *The Light* of Lahore, with the answer of the Aḥmadiyya editor.

Q. The Arya Samaj often blames us saying, "Though the Muhammedans believe in one God, they mix up the name of Muhammad with God when they utter the *Kalima*, which is a part of their faith." Kindly explain fully how to refute this objection.

A. Rather than adulterate the unity of God in any way, the addition of the expression about the Prophet emphasizes it. It has been made part and parcel of the very formula of faith as a safeguard against the common human weakness of deifying their religious founders. Krishna has been deified by the Hindus; Jesus by the Christians. Islam obviated this danger once for all by making every Muslim repeat a number of times every day, "Muhammad is but an apostle of God." So long as this declaration is there in the *Kalima*, there is no danger of the deification of the Prophet by the Muslims. The addition thus re-affirms and guarantees the undisputed unity of God.

The Names of Muḥammad in Worship

Yet the study of our devotions shows that Islam of to-day must be ever on her guard against what may be a tacit, though never explicit, deifying of the Prophet, whose position in these prayers is so immeasurably beyond that of humanity. The study of the Names of God and of the Names of the Prophet, as used in prayer, shows how vigilant this guard must be. Constantly are the same phrases addressed to both in worship. For the title *nūru 'n-nūr*, Light of Light, used for both, see chapter 16. God is addressed as *Yā man yujību daʿwata 'l-muḍṭarīn*, Thou who dost answer the cry of those in need: so is Muḥammad. Both are addressed as *mawlā*; both as *murādu 'l-mushtāqīn*, desired of longing hearts. In the noble prayer at the end of the burial service God is called:

The friend of all who are strangers, the Companion of all who are lonely.

Exactly the same words are addressed to Muḥammad.[1] Both are called in prayer *Al-Ḥabīb*; of both it is said *laisa lahu naẓīr wa lā mathīl*.[2] The name Maḥmūd is felt to be a donation to Muḥammad from Him whose Name is al-Maḥmūd, and devotions often play upon its letters:

The *mīm* of *majd* (glory), the *ḥā'* of *raḥma* (mercy), the *mim* of *mulk* (empire) and the *dāl* of *dawām*, everlastingness. *Fatḥu 'r-rasūl*, M. ʿUthmān al-Mirghanī, p. 24.

[1] For instance in *Wirdu 'ṣ-ṣalātu 'l-kubrā*, attributed to ʿAbd al-Qādir al-Jīlānī.
[2] *Ad-Durru 'l-fā'iq, Muṣṭafa al-Bakri*, p. 32.

Two other Names of God are believed to have been bestowed on Muḥammad as a divine gift, *ar-Ra'ūf* and *ar-Raḥīm* (*Shifā* I.93).

In all this there is as much need to-day as when it was written for the following warning:

> It is forbidden to us to be named with names like the Names of God Most High, like *Wāfī* and *Nūr* and *Wakīl* and so forth. It is a duty of the law and of the mind to avoid that, and if we use such a name for anyone it must be with a (mental) dissociation of it from its connection with God Most High. As for instance, if we say a certain man is *mu'min* (believer) our meaning is that he gives the endorsement of faith to God's promises and threats, and not the meaning attached to it as a Name of God (*al-Mu'min*, Faithful). As for God's naming of His servant Muḥammad *Ra'ūf* and *Raḥīm*, we only say this by way of recitation or as telling the story of what God said of him, naming him as God named him; and there is no harm in this for it was the Owner of the Name who endued him with it. And all the time, we believe that in himself he was before his Lord a lowly, humble, repentant, penitent servant. *al-Istighāthatu, 'l-kubrā*, Yūsuf an-Nabhānī, quoting from Ash-Sha'rānī, *al-Yawāqīt wa 'l-jawāhir*, mabḥath 13, who in his turn quotes from Ibn al-'Arabī.

The love of Muḥammad's people has piled up for him, with oriental lavishness and poetry, names and epithets numerous as the Names of God, whether these are regarded as ninety-nine, one thousand, or variant numbers. And like the Names of God the Prophet's names are strung together in hymns and litanies. A curious assignation of names of the Prophet, placing him in relationship with the whole creation, is the following:

For the people of Paradise he is the servant of the Generous One				
For the people of the Fire	,,	,,	,,	the All-Compelling One
For the people of the Throne	,,	,,	,,	the Praiseworthy
For the rest of the Angels	,,	,,	,,	the Glorious
For the Prophets	,,	,,	,,	the Giver of Graces
For the Devils	,,	,,	,,	the Queller
For the Jinn	,,	,,	,,	the Merciful
In the mountains	,,	,,	,,	the Creator
On the dry land	,,	,,	,,	the Powerful
On the sea	,,	,,	,,	the Watcher
For the sea monsters	,,	,,	,,	the Transcendently Holy
For the owls	,,	,,	,,	the Succourer
For the wild beasts	,,	,,	,,	the Giver of Sustenance
For the lions	,,	,,	,,	Him who is Peace

For the cattle he is the servant of the Trustworthy
For the birds „ „ „ the Forgiving One
In the Torah „ Ma'ūda Mauda[1]
In the Gospel „ Ṭāb Ṭāb
In the Holy Books the Requiter
In the Psalms „ the Distinguished
For God „ Ṭāhā and Yā Sīn
For the believers „ Muḥammad
as-Sirru 'l-a'ẓam, 'Abd Allāh al-Mirghanī.

Prayers concerning the cosmic Muḥammad, before whom all creation is believed to bow, will be found in Chapter 16. Prayers concerning Muḥammad as the heavenly Intercessor and Mediator have been noted in Chapter 2. Chapters 11(a) and 11(b) show the stupendous position believed to be his in the heavenly places and in relation to all other prophets. It must be the business of this chapter to study the attitude of the Muslim worshipper to Muḥammad not as regards the Last Day or the life to come, but as the guide and helper of his struggles here on earth.

THE PATTERN OF PRAYER

Muḥammad is the pattern of life for his people, ever occupied with his *sunna*.

> Followers of his steps in word and deed. *Aḥzābun wa awrād.* 'Abd al-Qādir al-Jīlānī. (Preface.)
>
> Order our goings in the way of the Best of Creation. Ibid., p. 16.
>
> I ask Thee, O our Lord, to employ us in his usages, to cause us to die in his community, to number us in his band, under his banner, and to make us his companions, to supply us from his reservoir, to give us to drink from his cup, and to give us the boon of his love. *Dalā 'ilu 'l-khairāt*, p. 157.

He is the pattern, for his people, of prayer as well as of the rest of life. One of their most frequent petitions is:

> We ask Thee for that which Thy servant and apostle Muḥammad asked of Thee. We seek refuge with Thee from that from which Thy servant and apostle Muḥammad sought refuge with Thee. (Constantly used in the manuals. Traditional, at-Tirmidhī from Abū Imāma.)

The much-used *ad'iya nabawiyya*, a collection of prayers which needs the careful critical study of Muslim scholars, historians, and orientalists,

[1] The name *Ma'ūda Mauda* is an echo of the Hebrew of Gen. 17.20.

are for the most part straightforward requests for sustenance, *rizq* (*urzuqnā khaira 'd-dunyā wa khaira 'l-ākhira.*—Supply us with the best of this world and the best of the world to come) or deliverance from Hell (*qinā 'adhāba 'n-nār*—deliver us from the sufferings or the chastisement of the Fire).[1] These are within the capacity of the simpler souls of the community and one or two of them are generally taught to children to use in the set prayers. Two examples will be found in Chapter 13. With the mystics among the Prophet's followers the *ad'iya* suffer a transformation "into something rich and strange", as they live on in the minds and hearts of men whose desire is towards the spiritual.

As they meditate on the picture of Muḥammad at prayer, on his vigils and fasts, on the mystery of his revelation, the Prophet's life with God becomes the pattern of spiritual attainment for his people.

> He who was satisfied with but a little. *Majmū'atu 'l-wirdi 'l-'āmm*, p. 31.
>
> He who used to put a stone against his noble belly from hunger. *ad-Durru 'l-fā'iq*, Muṣṭafā al-Bakrī, p. 27.
>
> Tradition tells us that when he sat down between the two prostrations (in the prayer-rite) it was as if he sat on hot cooking-stones, that is to say he returned rapidly to prostration because of his spiritual power. *Laṭā'ifu 'l-minan*, ash-Sha'rānī, p. 127.
>
> He who desired union with Thee, Thine intimate, turning away from all else but Thee that he might enjoy the Light of Thine Essential Being. He whose repair was to Thee and to none other, and who saw Thy Unity in Thy multiplicity (*kathratika*). He who made mention of Thee by night and fasted for Thy sake by day. *Wirdu 'ṣ-ṣalāti 'l-kubrā*, 'Abd al-Qādir al-Jīlānī.

Most of all, even in prayer-books which only touch on the fringe of the mystical life, worshippers meditate on the deeper mystery of the night ascension to heaven (*Qur.* 7.1, 60. 53.1–15). The mysterious sentences concerning that spiritual experience are more than any other Qur'ānic verses, the nexus between the whole system of Islam and the inner life of the mystics. They, and the whole embroidery of tradition on them, are also the food of the simple, in such narratives as al-Mirghanī's *Qiṣṣatu 'l-Mi'rāj*, with rhymed responses.

In these verses, unutterably precious to the deeper souls of Islam, is sought the basis in Qur'ān and *sunna* for any *ascensus mentis ad Deum.* In meditation on them Muḥammad is studied as the prototype of the

[1] This prayer forms a regular part of the Shī'a *namāz* and is taught also to Turkish children when they learn the prayer-rite.

mystical life of his people, not their Prophet, Law-Announcer, Ruler, Pattern of outward life only, but their spiritual leader.

> Make him to us a spirit and the very secret of our worship. And make his love to us a food aiding us to magnify him. And make our magnifying of him life in our hearts by which I may arise and with its aid make mention of him and make mention of his Lord. *al-Awrādu 'l-ikhtiyāriyya*, Aḥmad at-Tijānī.
>
> The presence-chamber of the prostration (in the set prayers) is like the presence-chamber of "two bow's-length or less" (*Qur.* 53.9) as is indicated by that tradition, "A man is at his nearest to his Lord during his prostration." *Laṭā'ifu 'l-minan*, ash-Sha'rānī, p. 127.
>
> The distance of two bows'-length was his request. His request was his goal. His goal was his attainment. *Durūd-Tāj* (one of the great devotions of Indian Muslims).

Probably many a Muslim mystic would feel the sense of uneasiness that may come to a Christian reader confronted with the sentence last quoted. Can the assumption of this prayer that *the goal has been reached*, at "two bows'-length or less" be true to the life of the seeker after God? If it were true that Muḥammad's *maqṣūd* was reached at even the least distance from Him whom the mystics call *Al-Maqṣūd*, could he be the pattern for those whose goal is God Himself? "I count not myself yet to have apprehended" (Phil. 3.13) was the record of another who had been caught up into heaven.

Although Muḥammad is accepted as the pattern of prayer, the worshipper, in following his practice is warned off the use of any phrases that belong to his prerogative of apostleship and prophethood, sealed and forbidden to any that come after.

> For he would be asking from God Most High Prophethood and Apostleship after our Prophet. And if not actually an impious unbeliever (*kāfir*) he would not be far from such wilful unbelief. For the command of God, Mighty and Majestic has gone forth concerning that, and He has made it known to us, therefore petition in contravention of God's command impinges on impious unbelief, since the worshipper has asked God for what is wrong, and God is Transcendent of wrong-doing. (Aḥmad at-Tījānī, *Aḥzāb wa awrād*, p. 91.)

Awe of the Prophet

There is, then, for these worshippers, a deep sense of awe in approaching one whose God-given prophethood and apostleship are thus believed to be a *ḥaram*, a forbidden holy of holies.

Thou hast commanded us not to raise our voices against his voice, but that they all should be subdued before the awe of him. We should not then speak aloud in our communing with him, but should meet him with lowered voices in our dialogue with him; and tongues should be satisfied with a murmur in petitioning him. And this order was given as a token of the greatness which Thou dost assign to his reverend apostleship, a tribute to the majesty of the power of his message, that the love of him may be concealed in our breasts. Shīʻa *Ṣalātun ʻalā 'n-nabī*, ʻAlī Zain al-ʻĀbidīn. *aṣ-Ṣaḥīfatu 's-sajjādiyya*, p. 33.

He affirmed that to magnify (the Prophet) is a stage beyond loving him. Then he said, It is our duty to love him and render him honour and magnify him more abundantly than the honour of every slave to his master or every son to his father. *al-Ḥirzu 'l-manīʻ*. As-Suyūṭī, p. 9.

For there is nothing unconnected with him, and all the current of events is enclosed in his mystery. *al-Wazīfatu 'sh-Shādhiliyya, Manbaʻu 's-saʻādāt*, p. 164.

This cosmic figure cannot be far from his follower at worship.

And al-Munāwī and others informed us that the Prophet is present at every session (for the *dhikr*) and the Companions also are present at any session which they desire to attend (of the Tījāniyya Order). *Al-Fatḥu 'r-rabbānī*, p. 13.

For except Muḥammad is the cause of it, no grace outward or inward comes our way, by which we obtain our special endowment in religious practice or ordinary life, and by which we are defended against what is undesirable in either or both of them. *Fatḥu 'r-rasūl*, M. ʻUthmān al-Mirghanī.

The result of such a belief is an attitude which comes very close to the Christian's offering of his prayer "through" his Divine Lord.

Let my petition to Thee reach Thee in him, and Thy mercy and goodness to me descend upon me in him. *Mukhtaṣaru adʻiyati Ramaḍān*, p. 27.

Prayer to Muḥammad

It is but a step from this to prayer addressed to Muḥammad himself. Sometimes to him is addressed the pathetic cry of the street-beggar "*Shai'an lillāh!*" "Something for God's sake!"

O Thou who art transfigured in radiance, have mercy on my abasement. O Thou who art exalted, set to rights my state. O Apostle of God, help! and supply of succour! O Beloved of God, on thee is reliance. O Prophet of

God, be to us a mediator. Thou, by God, art an intercessor who meets with no refusal.

O my lord, O apostle of God, O my support, my refuge, my apostle, thou sufficest me. I have placed in the praise of the apostle of God my confidence, for he, when I seek for sufficiency, suffices me. *Wirdun sa'diyya mukhtaṣar, Majmū'atu 'l-aḥzāb*, pp. 469, 471.

At the Pilgrimage

It is but natural that devotion to the Prophet should find strong expression in the Pilgrimage to the sites of his mission and to that tomb where his living presence is felt to reside.

Not without nearness (to him) can my heart's care be relieved. A visit would be healing for my sickness, could I attain it; I long for it even were I on my bier. *Dīwān fī madḥi 'n-nabī*, Abū Zaid al-Fazāzī al-Andalusī.

The *ḥaḍra* of Muḥammad, or *al-ḥaḍratu 'l-aḥmadiyya*, for the attainment of which so many prayers go up, seems to vary between a spiritual presence in the heart and a kind of presence-chamber like the levee of an eighteenth-century king, a spiritual reception of the blest. Many a vision and many a colloquy is reported at the Tomb of Medina.

I entered the Tomb and stood in the presence of the Chosen and asked his leave to make this anthology. And he gave me leave. And I asked his acceptance of it by people in general, and he was generous in giving true acceptance and told me that through it a man might attain to revelation from him and nearness to him in both worlds. *Fatḥu 'r-rasūl*, M. 'Uthmān al-Mirghanī, p. 126.

In the following prayer at the Tomb, the Prophet is asked to say to his follower, "Enter thou into the joy of thy Lord."

O Owner of this Tomb—say "Enter to my honourable presence and be dowered with the bliss of the sight of my beauty in my generous welcoming. May the sight of me abide with you in this world and the next." Ibid., loc. cit.

In the next prayer, written after a Friday night spent before the tomb, the Prophet is made into the spiritual meaning of all the familiar features of the Meccan sanctuary.[1]

[1] The famous *mīzāb* on the western side of the Ka'ba sent from Stambūl in 981/1573 is reputed to be of pure gold. At the "Yamānī corner" of the Ka'ba,

Call down blessing on him and speak in blessing to him who is the water-spout (*mīzāb*) of Thy presence, the roof of the Ka'ba of Thy perfections, the stone (Black Stone) of Thy divine Church, the south east corner (*rukn yamanī*) of Thy mysteries, the enclosure (*hijr*) of Thy safety, within which if a man enter he is safe, the stance of Thy friendship (*maqām Khullatika*), the *multazam* of Thine appointment, the water of Thy *Zamzam* and the spacious House of Thine irradiation. *Fatḥu 'r-rasūl*, p. 146.

The unforgettable cry of the Meccan pilgrimage (the *talbiya*) is *Labbaika!* (interpreted "Here am I at Thy service"). There seems little doubt that it passed into the Muslim pilgrimage from the primitive rites before it (Muslim. *Ḥajj*. 22). Muslim worshippers say that when Abraham gave the command for the Pilgrimage the people responded with their *talbiyya*. It is said to-day as each pilgrim puts on his sacred garment (*iḥrām*) and enters the "sanctified state" of the pilgrimage; shouted, as he first comes in sight of the city, with an emotion comparable to that of a crusader beholding Jerusalem; and raised again and again through the pilgrimage rites until the lapidation. This haunting cry which might become for Muslim souls their version of Mary's "Behold the handmaid of the Lord" in in the prayer-books given to Muḥammad to whom Islam gives all: *Labbaika! yā rasūla 'llāh!*

Love of the Prophet

No one can estimate the power of Islam as a religion who does not take into account the love at the heart of it for this figure. It is here that human emotion, repressed at some points by the austerity of the doctrine of God as developed in theology, has its full outlet—a warm human emotion which the peasant can share with the mystic. The love of this figure is perhaps the strongest binding force in a religion which has so marked a binding power. The witness to the Prophet in our prayers is not infrequently followed by the witness to the brotherhood of the community.

facing south is a reddish stone which pilgrims touch with their hands. It is a place of the answering of prayer.

The *maqām* of Abraham *Khalīlu 'llāh*, is the place where he stood when the Ka'ba had reached some height, to continue building, and which received the impress of his feet, the place also where he stood, mountains high to proclaim the pilgrimage. The *multazam* is the part of the Ka'ba from the Black Stone to the entrance door.

O God our Lord and Lord of all things, I am witness that Muḥammad is Thy servant and Thine Apostle. O God our Lord and Lord of all things, I am witness that all the worshippers are brothers. *Khalāṣatu 'l-maghnam*, 'Alī b. Ḥasan al-'Aṭṭās, p. 15, and frequently in the manuals. Based on *Qur.* 49.10.

And true it is that even the sinners of this community are better than the Jews and the Christians and the Magians. *al-Wirdu 'sh-shāfī*, Yūsuf an-Nabhānī (quoting from an *'aqīda* of 'Abd al-Qādir al-Jīlānī).

To Thee be praise and thanks for the grace of belonging to the community of the Best of Mankind. *Majmū'atu 'l-wirdi 'l-'āmm.*

Every detail of the human figure is treasured and loved, as well as the details of the mystical and super-human figure built over it.

The man of the stalwart staff
The man who wore sandals
The man of argument
The man of sound reason
The man of power
The wearer of the turban
The hero of the Night Ascent
The hero of the sword
The rider of Burāq
The noble rider
He who traversed the seven spheres
The intercessor for all creatures
The man who gave thanks when he abstained from taking food
The man for whom the palm trees wept and sighed at his departure
He of whom the birds of the desert sought influence
He to whom the very stones did homage at his self-restraint
He of whom the gazelles sought intercession in articulate speech
He to whom the lizard spoke at an open conference of the most learned
The devoted evangelist
The brilliant lamp
The man to whom the camel made its complaint
The man for whom the sparkling water burst forth in the midst of his comrades
He who was pure and yet purified
The light of lights
He for whom the moon opened out
He who was good and did good

The apostle to whom was given the privilege of access
The spreading dawn
The brilliant star
The trusty handle
The monitor of the people of the earth

. . . .

The man in whose presence the trees did obeisance
The man at whose light the flowers opened
The man at whose blessing the fruits matured
The man at whose promise the trees moved themselves from all directions
The man at whose light all other lights burst forth
The man to the skirts of whose robes wild creatures clung when he was travelling in the most desert lands.

Dalā'ilu 'l-khairāt, pp. 19, 22.

Miracles to match the Gospel miracles are recited to stir the loving wonder of the faithful.

Jābir related that the people thirsted on the day of Huḍeiba, and they came to the Prophet complaining of their thirst. Now there was a leather water-bucket before him with a little water in it. And he put his hand into the leathern bucket and made the water well forth from between his fingers as springs gush out. Jābir was asked, "How many were you?" He said, "Had we been a hundred thousand it would have sufficed us. We were fifteen hundred."

Among his signs was the blessing of a little food till it sufficed a great multitude. *Ṭahāratu 'l-qulūb*, ad-Dīrīnī, pp. 34, 35. (Cf. al-Bukhārī 7.6. Aḥmad ibn Ḥanbal 4.174. It was "barley cakes" that he was said to multiply.)

If, for the mystic, God Himself is *al-Maḥbūb*, the Beloved before whom all other loves go less, this is the place of Muḥammad for a very wide circle of his people.

Our beloved, our lord, our support, our mediator, our owner (*Maulānā*). (Outburst at the end of the most popular devotion of Indian Muslims, *Ganj il 'Arsh*.)

O God by the rank of Thy Prophet, by Thy love to him and his love to Thee I ask . . . double O Lord my love to him; adorn my hearing with the earrings of the joy of his speech. *Majmū'atu 'l-wirdi 'l-kabīr*, M. 'Uthmān al-Mirghanī, p. 86.

He to whom yearning loves fly without wings . . .
He in whom the hearts of the people of affection find rest . . .
He through whom we have found delight even in misfortunes . . .
He without whose love there is no solace to the believing heart

Awrād Muṣṭafā al-Bakrī, pp. 15, 36.

That Thou wilt give us to drink of the wine of his love and affection, and grant us a waft of his breezes, and wilt single us out for a special drawing of his mighty attraction, and wilt give us a perfect sincerity in loving him, and affection embracing all the people of his love. Ibid., p. 41.

Thou hast banished from my heart all dubiousness and doubt of this noble Prophet, and hast caused the love of him to prevail over the love of all kinsfolk and loved ones. *Dalā 'ilu 'l-khairāt*, p. 144.

O God the love of Thee and the love of Thine Apostle are dearer to me than myself and my family, more desirable than cold water. By his value in Thine eyes make me loved by him and by all who love him and who love Thee, in earth and heaven. *Ḥizbun 'aẓīmun li'l 'ashshāqiyya* (*Majmū'atu 'aḥzāb*, p. 391).

This type of prayer is supported by a group of traditions which are echoes of the Gospel words of Matthew 10.38,39; Luke 14.26,33.

The Prophet of God said None of you is a believer until I have become dearer to him than himself and his property and his son and his father and all men.

(In the Ḥadith of 'Umar) Dearer art thou to me, oh apostle of God, than all things save the soul within my body. And the Prophet said, "Thou wilt not indeed be a believer until I am dearer to thee than thine own soul." And 'Umar said, "By Him who sent down to thee the Book, indeed thou art dearer to me than my own soul"; and the Prophet said, "Now 'Umar thy faith is complete."

It was said to the Apostle of God, "When shall I be a believer" (another version has a true believer). He said, "When you love God." "And when shall I love God?" "When you love His Apostle." "And when shall I love His Apostle?" He said, "When you follow his way and seek to do his works and to love as he loves and hate as he hates, and to be the friend of his friends and the foe of his foes. For the faith of men increases with the measure of their love for me and their unbelief (*kufr*) increases with the measure of their enmity to me." *Dalā'ilu 'l-khairāt*, p. 19 ff. *Al Ḥirzu 'l-munī'*, p. 39. (Aḥmad ibn Ḥanbal, *3*.177,207,176,206,370. al-Bukhārī, *Imām* 8. Muslim *1*.28).

Yet another tradition echoes, John 20.29:

It was said to the Apostle of God, "Who is he who is strong in faith in thee?" He said, "He who believes in me though he never saw me. For he believes in me from a yearning love and a sincere one and the sign of it in him is that he prefers the vision of me to all that he possesses (or in another version to the fulness of the earth and gold). That man is the true believer in me and my sincere lover." *Dalā'ilu 'l-khairāt*, p. 22.

On this last tradition the following prayer is based:

O God I have believed in our lord Muḥammad though I have not seen him. Then deprive me not of the vision of him in Paradise, but grant me his companionship and make me to die in his Church, and give me to drink of his tank a thirst-quenching palatable, health-giving draught after which I shall never thirst again. Ibid., p. 50.

VISION OF THE PROPHET

The prayer-books are eloquent of the longing of his people to see the face of the Prophet they love; this is a special mark of nineteenth-century devotions. Notes are appended to some forms of prayer (usually to *Taṣliyāt*) giving encouragement and direction for their use so as to ensure such a vision.

An important note. Let him who desires to see the Prophet say, "O God call down blessing on Muḥammad and on the family of Muḥammad as Thou hast commanded us to call down blessing on him," seventy-one times. *Fatḥu 'r-rasūl*, p. 84.

Among the many prayers for the vision of the Prophet not only in the hereafter, but here and now, are some which imply what we should call "a vision" (*ru'yatu 'n-nabī*), what seems an external sight of the beloved face, whether in a dream (*fi 'l-manām*) as is so often recorded, or waking[1]—a witnessing of it (*mushāhada*), while others seem to imply the vision of the heart, a continual gaze (*murāqaba*) not on his face but on his essential being:

VISION IN SLEEP

(From Muḥammad b. Sa'īd b. Muṭraf.) One night I fulfilled the number of blessings of the Prophet and I fell asleep. I was dwelling in a room and, lo, the Prophet had come to me in through the door, and the whole room was lighted up by him. Then he moved towards me and said "Give me

[1] *Al Fatḥu'r-rabbānī*, of 'Abd Allāh ibn Ḥasanain, gives a list of those who have seen him waking, "And Shaikh Jalāl ad-Dīn as-Suyūṭī saw him at Cairo and kissed his hand." (pp. 12, 13.)

the mouth that has blessed me so often that I may kiss it." And my modesty would not let him kiss my mouth, so I turned away my face, and he kissed my cheek. Then I woke trembling from my sleep and my wife who was by my side awoke, and lo the house was odorous of musk from the scent of him, and the scent of musk from his kiss remained on my cheek about eight days. My wife noticed the scent every day. *al-Ḥirzu 'l-manī'*, As-Suyūṭī, p. 32.

Prayers for the Vision of His Face

We beseech Thee, Thee Thyself through Thyself, to show us the face of our Prophet. *Wird ṣalāti 'l-kubrā*, 'Abd al-Qādir al Jīlānī.

A calling down of blessing by which our thirsty hearts are made ready to behold his noble face. *Aḥzāb wa awrād Aḥmad at-Tījānī*, p. 138.

In mercy grant me to behold him who ever beholds Thee. Ibid., p. 146.

The Use of Imagination

Imagine that you are standing facing him, as though you are before him, face to face, and that he hears you and sees you even though he is far away, for he does hear, through God, and see through Him, and nothing, near or far, is hidden from him. *al-Faiḍ wa 'l-madad min ḥaḍrati 'r-rasūli 's-sanad*, M. 'Uthmān al-Mirghanī, p. 143.

I have filled my heart with him and my eyes and my hearing, and have come near to him in recollection through which he is with me. *Dīwān fī maaḥi 'n-nabī*, Abū Zayd al-Fazāzī.

Prayers for the Vision of His Spiritual Personality

Among the graces with which God honoured him (Aḥmad at-Tījānī) was the waking vision of the Prophet, continuously and ever, so that it was never absent from him for the twinkling of an eye. And (another grace was) his questioning of the Prophet on everything and asking his counsel in small things and great, and undergoing training at his hands. This is the highest of all graces granted to the people of knowledge. *al-Fatḥu 'r-rabbānī*, p. 74.

Abū'l Baqā al-Makkī used to say that this (Sanūsī) Order is founded on the absorption of the inner life of its founder in the spectacle of the Very Self of the Prophet, with the building up of his outer life on the following of him in word and deed, and the occupation of his tongue with the calling down of blessing upon him and his perseverance in this during the greater part of his solitary and his public devotions, till the magnifying of the Prophet dominated his heart and was mingled with his inmost being, so that he was moved at the very mention of him. And the vision of the Prophet's essential being reigned in his heart so that no created being other than the Prophet had any weight with him. *al-Fuyūḍātu 'r-rabbāniyya fī ijāzati 't-ṭarīqati 's-sanūsiyya*, p. 12.

O God, open our eyes through him to see him, and open our ears through him to hear from him and cause us to lose ourselves in his beauty. *Fatḥu 'r-rasūl*, p. 59.

So the thought of some has passed from vision to constant spiritual companionship:

Praise be to Thee, a praise that shall be to us a means to companionship, waking and sleeping, with the loved Beloved. *Majmū'atu 'l-wirdi 'l-'āmm*, p. 68.

To vivify our hearts by the light of his heart embracing all things, and to purify our souls by the purity of his unstained soul. *Wirdu 'ṣ-ṣalāti 'l-kubrā*, 'Abd al-Qādir al-Jīlānī.

Union with the Prophet

From desire for companionship, the longing heart turns, after the manner of all love, to desire for union:

To make our essential personality one with his in his beginnings and his end, through love of his character and the purest love to him. *Wirdu ṣ-ṣalāti 'l-kubrā*, 'Abd al-Qādir al-Jīlānī.

One of the commonest forms of this prayer is:

Unite me with him as Thou hast united the spirit and the soul, outwardly and inwardly, waking and sleeping, make him the spirit of my being under all aspects, in this life as in the next. *Majmū'atu 'l-wirdi 'l-kabīr*, pp. 13 and 45, and constantly in the manuals.

So the longing of man's heart for love and communion has built up a life-habit of devotion that might put to shame many to whom is given "the light of the knowledge of the glory of God in the Face of Jesus Christ" from whom Sadhu Sundar Singh in his *munājāt* heard the words:

The womb of Mary, where in a fleshly form I had My abode for a few months, was not a place more sacred than the heart of the believer in which for all time I have My home and make it a heaven.

II a

THE CALLING DOWN OF BLESSING: THE BLESSING OF THE PROPHET

Taṣliya, Durūd (in Indian manuals)

At the very least, one third of the manuals on which this book is built consists of variations on a single sentence, "May God call down blessing on our Lord Muḥammad and on the family of our Lord Muḥammad and greet them with peace."

Here is the *taṣliya*, the commonest of phrases on Muslim lips; the commonest of phrases in Muslim books, where some form of it follows every mention of the Prophet of Islam and has done so since the days of Hārūn ar-Rashīd; the commonest of phrases in Muslim devotion, whether it be as the sole and sufficing subject of whole books, or whether it be as the sudden conclusion applied to prayers and praises of the most various character, since all prayers should both begin and end with *taḥmīd* and *taṣliya* (*Adhkār,* an-Nawawī, p. 56). There is no end to its uses:

> A member of the Māliki school said: The calling down of blessing on the Prophet is an ordinance of Islam to which no numerical limit has been set and no fixed time has been allotted. *al-Ḥirzu 'l-manī'*, as-Suyūṭī.

In the Ādhān

The *Taṣliya* rings down from the minaret in the *mu'adhdhin's* call. At what moment in Muslim history it was inserted there it is hard to decide. An oft-quoted tradition may mark a stage at which the *ṣalātu 'alā 'n-nabī* was known as a response to the *ādhān*, but was not yet part of the *ādhān* itself.[1]

> When you hear the call to prayer, say after him what the *mu'adhdhin* says, then call down blessing on me, for whoso calls down one blessing on me,

[1] As was the case, Tor Andrae points out, as late as Al-Bukhārī †256/870, whose whole section on the Ādhān shows no sign of the *taṣliya*.

God shall call down on him ten blessings. (Muslim, from 'Abdullah b. 'Umar; also Aḥmad, Abū Dāwūd, at-Tirmidhī, an-Nasā'ī.)

(Many variants of this tradition of ten-fold reward are quoted in the manuals. It is said to be based on the Qur'ānic text: "He who does a good deed shall have attributed to him ten more" (6.160); "for there is no doubt that to bless the Prophet is one of the most important of good deeds." *Fatḥu 'l-karīmi 'l-Khāliq*, p. 11. (Commentary by 'Alī al-Makkī on Muṣṭafā al-Bakri.)

What work can arrive at such a result? What power or means can attain it? How could it come about that the Mighty King should call down blessing on his poor and lowly servant, but for his care to obey the Prophet, and the greatness of that Prophet's influence with the Almighty? Ibid., p. 8, quoting from Al-Fāsi, *Muṭāli'u 'l-musarrāt li sharḥ Dalā'ili 'l-khairāt*.

One of the manuals, an abridgment by as-Suyūṭī of a work on *Taṣliya* by Shams ad-Dīn as-Sakhāwī †902/1496, would even place the insertion of the *taṣliya* in the *ādhān* as early as the end of the first Islamic century:

And this insertion of the *ṣalāt* began in Sha'bān of the year 91 when An-Najm ibn al-Ṭandī the *Muḥtasib* ordered that they should call down blessings on the Prophet at every Call to Prayer except that of sunset when time did not permit of it (no source given). *al-Ḥirzu 'l-manī'*, p. 104.[1]

In the Prayer-Rite

There is silence in the manuals as to the moment when the *taṣliya* became obligatory also in the prayer-rite itself,[2] an obligation on which the devout conscience could still suspend judgment as late as ash-Sha'rānī (†973/1565).

As for the position of those who do not make the *ṣalātu 'alā 'n-nabī* obligatory in the last *tashahhud* they hold that the preoccupation of (the man engaged in) the prayer-rite is continuously with the presence of God himself, and perhaps the awe of that presence may so strongly dominate the heart of the worshipper that he may be unable to turn from the greatness of the divine interview to the thought of anyone else. One of the divines has said

[1] The Muḥtasib, though not a mosque official, had to see that the *ādhān* was duly given. The date 91 A.H. was perhaps suggested by the fact that that year (the year of the donation of the first golden waterspout) was one of changes and enlargements in the mosque.

[2] For references supporting a tenth-century date see Massignon, *Al-Ḥallāj*, p. 745, notes 4–7.

> that in such a case the calling down of blessing on the Prophet is an approved but not an obligatory practice, thus differing from those great ones whose vision includes both God, High in Majesty, and his creatures, and whose vision of God Most High does not preclude the vision of created beings. Nor should it, for the calling down of blessing on the Prophet in the presence of God only means that the Prophet is their *imām* in that worship.
>
> And we have a saying of Junaid that for the perfect man neither does the vision of God preclude the vision of his creatures nor *vice versa*, but to each is given his rights. He then who said that the calling down of blessing on the Prophet was not obligatory, did not do so from any belittling of the Prophet's rank, but only because of the overwhelming greatness of the divine irradiation in the heart of the worshipper. Al-Qushairī quoted from Abū Bakr ash-Shiblī that he once gave the call to prayer and when he reached the *shahādatain* he stood and said, "By Thy Might and Thy Majesty hadst Thou not commanded me to make mention of Thy Prophet, I should not have been able to mention him!" Possibly this happened to ash-Shiblī before he had reached perfection.[1] *Laṭa'ifu 'l-minan*, p. 127.

The prayer-manuals now in popular use, even though much of their material goes back to a date earlier than that of al-Sha'rānī, show no such suspension of judgment. For them the *ṣalātu 'alā 'n-nabī* is both primitive and of overwhelming importance:

> Know that the command to call down blessing on the Prophet was given in the second year of the *Hijra*, and it is said that it was on the night of the *Isrā'*; there is a tradition, without *isnād*, in *Faḍlu Sha'bān* by Ibn Abī 's-Saif, that the month of Sha'bān is the month of calling down blessing on the chosen Prophet because the verse commanding it was sent down in that month (i.e. *Qur.* 33.56). *Al Ḥirzu 'l-manī'*, p. 16.

Essential

The *taṣliya* has become an essential, sometimes it would seem, *the* essential of the life of salvation and devotion:

> If a man brings on the Day of Resurrection good works many as those of all the people in the world and does not bring with them the calling down of blessing on the Prophet, his good works are returned to him, unacceptable. *Fatḥu 'r-Rasūl*, M. 'Uthmān al-Mirghanī,

[1] Cf. the other anecdote in al-Qushairī concerning al-Kharrāz (died at Cairo in 286/899) who greeted a night vision of the Prophet with the words: "Pardon me! Loving God makes me forget to love thee," and heard the response: "Thou blessed one, he who loves God loves me also." *Risāla Qushairiyya*, Maliji's edition. Cairo 1319, p. 160.

and conversely:

One of the saints saw in sleep a hideous form, and he said, "Who art thou?" It answered, "I am thy misdeeds!" He said, "And how can I be delivered from thee?" It said, "By much calling down of blessing on the Prophet." *al-Ḥirzu 'l-manī'*, As-Suyūṭī, p. 23.

Muḥammad said: Gabriel came to me and said, "O Muḥammad, he who passes Ramaḍān without obtaining forgiveness and enters the Fire shall be banished from God Most High." And I said, "Amen." Then he said, "He who sees his parents or one of them and behaves without filial piety, when he dies and enters the Fire shall be banished from God Most High." And I said, "Amen." Then he said "He who, when thou art mentioned, fails to call down blessing on thee, when he enters the Fire shall be banished from God Most High." And I said, "Amen." *Fatḥu 'r-Rasūl*, M. 'Uthmān al-Mirghanī, p. 13.

And Ubayy b. Ka'b said, "O Apostle of God, many a time do I call down blessings on you for love of you. How much of my prayer shall I devote to you?" He said, "What you will." Ubayy said, "A quarter?" He said, "What you will, but if you do more it will be for your good." He said, "Half?" The Prophet said, "What you will, but if you do more it will be well for you." He said, "Two-thirds?" The Prophet said, "What you will, but if you do more it will be for your good." Then Ubayy said, "I will devote my whole prayer to you." The Prophet replied, "Then your anxieties will be met and your sins forgiven." Ibid., p. 12, note.

The Meaning of Ṣallā 'alā

Ṣallā 'alā with the general meaning "to pray for" is found in the Qur'ān (9.103) where Muḥammad is told to pray for (perhaps with this is included the sense of praying *over*) misdoers who have at length made application to enter Islam. In Christian Arabic the same phrase is used in the passage in James 5.14 where the sick man is told to send for the elders of the Church and they will pray over him[1] (here of course including the sense of for him). It is used in the Qur'ān (9.85) and in tradition for some kind of funeral prayer, whether that means praying over or for the dead man, or both. Our prayer-manuals use it for Muḥammad's prayers for *himself*.

That which the greatest of lords prayed for his noble self. *Fatḥu 'r-Rasūl*, p. 3.

[1] *Ṣallā 'alā* is here used both in the modern versions and also in a ninth- or tenth-century manuscript in the convent of St Katherine on Mt Sinai. (Gibson Catalogue, No. 154.)

But in the Qur'ānic verse which is basic for the whole of this devotion, the *ṣalātu 'ala 'n-nabī* is described as the action of God and His angels.

> "Verily God and His Angels call down blessing on (*yuṣallūna 'alā*) the Prophet. O ye who have believed, call down blessing on him and greet him with peace." (33.56.)

Here then is a universal communion in honouring Muḥammad:

> God Most High informed His worshippers of the rank which His Prophet holds with Him in the heavenly host, by praising Him in the presence of the angels of access, and by the *ṣalāt* of those angels for Him. Then He commanded *ṣalāt* and a greeting of peace from the people of the world below, so that the people of both worlds, above and below, might unite in His praise. . . .
>
> The honour with which God Most High honours Muḥammad is fuller and more universal than that with which He honoured Adam when He commanded the angels to prostrate themselves before Him, for it is not possible that God Himself took part with the angels in that earlier honouring. *al-Ḥirzu 'l-manī'*, p. 12.

There lies the rub. Some explanation must be given of the word *ṣalātun 'alā* which covers an activity in which God Himself takes part. We do not attempt to trace the history of Muslim thought on God's *ṣalāt* but only to note the explanations in our collection of manuals.

The early suggestion that God's *ṣalāt* means His forgiveness (al-Baiḍāwī in *Qur.* 2.152 gives the sense of forgiveness) is quoted but glided over in favour of the more acceptable idea that it means His magnifying of His servant.

> It has been transmitted to us from Ibn 'Abbās that it means that God praises your Prophet and forgives him and commands the angels to ask forgiveness for him. *al-Ḥirzu 'l-manī'*, as-Suyūṭī, p. 114.
>
> Opinions differ as to the meaning of *ṣalāt*. It is said that from God its meaning is mercy and complaisance, and from angels and men petition and asking forgiveness. And it is said that the *ṣalāt* of God is His mercy and the *ṣalāt* of angels prayer for blessing. And it is said that the *ṣalāt* of God is His mercy combined with magnifying and that of the angels is asking for forgiveness, and that of men, humble beseeching and petition. And it is said that God's *ṣalāt* for His prophets is praise and magnifying while His *ṣalāt* for others is His mercy.
>
> Ibn al-'Arabī said: *Ṣalāt* from God is mercy, and from human beings and others, angels and jinn, it is bowing and prostration and petition and praise, and from birds and owls it is praise. Each creature knows his own *ṣalāt* and

tasbīḥ . . . and al-Ḥalīmī set forth the meaning of God's *ṣalāt* for His prophet as His magnifying of him. *Fatḥu 'l-karīmi 'l-khāliq*, 'Alī al-Makkī, p. 15.

This last meaning is preferred because, with the sense of "magnifying",

> One meaning can be given to the word *ṣalāt* whether it is attributed to God or to angels or to the believers who are commanded to it. Ibid., loc. cit.

Perhaps the happiest English translation that can be used alike of God, angels, and men, is "to call down blessing upon . . .".

One form of the *ṣalātu 'alā 'n-nabī* asks God to take our place in this blessed action, just as God is frequently asked to reward the Prophet on behalf of his people.

> And replace us, with Thy pure and generous favour, in calling down blessing on him. *aṣ-Ṣalātu 'l-ghaibiyya*, Aḥmad at-Tījānī.

But here another explanation is felt to be necessary and is found in several of the manuals as follows:

> If you say, what is the explanation of the fact that although God commands us to call down blessing on the Prophet, we yet say, "O God call down blessing on Muḥammad," asking God to call down blessing instead of doing so ourselves, I reply that this is because the Prophet is pure, without blemish or failing, while we have both blemishes and failings. How shall one full of blemishes and failings call down blessing on the pure and perfect Prophet? Therefore we ask God to call down blessing on him, that the blessing may be called down by a pure God on a pure Prophet. *Fatḥu 'l-karīmi 'l-khāliq*, 'Alī al-Makkī.

After all explanations the worshippers feel themselves in the presence of a mystery on which some have loved to ponder, picturing a Divine *ṣalāt* continuous from before all worlds, in the *miḥrāb* of the essence of the Divine Being. Others have dwelt on it as a communion of love, "the calling down of blessing by the Beloved on his beloved". (Aḥmad at-Tījānī.)

> Call down blessing on him with that *ṣalāt* with which Thou didst call down blessing on him in the *miḥrāb* of Thy transcendent holiness and the Ipseity of Thine intimacy. *aṣ-Ṣalātu 'l-ghaibiyya*, Aḥmad at-Tījānī.

For Others than Muḥammad

While the overwhelming mass of this devotion is reserved for Muḥammad, its pattern sentence "O God call down blessing on our Lord Muḥammad *and on his family*", opens the door for a wider use.

It is extended to other prophets, and by Shī'a books to all the 'Alids. Shī'a writers prefer the form "On Muḥammad and his family" to "and upon his family", which might place the family in a different category.

> May God call down blessing on Muḥammad and on his family and his companions and his wives and his descendants and the members of his house [i.e. his descendants][1] morning and evening. And bless and greet with peace, O God, him and his father Abraham Thy Friend, and David Thy Caliph, and Moses Thine Interlocutor, and 'Īsā Thy Spirit, and Isaac Thy Sacrifice, and all their brethren the Prophets and Apostles. *Wirdu 'l-Asḥār*, Muṣṭafā al-Bakrī, p. 61.

The mention here of Isaac instead of Ishmael is surprising. Such lists of blessings on prophets are common, e.g. *Wirdu 's-saḥr* of Aḥmad al-Mar'āshī, or that which 'Abd al-Wahhāb ash-Sha'rānī is said to have learnt from al-Khiḍr (*Majmū'atu 'l-aḥzāb*, p. 196).

Similar callings down of blessing on Muḥammad's "brother Gabriel" and on all the angels are often found:

> O God, call down blessing on Thine Angels of Access and on Thy purified Prophets and Thine Apostles sent forth as messengers, and on the Bearers of the Throne, and on Gabriel and Michael and the Angel of Death, and Raḍwān treasurer of Paradise, and Mālik treasurer of the Fire, and Raumān and Munkar and Nakīr. And call down blessing on the noble Recording Angels, and call down blessing on all the people of Thine obedience, people of heaven and people of earth. *Ṣalātu Kunūzi 'l-Asrār*, 'Abd Allah al-Fāsī in *Fatḥu 'r-Rasūl*, p. 51.

The Prophet's family, always included in the blessing formula, are in *Dalā'ilu 'l-khairāt* spiritualized in a manner strongly reminiscent of the Gospels. (Mark 3.33–5):

> It was said to the Apostle of God, "Who are the family of Muḥammad whom we are enjoined to love and honour and treat with piety?"
>
> He said, "The people who hearken and fulfil their dues, whosoever believes in me and is true to me."
>
> It was said, "And what are the signs by which they may be known?"

[1] Evidently a widely used explanation. In *al-Ḥirzu 'l-Manī'*, as-Suyūṭī says that he could read this explanation in *Sharḥ muqaddimāti Abī 'l-Laith* of al-Imām Muṣṭafā 't-Turkumānī. Goldziher quotes the same passage as from *Al-As'ila wa 'l-Ajwiba* of Aḥmad b. Muḥammad al-'Abbāsī, a ninth-century Egyptian catechism (*Über die Eulogien der Mohammadaner, Z.D.M.G.*, vol. 50, p. 97).

He said, "The preference of love for me over all other love, and inward occupation with the remembrance of me, second only to the remembrance of God." *Dalā'ilu 'l-khairāt*, p. 21.

"The Family" in prayer means the whole community, although there should be a reference of special respect to his relatives. *al-Fatḥu 'r-rabbānī*, M. 'Abd Allah b. Ḥasanain, p. 66.

The spiritualizing of Muḥammad's family makes it possible to include all believers in the prayer of blessing, and this blessing of the whole family is a kind of spiritual almsgiving.

Muḥammad said, "If any Muslim has nothing wherewith to give alms, let him say in his petition, O God call down blessing on Muḥammad Thy servant and apostle, and call down blessing on the believers, men and women, and the Muslims, men and women. For that (petition) will be to him a giving of the legal alms." *Fatḥu 'r-rasūl*, M. 'Uthmān al-Mirghanī, p. 32.

Rewards of Taṣliya

No part of Muslim devotion is more of the people, more full of popular anecdote and traditions quoted without the dignified support of *isnād*. These may be trite and homely like that which says that the best way of finding a lost object is to say *ṣallā 'llāhu 'alā'n-nabī*. But for the most part they deal with the *ṣalāt* as a means to forgiveness of sins, and of escape from the terrors of the tomb and the Judgment Day to the joys of Paradise. We quote only a few examples from the lush growth of these popular sayings.

Forgiveness of Sins

Muḥammad said: Gabriel came to me one day saying, "Muḥammad, I have brought you such good news as I never brought to anyone before. It is that God Most High announces to you that any one of your people who calls down blessing upon you three times will have his sins forgiven; if he be standing, ere he sits down; if he be sitting, ere he rises up." *Fatḥu 'r-rasūl*, p. 13.

It is said that written on the base of the Throne are the words: I have mercy on him that yearns for Me; I give to him that asks of Me; and whoso approaches Me calling down blessing on Muḥammad I forgive him his faults be they as the foam of the sea. *Dalā'ilu 'l-khairāt*, p. 17.

It is narrated in a tradition that there was in Banū Isrā'īl a man given to excesses. And when he died they cast out his body. But God said by inspiration to his prophet Moses that he should wash the body and pray over it (*ṣalli 'alayhi*), "for I have forgiven him". Moses said, "Why hast Thou so done?" He said, "The man one day opened the Torah and found in it the name of Muḥammad and he called down blessing on him and for that blessing I have forgiven him his sins." *al-Ḥirzu 'l-manī'*, p. 73.

And, though dignified as a tradition, a real folk-story:

I heard a man in the Ḥaram at Mecca most abundant in his calling down of blessing on the Prophet, wherever he was, in the Ḥaram, or at Mount 'Arafat, or at Minā. I said, "O man, every prayer station has its appointed form of words. How is it that you do not employ yourself in petitions or offer performances of the prayer-rite to the extent that you call down blessing on the Prophet?" And he said, "I came as a pilgrim from Khorasān to this House, my father travelling with me. And when we reached Kūfa he fell ill, and his sickness increased. He died, and I covered his face with a veil and left him for a time. When I came back I unveiled his face that I might look on it and lo! it had taken on the form of a donkey's face. When I saw that, I was deeply impressed and disturbed and terribly grieved. And I said to myself, 'How can I display my father to the people (at the funeral prayers) in this condition which has come over him?' And I sat down beside him full of care. And sleep overcame me, and while I slept, behold I saw what seemed to me a man entering our room; and, coming to where my father lay, he uncovered his face and gazed at him, then covered it again. Then he said to me, 'Why so greatly troubled?' And I said, 'How should I not be concerned when this trial has come upon my father?' Then he drew back the cover from my father's face and behold it was like the rising moon.

"And I said to that man, 'By God, who art thou whose coming was thus blessed?' He said, 'I am the Chosen One', and when he said that I rejoiced greatly and caught hold of the hem of his garment and raised it on my hand saying, 'By God's truth, my Lord the Apostle of God, wilt Thou not explain to me this story?'

"He said, 'Your father used to take usury, and by God's command usurers shall have their faces changed to asses' faces at death, either in this world or the next, but it was your father's custom to call down blessing on me a hundred times every night before he lay down on his bed. And when he was exposed to this trial for his usury, the angel came to me who reports the doings of my people and informed me of what had happened to him and I besought God, who gave me the right to intercede for him.'

"Then I awoke and uncovered my father's face, and there it was like the moon when it is full, and I praised and thanked God and made my father ready and buried him and sat down by his grave for an hour. And as I was half asleep and half awake I heard a voice calling, 'Dost thou know the cause of this grace done to thy father?' I said, 'No.' The voice said, 'Its cause was his *Ṣalāt* and *salām* on the Apostle of God', and he enjoined me never to forsake the calling down of blessing on the Apostle of God under any condition or in any place." *al-Ḥirzu 'l-manī'*, as-Suyūṭī, pp. 120, 121.

Relief from the Terrors of the Tomb

A calling down of blessing which widens the narrowness of the tomb and solaces for me its loneliness and which will be companionable to me in my grave. *Fatḥu 'r-rasūl*, M. 'Uthmān al-Mirghanī, p. 130.

And in the niche of the tomb there will be spaciousness for thee, and a garden of rest a creation within it. The pleasaunces of that garden are freedom and it is lofty, magnified by the calling down of blessing on Muḥammad. *Tashṭīru 'l-qasīdati 'l-ḥaḍramiyya*, anon.

A curious thought about the after-death efficacy of the *ṣalātun 'alā 'n-nabī* is that it will create a passage between the believer's tomb and the Tomb of the Prophet.

A calling down of blessing by which there may be for me a road from my grave to the Prophet's Tomb. *Fatḥu 'r-rasūl*, p. 130.

Relief from the Terrors of Judgment

Muḥammad said: When a man is ordered to the Fire I shall say, "Bring him back to the scales," and I shall add to the scale (of his good deeds) something small as a finger tip, and that is his calling down of blessing on me. And the scale will be balanced and the cry will go up, "Happy is so and so." *al-Ḥirzu 'l-manī'*, p. 94.

A Reward of Glory

It is related that after the death of al-'Abbās Aḥmad ibn Manṣūr, a man of Shīrāz saw him standing in the miḥrāb of the mosque of that city, clad in a robe of honour and crowned with a jewelled diadem. And the man said to al-'Abbās, "What did God do with you?" He said, "He forgave me and honoured me and crowned me and gave me entrance to Paradise." He said, "And why?" al-'Abbās replied, "Because I was so abundant in blessing the Prophet of God." *Fatḥu 'r-rasūl*, p. 72.

And God Most High will say, "Oh My angels, here is one of My servants who abounded in calling down blessing on My Beloved. By My Might and Majesty and Generosity and Glory and Exaltedness, we will give him for every letter of his *ṣalāt* a palace in Paradise, and he shall come to Me on the Resurrection Day under the banner of Muḥammad, the light of his face like the shining of the moon when it is full, and his hand in the hand of Muḥammad My Beloved." *Dalā'ilu 'l-khairāt*, p. 124.

Spiritual Values

But the worshippers have seen in this devotion other and more inward values. That double *ṣalāt* of heaven and earth announced in the basic Qur'ān verse, gives to the believer's *ṣalāt* a semi-sacramental character, for it is an earthly and audible sign of a heavenly and potent activity. The humble little act of the earthly *ṣalāt* is believed, as we have seen, to set in motion the heavenly forces "and move the Hand that moves the world to bring salvation down". A phrase of such potency is felt in popular religion to be more full than most of mysterious half-magical *baraka*; but more spiritual minds see it as an inward purification and education, even a stepping-stone to the very presence of God.

A calling down of blessing which disciplines our (lower) selves with the best of discipline. . . .

A calling down of blessing which saves us from pleasures and lusts. . . .

A calling down of blessing which helps us to perform the prescribed ritual. . . . *ad-Durru 'l-fā'iq*, Muṣṭafā al-Bakrī.

A calling down of blessing, the light of which irradiates our hearts and spirits and minds, and of which the secrets are intermingled in our total being and our inmost life. *Yāqūtu 'l-ḥaqā'iq*, Aḥmad at-Tījānī.

And make our calling down of blessing on him a key, and by it open to us O Lord, the veil of acceptance, and accept, by the blessing of my Beloved (M), the litanies and invocations which I now recite, and my love and magnifying of Thyself. *Tashṭīru 'l-qasīdati 'l-ḥaḍramiyya*, anon.

Vision of the Prophet

But the most characteristic thought about this Muḥammad-centred devotion is that it is a sovereign means of vision of the Prophet and communion with him. His people rest assured that he appreciates each individual calling down of blessing upon him.

Muḥammad said: "No one greets me with peace without God returning my spirit (to my body) that I may respond to his greeting." *Adhkār*, an-Nawawī.

It was said to the Apostle of God: "Wilt thou see the blessing of those who call down blessing on thee, even though they are absent from thee or live after thy time? What is their standing with thee?" He said, "I hear the blessing of the company of my lovers and I know them, and the blessing of those who come after me is all made known to me." *Dalā'ilu 'l-khairāt*

He busies himself in calling down blessing on the Prophet until the Prophet's greatness masters his heart and pervades his inmost being. So that he is stirred by emotion at the mention of him, and the Prophet's graces are abundantly poured on him outwardly and inwardly, and he receives favours from no created being save the Prophet, and he sees him waking and sleeping and asks him concerning what he will. *ad-Durratu 'l-fardiyya,* Ahmad b. Sayyid as-Sanūsī.

Forms of the Ṣalātu ʿalā 'n-nabī

The forms of the *taṣliya* are an endless, intricate embroidery on the short basic phrase, ever seeking greater intensity, greater inclusiveness, greater duration. And when the worshipper has piled up all that his tongue can frame of extent and duration, he will ask God to double this!

My God, make every one of these blessings of the Prophet to exceed and excel the blessing of him by all and every the people of the heavens and of the earths who have ever blessed him, exceed and excel these as he excels all the rest of mankind through the excellence with which Thou hast favoured him. *Wirdu 'ṣ-ṣalāti 'l-kubrā,* ʿAbd al-Qādir al-Jīlānī.

Whole books are devoted to the embroidering of this one short sentence, many of them famous in Muslim devotion. Of these *Dalā'ilu 'l-khairāt,* the work of the Berber saint, Al-Jazūlī († 870/1465), is the most famous of all. It is known and recited from Morocco to Malaya, much as the *Imitation of Christ* is known in the Western Church. In Egypt its Litanies are often sung by the *fuqahā'* as the dead are carried to the grave.

Second only to it in fame are the *Ṣalawāti 'l-mashīshiyya,* the work of ʿAbdu 's-Salām ibn Mashīsh († circa 625/1227), the Moroccan saint whose tomb on Jabal ʿAlam attracts a huge annual pilgrimage. Like *Dalā'ilu 'l-khairāt* these *ṣalawāt* have had special commentaries devoted to them, and are used to-day by men of many types of piety.

Thus after morning and sunset prayer, the beginners in the *Shādhiliyya* Order are told to gather together in a circle for the orderly recitation "with attention of heart" of these *ṣalawāt,* after which follows the daily *dhikr*[1]. Similarly Aḥmad b. Idrīs († 1253/1837) founder of the Qādiriyya-Idrīsiyya Order and inspirer of the founders of the yet more popular Sanūsī and Mirghanī Orders, said that nothing equals the

[1] See *as-Silsilatu 'dh-dhahabiyya,* Muḥammad Aḥmad Al-Madanī.

ṣalawāt of Ibn Mashīsh except the prayers that were used by the Prophet or prayers that have a similar meaning.[1]

Forms connected with Saints

Shorter forms (*ṣīgha*) of the *ṣalātun 'alā 'n-nabī* are innumerable. Many are connected with the names of great saints of Islam. Thus 'Alī Zain al-'Ābidīn when he called down blessing on his grandfather, is held responsible for the much-used form:

> O God call down blessing on Muḥammad to the satisfaction of Thine own good pleasure, to the weight of Thy throne, to the inexhaustible supply of Thine imperishable words.

or again, Ma'rūf al-Karkhī, the famous saint of Baghdad, is said to have invented another much-used form:

> O God call down blessing on Muḥammad to the fullness of this world and the fullness of the next.

Named Forms

Many famous forms have their own names, we give only a few examples.

The Kamāliyya (beloved of the Bakriyya Order).

> O God bless and greet with peace and benediction our lord Muḥammad and his family—blessing to the number of the perfections of God and befitting those perfections.

The Fātiḥiyya (recommended above all other forms by Aḥmad at-Tijānī).

> O God call down blessing on our Lord Muḥammad, the Opener of what was closed, the Seal of that which went before, the Succourer of truth with truth, the Guide to the straight path, and on his family, as befits his status and his great position.

The Kalāmiyya (said to have been learnt by ash-Sha'rānī from al-Khiḍr).

> O God bless Muḥammad at the beginning of our speech
> O God bless Muḥammad in the course of our speech
> O God bless Muḥammad at the close of our speech

[1] Quoted in *Fatḥu 'r-rasūl*, p. 24.

The 'Aẓīmiyya (best-loved form of the Sanūsī Order).

My God, I ask Thee by that light of the Face of the great God which filled the bases of the Great Throne, and by which uprose the worlds of the Great God, to call down blessing on our Lord Muḥammad the great in rank, and on the family of the Prophet of the great God, etc.

Forms with Prophetic Sanction

But most characteristic of this devotion is the great number of forms for which a Prophetic blessing (generally given in a vision) is claimed by the author. It is interesting to note that these visions continue into modern times.

Space forbids our quoting more than one of these accounts of Prophetic sanction:

The Smile

It is narrated from aṭ-Ṭabarānī ... that in sleep he saw the Prophet as he was when he was among us and said to him, "Peace be to thee O Prophet and the mercy and blessing of God. God has inspired me with some words to say." And he said, "What are they?" "They are: O God ... bless Muḥammad to the number of those who have called down blessing on him and to the number of those who have not called down blessing on him. And bless Muḥammad even as Thou desirest that he shall be blessed."

And the Apostle of God smiled a smile that revealed his teeth, and light could be seen issuing from the spaces between his front teeth. *Fatḥu 'r-rasūl*, p. 24.

Note on Christian Equivalents

In countries where the *taṣliya* is on every lip from morning to night, the Christian Church should probably hearten herself by greater use, at least in her services, of ejaculations of praise to her Prophet, Priest, and King. The Urdu-speaking Church has a great popular cry for festivals, *melas*, processions and moments of emotion, *Jai Yishu*, Victory to Jesus! The common greeting of Christians in Chota Nagpur is *Yishu sahay*, "Jesus be your Helper!" Should the Arabic Church in her services return to the fundamental affirmation of the primitive Church, "Jesus is Lord"? Or should she, not only in her services, but in all moments of gladness, make fuller use of the old Hebrew joy-cry which is the closest equivalent to the *taṣliya*, *Hosanna*?

For indeed the *taṣliya* is the *Hosanna* of the Muslim world, with an almost parallel history. Like *Hosanna* (Save now!) the *taṣliya* is in form a prayer, but has taken to itself the value of an acclamation, a cry of praise, just as "God save the King!" in English hovers between the two meanings.

At what time in its history *Hosanna* became a popular acclamation is not clear, though the transition would be easy enough, from the fact of its use (with its context in Psalm 118.25,26) at an exultant moment in the joyful Feast of Tabernacles. We do not know whether "the people of the Hebrews" were consciously quoting the Psalm or only using a customary acclamation on the day when "the multitudes that went before, and that followed cried, saying, Hosanna to the Son of David" (Matt. 21.9), but the doings of that day consecrated *Hosanna* for ever to the Christ.

11 b

THE CALLING DOWN OF BLESSING: ABRAHAM AND ALL THE PROPHETS

Aṣ-ṣalātu 'l-ibrāhīmiyya

The form in almost universal use for the calling down of blessing on Muḥammad in the prayer-rite is that known as "The Abrahamic Blessings" (*aṣ-ṣalawāti 'l-ibrāhīmiyya*). It runs:

> O God call down blessing on Muḥammad and on the family of Muḥammad as Thou didst call down blessing on Abraham and on the family of Abraham. And bless Muḥammad and the family of Muḥammad as Thou didst bless Abraham and the family of Abraham, throughout the universe. Verily Thou art praiseworthy, glorious.

Two or sometimes three other lines are often added to these blessings, though not as a rule in the prayer-rite: "Show mercy . . . as Thou didst show mercy. Be compassionate . . . as Thou wast compassionate. Greet with peace . . . as Thou didst greet with peace." The Shī'a breviary extends it in one case beyond its traditional form:

> As Thou didst call down blessing on Idrīs and on Noah and on Elijah *aṣ-ṣaḥīfatu 's-sajjādiyya*, p. 413.

This introduction of the name of another Prophet into the sacred prayer-rite is based on *Qur.* 26.84, and still more for our writers on the traditional command of Muḥammad to use this particular form (traced to his orders in Aḥmad, ibn Ḥabbān, ad-Daraquṭnī). Such a command, together with that traditional morning prayer:

> I come this morning, a conformer to the religious practice of our Prophet Muḥammad and to the Church of our father Abraham, a monotheist, a Muslim. (*al-Wirdu 'sh-shāfī*, Yūsuf an-Nabhānī, and constantly as a morning prayer. Closely connected with *du'ā'u 't-tawajjuh* in the prayer-rite.)

raises the whole question of the position of Abraham and the other prophets in the devotional life of Islam.

Two trends are noticeable in the prayers in our manuals. The one, based on all the Qur'ānic stories of prophets, is to make list-prayers, naming them in a series, especially as exemplars in worship. Fuller meditations are found concerning a few of the prophets, especially Moses, which unfortunately, space forbids us to reproduce. There is singularly little, considering the high place allotted to him in the Qur'ān, concerning 'Īsā, and the list-prayers tend to break off before reaching him—possibly a conscious or unconscious reaction against Christian claims.

The second trend is towards a type of prayer or meditation based on the high doctrine of Muḥammad's personality and position, and glorifying him by placing all other prophets far beneath him, and in dependence on him.

This again leads to questionings as to the singling out of Abraham for mention in the prayer-rite together with one so exalted as Muḥammad, and various answers are given.

List-Prayers

These envisage Muḥammad as one of a family of prophets.

Call down blessing on our Lord Muḥammad the Beloved, and on his father Abraham the Friend, and on his brother Moses the Interlocutor, and on the Spirit of God 'Īsā the Faithful. *aṣ-Ṣaḥīfatu 's-sajjādīyya*, p. 481 (Shī'a).

Their names are recited in prayers. Thus in the favourite and endlessly re-printed devotion of Indian Muslims, *Ganj il-'arsh*:

Adam the Chosen One of God.
Noah the Delivered One of God.
Abraham the Friend of God.
Ishmael the Sacrifice of God.
Moses the Confidant of God.
David the Caliph of God.
'Īsā the Spirit of God.
Muḥammad the Apostle of God.

each Prophet has his special endowment (*ḥaẓẓ*) of virtue.

Liberality belongs to the Prophet of God, Abraham.

Satisfied acceptance (of God and His givings), belongs to the Prophet of God, Isaac.

Patient Endurance belongs to the Prophet of God, Job.

The making of signs belongs to the Prophet of God, Zachariah.

Expatriation to the Prophet of God, Joseph.

The wearing of wool (the ṣūfī garb) belongs to the prophet of God, Yaḥyā.

Wandering as a pilgrim belongs to the Prophet of God, 'Īsā.

Poverty belongs to the Prophet and Apostle of God our Beloved and Mediator. *Waṣiyya* of 'Abd al-Qādir al-Jīlānī in *al-Fuyūḍātu 'r-rabbāniyya*, p. 38.

In the above list the virtues are strongly ṣūfistic. The *ishāra* of Zachariah refers to a state of soul when it receives inward divine guidances, and the *ghurba* of Joseph to a state of separation from outward and inner possessions. The list is unusual in replacing Ishmael by Isaac. Though no one may aspire to the office of prophethood these virtues are imitable.

I ask Thee to form me on the fair pattern of Abraham and his companions when they said to their people, "We are clear of you and of what you worship." *Ṭahāratu 'l-qulūb*, ad-Dīrīnī, p. 97.

We may pray, too, to be their companions.

Make us, O Lord, the comrades of Muḥammad and Abraham Thy Friend and 'Īsā Thy Spirit. *Majmū'u tabāraka dhū 'l-'ulā*, p. 3.

In our manuals the prophets are often mentioned as examples of trials suffered and of God's deliverance, of prayers offered and answered.

Consider and understand the trials given to the prophets through the contradictions of their followers; as in the story of Adam with his sons, and Seth with his people; and Noah, when he said, "Oh my people, if my abode with you and my reminding of you through God's signs is heavy upon you, then in God do I trust, put together your case then and gather your associates" (*Qur. 10.7*), and Hūd and Ṣāliḥ with their people, and Abraham with Nimrod and with his father, and Jacob with his brother, and Joseph with his brethren, and Job with his trial, and Moses with the Children of Israel after they were saved from the sea. *al-'Aṭiyatu'l-haniyya*, 'Alī b. Ḥasan al-'Aṭṭās, p. 73.

They are examples of prayer.

Abraham used to hear the throbbing and boiling of his heart during his prayers. This is the fear of the Beloved, the Friend, in spite of all that has been given to him of honourable rank. Oh the wonder then that the heart of a man whose back is burdened with sin can ever be at rest! *Ṭahāratu 'l-Qulūb*, ad-Dīrīnī, p. 147.

But most of all are they patterns of answered prayer and of God's deliverance.

Thou who didst heal the plague of Job, Thou who didst ease the anxiety of Jacob, Thou who didst save Noah from the people of wrongdoing, Thou who didst save Lot from the people of vice, Thou who didst save Hūd from the people of 'Ād, Thou who didst save Muḥammad from the people of scorn. *Shī'a prayer of Nuṣfi Sha'bān.*

An answer! an answer, O my God! Thou who didst answer Noah when he called, Thou who didst succour Abraham against his foes, Thou who didst restore Joseph to Jacob, Thou who didst heal the plague of Job, Thou who didst grant the petition of Zachariah, and accept the praise of Dhū 'n-Nūn the son of Mattā. *Majmū'u aḥzābi wa-awrādi wa-ad'iya*, p. 108.

Thou who didst cleave the sea for Moses and give life to the dead for 'Īsā, who didst make the fire coolness and comfort for Abraham, call down blessing on our lord Muḥammad, and grant me from my affair relief and a happy issue. *Wirdu yawmi 's-sabt* in *Majmū'u aḥzābi wa-awrādi*, etc., p. 108.

So in ash-Shādhilī's *Ḥizbu 'l-baḥr* the unofficial but widely used *Itinerarium* of Islam:

Subdue to us this sea as Thou didst subdue the sea to Moses, the fire to Abraham, the mountains and iron to David, the wind and the devils and jinn to Solomon. And subdue to us every sea of Thine in earth and heaven, in the Kingdom of this world and the Kingdom supernal, the sea of this world and the sea of the other. And give us a favourable wind according to Thy knowledge, and be to us our Travel-Companion and replace us in the care of our families. *Ḥizbu 'l-baḥr.*

Muḥammad and the Other Prophets

In the second type of prayer, Muḥammad is made to gather up into his own person the privileges of all the other prophets.

Muḥammad the Law of the Torah of Moses and the Lexicon of the Injīl of 'Īsā. *Wirdu 'ṣ-ṣalāti 'l-kubrā*, 'Abd al-Qādir al-Jīlānī, p. 131.

He was Thy Friend before (Abraham) the Friend. He had converse with Thee before Moses the glorious. *al-Jawāhiru 'l-mustaẓharāt*, M. 'Uthmān al-Mirghanī, p. 150.

Adam knew him and made petition through him, and he (M.) took a covenant from all the Prophets to himself. He took the purity of Adam, the lamentation of Noah. A part of his teaching contains the knowledge of Idrīs. Included in his ecstatic experiences is the grief of Jacob. Within the mystery of his ecstasy is the endurance of Job. Enfolded in his bosom is the weeping of David. A part only of the riches of his soul exceeds the wealth of Solomon. He gathered into himself Abraham's friendship with God. He attained the converse of Moses, God's interlocutor, and was more exalted than the highest Kings. He excels the Prophets as the sun excels the moon, the ocean the drop. *Ṭahāratu 'l-qulūb*, ad-Dīrīnī, p. 40.

So he is seen as supreme over prophet and saint alike; and all their excellence is said to come by way of him.

Call down blessing on him whom Thou didst create from Thy light, and didst make his speech from Thy speech, and preferredst him over Thy prophets and Thy saints, and didst cause the perfection of all Thy saints to have its course from Thee to him and from him to them. *Wird 'ṣ-ṣalātu 'l-kubrā*, 'Abd al-Qādir al Jīlānī, p. 101.

Thou (Muḥammad) art he through whom, after his fall, Adam made successful petition, he who was thy father! And through thee the Friend made supplication and his fire was made coolness, dying away in the light of thy splendour. . . . And through thee the Christ came, bringing good news, announcing the attributes of thy beauty, praising thy exaltation. *al-Qaṣīdatu 'n-nu'māniyya*, anon.

And all of them in comparison with the Apostle of God are as a spoonful of the ocean, a single spear of the rain, standing before him with the limitation of their drop of knowledge, their (spear) point of wisdom. And he it is who perfects its meaning and its form. *Al-Burda*, Al-Būṣīrī.

Why the Abrahamic Blessings?

To western readers, conscious of the constant preoccupation of the Qur'ān with Abraham, of Muḥammad's earnest endeavour to vindicate his faith as the true faith of Abraham, there is little of surprise in a request that Abraham's blessings should be his. But for those to whom Muḥammad is the "unique Beloved", eclipsing all other prophets, who are but his spiritual dependents, the question arises as to whether the request that God shall bless Muḥammad and his family as He blessed Abraham and his family is not demeaning to the former?

To these questions as-Suyūṭī supplies the answers in *al-Ḥirzu 'l-manī'*, answers which reveal some of the thoughts of Muslim worshippers concerning Abraham.

(*The question stated.*) By common consent the thing compared is less than that to which it is compared and yet here the reverse is the case, for Muḥammad alone is greater than the whole family of Abraham and than Abraham—even more so when the family of Muḥammad is added!

(*A suggested answer.*) Muḥammad said this (i.e. ordered this form of blessing) before he knew that he was greater than Abraham; for Muslim traced a tradition from Anas that a man said to the Prophet. "O Best of Creation," and he replied, "That is Abraham." Ibn al-'Arabī, in reference to this question, said that Muḥammad asked for equality with Abraham and commanded his community to ask for this. And God, unasked, granted him more—that his excellence should exceed that of Abraham.

(*Objection to this answer.*) It is objected that had this been the case Muḥammad would have altered the form of the prayer when he knew that he was greater than Abraham.

Further Suggested Answers

The singling out of these two (Abraham and Muḥammad) in the *ṣalāt* is because Abraham is the Friend and Muḥammad the Beloved. Or it is because Abraham was the announcer of the sacred Law, when God Most High said to him, "And proclaim among men the pilgrimage, they will come to thee on foot and on every clean-run camel" (*Qur.* 22.27), while Muḥammad was the announcer of the whole practice of religion, according to the word of God Most High, "Our Lord, we have heard a caller calling to faith" (*Qur.* 34.192).

Or because of Abraham's petition to God, Mighty and Majestic, when in a dream he saw Paradise, and on its trees written *la ilāha illā 'llāh, wa Muḥammadu rasūlu 'llāh* and he asked Gabriel the significance of that "Muḥammad", and was informed by him concerning Muḥammad and his spiritual position. Then Abraham said, "O Lord make my name current on the tongues of the community of Muḥammad," as He said, "And give me a goodly mention among them that come after." (*Qur.* 26.84.)

Or because Abraham was of a higher excellence than the rest of the prophets.

Or because God named him the Father of Believers, in His word, "The nation of your Father Abraham". (*Qur.* 22.78.)

Or because of the command of the Prophet to follow Abraham, especially in the elements of the Pilgrimage.

Or because when he built the House (the Meccan sanctuary) Abraham prayed saying, "O Lord, whosoever of the old men of the community of Muḥammad shall make pilgrimage to this House, bestow on him (a bestowal) from me and from my household."

Then Ishmael prayed (similarly) for the full-grown men; then Isaac for the youths; then Sarah for the free-women; then Hagar for the bond-women. And for this reason Abraham and his household are singled out for mention.

(But after all the two prophets are not compared.)

The comparison is only concerned with the calling down of blessing in the two cases, there is no comparison of the rank of the two prophets. *al-Ḥirzu 'l-manī'*, pp. 36, 37.

12a

THE WORSHIP OF PENITENCE: THE SINNER DESTITUTE BEFORE HIS LORD

Al-mudhnibu 'l-faqīr li rabbihi

The prayer-rite is a rite of praise, and penitence has no place in its *arkān*, but this act of praise is performed by sinful men, and it is a generally followed *sunna* (rule of conduct) to insert a forgiveness-seeking prayer.[1]

> When he performs his prayer-rite the last thing he shall say between the *tashahhud* and the greeting of peace is: "O God forgive[2] me my former and my latter (sins), my open and my secret (sins) and my extravagances and what Thou dost know, for Thou art the Former and the Latter." *Adhkāru 'n-Nawawī*, p. 33. (Tradition, Muslim from 'Alī.)

This brings us to the question of the sense of sin and the worship of penitence in Islam.

It is a common remark of Europeans living in Arab lands that a sense of personal sinfulness is rare amongst the people of Islam. That this should be a first impression is not surprising in Near Eastern countries where popular etiquette is not averse from the happy announcement of one's own good qualities, and where a correspondent will send to a well-known paper such a prayer as the following:

> Not for a day was I a sinner or an evil doer that this bitter, painful punishment should be laid on me. But I call Thee to witness, O Lord, that I have known nothing all my life but feelings of love, compassion, mercy, sincerity, manliness, chastity, purity, cleanness, honour, nobility, and absorption in love of country and humanity. These are all the sins or some of the sins for

[1] The form varies. In the Ḥanafite rite the forgiveness-seeking for parents is commonly used here.

[2] The modern Aḥmadiyya movement of India appears to have an objection to the word "forgive", and in its translations of this prayer for missionary use renders it by some such phrase as "make me to prosper".

which, and in the prosecution of which, I meet with censure and malice. *'Abd al-Hādī al-Ḥadīdī* in *Rawza 'l-Yūsuf*, Cairo, Oct. 1936.

Pride is a universal disease of the human heart, and may be less deeply rooted in the man of naïve conceit than in one too proud to lay himself open to the charge of conceit. Looking deeper we may find the sense of sin alive in Muḥammad's community.

On this point Dr Kraemer writes: "The curious thing is that, in many utterances and institutions of practical religious life in Islam, the need for forgiveness and redemption is breaking through. For instance, Indonesian Mohammedans practically put the visit to the sepulchre of the prophet in Medina above the pilgrimage to Mecca, thus coming into flat contradiction with one of the fundamental tenets of Islam. They regard this visit to Medina as an effectual means of cleansing from sin."

With these remarks we turn to see what the manuals teach us about the worship of penitence.

The Muslim and Christian worshipper alike regard themselves as set in a world of temptation and testing (*ibtilā'*) and exposed to forces urgent to evil outside themselves as well as within.

> My God, Thou hast created me, a body, and with it hast given to me instruments of obedience or disobedience, and hast appointed for me in my own nature a soul clamant for selfish ends, and after this Thou hast said to me, "Abstain, my servant!" Through Thee (only) can I guard my innocence. Keep me then from evil. Through Thee (only) can I be shielded from sin. Then do Thou keep me. *Munājātun* attributed to 'Alī Zain al-'Ābidīn, *Aṣ-ṣahīfatu 's-sajjādiyya*, p. 159.
>
> When Iblīs was cast out God cursed him; and lo he said, "O Lord by Thy Might and Majesty my desire for the son of Adam shall never cease so long as the spirit remains in him." And God, Mighty and Majestic, said, "By My Might and Majesty I will not deprive him of the opportunity of repentance so long as the spirit remains in him." *Ṭahāratu 'l-qulūb*, ad-Dīrīnī, p. 98.

The Most Dreaded Sins

While the prayer-manuals do not contain such detailed and searching confessions as those of the Jewish Day of Atonement, it is yet possible to see what forms of sin are most dreaded by the Muslim conscience. There is a well-known division (based on *Qur.* 4.30), not unlike that in Latin Christianity between mortal and venial sins, of sins into "great and small". In the life of conscience this does not play a very great part, for the educated conscience learns to find in all sin that estrangement from God which is mortal. "The good deeds of the ordinary righteous man are evil deeds for those close to God." (*Risāla Qushairiyya*, p. 35.) Moreover, the Muslim Church does not appear to have decided officially on her list of *kabā'ir*. Our manuals quote a tradition pointing to the early days of the Islamic community.

> (From Abū Huraira.) The Apostle of God said avoid the seven mortal sins. He was asked, "And which are they, O Apostle of God?" He said, "Associating aught with God, and wizardry, and the killing of men, which God has forbidden except with right, and consuming the property of orphans, and taking usury and absenting himself on the day of a military expedition and calumny against believing well-conducted women." *Ṭahāratu 'l-qulūb*, ad-Dīrīnī, p. 99.

The same writer quotes a summary of pious opinion on the subject:

> Abū Ṭālib al-Makkī said: "I collected them from all the sayings of the Companions, and I found them to be four sins of the heart, which are associating (aught else) with God Most High, and persistent disobedience towards Him, and despair of God's mercy and assurance against His stratagems. And four sins of the tongue which are false witness, and slander of chaste women unaware, and perjury which is an oath sworn with the determination to lie, and scoffing to which God has attached the result of corruption. And three sins of the belly, the drinking of wine, and consuming the property of orphans, and eating of the fruit of usury while knowing that he does so. And two of the secret parts, adultery and unnatural vice. And two of the hands, murder and stealing, and one of the feet, escaping from service in an army, and one of the whole body, disobedience to parents." Ibid., p. 100.

But these lists do not appear in confession and in prayer against temptation. In most of the manuals the only named sins—named rather in anxious prayer against them than in confession—are those sins against the Godhead most horrible to the Muslim soul, *shirk*, sin against the Unity, the sin of sins, and *kufr*, the sin of impious unbelief against *Al-Qayyūm* the Self-existent One, and His manifestations in Islam, a sin which carries with it not mere absence of belief but that coupled with ingratitude.

If for the men of the Chinese civilization the essential sin was that which broke the due proportions of the rightly adjusted life; if for an

African, now rapidly passing, the essential sin was that which broke the unity of the tribe; if for Israel of old the essential sin was unfaithfulness to Jehovah's covenant; for Islam, not only yesterday but to-day, the essential sin is unfaithfulness to that revelation of the Divine Unity which it is Islam's business to proclaim with passionate insistence. More than 150 times does the root *sharak* echo through the Qur'ān with terrible protest and threat whether against Arab idolatry or a misconceived doctrine of the Trinity. This sin, if conscious, may be unforgivable. How must the believer guard against slipping into this horrible pit!

> And Thou art the Forgiver of every sinful action save only *kufr* and *ishrāk* of terrible results. (Poem by M. Ibn ash-Shahīd of Algiers in *Majmū'u 'l-qaṣā'idi wa'l-ad'iya.*)

A constantly printed little prayer is the following, attributed to the Prophet:

> I take refuge with Thee lest I should fall knowingly into the sin of associating aught with Thy Godhead and I ask Thy forgiveness for such sin unknown to me. *Majmū'u 'l-wirdi 'l-'āmm*, p. 87, and frequently in the manuals.

The saints, with their spiritual penetration saw the essential nature of this sin of association where there was no formal expression of it.

> Ash-Shādhilī said: O God I repent towards Thee; then give me refuge and bind me and strengthen me and succour me and stabilize me and keep me clear from sin and shelter me in the midst of mankind and do not disgrace me in the eyes of Thine Apostle. Then it was said to me, "Thou art an associator (*mushrik*)." I said, "How?" And it was said to me, "Thou didst fear disgrace in the eyes of created beings; thou art only afraid of being put to shame before men, but thy heart should be dependent on God, not on men." *al-Mafākhiru 'l-'aliyya*, Aḥmad b. 'Ibād.
>
> O God, if without my knowledge impious unbelief (*kufr*) entered into my surrender (*islām*) to Thee, I repent and say with singleness of heart, "There is no god but God and Muḥammad is the Apostle of God." O God, if without my knowledge associationism (*shirk*) entered into my declaration of Thy Unity, I repent and say with singleness of heart, "There is no god but God and Muḥammad is the Apostle of God." *Ḥizbu 'l-ḥifẓ*.

The ordinary man, less prone to refinements of spiritual thought, is thankful enough to find prescriptions against *shirk* or *kufr*, and these are not wanting:

> Say *yā aiyuhā 'l-kāfirūn* (*sūra* 109) then sleep on thy right side for this is immunity from *shirk*. *Rabī'u 'l-fu'ād*, 'Abd Allāh ash-Sharqāwī, p. 135.

and against *kufr*, *ḥamd* may be efficacious; does it not include that element of thankfulness the lack of which is part of the blackness of *kufr*?

> Praise be to God—a praise the blessed power of which makes us safe from unbelief. *Majmū'atu 'l-wirdi 'l-'āmm*, p. 53.

The other words in our manuals descriptive of sin will be found set out in vocabulary form in Chapter 12b. Here we may note that in studying this vocabulary the reader accustomed to Christian Arabic will remark the absence of a group of familiar words concerning the vileness, corruption, and defilement of sin—such words as *khubth*, *najāsa*, *danas*, and *fasād*. These words, so common in Christian confessions of sin, and necessary in Bible translations to represent such words as *aselgeia*, *akatharsia*, have hardly found their way into the Muslim prayer-manuals, although *khabīth* and *fasād* are Qur'ānic words, and the Prophet is often described as *ma'ṣūm min al-adnās*, "immaculate".

THE SENSE OF SIN

As men grow in depth they pass from the consciousness of sins to the consciousness of sinfulness, of an inward state or sway of sin. The Arabic language has no love of abstract nouns, preferring verbal expressions.[1] But the absence of a noun need not imply the absence of an experience. The Old Testament, for instance, no more than our prayer-manuals, has any word corresponding to the English use of "conscience". Yet the fifty-first Psalm is for all men the cry of stricken conscience. The absence of convenient nouns demands a rather close scrutiny of Arabic devotions to note the expression of the sense of inward sinfulness.

[1] Here is one of the difficulties of New Testament translators in rendering into Arabic a language rich in abstract nouns. Such words as *adikēmata, erga asebeias, hamartēmata* pass much more readily into Arabic than *adikia, asebeia, hamartia.*

Thou God Seest Me

One common thought, that of the all-seeing eye of God, is clearly a stirrer of conscience. Already in Israel and in Christianity it had proved so.[1] In these prayers it is based on that strong recurring note of the Qur'ān, beating like a drum through the book, *wa 'llāhu bi mā ta'malūna baṣīr*, "God is the observer of your doings." The thought that the all-seeing eye notes wrong within us of which we ourselves are unaware brings us very near to the sense of *sinfulness* as against merely having-committed-sins. Whatever theology may have striven to express of remote transcendence, these Muslim worshippers have the sense that all is naked and open before the eyes of One *with whom they have to do.*

Nothing was ever invisible nor will be invisible to Thee: from Thee no secret is hid, nor does aught stray away from Thee under cover of darkness. *al-Ḥizbu 's-saifī*, and frequently in the manuals.

I beg Thy forgiveness for all that Thou knowest. For Thou knowest that of which we do not know, Thou being the knower of the unseen. *Dalā'ilu 'l-khairāt*, Ḥizb for Tuesday, and frequently in the manuals.

Fear

In the work of conscience, in Islam as in other religions, a sense of fear and danger has its part to play, drawn out, as always, by the thought of death:

And sincere repentance is always demanded from the worshipper, especially at bedtime for fear lest in that sleep he may draw his last breath. *Khaṭwa* to *al-Ḥusūnu 's-saba 'atu 'l-manī'a*, M. al-Fatḥī al-Marrākushī.

Indeed I know that any one of my sins is enough to bring on me Thy painful chastisement. *Du'ā'un fī qaḍā 'l-ḥawā'ij*, 'Alī Zain al-'Ābidīn.

O Lord old age and shame draw in on me, for carelessly I gave no thought to death.

O Lord my sins have blackened my record, and what can I do when that record is published?

O Lord Thou knowest my sins. Wide is Thy giving and destitute Thy servant. O Lord, these two have I obeyed, myself and Satan; these two I did not resist, I (am full of) hidden sin. *al-Qaṣīdatu 'l-muḍarra'*, Al-Būṣīrī.

[1] We may compare with the Qur'ānic *al-Baṣīr*, Hagar's, "Well of Him that liveth and seeth me," echoed so long after in the experience of another who had been seen beside a well, and who said, "Come see a man which told me all things that ever I did." (Gen. 16.14, John 4.29.)

This sense of fear is seen to be a salutary and desirable quality:

> The true believer sees his sin as a mountain overhanging him and dreads its fall on him. The hypocrite sees his sin as a fly that alighted on his face and which he brushed away. *Ṭahāratu 'l-qulūb*, ad-Dīrīnī, p. 103.

> The fire of fear burnt out the growth of concupiscence from our hearts. *Fatḥu 'r-rasūl*, M. 'Uthmān al-Mirghanī, p. 103.

> Give us a portion of the holy fear of Thee that will be a barrier between us and disobedience. *al-Munājātu 'l-injīliyyatu 'l-wusṭā*, 'Alī Zain al-'Ābidīn.

Against Thee Only Have I Sinned

How far do these prayers conceive of sin as *against* God? Can this thought, so rich and deep in Judaism with its sense of a covenant between the Lord and His worshippers, so rich and deep in Christianity with its sense of love exposing Itself to the wounding—find its place also in Islamic devotion, in spite of the stiffest doctrine of divine transcendence ever formulated?

At first sight one would say, No. The Qur'ānic shout of confidence that neither those who retire from battle nor those who reject the Prophet's message can injure God one whit (*3*.144,176,177) is often in the prayers caught up into a formulary of *tanzīh*.

> Thou whose empire suffers no loss from the disobedience of rebels, whose dominion is not increased by the faith of the affirmers of Unity. *al-munājātū 'l-injīliyyatu 'l-wusṭā*, 'Alī Zain al-'Ābidīn.

> O Thou whom sins harm not and who sufferest no loss in giving pardon. *Ḥizbu yawmi 'l-khamīs*, M. 'Uthmān al-Mirghanī.

Such phrases would seem to bring a strange sense of breakdown of communication between the sinner and the God who is *not* the Sinned Against. That word "against" was a bridge, if only where wrath and terror meet. Whatever theology may have to say, this is intolerably arid for personal religion. The experience of the worshipper belies it, and the prayer-manuals usually show much more kinship with another and warmer climate of the Qur'ān, a single *wird* sometimes combining both ways of thought. A sense of sinning *against* Allah is reached by the presupposition of a covenant between Him and the believer, a thought deeply embedded in the tissue of the Qur'ān. One of the commonest openings for a Muslim confession of sin is:

> I am Thy servant, and I have not been obedient to Thy covenant and promise. (Numerous uses in the manuals.)

Given a covenant between two parties, however unequal, the one can sin against the other. And this idea is extended in prayer to cover a more individual pact of spirit than any inherited share in some primitive pact with the pre-creation *ṣūra* of Adam, with Abraham or with the people of the *Sharī'a*.

> I ask Thy forgiveness for all that I promised Thee in my soul and then failed to fulfil.
>
> I ask Thy forgiveness for every work which I purposed to do for Thee alone and into which I admitted human respect. (Said to have been taught by al-Khiḍr to Muḥammad.)

And thus the author of *Dalā'ilu 'l-khairāt* can say:

> I have faults in that which is between me and Thee. *Dalā'ilu 'l-khairāt*, p. 57. See also the Shi'a prayers for Yawm 'Arafat.

So religion builds the bridge, that bridge of trembling hope and fear, which theology seemed likely to pull down. The sinner in these prayers does not conceive of himself as a child returning to his Father, but neither is he a lonely mortal before an unknowable and unresponding Remote.

> And if one of you loses delight in his converse with God or his religious observances let him betake himself to repentance and much seeking of forgiveness, for what happened to him is only the result of some sin into which he fell. *Rabī'u 'l-fu'ād*, 'Abdallah ash-Sharqāwī.
>
> O God Thou art not veiled from Thy creatures except when sin veils their sight of Thee. He who travels towards Thee is near to Thee except when the burden of sin separates him from Thee. O may my prayer for forgiveness make thin the veil of my sin. *Maṭālibu 'd-dunya wa 'l-ākhira*, 'Alī Zain al-'Ābidīn.

The Enemy Within

"The self urgent to evil" (*Qur.* 12.53) is the great Qur'ānic phrase for the lower nature that has to be mastered. Our prayers describe these urgings by two words constantly used with a sense of guilty malaise. *Hawā*,[1] predilection, inclination, "my own sweet will", waywardness

[1] *Hawā* has had a curiously variegated career. In those of our prayer-manuals which have a Shādhili descent it is used simultaneously for sinful inclinations that must be given no quarter, and for spiritual longing recognized and codified as an early stage in the "way" of the soul.

as of the wind (for whose wanderings the verb *hawā* is used), and *shahwa*, desire, appetite, passion, "carnal lust", not always in the literal sense but often also in the sense in which "carnal" is used in the New Testament for the thoughts and desires of the natural man. The prayers seem to echo that saying of Abū Muḥammad al-Jurairī, "He who is mastered by his lower self becomes a captive in the power of his selfish desires (*shahawāt*), confined in the prison of his own inclinations (*hawā*)." (*Risāla Qushairiyya*, p. 51.)

The classical Qur'ān text (79.40) about the conquest of *hawā*, "He who fears his Lord's assize and denies his soul its lower desires, for him Paradise shall be his place of repair," is turned in our manuals into a prayer, and again and again the prayers reflect the inward struggle.

> Make us those in whose hearts the door of selfish desire is locked. *Majmū'atu 'l-wirdi 'l-'āmm*, p. 8.
>
> Make us those who preoccupy themselves against selfish appetites (*shahawāt*) by the remembrance of Thee, and contend against the claims of greatness through clear knowledge (of Thee) and put out the fire of selfish desire (*hawā*) through the sprinkling of the water of life. *Al-munājātu 'l-injīliyyatu 'l-wusṭā*, 'Alī Zain al-'Ābidīn.

The Sinner's Weakness

The inward struggle results in a sense of weakness touchingly expressed in many of the prayers of deeper experience:

> I have lost my purpose, I am stripped of will, lacking in strength and power. . . . O God my soul is a ship wandering in the seas of (her own) will where there is no refuge and no shelter from Thee but in Thee. Appoint for her, O God, in the Name of God, her course and its harbour. *Ḥizbu 'l-fatḥiyya* and *Ḥizbu 'l-ḥifẓ*, 'Abd al-Qādir al-Jīlānī.
>
> My breast is oppressed, my thoughts wander, I am bewildered. Lord have mercy on one whose disease is great, whose cure is impossible to him, whose sickness increases while his means of healing decrease, whose strength lessens while his will grows stronger. Thou art his refuge and strength, his help and healing. *al-Ḥizbu 'l-kabīr*, 'Abd al-Qādir al-Jīlānī.

Sinfulness

Have we not in these prayers of the inner struggle a sense of sinfulness far more interior than the usual acknowledgment of *dhunūb*, and approaching that sense, so well known to Christians, of a sinful nature to be forgiven and redeemed as well as sinful acts? A phrase expressing natural bent (*inṭiwā'*) comes very close to this conception:

> I ask forgiveness of the great God for those forbidden things towards which my inmost thoughts inclined. *Majmū'atu 'l-wirdi 'l-'āmm*, p. 7.

The use of the word *'aib*, as though a moral defect resembled some blemish of the skin that one would fain cover from sight, has produced a curious sentence quoted in one of our manuals from 'Abd al-Wahhāb ash-Sha'rānī, which comes very near to implying a *state* of sinfulness. The picture is like Isaiah's description of his sinful nation. "From the sole of the foot even unto the head there is no soundness in it." (Isa. 1.6):

> My brother, the most devout of persons in religious practice, if the real man were revealed, would see himself all blemishes which had run together and joined each to each until they became the very form of the man. *al-Fatḥu 'r-rabbānī*, Aḥmad at-Tījānī.

The following confessions surely express the worshipper's sense not of sins only but of sinfulness:

> My God, my Lord and Master, this is the position of him who now makes confession of many a fault, many a disobedience, many a misdeed, of lack of moral control. I sinned as I did from inability to deny my own sinful desires. Thy case against me is a clear one, Thy judgment on me must take effect, and there is none that can help my weakness against Thee, save Thee Thyself. *Ḥizbu 't-taḍarru'*, Aḥmad al-Tījānī.

> How shall I not fear Thy punishment with the evil of my state? *Wirdu 's-sattār*, Muṣṭafā al-Bakrī.

> O God I confess before Thee that I do not know a single believer on the face of the earth with more of disobedience and transgression than I, nor in a worse spiritual condition, nor with less of holy fear than I, O Thou Guide of the erring. O God my sins outweigh the sins of them all the first and the last. *Ḥizbu 'l-imāmi 'r-Ramlī*.

Repentance

Although there have been questionings amongst the doctors (Ibn Ḥanbal for instance) as to the necessity of repentance for those who are Muslims, the chosen people, who "have Abraham (and Muḥammad) to their father", our prayers show that the worshipping soul knows this experience described by the root *tāb* to come back (synonym *anāba*, Muḥammad being described as *al-mutawāḍi'u 'l-munīb*, the humble repentant one). The word *tawba* does not occur in the sunnī prayer-rite but Shī'as say *Astaghfiru 'llāha rabbī wa atābu ilaihi* (and I repent towards Him).

Ash-Shādhilī said, If you failed to show the fear of God in right behaviour, do not fail to show it in repentance and return to Him. *al-Mafākhiru 'l-'aliyya*. Aḥmad b. 'Ibād, p. 53.

He (M.) said I repent towards God a hundred times every day. *Ṭahāratu 'l-qulūb*, ad-Dīrīnī, p. 4.

The teaching of the Qur'ān that God loves penitents, *yuḥibbu 't-tawwābīn* (2.222), is echoed in the prayer-manuals.

I am near to the rebellious one when he has ceased from his rebellion and I am far from the obedient one when he ceases to obey. *al-Ghawthiyya*. Cf. Ezek. 18.21–4.

But echoed still more is the message that God Himself is *at-tawwāb* (*Qur*. 9.15,119; one of the Ninety-Nine Names)—the Prone to Return, to Relent. The prevenient turning of God to the sinner is seen to underlie all turning of the sinner to God. A commonly used form is:

We ask Thee for a turning first on Thy part towards us, and then a resultant turning on our part towards Thee. *al-Wirdu 'l-kabīr* (Shādhili).

A man said to Rābi'a, "My sins are many; if I repent will God turn towards me?" She said, "Nay if He has already turned towards you, you will repent." *Ṭahāratu 'l-qulūb*, p. 96.

This sense of God's turning towards the sinful has made of repentance a meeting place. The modern Indian Christian mystic, Sadhu Sundar Singh, in his *munājāt* heard words from his Lord that are endorsed by the experience of some of the writers of our Muslim prayers:

With My finger I wrote upon the ground the sinful state of each of those who brought the sinful woman to Me for condemnation . . . with My finger too I point out in secret to My servants their wounds of sin; and when they repent, with a touch of the same finger I heal them. . . . When a man turns towards Me in repentance, I cleanse the temple of his heart with the whips of love and make it a heavenly abode for the King of Kings.

A Turning of the Whole Man

The adjective *nuṣūḥ*, sincere, is the companion of the noun *tawba*.

We ask Thee for sincere repentance before death. *Awrād Aḥmad at-Tījānī*, p. 7.

That I may be sincere to Thee in repentance because I fear Thee, and that I may be single-hearted in this sincerity because I love Thee. (Shī'a *Du'ā'un* for the 28th day of Ramaḍān.)

Lightly as the word *tubt* (I repent—used for instance by a servant in apologizing for some small fault) is taken on the lips of men in ordinary speech, Islam has seen that sincere repentance calls for a re-alignment of life.

Mu'ādh b. Jabal said, O Apostle of God who art to me as father and mother, what is sincere repentance (*tawba nuṣūḥa*)? He said, that a man be contrite for the fault that befell him and apologize to God, then, as milk returns not to the udder, he shall not return to it. (aṭ-Ṭabarī, 1.38.)

Tawba then, is the word most commonly used in Muslim religious books for "conversion", which comes so near to its meaning of "turning". A single story from the manuals will illustrate this use of the word:

Dhū 'n-Nūn al-Miṣrī said: "As I was making my perambulation of the House (the Ka'ba) I saw a youth wearing a woollen garment (sign that he was a Ṣūfī) and strutting. He was saying as he went, 'My God, this is the step of one whose boast is in other than Thyself, who glories in other than Thee. How can it become the step of one who has no other love than Thee?' I asked him, 'What is this story?' He replied, 'Oh, uncle, look at yonder slave of the Emir of Mecca!' I stepped forward," Dhu 'n-Nūn continued, "and there was a youth trailing his mantle vaingloriously on the ground. And I said to him, 'My boy, you are strutting because you are the slave of the Emir of Mecca, and this poor Ṣūfī is behind you although he is the slave of the King of heaven and earth. Go back and let him take precedence, he is more worthy than you to bear himself proudly.' Then I saw the boy step back and change colour, and he said to the poor Ṣūfī, 'Step forward for, by God, you are worthier than I. Blessed is he who is like you.' Then he ended his perambulation and went away with bowed head, for the words were working in him. And he returned to his master and bought his freedom from him, and having sold all his possessions and donned a woollen robe he returned to the Ka'ba on the third day, and meeting me he said, 'O Shaikh I wonder if God Most High will receive me after all those great sins.' So I said to him, 'Be cheered, my son, for you are dear to God. Don't you know that He calls those who are wandering away from Him? Then how much more those who are coming towards Him? Be single-hearted in your resolve, for He will receive you in spite of your past doings.' He answered, 'O Uncle you have healed my heart after it was all but broken, may God reward you with good for your exhortation!' Then he went away and on the seventh

day a man came to me and said, 'O Shaikh, may God give you a great reward in that repentant youth, for he has died.' I said to him, 'Will you not show him to me?' And he conducted me, and I found the boy at rest, his face like the full moon. And I asked how it had been with him. They told me that he had entered that place and made his ablution and remained before the *miḥrāb* weeping for his soul. 'And in the morning we found him dead.'"
Ṭahāratu 'l-qulūb, ad-Dīrīnī.

Restitution

We have to admit that with the great riches in the manuals of prayer regarding sin as self-wronging goes in many cases an apparent oblivion as to the wronging of others.[1] For the most part there is little in them of that delicacy of conscience towards others, which caused as-Sarī aṣ-Ṣaqalī to ask forgiveness for thirty years because he had rejoiced that his shop had been saved from a fire in which those of fellow-Muslims had been burnt. Yet Miss E. Mitchell, who lived for many years among Muslims in Faizabad, reports that it is there customary for a man upon his deathbed to seek the forgiveness both of his friends and of his enemies.

The typical reference in the prayer-manuals to sins against fellow-creatures runs as follows:

> O God I have sins between Thee and me and sins between me and Thy creatures. O God forgive me for Thy part in them, and, for Thy creatures' part, do Thou take the responsibility and pardon me of Thy generosity.
> *Dalā'ilu 'l-khairāt*, p. 57, and frequently in the manuals.

But although the prayers show little trace of that grief for the wronging of others which is part of the anguish of penitence, instructions on repentance often include the duty of restitution or reparation:

> When a man had in his presence said, "I ask forgiveness of God," 'Alī rejoined, "May thy mother be bereaved of thee, hast thou any perception of what asking forgiveness means? Asking forgiveness is one of the stages to be passed through by exalted souls. It is dependent on six aspects, first remorse for the past, second determination never to return to past sin, third payment to created beings of their rights so that thou mayest meet God Most High free from all responsibility, fourth that thou shalt determine to

[1] Though in the Dantesque hell of al-Jīlānī sinners against others are placed lower than those who fail to fulfil obligations of the sacred law. *Insān Kāmil*, Bāb 58.

give to every religious duty its due form and full performance, fifth that thou shalt afflict the flesh that has grown on thy bones and reduce it by thine attrition till the skin cleaves to the bone and a new flesh shall grow between them, and sixth that thou shalt make the body taste the pains of obedience as thou didst make it taste the sweets of rebellion. When thou hast done this thou canst say, 'I ask forgiveness of God.'" *Majmū'u 'l-awrādi 'l-'āmm*, p. 9.

(Jacob had been blamed for "failing to nourish orphan neighbours.") So after this Jacob used to order a crier to announce at dinner time and at supper time, "Whoever desires to dine or to sup let him come to the family of Jacob." For this cause it is said, "He who has sinned let him perform a good deed corresponding to the type of wrong that he did by his transgression." *Ṭahāratu 'l-qulūb*, p. 105.

The Broken and Contrite Heart

O Lord endow me with a lowly, humble, prostrate heart, and a weeping eye . . . and sincere acceptable repentance. *Awrād Aḥmad at-Tījānī*, p. 40.

Here we come to the experience of the grief of penitence; described by the words *nadāma*, contrition, *kamad*, wearing grief, attrition, remorse. (*Ḥazan*, mourning grief, though used in *ṣūfī* literature does not appear to have found its way into the manuals.)

And it is said he who turns from transgression from fear of the chastisement of God Most High is repentant (*tā'ib*) and he who returns from shame at God's gaze on him is contrite (*munīb*) and he who returns for God's greater glory is a penitent (*tawwāb*). *Ṭahāratu 'l-qulūb*, p. 96.

O Lord, if contrition (*nadam*) is repentance before Thee, well, I am the most contrite of contrite souls. And if the forsaking of disobedience is to return to Thee, well, I am the most contrite of contrite souls. *Du'ā'un fī 't-tawba. aṣ-Ṣaḥīfatu 's-sajjādiyya*, p. 276.

Make us to be those who taste the bitterness of attrition (*kamad*) till they are saved from their defects. *al-Munājātu 'l-injīliyya*, p. 222.

Qur'ānic Examples

Two Qur'ānic types of sin (supported by traditional additions to the Qur'ānic stories) are held up before the readers of our manuals, the sin of Iblīs and the sin of Adam,[1] and two Qur'ānic types of penitent, Dhū 'n-Nūn (Jonah) and Adam. The Qur'ānic prayers of both are constantly employed.

[1] In spite of the protest sometimes made that his fall should not be regarded as "sin" because he was a prophet.

The Qur'ānic Types of Sin

Beware of pride for pride prevented Iblīs from prostrating himself to Adam. Beware of greed for greed led Adam to eat from the tree. And beware of envy for it was only from envy that one of the two sons of Adam killed his fellow. *al-Mafākhiru 'l-'aliyya*, Aḥmad b. 'Ibād, p. 20.

The Typical Penitents

Jonah

My soul is darkened and Thy servant is in grief and care and anxiety. The whale of selfish desires has swallowed him and he calls to Thee with the call of the beloved, the preserved from sin, Thy prophet and servant Jonah the son of Mattā, saying to Thee, "There is no god but Thee, glory be to Thee, lo I was one of the wrongdoers." (*Qur.* 21.87.) Answer me, then, as Thou didst answer him and help me with love in my isolation and loneliness. *Munājātu 'sh-Shaikh Abū 'Ḥasan ash-Shādhilī.*

Adam

It is narrated that Adam, when he ate of the tree, and the raiment of Paradise was stripped from him, wandered fugitive and began to hide himself among the leaves of the garden. And his Lord called to him, "Dost thou fly from me, O Adam?" He said, "Rather am I ashamed before Thee O Lord." And God Most High said, "Did I not create thee with My hand? Did I not cause my angels to prostrate themselves before thee? Did I not breathe into thee of My spirit? Did I not give thee a dwelling in My paradise, in My neighbourhood? Why then hast thou disobeyed Me? Go out from My neighbourhood, for he who disobeys Me cannot dwell near Me."

Then Adam said, "Glory and praise be to Thee O God. There is no god but Thee. My Lord I have done evil and wronged myself. Therefore have mercy on me, Thou who art the most merciful of them that show mercy. And turn Thyself to me, Thou who art Prone to Relent, and Compassionate." And these are the words which Adam learnt from his Lord. . . . And some of the traditionists say that he said: "O God, by the reverence due to Muḥammad, forgive me," and He forgave him. *Ṭahāratu 'l-qulūb*, ad-Dīrīnī, p. 95.

Adamic Prayer for Pardon

The *Imām* Aḥmad narrated that Abū Huraira said, The Apostle of God said: When Adam was sent down to earth he circumambulated the *Ka'ba* for a week and performed a prayer of two prostrations behind the prayer-platform. Then he said, "O God Thou knowest my secret and my outward life, receive then my apology. Thou knowest my need, then grant my request. Thou knowest how I stand, then forgive all my sins for there is none that forgiveth sins but Thee." *al-Mukhtārātu 'l-ḥusān*, 'Alī Ḥasan Sharīf, p. 26.

The Type of Contrition

Your father Adam wept over one sin three hundred years. Whenever he saw the angels mount to heaven he said, "How I long for home!" *Ṭahāratu 'l-qulūb*, p. 142.

This thought must have been current in pre-Islamic Christianity. Cyril of Jerusalem in the fourth century said:

He (God) cast him out from Paradise, for because of sin he was unworthy to live there; but He put him to dwell over against Paradise (LXX of Gen. 3.24), that, seeing whence he had fallen, and from what and into what a state he was brought down, he might afterwards be saved by repentance. (*Lecture 2* to those preparing for Baptism.)

11 b

THE WORSHIP OF PENITENCE: THE VOCABULARY OF SINNING IN THE MANUALS

We give this vocabulary not because the words are difficult but because they differ from those to which Christian readers may be accustomed.

Sin as Evil

(*a*) Verb *sharra*. Nouns *sharr*, *shurūr*

Evil in itself, often coming close to the Hebrew *ra*ʿ. As was noted in Chapter 6, many prayers show an implicit belief in dual powers—good and evil—at work within all created things, and such forms are common as:

> Give me the good of all things and fend off from me the evil of all things. *Wirdu 'ṣ-ṣubḥ* also called *Ḥizbu 'l-ibtihāl*, Qādiriyya.

But a study of the word *sharr*, as used in the prayer-manuals, raises the question whether the writers can be said to use the word *sharr* of an evil *principle*, or whether they did not conceive of multitudinous separate particles of evil. One well-known prayer certainly seems to envisage a general principle of evil.

> Indeed if Thou leavest me to myself that self will bring me near to evil and put a distance between me and good. *Ḥizbu yawmi 'l-arbiʿā'*, M. ʿUthmān al-Mirghanī.

Here the word *sharr* would seem to correspond to the English word "evil" in its sense as the "principle of evil" which cannot be pluralized without an alteration in its meaning, confining it to a more limited concrete sense. ("Of two evils choose the lesser.")

This absolute use of the word is unusual in our books of Muslim prayer. Here far more commonly it is used in construction and indicates the evil of some created being, thing, or circumstance. The idea of absolute good and evil is perhaps foreign to minds which would prefer to see both contingent upon unlimited momentary acts of the will of the Creator. *Sharr, shurūr* in these prayers, therefore usually represents not absolute evil, but the evil or evils of specific parts of creation. When the word is applied to the evil of ourselves or of our deeds, it must be recognized as one of the names for sin.

I take refuge with Thee from the evil of what I have done. *Wirdu 'l-ghurūb,* Muṣṭafā al-Bakrī, and constantly in the manuals.

Protect us O God from the evils of our (lower) selves and the illusion of our works, and from the evil of Satan's snares, and make us to be of that inner circle of Thy servants over whom he has no authority. *Majmū'u aḥzāb wa awrād,* etc., 'Abd al-Qādir al-Jīlānī.

(*b*) Verb *sā'a.* Nouns *sū', sai', sai'āt, isā'a.* The sinner, *al-musī'*

This root represents a more transitive aspect of evil, evil that hurts or does harm. If the opposite of *sharr* is *khair,* that of *sū'* is *ḥasan,* a couple which comes very close to the Greek *kakos-agathos.* The sense of the evil that hurts may be observed in one of the numerous Qur'ānic uses of the root: *sā'a ṣabāḥu 'l-mundharīn* (9.10) "evil shall be the morn of them that were warned", where the word "evil" might be replaced by "hard". But the Qur'ān has given the word *sū'* for ever its place in Muslim thought about sin, through the phrase *inna 'n-nafsa la ammāratun bi 's-sū'* (12.52), "Verily the self is urgent to evil"—the Arabic equivalent to the Hebrew *yetzer ha-rā'.* This great phrase, recognized by the Ṣūfī world as the picture of the unregenerate, concupiscent self and of the standpoint from which the soul must start on its journey to God, is hard to reconcile with some modern Muslim claims about Islam's belief in the innate goodness of human nature.

Such a phrase, with its history in religious thought, naturally enters into the life of prayer, and much more fully than *sharr* represents human sinfulness.

Deliver me from one who, endeavouring to slay me
Contrives against me libels with stealth and subtlety
And also from this self which urges me to evil
And from rebelliousness, to sin's disaster calling.

Riyāḍu 'l-madḥ, Ja'far aṣ-Ṣādiq al-Mirghanī.

My God, Thou art the Forgiving One and I the sinner (*musī'*) and who will show mercy on the sinner save the Forgiving One? (Constantly used throughout the manuals.)

Sin as Wrong-doing

Verb *adhnaba*. Nouns *dhanb, dhunūb*. The sinner, *al-mudhnib*

This, whether in the Qur'ān, in the devotional manuals, or in Muslim speech, is by far the commonest word for sin, or rather for sins, for *dhanb* expresses not sin but a sin, a single, articulated act of transgression.

In view of its very general use by Muslims (Christian Arabic, for reasons which we shall see below, having given preference to *khaṭī'a*) we must be thankful that the most widely used translation of a sentence in the Lord's Prayer employs this word which all can use: *wa'ghfir lanā dhunūbanā kamā naghfiru naḥnu aiḍan li 'l-mudhnibīna ilainā.*[1] So common, so universal is the use of this word that it hardly seems necessary to give examples from our prayer-manuals.

Sin as Guilt

(*a*) Verb *jarama*. Nouns *jaram, jurm*. The sinner, *al-mujrim*

This root expresses sin as crime or misdemeanour, a word of the law-courts. The Old Testament use of *rāshā'* may be compared, and the New Testament *enochos*, as at 1 Cor. 11.27, James 2.10.

The commonest use in Muslim devotions, echoing the Qur'ān (*20.74*), is the participle *mujrim* for the sinner as the one who is guilty, the criminal.

> My God, Thy longsuffering in regard to my constant criminal acts encourages me to ask Thee for that to which I have no right. *Mukhtaṣaru ad'iyati Ramaḍān*, p. 6.
>
> One of the generous acts of the noble is compassionate kindness to captives, and I am a captive through my crime, the captive of my criminality, bound by my own deeds. *Munājāt*, 'Alī Zain al-'Ābidīn. *Aṣ-Ṣaḥīfatu 's-sajjādiyya*, p. 240.

(*b*) Verb *athima*. Nouns *ithm, āthām*

Whereas the *mujrim* is a guilty one sentenced, or liable to sentence, by a tribunal outside himself, *ithm* seems to carry with it more of the sense of inward guilt, of wickedness not necessarily apparent, so that the Qur'ān uses the adjective "manifest" (*ithmun mubīnun*) with it when the guilt of the action is clear to all. (Cf. *4*.19 and 111.) A perfect

[1] The Jesuit translation of Beirut has in the second limb of the petition *li man asā'a ilainā*. The Book of Hours of the Greek Orthodox Church has: *utruk lanā mā 'alainā kamā natruku naḥnu li man lanā 'alaihi*, "forgive us our debts." Matt. 6.12.

example of its meaning of inward guilt is found in the Beirut American translation of Ezra 9.15, *hā naḥnu amāmaka fī āthāminā*, a verse which Moffat translates "Here we stand guilty before Thee."

> We ask Thy forgiveness for all our sins and guilt. *Ḥizbu 'l-ḥamd*, 'Abd al-Qādir al-Jīlānī.

Sin as Self-wronging

Verb *ẓalama*. Noun *ẓulm*. The sinner, *ẓālim*

Ever present with this word is the sense of wronging, oppression, injustice. Thus those with a sense of injury pray:

> And appoint for us vengeance on any who oppressed us. *Ḥizbu yawmi 'l-Khamīs*, M. 'Uthmān al-Mirghanī.

Ẓulm sometimes has the sense of the New Testament *hubris*. It is one of the most characteristic notes of Muslim thought about sin.

> (As there are three Names for God the Forgiver) the Servant also has three several names for the degrees of his rebelliousness. The first of them is *ẓālim*, as He said, "and some of them are wrongers of themselves". (*Qur.* 35.32.) The second of them is *ẓulūm* (habitually wronging); He said, "(Man) is unjust, ignorant" (33.72), and the third is *ẓallām* (wronging exceedingly). He said, "Say, O my servants who exceeded against yourselves" (4.110). Now he who goes to excess in rebellion is *ẓallām*. (*Lawāmi'u 'l-bayyināt*, Fakhr ad-Dīn ar-Rāzī, p. 161.)

From the Qur'ān comes the cadence, echoed incessantly in Muslim prayer *ẓalamnā anfusanā* (7.22), *ẓalamtu nafsī* (27.44), "I have wronged myself", the normal form of confession and one attributed to the Prophet.

The Apostle of God used to say when he stood up for the prayers . . .

> Thou art my Lord, I thy servant.
> I have wronged myself and I confess my sin.
> Forgive me then all my sins, for there is none that
> forgiveth sins save Thee.
> *Adhkār*, an-Nawawī, p. 21, constantly used in the manuals.

What is the story of this thought of self-wronging which is so widespread and constant a note of Muslim confession that there is no need to give examples. Did the phrase and the idea spring to birth first in the Qur'ānic *sūras*? We have not been able to trace this thought in Jewish worship. Is it Christian? It is not *un*-Christian. The Prodigal

Son undoubtedly wronged himself, though on his return his confession was of sin "against heaven and before thee". Yet so far the only trace of the thought in Christian worship prior to Islam which has come under the present writer's notice is a phrase in the Festival Evening Service of the East Syrian Church, where the faithful sing in the first anthem "Thou hast clothed us with a mortal nature *which our trespasses ever painfully oppress.*"[1]

The Entail of Sin

(*a*) Verb *janā ʿalā*

Although the nouns *janāya, janīya* are used for crime or misdeed with no particular overtone of meaning, the verb with its preposition (which is not Qur'ānic) has found its way into Muslim devotions with a fuller significance. With apparently a primary sense of fruit-gathering it has come to mean involving oneself or another in the fruits of wrongdoing, as when a sinner involves his child in disease.

> I acknowledge Thy grace to me, and this is what I have brought upon myself. *al-Wirdu 'sh-shāfī*, p. 65 (traditional).
>
> What my hands have brought upon me. *Duʿā'un ʿinda 'l-Kaʿba. aṣ-Ṣaḥīfatu 's-sajjādiyya*, p. 368.

(*b*) Verb *wazara* or *wazira*. Noun *wizr, awzār*

This verb means to carry the burden of sin, like Christian in the *Pilgrim's Progress.*

> By Thy mercy relieve my back from the weight of the burden (of sin). *al-Munājātu 'l-injīliyyatu 'l-kubrā*, ʿAlī Zain al-ʿĀbidīn.

Sin as Disobedience

(*a*) Verb *ʿaṣā* (synonym *marada*). Nouns *maʿṣiya, ʿiṣyān*. The sinner is *al-ʿāṣī*, the rebel

ʿAṣā Ādamu rabbahu is the Qur'ānic phrase for "man's first disobedience". Sin is here disobedience, rebellion, revolt.

[1] The root *ẓlm* so characteristic of Muslim thought of sin is very rare in this connection in Christian Arabic. Sinai MS. 154, however, of the eighth or ninth century contains the sentence *qāla shaikhun min al-abā' kamā anna 'n-nāra taḥriqu 'l-ḥaṭab kadhālika tuqā 'llāhi yaḥriqu 'ẓ-ẓulm wa 'sh-shahawāt.* One of the fathers, an elder, said, "As fire burns up wood, so the fear of God burns up wrongfulness (*ẓulm*) and evil desires."

The people of obedience make mention of the God of Grace and the people of disobedience make mention of the God of Mercy. *al-Ghawthiyya*, 'Abd al-Qādir al-Jīlānī.

A prayer constantly used in the manuals is that said by Al-Qushairī to have been ever on the lips of Ibrahīm b. Adham:

O God, transfer us from the degradation of disobedience to the glory of obedience. *Risāla*, p. 8.

(*b*) Verb *khālafa*. Noun *mukhālafa*

Sin as breaking of regulations, contravention.

Keep us from all things unlawful and all contraventions of the divine law. *Majmū'atu 'l-wirdi 'l-'āmm*, p. 17.

(*c*) Verb *ta'addā*

Sin as passing the limits, transgression, violation of law. (Compare English "trespass".)

Verily God loveth not the transgressors. *Qur.* 2.190.

I acknowledge that in which I have contravened Thy command and transgressed against it. *al-Munājātu 'l-injīliyyatu 'l-kubrā*, 'Alī Zain al-'Ābidīn.

Sin as Error

(*a*) Verb *khaṭi'a*. Noun *khaṭī'a*. The sinner is *al-khāṭi'*

Both the Old and New Testaments have frequently used words for sin with a root-meaning of error, missing the mark. The Old Testament *ḥaṭa'* is the same root as the Arabic *khaṭi'a*. In the story of the Hebrew language, this root all but forgot its original sense and, from meaning a fault by accident or error, came to have at once a more general and a more ethical significance. Yet it was probably that original meaning that led the New Testament writers (following the Septuagint) to choose as their most frequent word for sin a Greek root with a similar history. But in New Testament usage *hamartanō* and the connected nouns have forgotten their original sense of missing the mark and error, in a graver ethical significance. When Bible translations into Arabic became necessary it was perhaps natural that many of the translators should use the Arabic verb of kindred meaning, *khaṭi'a* and its nouns, to translate the *hamartanō* group. It was natural and linguistically exact, but the resultant general use by Christians of *khaṭi'a* as their predominant word for sin may give a wrong impression to their Muslim friends.

For *khaṭi'a* is by no means so advanced in Muslim Arabic along the pathway from sheer error to ethical wrong as was *hamartanō* when the Church took it over from the Septuagint and from common speech.

We have in the Qur'ān several contemporary shades of meaning for the one root. When in *4*.91, it is said that a believer kills not a fellow believer *'illā khaṭa'an*, the meaning is at the level of pure error or accident. The word is still so used in Arabic speech to-day, for a guest returned to the writer's house to say *akhṭa't*, not with the meaning that she had sinned, but that she had by mistake left a sunshade there.

On the other hand, in the speech of Abraham in *26*.81, the word seems to have passed from the sense of sin by error to that of sin in general.

Our prayer-manuals likewise exhibit the word with several stages of meaning, but its general tendency is towards the thought of error or slip, a fact often insufficiently remembered by Christians who use the word with a wider and deeper meaning.

> He who when I (M.) was mentioned missed blessing me, missed the road to Paradise. (Tradition quoted in *Ḥizbu yawmi 'th-thulāthā*, M. 'Uthmān al-Mirghanī.)
>
> I repent towards Him of every sin I have committed, intentionally or in error. Forgive me what I did in error and what I did intentionally. *Majmū'atu 'l-wirdi 'l-'āmm*, and so constantly.

There is, however, an interesting group of passages which appear to have a Christian or a biblical origin and in which the word *Khaṭī'a* is used as in the Christian writings:

> Thou hast forgotten the words of our Lord 'Īsā: The love of this world is the foundation of every sin and of sin in general. Not one sin can be driven out of a man who loves the world. *Khatma* to *Al-Ḥusūnu 'l-manī'*.
>
> O God put between me and my sins the distance that Thou hast put between the east and the west. O God cleanse me from my sins as a white robe is cleansed from dirt. O God wash me from my sins with snow and water and ice. *Adhkār*, an-Nawawī, p. 21.

(*b*) Verb *'athara*. Noun *'athra*

Sin as stumbling and falling, a lapse. *'Athara* is not used in the Qur'ān in this connection. In the Bible the stumbling-block is a familiar idea, and this root is used in the Arabic versions. A perfect example in both

[1] This echo of Ps. 51.7 and Ps. 103.12 is attributed to the Prophet. (At-Tirmidhī from 'Ā'isha and Al-Ḥākim from Abū Umāma.)

the American and the Jesuit Beirut translations of Ezek. 14.3 is *ma'tharata ithmihim*, the sin that trips them up.

> We ask the forgiveness of God for the slips of the tongue. *Wirdu 's-sattār*, Muṣṭafā al-Bakrī.

(*c*) Verb *Zalla*. Nouns *zalla* and *zalal*

Sin as slipping on the path or from the path. (*zaigh* is also used for deviation from the right path.) This is the word commonly used for the sin of Adam, echoing *Qur.* 2.38, where Satan caused Adam and Eve to slip. In the Nestorian Church services Satan's constant epithet is "He who causeth to slip without mud."

> I slipped with a slip that debarred me from the (soul) stage I had reached. *Risāla Qushairiyya*, p. 36.

Sin as Flaw, Defect, Shame

Verb *'āba*. Noun *'aib*, *'uyūb*

This is not a Qur'ānic word, the root being only once used (*18*.80) and then of the damaging of a ship. But of all the words for sin it is perhaps that which comes nearest to our conception of a fault in character, for it contains the idea of blemish with the sense of shame that goes with that. It is used of physical defect as in Dan. 1.4, where the king sought for youths *lā 'aiba fīhim, ḥisānu'l manẓar* (without blemish, goodly to look at). This idea of the unsightliness of physical defect seems to have passed over into the spiritual use of the word, for the prayer-verb invariably used with it is "cover". A synonym for *'aib* is *'awra*, used of the parts of the body that must be covered, and hence spiritually "cover our shames".

A universal form is the following:

> Cover our defects, forgive our sins, cleanse our hearts, enlighten our graves, dilate our breasts, cover our shames, pardon our wickednesses and let us die the death of the righteous. *Wirdu 's-Sattār*, and constantly in manuals.

> Praise be to God who when I call to Him answers me and covers all my shame when I disobey Him. *Mukhtaṣaru ad'iyat Ramaḍān.*

Sin as Excess, Prodigality

Verb *asrafa*. Noun *isrāf*. The sinner is *al-musrif*

(Cf. *Qur.* 39.53 of those who had left Islam.) This is the sin of the Prodigal Son in the Gospel, excess and self-squandering, self-ruin.

I have gone too far. *Majmū'atu 'l-wirdi 'l-'āmm*, p. 14.

If I have ruined myself, yet Thou art generous of Thy mercy to prodigals. *Du'ā'un fī yawmi 'l-ithnain*, 'Alī Zain al-'Ābidīn.

Sins of Omission

taqṣīr	falling short
nisyān	forgetting
nuqṣān	doing too little, lacking, shortcoming
tark	leaving undone

"Thee do we worship." We worship God by confession, and acknowledge faults and weakness and shortcoming. *Awrād*, 'Abd al-Qādir al-Jīlānī, p. 8.

We ask forgiveness of the great God for every great sin, sin of premeditation, sin of carelessness, error, forgetfulness, shortcoming, or slips of the tongue. *Wirdu 's-sattār.*

Couplets Used in Confession of Sin

tafrīṭ—taqṣīr	Overdoing it. Falling short.
mā asrartu—mā a'lantu	What I did in secret and what I did openly.
sirran—jahran	Secretly. Openly.
ẓāhiran—bāṭinan	Outwardly. Inwardly.
hazalī—jiddī	My lack of seriousness. My over-seriousness.
'amadan—sahwan	By premeditation, by carelessness.
tarkan—'amalan	By omission, by commission.
ṭaw'iyyan—karhiyyan	Willingly, against my will.

12 C

THE WORSHIP OF PENITENCE: THE FORGIVING LORD

Istighfār, Forgiveness-seeking

Ritual Use

One of the conditions for a valid prayer-rite according to the Ḥanafites is:

> The saying of "I ask forgiveness of God" between the two prostrations. *Shurūṭu 'ṣ-ṣalāt*, M. ibn 'Abd al-Wahhāb, p. 27.

Many traditions are quoted in the manual to show that this was the Prophet's personal habit; he is sometimes called "The Prince of Forgiveness-seeking", *sayyidu 'l-istighfār*.

> The Apostle of God used to say between the two prostrations My Lord forgive me, My Lord forgive me.[1] *Adhkār an-Nawawī*, p. 28. *al-Kalimu 'ṭ-ṭayyib*, pp. 40, 41.

or, a much-used form known as the "seven supplications":

> O God forgive me, and have mercy on me, and sustain me, and guide me aright, and restore me, and preserve me in health, and pardon me.

Some brief form of *istighfār*, then, even among those who do not make it a condition of validity, is *sunna* in the prayer-rite. It is often said just after the final *salām*.

Expiation

Forgiveness is to be asked of God but are there any words and works that will ensure it?

[1] Other forms of Prophetic *istighfār* are quoted. A modern explanation, to make these numerous forgiveness-seekings accord with the doctrine of the sinlessness of the Prophet, is that *istighfār* need not imply that one has sinned. In relation to sins actually committed it means "asking forgiveness", in relation to sins that one *might* commit, it means "asking protection" against them. There is no trace of this idea in the prayer-manuals.

Islam has no doctrine of atonement, and modern Muslim writers, in reaction against the teaching of Christianity, indignantly repudiate the whole idea of God's atonement, of the atonement of the Righteous for the unrighteous, as immoral and unworthy. This does not mean, however, that our prayer-books do not recognize certain holy words and right acts offered by the sinner himself as having atoning power. We have here to do with the verb *Kaffar*, to cover or conceal, and thus to cover a crime by a meritorious act, to expiate. (*Kafāra* is also the word used in Christian Arabic for the Atonement.) *Kaffir ʿannā sayyiʾātinā*, "Cover our sins away from us," is a very frequent prayer. Our manuals quote numerous traditions as to the atoning power of various acts of worship. The *taṣliya* is one of these sacramentals.

> As for calling down blessing on the Prophet after committing a sin, if he wishes to expiate it, we have already referred to the tradition of Anas, "Call down blessing upon me, for the blessing will be to you an atonement." *al-Ḥirzu 'l-manīʿ*, as-Suyūṭī, p. 119.

The prayer-rite itself is a sacramental, atoning for all except mortal sins in the space between the performances of it. (*Iḥyāʾ* 4.1b.)
A frequently quoted tradition is:

> I heard the Apostle of God say, If there were in the courtyard of one of you a river in which he was accustomed to wash himself five times daily what do you think that would leave of his uncleanness? They said, "Nothing at all." He said, "So the five prayer-rites remove sins as water removes dirt." Aḥmad. 1.71. Mālik, *qismu 'ṣ-ṣalāti fī 's-safar* (quoted with his usual freedom as to details by al-Ghazālī, *Iḥyāʾ*, 4.1b).

So the Jews had explained that the morning and evening sacrifices were intended to atone, the one for the sins of the night and the other for the sins of the day, that Israel might ever be guiltless before God. (*Pesiqta* ed. Buber, p. 61, *b*.)

This expiatory power of holy words is based on *Qur.* 33.98, and the verse is very generally referred to the *dhikr*, for which traditions claim forgiveness-winning power. That the rites on which such reliance is placed may (through a slip or through *ghafla*, inattention, or some wrong condition of heart) themselves stand in need of forgiveness is felt by the deeper souls and attested by prayers seeking forgiveness for slips in the prayer-rite. (Among the Shīʿa such a petition is an obligatory part of the rite), and by *kafāratu 'l-majlis*, prayers often offered for forgiveness of any flaw at the end of a *dhikr* gathering. One of the manuals quotes the saying of *Rābi'a*: *Istighfārunā yaḥtāju ilā 'l-istighfār.* Our very asking for forgiveness needs a further asking for forgiveness. The following is advice as to penance:

And tradition informs us that pardon of a sin is to be hoped for if it is followed by eight things: Four of them in the heart, to wit, repentance and determination not to repeat the sin, with desire that it shall be rooted out and fear of punishment with hope of pardon. And four in the members, to wit that the man shall pray four *rak'as* in the mosque then ask forgiveness of God seventy times and say *Subḥāna rabbī 'l-'aẓīm wa bi-ḥamdihi* a hundred times, and give alms, then fast for a day. God Most High said: Good works remove sins. *Ṭahāratu 'l-qulūb*, ad-Dīrīnī, p. 98. (The reference is to *Qur. 2.115.*)

Insurance Value

The manuals show the natural human tendency to treat forgiveness-seeking phrases as a kind of insurance, especially at night and at the times of the great fasts and feasts. A single example will suffice to show the quality of this tendency of popular religion. It is the recommendation attached to an *istighfār* attributed to 'Abd Allāh b. as-Sulṭān, much printed in little popular manuals:

'Abd Allāh ibn as-Sulṭān used to recite this *istighfār* every night of the month of Rajab. Now he was notorious for drinking wine and adultery and vice and debauchery and failure to observe the prayer-rite and the Fast. And he lived in the time of the Apostle of God. Now when 'Abd Allāh ibn as-Sulṭān died, no one went to wash his corpse or to say prayers over him, or to attend his funeral.

Then Gabriel descended to the Prophet saying, "Muḥammad, your Lord sends you His *salām* and His special greeting and honour, and says to you, "Rise up and go to the burial of 'Abd Allāh ibn as-Sulṭān and wash him and shroud him and pray over him."

And the Prophet went walking on tiptoe and descended smiling to the tomb. His Companions wondered at him and on their return asked him, "Why did you go on tiptoe?" Then the Prophet said, "I saw such dense crowds of angels that there was no space left except for the tips of my toes." They said, "And why were you smiling?" He said, "I saw a company from Paradise which came to the tomb, and behind it were a thousand houris, in the hand of each of them a flask filled from the reservoir of *al-Kawthar*, and each of them was saying, 'I will arise and give him to drink', that was the reason of my smile."

Then the Prophet said, "Arise, and we will go to his house and ask his wife what he used to do during his life-time."

Now when they came to the door of the house it was shut, and when they knocked the woman said, "Who knocks at the door of the house of people of vice and debauchery?" And the Companions said, "O Mother of Excellence, open to the Prince of Apostles and Seal of the Prophets." Then she opened the door and they asked about the habits of her husband, and the woman said, "O Apostle of God, I saw nothing but ugly doings from him, and wine-drinking and vice and debauchery. And I never saw him perform a single prayer-prostration all his life long nor ever fast, but I noticed that when the month of Rajab came he used to rise up and pray this petition, and he said it so often that I learnt it by heart." And the Prophet said to 'Alī, "Write this *istighfār*." So the woman said it and 'Alī wrote it down. And the Prophet said, "He who recites this *istighfār*, or has it in his house or among his belongings to him God appoints the reward of . . ." *Al-majmū'atu 'l-mubāraka*, 'Abdu Muḥammad Bābā, pp. 12–14.

The longing for safety expresses itself also in an effort to make forgiveness-seeking forms that are all-inclusive, covering all manner of sins (not however providing for detailed confessions of any one wrongdoing) and extensive in time, sometimes to cover a whole life-time. And when all is said and done, there is always, as we have seen, reliance on the final *shafā'a* of the Prophet.

In Thee Alone Is My Hope

Yet men of deep spiritual experience know that ultimately the sinner's only hope is in the God against whom he has sinned. The form that more than any other may be regarded as the *Confiteor* of Islam strikes this note:

I ask forgiveness of Thee and repent towards Thee. I have done wrong; I have wronged myself; then forgive me, for there is none that forgiveth sins save Thee.[1] (*Majmū'u 'l-awrādi 'l-kabīr* (for daily use) and constantly throughout the manuals. The final phrase is based on *Qur.* 3.135.)

Our God and Lord and Master, if we weep till our eyelashes fall out, and wail till our voices fail us, and stand till our feet shrivel, and bow till our joints are dislocated, and prostrate ourselves till our eyeballs burst, and eat the dust of the earth all our lives long, and make mention of Thee till our tongues fail, we shall not thereby have earned the wiping out of one of our misdeeds. (Attributed by a tradition with *isnād* to 'Alī Zain al-'Ābidīn. "In his *munājāt* at night." *aṣ-Ṣaḥīfatu 's-sajjādiyya*, p. 165.)

[1] Al-Ḥallāj was heard murmuring this form throughout his final trial. (Massignon, *Ḥallāj*, p. 251.)

And forgive me what only Thy forgiveness can include, what only Thy pardon can wipe out, what only Thine indulgence and generosity can atone for. *al-Ḥizbu 'ṣ-ṣaifī.*

My God, if we consider Thy generosity, the marvel is that any perish. If we consider Thy justice, the marvel is that any are saved. My God if it is Thy generosity that calls us to account we shall attain to Thy good pleasure. If it be Thy justice that calls us to account we shall not attain even to Thy forgiveness. My God how can I hope in Thee, I being I? And how can I help hoping in Thee, Thou being Thou? If we are powerless to avoid a sin which Thou hast written down for us, Thou art powerful to forgive us for it. (Yaḥyā b. Mu'ādh ar-Rāzī. An oft-quoted prayer of Shī'a prayer-writers.)

Many a prayer in our manuals strikes the same note as that attributed to Yaḥyā b. Mu'ādh ar-Rāzī in *Tadhkirātu 'l-Awliyā'*.

My God, of Thy mercy forgive my sins. O my Lord, though my sinful deeds make me feel Thy justice, yet the greatness of Thy compassion makes me hope in Thee. O Lord, I have not merited Paradise by my deeds, and I cannot endure the pains of Hell, so I entrust myself simply to Thy grace. If on the Day of Resurrection I am asked, "What hast thou brought unto Me?" I shall reply: "What can one straight from prison, with unkempt hair, and tattered garment, burdened with wordly cares and full of shame, bring unto Thee? Wash me from my sins, give unto me the robe of the redeemed, and in Thy mercy cast me not away from Thy Presence." (Translation, Dr Margaret Smith.)

Reasons for the Hope of Forgiveness

The man who feels himself unforgivable and yet throws himself upon God for forgiveness must find his reasons for forgiveness not in himself but in God. Where shall they look for it, who have not Calvary before their eyes?

His Arbitrary Favour

There are those who find hope in the incalculable, arbitrary exercise of His favour:

My God, how many good deeds from those whom Thou dost not love have no reward, and how many misdeeds from those whom Thou lovest have no resulting burden. Then make my misdeeds the misdeeds of one Thou lovest and let not my good deeds be the good deeds of one Thou hatest. (Attributed to ash-Shādhilī in *al-Mafākhiru 'l 'aliyya*, p. 159.)

For such a worshipper there is at least hope of forgiveness because there is a living God, whose living volitions are beyond the calculation of the system-maker.

His Past Goodness and Past Forgiveness

My Master, my Master, if Thou hast shown mercy to any like me, then be merciful to me. If Thou hast received any like me, then receive me.

O God, Thy pardon of my sin, Thy passing over my errors, Thy covering of the ugliness of my doings, Thy long patience with my many wickednesses whether I did them in error or of set purpose, have made me ask in hope that to which I have no right. *aṣ-Ṣaḥīfatu 's-sajjādiyya*, 'Alī Zain al-'Ābidīn, p. 125.

My God, though my sin has made me fear Thee, yet my confidence in Thee (my good opinion of Thee) came to my rescue. My God, it is as though I stood before Thee with my sinful soul, and the fulness of my trust in Thee overshadowed it, and Thou didst with me after Thy wont, and coveredst me with Thy pardon. Ibid., p. 153.

His Nature and His Name

The soul longing for forgiveness dwells on those Names of God which promise it, to the exclusion of others in a contrary sense. The Names so used in forgiveness-seeking prayers are *Raḥīm*, *Tawwāb*, *Ghāfir*, *Ghaffār*, *Ghafūr*, *'Afuww*, *Ḥalīm*, *Karīm*.

Forgive and show mercy for Thou art the Best of them that show mercy. *Dalā'ilu 'l-khairāt*, p. 97, and constantly in the manuals.

Verily God is the Wont to Forgive, the One that shows mercy.—A Qur'ānic couplet (*10*.107 and six other uses) constantly used in forgiveness-seekings.

My God, Thou art the Forgiver (*al-Ghāfir*) and I the wicked one. Does any one, save the Intensely Forgiving (*Al-Ghaffār*), show mercy to the wicked? *Awrād Aḥmad at-Tījānī*, p. 49.

My God, wipe out our sins by the influence of Thy Name, the Intensely Forgiving (*Al-Ghaffār*). *Majmū'u 'l-awrādi 'l-kabīr*, Mirghaniyya.

O God, Thou art the Pardoning One (*Al-'Afuww*), the Lover of Pardon, pardon then me.

Praise be to God who rewards well-doing with well-doing, and evil-doing with generosity and long-suffering (*ḥilm*) and forgiveness. *Majmū'u 'l-wirdi 'l-'āmm*, p. 13.

My God Thou art the Generous One (*al-Karīm*) and I the mean object; will anyone show mercy on the mean save the Generous? Ibid., p. 42.

In the less spiritual of the prayers there is a touch of irresponsibility in the appeal by such names—He must pardon, *C'est son métier*, "My God, sins are our nature and pardon is Thine" (Shī'a *munājāt*), a suggestion of the inevitability of pardon. But the deeper prayers have no hint of this.

He is Great, Forgiveness is Easy to Him

One of the most constantly used and most characteristic of Muslim forgiveness-seekings, muttered by the peasant woman as she goes about her tasks, as well as by the dervish in his spiritual warfare, is the following:

> I ask forgiveness of the Great God for every sin. (Constantly used throughout the manuals.)

"This is a strain which Jesus prolongs and deepens. He more than anyone else is sure that there is such a thing as forgiveness, not because it is small, but because it is great and father-like."[1] The thought of God's greatness, however, leads to a certain moral shallowness in some forgiveness-seeking prayers that are unable, without the revelation that "His nature and His name is love", to attribute any moral cost to God's forgiveness.

> I ask Thee everything O Lord, by Thy power over everything, till Thou dost not hold me responsible for anything, O Thou in whose Hand is the empire over everything. (*al-Ḥizbu 'l-kabīr*, Qādiriyya.) This prayer is said to have been taught by Sufyān ath-Thawrī to Aḥmad b. Ḥanbal, who certainly used it in no light spirit. A vision is recorded, of M. b. Khuzaima who saw Aḥmad b. Ḥanbal after his death and learned that God had commanded his use of this prayer. (*Ṭahāratu 'l-qulūb*, ad-Dīrīnī, p. 234.)
>
> My God my sins do not harm Thee and Thy pardon does not impoverish Thee. Then forgive me what does not harm Thee and give me what Thou wilt not miss. *Munājāt, aṣ-Ṣaḥīfatu 's-sajjādiyya*, p. 234.
>
> His sins, great though they were, are nothing in comparison to the wideness of the mercy of the Most High and the greatness of His generosity. If He will He can forgive them in less than the twinkling of an eye. *al-Fatḥu 'r-Rabbānī*, M. 'Abd Allāh b. Ḥasanain, p. 26.

Because of His Declared Readiness to Forgive

He loves to forgive. It is not on Qur'ānic texts that they base this confidence so much as on an oft-quoted tradition.

[1] Mackintosh. *The Christian Experience of Forgiveness*, p. 12.

Had you not sinned and asked forgiveness, God would have brought another people that sinned and asked forgiveness, so that He might forgive them. *Majmū'u 'l-awrādi 'l-kabīr*, p. 7, Mirghaniyya.

Other traditions also are used to the same effect:

O people of love, does not God the Truth shine forth at the time of the night vigil and cry, "Is there any repentant one that I may relent towards him? Is there any forgiveness-seeker that I may forgive him his sins in their entirety? Is there any seeker of gifts, that I may abound towards him in graces and bestowals? *al-'Aqīdatu 's-saniyya* of 'Abd al-Qādir al-Jīlānī.

The confidence is based also on the knowledge that forgiveness has been part of the experience of saints:

Muḥyī b. Mu'ādh said, "If pardon were not above all dear to God he would not have submitted the people whom He honours most to the trial of sinning." *al-Mukhtārāt al-ḥusnā fī faḍli wa aḥkāmi Ramaḍān*, p. 25.

Verbs of Forgiving in the Manuals

Besides the very common *ghafara li*[1] (nouns *ghufrān* and *maghfira*) '*afā* (*noun* '*afw*), to efface and so to forgive, and *kaffara* and *satara* which have already been noted, the following may be remarked:

maḥaqa, to obliterate and make the traces disappear:

Forgive me what nothing can obliterate save Thy pardon. *Awrād Aḥmad at-Tījānī*, p. 29.

maḥā, to erase:

Erase our misdoings from the book of the wicked. *Wirdu 's-saḥr*, Shādhiliyya.

aqāla, to rescind. The verb generally used with '*atharāt*.

samaḥa li, to be indulgent, clement and to accord pardon:

Pardon and let off a debtor. *al-Qaṣīdatu 'l-mīmiyya*, Muṣṭafā al-Bakrī.

tajāwaza 'an, to pass over, overlook.

My God Thou hast commanded us to overlook (the wrong done by) the evil-doer, overlook then our wrongdoings with Thy beautiful generosity. *Du'ā'u nuṣfi Sha'bān.*

[1] It is perhaps not fanciful to see some significance in the preposition. It is the *sins* which are forgiven "*to*" the person. This may a little have dimmed the sense that the whole person, not only each several wrong action, stands in need of divine forgiveness.

ṣafaḥa ʿan, to turn away from.

Thou hast enjoined us to excuse sinners (against us) and Thou Thyself art the most generous of excusers. *al-munājātu 'l-injīliyyatu 'l-kubrā. aṣ-Ṣaḥīfatu 's-sajjādiyya*, p. 195.

The following metaphors of pardon are also used:

To break the chains of sin:

O God loosen the fetters of my disobedience. My God we are the captives, set us free, then, from our chains. *Ḥizbu 'l-barr*, ash-Shādhilī.

To dissolve sin:

God melted away his sins as salt melts in water. *Fatḥu 'r-Rasūl*, M. ʿUthmān al-Mirghanī.

To clothe with pardon, grace, etc., a very common metaphor. Compare the "wedding garment" in the New Testament.

(The sinner.) He who is naked of the robe of piety. *Nafḥu 'ṭ-ṭīb*, p. 8.
(The forgiven one.) And He will robe him on the Resurrection Day with forgiveness. *al-Majmūʿatu 'l-mubāraka*, ʿAbduh M. Bābā, p. 3.

Forgiveness-seeking for Others

The forgiveness-seeker stands before his Lord as a member of a family and of the brotherhood of Islam. This is not forgotten; very many forgiveness-seeking forms include the parents of the speaker.[1] (al-Bakrī enlarges the prayer for parents to *aṣḥābu 'l-ḥuqūqi ʿalayya*, those who have claims upon me.) The whole community, "men and women, living and dead" (the latter sometimes described as "those who preceded us in the faith") may be included, while the dervish orders make special mention of their shaikhs and leaders, and sometimes of their fellow-members under the phrase "our brothers in God". The following is a wide form:

Forgive us and our fathers and our mothers and our friends and comrades and those that love us and our shaikhs and the shaikhs of our shaikhs, and our teachers, and those who had a favour to us, and those who enjoined us to pray for them and those whom we so enjoined and those blessed people of

[1] Frequently with the phrase added, "as they fostered me when I was little", from *Qur. 18.24*, basic for prayers on behalf of parents. In the Shīʿa *namāz* the petition for parents is an integral part of the rite. The inclusion of women (*al-muslimāt*) in the prayer for forgiveness is referred to a tradition from Ibn ʿAbbās. (Ibn Abī Shaiba and ʿAbd ar-Razzāq, *al-Ḥirzu 'l-manīʿ*, p. 28.)

piety who have passed to Thee by death. *Fatḥu 'r-Rasūl*, M. 'Uthmān al-Mirghanī.

There are times and seasons when such general forgiveness-seekings are enjoined, as for instance on the last night of the Pilgrimage month. But the greatest of all opportunities for intercession is the pilgrimage itself.

Muḥammad, one of whose petitions was "O God forgive the (Mecca) pilgrims and forgive those for whom the pilgrims ask forgiveness." *ad-Durru 'l-fā'iq*, al-Bakrī.

This comes to a head on the Night and the Day of 'Arafat. A British Muslim who made the pilgrimage thus describes the scene on that night, when he left his tent shortly after midnight:

As I walked along in the direction of the Holy Mountain, I found a great many pilgrims engaged in calling out the names of such of their absent friends as had begged to be remembered on the night of 'Arafat. The Prophet recommended his followers to perform this act of remembrance and said that whosoever among them should thus create seventy pilgrims by proxy would be rewarded with seventy palaces in the world to come and the praises of seventy thousand angels. Imagine then with what zeal and devotion my fellow-pilgrims lifted up their voices. After each name loud cries of "Here I am, O Allah" (*labbaika*) were uttered by one and all. *With the Pilgrims to Mecca*, Hajji Khan.

A North-African Hymn of Forgiveness-Seeking

We close with an example of the popular verse, only to be compared with evangelistic hymns in Christendom, so common in many of the orders (particularly the Shādhiliyya and the Mirghaniyya), and widespread, especially throughout North Africa. Our example is from a book unattached to any order:

With Thy Beautiful Names have I opened my petitioning,
And from Thee besought pardon: grant me my suit.
My God we are caught in the sea of our blemishes,
Offences and crimes are piled up on every side.
And Thou art forgiver of every sinful action
Save only *kufr* and *ishrāk* of terrible results.
And we know that God is the Unique, the Creator
Whose favours mount up beyond the counting of a reckoner.
And therefore have we held out our hands towards our Lord,
At the Door of the Pardoner, eraser of blemishes.

In Thee, generous Lord, we hope—that Thou wilt grant repentance
  Sufficing to erase the Recording Angel's script;
And do Thou in everything grant us sincerity;
  And do Thou grant Thy succour to neighbour and to friend.
And grant to an Obedient One[1] a lust-driven rebel,
  And cause that Obedient One to intercede for him.
O Merciful, grant us our hopes and our petitioning,
  Thou generous in goodness to rebel and to penitent.
  (Muḥammad b. ash-Shāhid al-Jazā'irī, in *Majmū'u 'l-qaṣā'id wa 'l-ad'iya.*)

[1] The reference is to Muḥammad.

13 a

THE WORSHIP OF PETITION: TRADITIONAL PETITIONS

Du'ā'un Ma'thūr

The Muslim prayer-rite is primarily one of praise and adoration, yet there is a recognized place for a petition at the end of the second *rak'a*, before the final *salām*. This is not among the obligatory *arkān* (bases) of the rite and may be a later addition growing out of human need. In Judaism there was just such an opportunity for free prayer. "Tachanun ist im ältesten Gottesdienste das Privatgebet, das nach Vollendung der öffentliche Gebete der einzelne in stiller Andacht verrichtete." (Elbogen, *Der Jüdische Gottesdienst*, p. 14.) We may perhaps see in Luke 1.10 such an opportunity for private prayer in the public service of the Temple before the blessing.

The absence of any obligatory form for this petition-space in the Muslim prayer-rite gives a freedom that might be richly used. It was an important and interesting innovation when in 1940 King Farouk of Egypt appealed by wireless to Muslims everywhere to unite in prayer for peace, at the end of the sunset prayer-rite on the eve of Mid-Sha'bān.

We believe that nothing would more contribute to a revival of real prayer in Islam than that the masses, accustomed to use all their lives long the one or two *ad'iya* learnt in childhood, should by their leaders be taught some of the wealth of petitions available, and be trained to vary this part of the prayer-rite with the variation of temporal and spiritual needs.

Ṣalātu 'l-istikhāra

There is one use of the prayer-rite which is purely petitionary, *ṣalātu 'l-istikhāra*, a prayer for guidance, when two *rak'as*, *extra* to the regular performance, may be said with intention and followed by the worshipper's petition.

A famous use of this custom was that by Saladin in 1192. He was in great perplexity as to whether to defend Jerusalem against the expected attack of the Crusaders. He longed to do so, but his emirs dreaded being boxed up in a walled city. Bahā' ad-Dīn tells us that he had resort to *ṣalātu 'l-istikhāra* as follows. He performed the ablution, gave alms secretly, then, between the *ādhān* and the *iqāma* in the mosque al-Aqṣā, performed two private *rak'as* and made his request with tears.

Next day spies reported discord in the Crusaders' camp as to the attack on Jerusalem, which did not take place.

The Place of Petition in the Prayer-Life

A few of the prayer-manuals show that refinement of some of the *Ṣūfī* saints which tends rather to look down on *du'ā'* as seeking something from God rather than God Himself. An extreme case extends this even to the giving of thanks:

> He preferred *dhikr* to *shukr* because invocation means being busied with Him, while thanksgiving means being busied with His grace. *Lawāmi'u 'l-bayyināt,* Fakhr ad-Dīn ar-Rāzī, p. 29.

A Christian, with the teaching and example of Christ before him, cannot endorse the effort to degrade petition and thanksgiving, a refinement which would make a dichotomy between his life in God and his life in this world, united by the Incarnation.

Nor is this attitude that of most of the prayer-manuals which are better represented by the following:

> My Lord I pray to Thee with the petition of one whose petition was never made to any other. I hope in Thee with the hope of one whose hope never had any other for its goal. My Lord, how can I refrain from turning my longing gaze towards Thy grace, while I, in this creation of Thine, am only one of Thy babes. *al-Munājātu 'l-injīliyyatu 'l-Kubrā,* 'Alī Zain al-'Ābidīn.
>
> My God, Thou hast satisfied our hunger and quenched our thirst, now give us the strengthening benefit of that nourishment. Thou hast provided for us and increased Thy gifts and made them good to us, now give us yet more. *al-Wirdu 'sh-shāfī,* Yūsuf an-Nabhānī, p. 70.

The teaching of the Qur'ān is clear, whether implicit in the complete naturalness with which the prophets make petition for earthly as well as heavenly good, or explicit in such texts as the following, constantly quoted in the prayer-manuals:

> Call upon Me and I will answer you. (*40.60.*)
>
> My Lord would not care for you but for your calling on Him. (*25.77*).

The latter is explained as follows in one of the manuals:

> That is to say, your only power with Him is your cry to Him in difficulties. And it is said to mean, "I did not create you from any need in Me for you, save that you should call upon Me and I should answer you, and you should seek My forgiveness and I should forgive you." *Majmūʿātu 'l-wirdi 'l-ʿāmm*, p. 99.[1]

Of traditions, the following are favourites:

> The Prophet said, "Nothing is more honourable in God's eyes than petition." "Petition is the most honourable part of worship, and he who asks not incurs God's anger." "Petition is the weapon of the believer and the pillar of the faith and the light of heaven and earth." Ibid., pp. 99, 100.

Adʿiyatun maʾthūra

The child learning to perform the prayer-rite is told that it is a *sunna* (rule of behaviour) that in the last *jalsa* (*quʿūd*) of his last *rakʿa* he shall say a *duʿāʾun maʾthūr*. (*Durūsu 'd-dīnī 'l-islāmī*, p. 115.) It is customary at this point to teach children either one of the prayers attributed to the Prophet (*adʿiyatun nabāwīya*), or one of the *adʿiyatun maʾthūra*, prayers handed down from the saints in tradition, or one of the petitions found in the Qur'ān. Perhaps the prayer most commonly taught is:

> Grant us, O Lord, good things in this world and good things in the next, and save us from the torment of the fire.

In the teaching of young children, the prayer may end here, or it may continue:

> O God I take refuge with Thee from the torment of the grave and from the torment of the fire and from the seduction of life and of death and from the seduction of Anti-Christ (*al-Masīḥu 'd-Dajjāl*).

It is regrettable that the prayer thus taught to a child too often remains with him through his life as an invariable use, and he remains unaware of the admirable freedom of this part of the rite, or of the whole body of the *adʿiyatun maʾthūra*.

[1] Compare *Exodus Rabba* 21.55. Why did God bring Israel into the extremity of danger at the Red Sea before saving him? Because He longed to hear Israel's prayer.

Many of these are quoted in this book. Here it will suffice to give three more examples from the manuals, one because of its dependence on the Lord's Prayer and two more because of their beauty.

1.

Our Lord Allah which art in heaven
Hallowed be Thy name.
Thy command is in heaven and earth.
As Thy mercy is in heaven so appoint us mercy on earth.
And forgive us our sins and errors, Thou Lord of good things. (Abū Dāwūd I.101. Aṭ-Ṭabarānī. Al-Hākim, *Mishkāt al-Masābīḥ. Kitābu 'l-Janā'iz.*)

This is said to be a word powerful against sickness uttered by the Prophet. *al-Wirdu 'sh-shāfī*, Yūsuf an-Nabhānī, p. 33.

2. *The Prayer of Light*

This traditional prayer appears here and there in the manuals. It is referred (under slightly variant forms) by "weak" traditions to the Prophet, either as what he said when the *mu'adhdhin* called to the morning prayer (*Adhkāru 'n-Nawawī*, p. 16) or as what he said after the night prayers and before the dawn broke (At-Tīrmidhī from Ibn 'Abbās). Other books refer it to *Al-Jāmi'u 'ṣ-ṣaghīr* of aṣ-Ṣuyūtī. The Shī'a breviary gives it to 'Alī Zain al-'Ābidīn.

We quote it in a full form as it appears in the margin of *Dalā'ilu 'l-khairāt ma'a 'l-aḥzāb.*

> O God appoint for me light in my heart and light in my tomb and light before me and light behind me; light on my right hand and light on my left; light above me and light below me; light in my sight and light in my perception; light in my countenance and light in my flesh; light in my blood and light in my bones. Increase to me light, and give me light, and appoint for me light, and give me more light, give me more light, give me more light!

Other prayers of light, often beautiful, have sometimes a touch of magic about them. They are often protective in the sense that the petitioner begs to be so filled with awful divine light that, like Moses when his countenance shone, he will strike awe into beholders and so be defended from his foes. This is one of the recurring notes of the prayers of 'Abd al-Qādir al-Jīlānī † 561/1166. We give a version which appears in *Ḥizbu 'l-qasam* attributed to him, as it is repeated with an additional final sentence by Al-Būnī † 622/1225. Did he import it from al-Jīlānī, or what is its source?

Lord, plunge me into the sea of the Light of Thy Majesty that I may come forth with the shining of that majesty upon my face, from which the envious eyes of jinn or man will glance off harmlessly, unable to throw the dart of malicious envy. And screen me from them with the veil of light that has light for its inner essence and fire for its outer showing. I ask Thee by Thy Name of Light and by Thy Countenance that is Light, O Light of Light, to veil me in the Light of Thy Name in a veil of protection against all my own shortcomings, inward or outward, for Thou art the Light of all and dost illuminate all with Thy Light. *Sharḥu 'smi 'llāhi 'l-a'ẓam*, Aḥmad al-Būnī.

A more inward prayer of light is this of Aḥmad at-Tījānī:

O Light of Light who dost illumine the obscurity of non-being with the effulgence of Thy Light, make Thy Light the lamp of my subconscious being and of my mind and my soul and spirit and heart and body and all of me and each part of me, till I shall be only light and flooded with the Light of Thy Unity. *Awrādu Aḥmad at-Tījānī*, p. 139.

3. *The Old Age Prayer*

This lovely prayer, again, appears in both Sunni and Shī'a manuals from 'Abd al-Qādir al-Jīlānī onwards. It is traditional, aṭ-Ṭabarānī quoting it as the prayer of an Arab whom the Prophet overheard in passing:

O Lord may the end of my life be the best of it, may my closing acts be my best acts, and make the best of my days the day when I shall meet Thee. *Riyāḍu 'l-Janna*, Yūsuf an-Nabhānī, p. 92.

13 b

THE WORSHIP OF PETITION: THE BEGGAR AT THE DOOR

as-Sā'ilu bi 'l-bāb

The metaphor is a general one, almost inevitable in any religion that knows a God at whose door men may knock. It runs through Jewish and Christian prayer, but in Muslim prayer it is so much at home and so significant that a chapter must be given to it.

Human Doors to God

There is a development, we think not true to the broad, main stream of Muslim thought (yet understandable to those who know the comfort of a voice saying, "I am the door", John 10.9), which regards spiritual leaders as the door to God.

In the dervish orders the shaikh is his disciple's way to God:

> Without the link there would be nothing linked. For the shaikh is the door of God, and there is no access to God save through His door. Therefore Sīdī Muṣṭafā 'l-Bakrī said: Haunt the door of the Master and thou shalt be through this a chosen friend: . . .
>
> He haunted the thresholds and stood at the door like a doorkeeper.
>
> For all who travel arrive, and he who haunts the threshold enters.
>
> And Rābi'a al-'Adawiyya said, "Cleave to the door if thou desirest access." *as-Silsilatu 'dh-dhahabiyya*, pp. 5, 7.

Outside the special teaching of the orders, Muḥammad is sometimes referred to in prayer as God's door:

> He who is Thy very door itself. Bless the Door of Love. *Fatḥu 'r-Rasūl*. M. 'Uthmān al-Mirghanī, p. 58.

Sometimes men are spoken of as clients at Muḥammad's door:

> Servants of his door . . . cleaving close to Him, spending themselves in his path. *Ṣalātu sīdī Muṣṭafā 'l-Bakrī* (printed with *Bashā'iru 'l-khairāt*, p. 26).
>
> If all doors are barred, O Banner of Guidance, then thy door, O lord of

Mediation, is my goal. How can my confidence in thy door be seen to be a disappointment. *Manhal ash-shifā*, (no author given) in *Kitāb laṭīf*, Tunis.

At the door of the Best of Creation my purpose has stationed me, from my knowledge that the Chosen One is generous in succour. I come, bringing no knowledge and no piety, rather all is defilement, my lord, with me. *Awrādu wa aḥzābu Aḥmad at-Tījānī*, p. 148.

God's Doors

For the wide consciousness of Islam, however, the suppliant stands at the door of God Himself. Ask a villager in Arab lands where he is going, and if he does not wish to say, he will reply, *'alā bābi 'llāh*, for every place may be so described. God has many doors. Most of our prayers knock at "the door of His bounty":

Open to me the door of Thy generosity which Thou dost never close to Thy dear ones and Thy purified. *Du'ā'un fī 'sh-shakwā*, 'Alī Zain al-'Ābidīn. *aṣ-Ṣaḥīfatu 's-sajjādiyya*, p. 65.

The prayer attributed to Muḥammad on entering the mosque is:

Open to me the doors of Thy mercy. *al-Ḥirzu 'l-manī'*, p. 99.

It may be compared with "Open to us the door of compassion", in the preparation for the Liturgy of the Greek Orthodox Church.

Characteristic of lands where *ṣabr* is so great and so well-practised a virtue, is the thought of the door of patience:

Endow me with patience, for patience is the greatest of Thy doors. For Thou hast said, and Thy word is truth, "They that endure . . . to them is the reward of the abode, the gardens of Eden shall they enter. . . . And the angels will enter to them by every door. . . . Peace be to you through what you have endured, how excellent then is the reward of the abode." *Munājātun 'aẓīma*. Anon. The Qur'ān quotation is from *13.22*.

As the patient camel when made to kneel on stones tries to kneel, so the believer stands at his Lord's door patient with Him over his misfortunes. *Ḥizbu 'l-ḥifẓ*, 'Abd al-Qādir al-Jīlānī.

The Rich Man's Door

Most of the prayers of the door seem to be built on the picture of a rich man's house with a courtyard where travellers alight, and a door thronged by beggars. To the first, openhanded hospitality is shown, to the second openhanded generosity.

For Thou art the Generous One at whose door stand the beggars, Thou, wider in glorious generosity than all to whom the hands of poor clients are outstretched. *Ḥizbu 't-taḍarru'*, Aḥmad at-Tījānī.

I take up my station at Thy door, the poor expectant one. *aṣ-Ṣaḥīfatu 's-sajjādiyya*, p. 150.

Night and morning find me at one of the doors of Thy bestowal, a beggar, beseeching. *Du'ā'* for Monday. Ibid., p. 317.

Thy little slave is at Thy door, Thy poor one is in Thy courtyard. Thy beggar is in Thy courtyard. Thy destitute one is in Thy courtyard. (Traditional prayer of 'Alī Zain al-'Ābidīn when he made a prostration in his cell. Ibid., p. 330.)

We, Thy destitute, weak and poor servants, are standing at the threshold of the courtyards of Thy Majesty. *Ḥizbu fawātiḥi 'l-baṣā'ir*, 'Abd al-Qādir al-Jīlānī.

The Muslim worshipper is trained in so awful a sense of the infinite, distant majesty of God, ever present yet ever distant in the solitude of His incomparability, that he will not, when thinking theologically, urge upon his Lord any standards of human behaviour. It is all the more touching to note that so deep-rooted is his sense of the duty of host to guest that he is unable to think of a God who is not bound by the great standards of eastern hospitality. In prayers which picture travellers, short of provisions, arriving at the great house, the worshipper speaks to God in the assurance that He would be ashamed that any failure in divine hospitality should be attributed to Him:

O Best of those besought, O most glorious of those sought, Thy servants the Arabs, when a fugitive seeks shelter at the ropes of their tents, will shelter him. And Thou, Creator of the Arabs and the non-Arabs, at Thy door I seek shelter, in Thy courtyard I alight. *aṣ-Ṣaḥīfatu 's-sajjādiyya*, p. 101.

Oh be generous in Thy kindness, my God, to one whose travel-provision is small; Penniless he stands at Thy door, O Thou Friend. His sin is a great sin, do Thou forgive that great sin. Lo he is a stranger, a sinner, a miserable slave. *Qaṣīdatu Sīdī Abī Bakrī 'ṣ-Ṣiddīq. Majmū'u 'l-qaṣā'id wa 'l-ad'iya*, p. 52.

Thou who givest to a slave when he asks of Thee, and when he hopes for what is in Thy house sendest it to him, and when he approaches Thee dost draw him nearer. My God, who ever came seeking Thy hospitality without Thy giving it to him? Who ever halted his camel at Thy door hoping for Thy liberality, without Thy bringing him in? Is it seemly that I should return from Thy door driven away with contumely when I know no other lord than Thee whose quality is beneficence? *Munājātun 'aẓīma* (no author given). *Majmū'atu 'l-aḥzāb*, p. 447.

As with the traveller, so with the beggar. It is beneath the dignity of the rich house that the crowd of beggars at the door shall not receive their bounty:

> Far be it from Thee to send off with reproaches the beggar from Thy door, when Thou art the Generous King. *Ḥizbun 'aẓīm*. 'Ashshāqiyya.

> Thy generosity is wider, Thy glory greater than that a poor man could stretch out his hands asking Thee to pour down pardon and be turned away ashamed. *Ḥizbu 't-taḍarru'*, Aḥmad at-Tījānī.

> My Lord, I stand a beggar at one of the doors of Thy bestowal, turning away from the exposure of my case to others. It is not consonant with the lovely bestowals of grace to turn away a heartbroken beggar, a needy one hoping for Thy generosity. *al-Munājātu 'l-injīliyyatu 'l-kubrā. aṣ-Ṣaḥīfatu 's-sajjādiyya*, p. 196.

In the *Ghawthiyya* this conviction is turned into a saying of the Lord Himself:

> He said to me: O succour of the Almighty, if a thirsty one came to thee in a day of burning heat and thou didst own cold water for which thou hadst no use, wert thou to refuse him thou wouldst be of all misers the most miserly. Then how can I refuse them My mercy when I have set My seal to My Name of "the Most Merciful of them that show mercy"? *al-Ghawthiyya*, 'Abd al-Qādir al-Jīlānī.

Destitution

Into these prayers of the beggar at the door the Muslim soul has poured all its sense of sin and destitution and of hopelessness in all other than God:

> Lo I Thy servant am at Thy door;
> Thine abject one at Thy door;
> Thy captive at Thy door;
> Thy destitute one at Thy door;
> Thy client at Thy door,
> O Lord of the Worlds.
> A weary one is at Thy door,
> O Thou Helper of them that seek for help.
> Thine anxious one is at Thy door
> O Thou who dost lift away the care of all the careworn.
> And I, Thy rebel, O Thou who seekest for penitents,
> Thy rebel who acknowledges his fault is at Thy door.

O Thou who forgivest sinners,
    One who confesses his sin is at Thy door.
O most Merciful of the merciful,
    He who has erred is at Thy door.
O Lord of the worlds,
    He who has wronged is at Thy door.
The lowly, fearful one is at Thy door.
    Have mercy upon me, my Lord.

What is the source of this moving prayer found in *Ḥizbu 'l-waṣīla* attributed to 'Abd al-Qādir al-Jīlānī, and in *Ḥizbu 'l-maghnā* attributed to Aḥmad at-Tījānī, and elsewhere in the manuals?

I have naught but my destitution
    To plead for me with Thee.
And in my poverty I put forward that destitution as my plea.
I have no power save to knock at Thy door,
    And if I be turned away, at what door shall I knock?
Or on whom shall I call, crying his name,
    If Thy generosity is refused to Thy destitute one?
Far be it from Thy generosity to drive the disobedient one to despair!
Generosity is more freehanded, graces wider, than that.
In lowly wretchedness I have come to Thy door,
    Knowing that degradation there finds help.
In full abandon I put my trust in Thee,
    Stretching out my hands to Thee, a pleading beggar.

Munājātu 'l-Imāmi 'sh-Shāfi'ī.

My God, in my very riches I am poor, how great then my destitution when I am poor! My God, I am ignorant in my very knowledge, how shall I not be crassly ignorant in my ignorance! My God, from me comes what accords with blame, but from Thee comes what accords with generosity. My God, Thou didst show Thyself kindly and compassionate to me before my evil deeds were done. Wilt Thou then deprive me of Thy kindness and compassion after those deeds?

O God, how near Thou art to me, and how far am I from Thee!

Ṣalawātun nājiya, Abū 'l-Mawāhib.

THE EVER-OPEN DOOR

These moving prayers which the Christian penitent can share with his Muslim brother, show an underlying sense that this door stands open when all other doors are closed against the sinner.

Thy door is open to the beggar . . . all means have failed Thy servant and all doors are locked against him. *Al-Ḥizbu 'l-kabīr.* Qādiriyya.

Thou who dost open when the busy doors of kings are locked. *Ḥizbu 'l-alīfi 'l-qā'im,* 'Abd al-Qādir al-Jīlānī.

His door never closes and the beggar is never turned away. *Mukhtaṣaru ad'iyati Ramaḍān.*

Night Communion

The most haunting of Muslim night prayers is from one to whom the door has been opened:

> My God and my Lord, eyes are at rest, stars are setting, hushed are the movements of birds in their nests, of monsters in the deep. And Thou art the Just who knowest no change, the Equity that swerveth not, the Everlasting that passeth not away. The doors of kings are locked, watched by their bodyguards; but Thy door is open to him who calls on Thee. My Lord, each lover is now alone with his beloved, and Thou art for me the Beloved.[1] *Ṭahāratu 'l-qulūb,* p. 150.

[1] What is the origin of this prayer which appears, with slight variations, here and there in Muslim worship? It is given as the nightly prayer on the roof, of Rābi'a (Margaret Smith, *Rābi'a the Mystic,* p. 27). Ash-Shaṭṭanawfī in *Bahjat,* attributes it, in a full and picturesque form to "a prophet of Israel". In Shī'a worship it is traced with an *isnād* to 'Alī Zain al-'Ābidīn, and by a picturesque tradition from Ibn Ṭawūs al-Yamānī, as a prayer that he heard 'Alī saying with tears as he made his *ṭawāf* of the Ka'ba one night from the *'ishā,* till the *saḥar* (*aṣ-Ṣaḥīfatu 's-sajjādiyya,* pp. 120–3). In this form the "kings" are specified as Banū Umayya.

14

THE ELEMENT OF GREETING

Taḥiyya, Salām, Malā'ika

Twice during the prayer-rite occurs a moment of greeting. The first, known as the *taḥiyya* or the *taḥiyyāt lillāh*, occurs when the worshipper is in the sitting position at the end of the second *rak'a*. The greeting that he then says is:

> Salutations and blessings and ascriptions of goodness belong to God. Peace be to thee, O Prophet, and the mercy of God and His blessings. Peace be to us and to the righteous worshippers of God.[1]

Although this only became obligatory in the set prayers under ash-Shāfi'ī (it has been thought by some to be a beautiful Islamization of former heathen greetings to idols), there is a final and twofold greeting which is primitive. This latter corresponds with the prayer of peace at the end of the Jewish *'amīda* when, after a brief silence for personal prayer, the twofold prayer is said:

> May there be great peace from heaven and life for us and for all Israel, and say ye Amen.
>
> He who maketh peace in His high places, may He make peace for us, and for all Israel, and say ye Amen.

In Islam the final peace-greeting is known as the *salām*:

> The best form of the peace-greeting is that the worshipper shall say turning to the right, "Peace be to you and the mercy of God", and turning to the left, "Peace be to you and the mercy of God."

These words end the prayer-rite. The worshipper makes his intention to withdraw from the rite and then:

> It is incumbent on the worshipper to say after he has finished the prayer-rite:

[1] There are very slightly variant forms of this, all with traditions behind them. "Ascriptions of goodness", *ṭayyibāt*, akin perhaps to the *Ṭūbā* of the beatitudes in the Sermon on the Mount.

Thou O God art peace and from Thee is peace and to Thee peace returns. (Some here add: Greet us then, O our Lord, with peace, and bring us to Paradise to Thine abode, the dwelling place of peace.) *Adhkāru 'n-Nawawī*, p. 34, *Majmū'atu 'l-awrādi 'l-kabīr*, p. 21.

"Thou O God art peace and from Thee is peace and to Thee it returns" is one of the richest sentences in Muslim worship, carrying us far beyond the idea of a spoken greeting given and returned. Some would explain it as meaning, "Thou O God art peace, in the sense that Thy Name is Peace" (*Qur*. 59.23). Others think of the spiritual quality of peace rather than of one of the Names of God. In either case the two-fold flow of peace suggests an experience of worship akin to what is explained (from the Christian point of view) in the following words:

"Without Him was not anything made that was made" (John 1.3). The whole created universe is a manifestation of the Son, that is of that side of God which is turned towards us and which alone we see. . . . But the Son eternally loves the Father, consequently there is in Him a continual response of the universe to the source of all being. The stream that flows out from the Throne is ever returning whence it came. Practical devotion therefore consists in entering into the stream, identifying ourselves with the perfect sacrifice of the Son to the Father which we plead in the Eucharist, and thus going home to God in and "through Jesus Christ our Lord". All things are returning to unity in him through whom they took their origin, even our Lord Jesus Christ. W. K. Lowther Clarke in *Liturgy and Worship*, p. 7.

The Muslim prayer of peace is attributed to the Prophet:

The Apostle of God used to say when he finished the prayer-rite, "I ask forgiveness of God" (three times), and he said, "O God Thou art peace and peace is from Thee. Blessed be Thou the Majestic the Revered." *al-Kalimu 't-ṭayyib*, p. 44 (Muslim, Aḥmad).

These greetings of peace in the prayer-rite will be seen to embrace the thought of God's greeting, of greeting the Prophet, of the greeting of all believers, and of the greeting of the angels.

God's Greeting

The phrases "Salutations belong to God" and "Greet us O Lord with peace", rich as they are in spiritual possibilities, are not much developed in the manuals. Muslim thought about the joys of the saints in Paradise has included among them a greeting, from God to His saints, based on *Qur.* 36.58, perhaps like the "Well done good and faithful servant" of the Gospel parable. 'Abd al-Qādir al-Jīlānī in his *'aqīda* sees the divine *taḥiyya* as given to the soul of the believer, or perhaps of the mystic only, immediately after death. Of that soul he says:

> When it is snatched away to its Lord at its departure from the body, His beginning with it is the greeting. *'Aqīda* in *Majmū'u aḥzābi wa awrād*, 'Abd al-Qādir al-Jīlānī.

Others would believe that in this prayer we dare to ask God's greeting for the believers yet on earth, to whom it must come like the kiss of peace to the sinful prodigal in another Gospel parable. It is probable that the Hebrew worshippers of old, when they sang "The Lord shall bless His people with peace", thought of that "blessing" as a salutation of peace. In any case Muslim worshippers rightly feel that these phrases lift the whole prayer of greeting from earth to heaven:

> The worshipper when (in the *taḥiyya*) he begins with the supernal world is permitted to enter the sanctuary of the Living Deathless One and to have the solace of intimate converse. *al-Ḥirzu 'l-manī'*, as-Suyūṭī, p. 41.

The Greeting of the Prophet

The sentence just quoted continues:

> And he (the worshipper) is aware that this privilege is his through the Prophet of Mercy, and he turns, and lo the Beloved (Prophet) is present, and he goes toward him with the Greeting, "Peace to thee O Prophet." Ibid., loc. cit.

So the universal "Salve Muḥammad" ascends, "Peace be to Thee O Prophet, and the Mercy of God and His blessings." It is an offering of love to Muḥammad from his people, sometimes, as here in the prayer-rite, addressed directly to him, but often in other devotions sent to him, as it were, by way of God.

> O God bring to the spirit of our lord Muḥammad a greeting and a *salām* from me. *Dalā 'ilu 'l-khairāt*, p. 41.
>
> Greet him with the special greeting which Thou dost reserve for him. *Ṣalāt* in *Fatḥu 'r-rasūl*, p. 40. Abū 'l-Ḥasan ash-Shādhilī.
>
> Greet him and the Family and the Companions with the *salām* of a lover to his loved ones. *Ḥizbu 'n-najāt*, 'Alī Wafā. In *Majmū'atu 'l-Aḥzāb*, p. 171.

That this greeting sent by way of heaven is felt to be a real communion with the Prophet is shown by the following:

O God cause our *salām* to reach him and cause a *salām* from him to return to us. *Fatḥu 'r-rasūl*, M. 'Uthmān al-Mirghanī, p. 51.

And it has come down to us that some of the saints used to hear him reply to the *salām* in the prayer-rite. *Fatḥu 'l-karīmi 'l-khāliq*, 'Alī al-Makkī, p. 12.

The greatest *salām* of a Muslim's lifetime is that which he utters before the Prophet's tomb at Medina. Directions for this by as-Suyūṭī, who died in 911/1505, show the greatness of the moment and may be compared with those of the modern guidebook issued for Egyptian pilgrims.

When he enters the Prophet's mosque it is preferable that he shall offer a prayer of two prostrations in the "Garden" (the pillared space west of the tomb). Then he shall approach the Noble Tomb in the direction of its *qibla* and stand in front of it four cubits from the head of the Tomb, in such a way that the lamp is above his head and the nail in the wall of the noble enclosure is facing the lamp (it is a silver nail driven into red marble); and he who is facing the nail is confronting the face of the Prophet.

Let him stand gazing down at the lower part of the Tomb-enclosure opposite to him, his eyes abased, in the station of awe, lowliness, and reverence. Then let him say, "Peace to Thee, Thou Joy of God's creation! Peace to Thee Thou beloved of God! Peace to Thee Thou lord of the divine messengers! Peace to Thee Thou seal of the Prophets! Peace to Thee Thou leader of the Festal Band! Peace to Thee Thou bearer of glad tidings! Peace to Thee Thou warner! Peace to Thee and to the Pure Ones, people of Thy house! Peace to Thee and to Thy pure wives, mothers of the faithful! Peace to Thee and to all the Companions! Peace to Thee and to all the Prophets and Apostles and to all the righteous worshippers of God! *al-Ḥirzu 'l-manī'*, p. 111 f.

To-day's guidebook says:

Then let him turn to the Noble Tomb in silence and reverence and humility and deep regard, calling to mind the greatness of the Prophet and that he is alive in his Tomb, the hearer of his prayer, and let him greet him saying with a subdued voice: Peace be to Thee O Apostle of God! Peace be to Thee O Beloved of God! Peace be to Thee O Best of God's creation! Peace be to Thee O *imām* of the pious! Peace be to Thee O mercy of the universe! *Dalīlu 'l-ḥajj*, Muḥammad Ḥasanain Makhlūf, p. 58 (for the four Sunni rites; the directions in the Shī'a guide books are practically the same).

Shī'a worshippers, if the pilgrimage to Kerbela is not possible, will climb on to a high rock or a house-top and give the greeting of peace in the direction of Kerbela.

"He is alive in his tomb", says the guidebook of the Prophet, and there is among Muslim worshippers a strong sense of living presence in the tomb at Medina, backed by many a vision and many a tale of sounds heard issuing from the sepulchre. That the *spirit* of Muḥammad is in the heavenly places (and is as we have seen in Chapter 11a for many of his people the focal point of the universe) all Muslims will agree. A common form of the *salām* seems to point to the separation of spirit and body:

> Peace be upon him and upon them (the Family), upon their spirits and their bodies. *Du'ā'un baina raka'āti nawāfili yawmi 'l-jum'a* (Shī'a).

yet they cannot think of the body in the tomb as dead.

> His body is sanctified, rendered august, purified, illuminated in the House and the sanctuary. *Durūd Tāj*, p. 3.

For all men a dim life within the tomb is envisaged, the life of the *nafs* without the spirit. For sinners a life of anguish, constriction, and loneliness, relieved by God's mercy for those who are His. Even for the Prophet, then, there is a life within the tomb as well as the heavenly life, though the nature of this and its relationship to his heavenly life is not made clear in the manuals. Many prayers envisage greetings sent to him at Medina as being there received. Sometimes this is thought of as through a momentary return of the spirit to the body.

> Our sending of the Greeting, the peace, to him from our country to Medina the enlightened, if it is not possible for us to be there face to face, is by way of our saying a greeting to him in our own city which will reach him, as many traditions and recorded sayings tell us. He said: No one greets me without God returning my spirit to me so that I may reply to his greeting.[1] *Fatḥu 'l-karīmi 'l-khāliq*, 'Alī al-Makkī.

But in the daily prayer-rite the majority of worshippers picture their *salām* as reaching the Prophet's spirit in the heavenly world, and for many it is brought to him by the ministry of angels.

> God has angels wandering over the earth who bring to me the *salām* of my community. *Fatḥu 'r-rasūl*, M. 'Uthmān al-Mirghanī, p. 61.

> It is related that the Prophet said: No one will greet me after my death without his greeting being brought to me by Gabriel, who will say,

[1] (Tradition from Abu Dāwūd, *Shifā'* 269.) M. 'Uthmān al-Mirghanī explains the return of the spirit to the body as the return of the power of utterance. "For he is ever living and his spirit is never separated from him." (*Fatḥu 'r-rasūl*, p. 48.)

"Muḥammad, So and So, the son of So and So, greets you with peace," and I shall say, "And peace be unto him and the mercy of God and His blessings." *Fatḥu 'l-karīmi 'l-khāliq*, 'Alī al-Makkī, p. 12.

The question of the Prophet's appearance simultaneously to believers in different places, and his simultaneous answers to innumerable greetings is thus dealt with:

I reply that this is a thing transcending common rules "As the sun is in the midst of the heavens, yet enlightens the lands to the East and West."—That answers the question to a nicety. And if our lord 'Azrā'īl (the angel of death) seizes at one moment a hundred thousand souls, the seizing of one no deterrent to his seizing another, while all the time he is busied in the worship of his Lord, how much more is this possible to our Prophet, the origin of all existence? *al-Fatḥu 'r-rabbānī*, M. ibn 'Abdallāh aṭ-Ṭaṣfāwī, p. 13.

The Greeting of All Believers

The *salām* is a right of every Muslim, living or dead,[1] absent or present, and it is the greeting of the people of Islam, differing from the *ṣalāt* (*'alā 'n-nabī*) which is the right of the Apostle. And so the worshipper says, "Peace be to us and to all the righteous worshippers of God." *al-Ḥirzu 'l-manī'*, p. 30. (It is also the right of the man who gives the *salām* to receive a reply, al-Bukhārī, *Janā'iz* 4.)

The *salām*, then, whether in the prayer-rite or by the wayside, is the daily greeting of the family of Islām, but it is for the household of Islam only.

The Qāḍī 'Iyāḍ said: In the *tashahhud*, 'Alī used to say, "Peace be to the Prophet of God. Peace be to the prophets and apostles of God. Peace be to us and to the believers, men and women, the absent and the present. O God forgive Muḥammad and accept his intercession and forgive the members of his house, and forgive me and my father." 'Alī only said that by way of instruction for others who were present, for it is established by tradition that his father had died a Kāfir (prayer for such being forbidden). *al-Ḥirzu 'l-manī'*, p. 40. (The prohibition is based on the case of the prayer of Noah, *Qur. 11*.45,46.)

In those Arabic lands where there are communities other than Muslim, *As-salām 'alaikum* is withheld from members of those communities. It is a constant sorrow for those Christians who live

[1] Cf. *Berakh.* 17.a, May it be Thy will O God to establish peace in the upper family and the lower family.

amongst Muslims whom they love that this greeting which they hear on every side is denied them. Arabs of Arabia and other Muslims who have never lived where there is a non-Muslim community accord the greeting of peace to non-Muslims. The writer first received it, a precious benefaction from a penniless man, an Afghan stowaway on a boat in the Persian Gulf.

The *taḥiyya* in the prayer-rite is then the greeting of the beloved community. It contains a sort of sketch for what Christians know as the communion of saints, and it looks back possibly to Christian worship, where every ancient liturgy has its exchange of fraternal greeting, whether in the universal "The Lord be with you" of the minister with the people's reply "And with thy spirit," or in the ancient Kiss of Peace (2 Cor. 13.12, now usually changed into a hand clasp) which still makes so living a moment, for instance, in the Coptic liturgy. This has been revived in some of the churches in India to express the new-found brotherhood in Christ. With the handshake go the words "*Jesu sahay*" (Jesus be your helper).

> You must picture yourself in a village church after the blessing has been given. The people do not hurry away, but stand in their places, the men on one side, the women on the other. Then there takes place a very orderly procession of the women. Moving up in a long line towards the east end, they go down along the men's side to the west, shaking hands and saluting each man as they go. After the women have gone out, a similar procession takes place amongst the men. *Worship in other Lands*, H. P. Thompson, p. 39.

A companion picture from Islam comes from a visitor to Fez.

> When the prayer was over, each of the worshippers shook hands with his neighbour and invoked peace for him and for the whole world. *Desert Encounter*, Knud Holmsboe, p. 26.

The lovely Muslim form of the greeting of the brethren is supported by tradition.

> A man came to the Prophet and said, "Peace be to you," and the Prophet having responded to his greeting the man sat down. Then the Prophet said, "Ten!" Another man now came saying, "Peace be to you and the mercy of God!" And his greeting was returned and he sat down. Then the Prophet said, "Twenty!" Next another came who said, "Peace be to you and the mercy of God and His blessings!" And the Prophet said, "Thirty!" *al-Kalimu 'ṭ-ṭayyib*, p. 80. (at-Tirmidhī, Abū Dāwūd.)

This, then, is the daily greeting of the household of Islām, sanctified by its use in the daily worship. Small wonder that it carries its *baraka.*

(Anas said.) The Apostle of God said: My son when you enter the house of your family, give the greeting of peace. It will be a blessing to you and to the people of your house. Ibid., p. 28 (at-Tirmidhī).

Even on entering an empty house the greeting should be given:

It is approved that he should give the greeting of peace whether there are human beings in the house or no in accordance with the word of God, "and when you enter a house *sallim* on yourselves, a greeting from God (from *chez* God) blessed and good". (*Qur.* 24.61.) *Adhkār an-Nawawī*, p. 13.

Here we have the very ancient idea of the *baraka* inherent in the salutation itself. (Cf. Matt. 10.12,13.)

The Greeting of the Departed

In the *taḥiyya* the greeting is for the whole family in heaven as on earth. Special greetings are often sent individually in devotions to the great ones besides Muḥammad.

Blessing and peace be to Thee (Moses) Addressed of God!

Blessing and peace be to Thee ('Īsā) Spirit of God!

Peace be to all the Prophets and Apostles! Peace be to the righteous servants of God, inhabitants of heaven and earth!

Unite peace to the people of peace in the abode of peace, a salutation and greeting of peace. *Ḥizb* (unnamed), 'Abd al-Qādir al-Jīlānī in *Majmū'u 'l-aḥzāb*, p. 40.

Semi-magical prayers have a greeting to Noah and once to Jarjīs, who may be the St George, beloved and appealed to by Muslims as well as Christians in Jordan and what is now Israel.[1]

Peace be to Noah in all the worlds (three times) and Peace be to Jarjīs. *Du'ā'u 'l-āyāt*, attributed to Uwais al-Qaranī.

The greeting of peace is the greeting not only of the prophets and great ones among the departed, but the regular greeting for the visitation of cemeteries.

Buraida said: The Apostle of God used to teach them when they went out to the burial grounds to say, "Peace be to you, people of the houses,

[1] Offerings to St George are placed by Muslims on the "High Place" at Ajlūn, as formerly, and perhaps still, in his ruined Church at Aṭ-Ṭayyibeh.

believers and Muslims, Verily we, if God will, shall be joined to you. We ask God's pardon for ourselves and for you. *al-Kalimu 'ṭ-ṭayyib*, p. 62. (Muslim. Aḥmad.)

In households where women are secluded, the Friday visitation of the cemeteries is often for them the one open-air expedition of the week, and they have their own pieties for that visitation. In Egypt, on arrival at the cemeteries, the greeting of the older woman is:

> Peace be to you, O community of *lā ilāha illā 'llāh!* ye are the forerunners and we are those who will come after you. Peace be to you (my son, my father)! May God at my desire soften the bricks under your head!

The Greeting of the Angels

In the final salutation of peace as the worshipper turns his head to right and to left he

> makes the intention to close the prayer-rite with the salutation, and in the *salām* he intends the salutation of those angels and Muslims who are on his right, and similarly in the second (those on his left). *Iḥyā'*, 5.9.

This salutation of the angels raises the whole question of their place in the life of worship in Islam. The religion came into being at a time when the surrounding Christian churches were much absorbed with the thought of the angelic world and dedications of churches to St Michael were common.

> And the third (church) he called by the name of Michael, Chief of the Angels, who is the Mediator for the human race, that wrath may be turned away from them and mercy may rest upon them. *Martyrdom of Simon*, trans. by Margaret Dunlop Gibson. *Cod. 539, Arabic, Mount Sinai.* Composition probably contemporaneous with the rise of Islam. Date of MS., A.D. 797.

This development, far beyond the teaching of Christianity, came into the churches of the lands around Arabia partly through their inheritance of Jewish ideas and partly through the ferment which the new wine of Christianity set up among those who tried to accommodate the Christian teaching to various gnostic systems in which hierarchies of angels, of principalities and powers played their parts. In a world where these ideas were at work, Islam was born, and the angels have their part in its cosmogony and religious scenery.

The prayer-manuals make great use of the Qur'ānic data concerning the angelic world and the names of angels, as well as of numerous traditions. Such texts as "Appointing the angels messengers with wings, two and three and four" (35.1) are often introduced into passages of praise.

For Islam the angelic world is not essentially superior to the human world. It was created from light (Muslim 7.221, al-Baiḍāwī 1.52) generally now interpreted (as in most of our manuals) as the Nūr Muḥammadī; in the Ghawthiyya, however, as *Nūru 'l-insān*.

> Then I asked, "O Lord of what didst Thou create the angels?" He said to me, "O Help from the Almighty, I created the angels from the light of mankind, and I created mankind from My light." *al-Ghawthiyya*, 'Abd al-Qādir al-Jīlānī.

But the angelic beings live in a world of light inaccessible to the earthbound, and are known to be obedient to their Lord. Certain of them are distinguished as the *muqarrabūn* (angels) and of these brought near al-Baiḍāwī says (on *Qur.* 4.170) that they are "the Cherubim who surround the throne or even more exalted angels." Angels played their great part in the story of Muḥammad's revelation, and in general the devotions regard them with awe and reverence.

> O God bless Thine angels and the *muqarrabūn* who praise Thee night and day unceasingly and do not disobey the commands of God to them, but execute His orders. . . . O God, as Thou didst choose them to be ambassadors to Thy Prophet and faithful agents of Thine Inspiration and witnesses of Thy creation, and hast rent for them the enclosure of Thy veils . . . so call down blessing upon them. *Dalā'ilu 'l-khairāt*, p. 165.

They are constantly mentioned in prayer as examples of the fear of God and of obedience.

> O God Thine angels are on their guard from fear of Thee, attentive, obeying Thee, carrying out Thy command, and they cease not night or day from Thy praise. (Shī'a prayer for the Day of 'Arafat.)

We learn, however, of cases of disobedience other than the great rebellion of Satan.

> God has an angel whom He, Most High, commanded to root out a city against the will of its inhabitants, and that angel was merciful to them and did not proceed to root it out. And God Most High was angry with him and broke his wings. Now when Gabriel passed by him that angel complained to him of his plight. And Gabriel petitioned God for him and ordered

him to call down blessing on the Prophet, and God forgave him and restored his wings to him by the *baraka* of that blessing on the Apostle of God.[1] *Fatḥu 'r-rasūl*, M. 'Uthmān al-Mirghanī, p. 62 (al-Mustatrif and ash-Shifā').

The world into which Islam was born was instinct with angels, as with *jinn*, a man might start one from any bush; and this sense of angelic presence as of the presence of the *jinn*, is still vividly alive in folk religion.

The Prophet said: When you hear a cock crow, ask God for a favour, for the cock saw an angel. *al-Kalimu 'ṭ-ṭayyib*, p. 88. (The Matāwila in Syria say the *shahāda* when the cock crows at dawn and connect it in some dim way with the denial of St Peter.)

It is necessary to end the gathering with sweet incense because of the angels and the *jinn*, and cut off any disturbing connections. *al-Fatḥu 'r-rabbānī*, p. 14.

Great Angels

Much use is made in devotions of the names of the archangels given in the Qur'ān, Jibrīl and Mīkā'īl and two more great angels there mentioned but not by name, the Angel of Death ('Azra'īl) and the Angel of the Last Trump (Isrāfīl).

O God, Lord of Jibrīl and Mīkā'īl and Isrāfīl, Creator of the heavens and the earth, deliver me from the heat of the Fire and the suffering of the grave. *Riyāḍu 'l-Janna*, Yūsuf an-Nabhānī (traditional, traced to 'Ā'isha by aṭ-Ṭabarānī).

I beseech Thee O God by virtue of Jibrīl who was entrusted with them (i.e. the two names Ar-Raḥmān Ar-Raḥīm at the inspiration of the Qur'ān), and by mystery of Mīkā'īl and Isrāfīl and 'Azrā'īl and every angel in heaven and earth. *Manba'u 's-sa'ādāt*, p. 6.

The faithful one Jibrīl on my right, the faithful one Mīkā'īl on my left, the faithful one Isrāfīl before me and the faithful one 'Azrā'īl behind me, and God behind them enclosing all. *Fatḥu 'r-rasūl*, M. 'Uthmān al-Mirghanī, p. 54.

This often-recurring quartette of names is constantly written at the four corners of charms. It occurs again in an initiatory catechism of the weaver's craft in answer to the question "Who are the four *pirs* of reality?"[2] It brings to mind the English nursery rhyme (perhaps a descendant of an ancient charm):

Four corners to my bed.
Four angels to my head.

[1] An echo of *Qur.* 23.58.
[2] *Les corps de métiers en Asie Centrale*. R.E.I. 1927, p. 254. (Catechism in Turkish.)

Other angels besides these four are individualized in the prayers.

Bless Jibrīl and Mikā'īl and Isrāfīl and the Angel of Death, and Riḍwān, Keeper of Paradise, and Mālik (see *Qur.* 43.37) Keeper of the Fire and the Spirit of Holiness, and the Faithful Spirit, and the Bearers of Thy Throne and the angels of Access and my two Guardian angels. *Mukhtaṣar ad'iyati Ramaḍān*, p. 98.

Guardian Angels

Of the Qur'ānic data concerning guardian angels, Professor Margoliouth wrote:

According to another text (*Qur.* 13.11), "He (a man) has successors before him and behind him, guarding him by Allāh's order," i.e. angels who relieve each other; different, it would seem, from those who are employed in taking notes of his actions (82.11). These are described as seated one on his left hand and one on his right hand taking down the words that he utters (50.17). On Judgment Day the two will accompany the soul, the one driving, the other testifying. Thus each one is in charge of four angels, who are relieved at the end of the day. *What did they teach?—Muḥammad.* D. S. Margoliouth.

The prayers in the popular manuals, however, do not seem to know any distinction between the recording and the guardian angels. Of two angels for these duties they are vividly aware.

Peace be to the two noble recording and guardian angels and the mercy of God and His blessing! *Ḥizbun li 'Abd al-Wahhāb ash-Sha'rānī* (by inspiration of al-Khidr), *Majmū'atu 'l-Aḥzāb*, p. 196.

(Of a New Year's prayer.) He who offers this petition on the first day of Muḥarram will be entrusted by God to two angels who will guard him from Satan. *Manbā'u 's-sa'ādāt*, p. 266.

Welcome! Welcome! to the new morning and the happy day and the two noble recording, just, and guardian angels! Write, in the bright dawn of this our Day! *Ḥizbu shaikhi Ḥamīd al-'ārif*, *Majmū'atu 'l-aḥzāb*, p. 310.

The Angels and Human Worship

Endless traditions of encouragement are quoted in the prayer-manuals to show the deep interest of the angelic world in the worship of human beings, their love for its varied phases, their participation in it and their prayer on behalf of the worshippers. All human worship is overshadowed with the rustling of wings.

(Friday, the day of prayer.) It is a day witnessed, a day which the angels witness. *Ṭahāratu 'l-qulūb*, ad-Dīrīnī, p. 126.

(From Abū Huraira.) The Apostle of God said: God has wandering angels who, when they pass by a *dhikr* circle say to one another, "Sit down here." And when the people offer a petition they say *Amen* to their prayer. And when the worshippers call down blessing on the Prophet those angels join in the blessing till they finish; then the angels say to one another, "Blessed are they, they will not go away unforgiven." *al-Ḥirzu 'l-manī'*, as-Suyūṭī, p. 90.

If the night of mid-Sha'bān is All Souls' Day for the Muslim world, the still more famous Night of Power (feast of the Inspiration of the Qur'ān) is Michaelmas. Then "the angels and the spirit descend", and there is "peace till break of day". (*Qur.* 97.4,5.)

Ibn 'Abbās said, When *lailatu 'l-qadr* comes, God commands Gabriel to descend with seventy thousand angels, inhabitants of the Lotus Tree of the Boundary. And with them are aloe-sticks (torches) of light and they set up their torches in the mosque of the (Meccan) sanctuary and in the Medinan sanctuary and Jerusalem and Mount Sinai. And Gabriel sets up his torch on the very roof of the Ka'ba. Then the angels separate over the lands of earth and visit every Muslim whom they find at the prayer-rite or engaged in *dhikr*, and salute him and clasp his hand and say *Amen* to his petition, and ask forgiveness for all the community of Muḥammad and pray for them till daybreak. *Ṭahāratu 'l-qulūb*, p. 72.

"On such a night as this," when he feels the air to be pulsing with angelic movement, many a worshipper has a vision of the heavenly world.

People differ in this revelation. Some of them see light like a sudden flash of lightning. Some have the veils withdrawn for them from the highest heaven and see the angels there after their various fashions, standing, sitting, bowing, or prostrating themselves and giving thanks and praising; and they behold Paradise and its houris and its palaces and its lights and its trees and its fruits; nay, they behold even the Throne of ar-Raḥmān which is the roof of Paradise; and they behold the abodes of the prophets and the saints and the martyrs and the righteous and the single-hearted. *al-Mukhtārātu 'l-ḥusnā fī faḍli wa aḥkāmi Ramaḍān*. Ḥasan 'Alī Sharīf, p. 17.

Part 4

OUTSIDE THE PRAYER-RITE

15

THE SAINTS IN WORSHIP

Awliyā'u 'llah, Ahlu 'l-Bait

> Ah surely the friends of God, to them is no fear neither shall they grieve—who believed and were God-fearing, theirs are good tidings in the life below and in the other life. To the words of God there is no reversal, that is the supreme attainment. *Qur. 10.62–4.* (The "good tidings" are often interpreted as visions.)

These are the glowing words which the Muslim recites as he visits the tombs of the saints, adding his voice to the testimony of his Book on "the supreme achievement". The Qur'ān, in no set doctrine, since that is not its way, but in many a promise, makes certain the blessedness of those whose beliefs and actions were alike Godward, "Who will pay them in full their reward and of His free grace give them more." (*4.117.*) In the world to come they shall hear the greeting of "Peace, a word from a merciful Lord." (*36.58.*) And surely their beatitude, *Ṭūbā lahum*, the word of the Sermon on the Mount (*13.29*), has its beginning in this life also.

Islam has been rich in saints, and if, as with those of other religions, her scribes and lawyers have sometimes made life hard for them, her people honour them.

There are humble folk-devotions, relics of a dim past of animistic belief in sacred stones, "high places", and haunting spirits. Such devotions, obscure, ignorant, and often full of faith, may play their part when an Egyptian peasant woman vows oil or lentils to the inhabitant of a whitewashed tomb among the mudbrick houses, or when an Arab village sacrifices a sheep to the walī of the neighbouring hilltop.

Our business here is not with these but with what the prayer-manuals have to tell us of the place of the saints in more literate devotion.

The Portrait of the Saints

The picture of the saints given by these books (not written for instruction but for devotion) is not very clear as to the saintly hierarchy which Muslim thought has evolved (and which differs slightly from author to author) under the leadership of the *quṭb* of his age, the Pole-saint, pivot of the world, of whose kind only one at a time is on earth. The following prayer shows such a hierarchy.

> Peace be to you, ye men of the mysterious other world! Peace be to you ye sanctified spirits! Ye lieutenant saints (*nuqabā'*), ye overseeing saints (*ruqabā'*), ye saints of permutation[1] (*budalā'*). Ye pillars of the earth, four pillars (*awtād*), ye two imāms, thou Pole-saint (*quṭb*) thou unique! Ye faithful ones, aid me with succour, turn to me a glance, be merciful to me, bring me my desire, my aim. Rise up to fulfil my need with our Prophet Muḥammad. May God Most High greet you with peace in this world and the next![2] *al-Fuyūḍātu 'r-rabbāniyya*, p. 104 (*Qādiriyya*).

Few prayers are as definite as this concerning the hierarchy, but many are clear that God has His friends everywhere on earth and in heaven. *Walī*, *awliyā'*, is the most general word for saints, combining the ideas of nearness, protection, and friendship. Thus the time-keeper of the Yūsufiyya Mosque at Fez, after greeting the Prophet, his Companions and Followers, Mūlai Idrīs and the local saints of Fez and Marrakesh, continues:

> May God reward, on our behalf, the saints (*awliyā'*) of the east and the saints of the west, south, and north, of land and sea, of heaven and earth, of the Throne and the Seat, with even greater favour than is their desert, and may He be well-pleased in them. *Majmū'atu 'l-wirdi 'l-'āmm*, p. 91.

The general portrait of the saints we can put together from many touches in our manuals. They are:

> God's purified, God's friends, those that are brought near, *al-muqarrabūn*. (A word which Nicholson translates, "the favourites of God", those who in the Scottish phrase are "far ben".) Ibid., p. 8.

They are dear to God. On the tomb of Mu'īnu 'd-dīn Chistī, Ajmīrī, is written "This is the dear friend (*ḥabīb*, a friend loving and beloved) of God, who died in the love of God."

[1] Of whom only a given number, often forty, are in charge of the world at one time. They relieve one another and hence are saints of permutation.

[2] This prayer which is taken from al-Jīlānī's *Ghunya* has a note appended to it explaining that the saints are on different days of the month at different points of the compass, a matter, which, with knowledge and care, can be arranged for in addressing them.

> Make me one of the lovers that are beloved, that are brought near, that have personal knowledge, that yearn for Thee. *Dalā'ilu 'l-khairāt*, p. 63.

Poverty is their bride:

> When you see one burning with the fire of poverty, broken by his exceeding destitution, draw near to him, for there is no veil between Me and him. Prize as a spoil the intercession of the poor, for they are with Me and I with them. *al-Ghawthiyya*, 'Abd al-Qādir al-Jilānī.
>
> In regard to struggling mortals they are "Lamps in the darkness". (*Dalā-'ilu 'l-khairāt.*)
>
> For they are the people of protection and hope and deliverance and penetrating vision. (Preface to *Majmū'u Ṣalawāt*, Muṣṭafā 'al-Bakrī.)

THEIR WORK OF INTRODUCTION AND INTERCESSION

We have already spoken of these "near ones" as sharing with the Prophet in the work of mediation which his people assign to him. (See Chapter 2.) Before dealing with what our prayer-books have to show us of reliance on the intercession of the saints we must note that in several directions in our day (as by Ibn Ḥanbal in his day) this is regarded as a non-Islamic development, derogatory to the soleness of God. In Arabia the Wahhābites will have none of it; and in India (a land of saints) a modernist Aḥmadiyya author writes:

> However glorified the position of these Awlias in the eyes of God and the world, the fundamental creed of Islam cannot tolerate the slightest thought of their being sought help from. It will not do for us to forget that in every prayer, a Muslim is required to pray in the terms—"*Thee* (i.e. Allāh, Thee alone) do we worship."

WASĪLA WITH THE PROPHET

It is a strange development that the Prophet who is regarded as his people's Mediator should himself be approached through saintly mediation. Yet the guide to the Pilgrimage by an official of the Azhar orders this indirect approach to him through the saints buried in his neighbourhood. We give two examples:

> Then he shall move opposite Abū Bakr and say, Peace be to thee O caliph of the Apostle of God! Peace be to thee O true friend of the Apostle of God! I bear witness that thou didst fight the good fight in God with true endeavour. May God reward thee with good on behalf of the community of Muḥammad. May God be well-pleased with thee and make thee well pleased. And may

He make Paradise thy future and thy dwelling place. And may God be well pleased with all the Companions. *Then he (the pilgrim) shall seek his mediation with the Apostle of God.* . . . Then he shall go out from the mosque to (the cemetery) *Al-Baqī'* and greet its inhabitants and offer any prayer that suits him *and seek the mediation of the people of those graves with the Apostle of God. Dalīlu 'l-hajj*, Ḥasanain Makhlūf, *Wakīlu mashā'ikhati 'l-Azhar.*

In Shī'a Devotion

For Shī'a worshippers, the royalists of Islam, whatever other saints God may have graced, the saints *par excellence*, the intercessors, the mediators, are *ahlu 'l-bait*, the people of the household, the family of the Prophet. And this because, for them, the *Nūr Muḥammadī*, that primal, pre-creation light from which all other prophets, angels, saints, and common mortals were created, passes down unimpaired, in all its heavenly authority through the blood-royal, through 'Alī and Fāṭima and the imāms descended from them. Here then is a "divine right" and an "apostolical succession" of more than royal authority.

Prayers for Pilgrims to the Tomb of the Imām 'Alī ar-Riḍā at Mashhad (Meshed).

(From the "Permission for the First Entrance".[1]) I have come to Thee my God, drawing near to Thee through the son of the daughter of Thy Prophet Muḥammad.

(From the "Permission for the Second Entrance".) Here am I seeking Thy permission and the permission of Thine Apostle.

Let me enter, O God!
Let me enter, O Apostle of God!
Let me enter, O our Lord, Commander of the Faithful.
Let me enter, O our lady Fāṭima the Fair, mistress of the women of the two worlds.
Let me enter, our lord Ḥasan, son of 'Alī.
Let me enter, our lord Ḥusain, son of Alī.
Let me enter, our lord 'Alī, son of Ḥusain, ornament of worshippers.
Let me enter, our lord Muḥammad, son of 'Alī.
Let me enter, our lord Ja'far, son of Muḥammad.
Let me enter, our lord Mūsā, son of Ja'far.
Let me enter, our lord 'Alī, son of Mūsā.
Let me enter, our lord Muḥammad, son of 'Alī
Let me enter, our lord Ḥasan, son of 'Alī.

[1] I.e. the entrance to the first building.

Let me enter, our lord Ḥujjat, son of Ḥasan, lord of the age.

Let me enter, O ye angels on duty, standing, surrounding, guarding this noble and blessed precinct, and the mercy of God and His blessings be upon you. (From a pilgrim's leaflet kindly contributed by Dr Donaldson from Meshed.)

At the still holier shrine of Najaf, before the visit to the tomb of 'Alī, the worshipper says:

Facilitate my visit to him, O my Lord, through his goodness. And as Thou hast not deprived me of a visit to him, so let me not be deprived of his protection; but continue Thy gifts of grace to me O God, and as Thou hast given me the grace of knowing him, so make me of his party (*shī'a*) and bring me into Paradise through his intercession. *Miftāḥu 'l-Janān*. The Arabic of these prayers written by a Persian scribe in Lahore is a little doubtful.

That this coming to the sanctuaries of the *imāms* is felt to be a real grace of God, the following prayer, to be said on entering the *ḥaram* at Najaf, bears witness:

Praise be to God who has guided us here, and had not God guided us we should have had no guidance. Praise be to God who brought me through His lands and mounted me on His beasts and led me by stages from afar, and kept off from me what was dreadful. . . . O God this *ḥaram* is Thy *ḥaram* and this place is Thy place. *Majmū'u suwarin wa ad'iya* (Delhi), p. 52.

How this overwhelming belief in the spiritual potency of the *imāms* colours daily life is shown by some notes from Miss E. Mitchell who lived among Shī'a Muslims in Faizabad.

When the child can speak clearly it is taught the names of the twelve *imāms*. At the New Year the requests of the household for the year are written down—the paper is folded up and fastened and weighted with a little ball of flour to make it sink. The head of the house rises early to take it to the river and throw it in. "It will find its way to the *imām*", the women say hopefully. The idea is prevalent that daily when the lamps are lit in the evening and the rooms swept after the evening meal, the spirits of the *imāms* enter the homes and, making circuit of the rooms, pass out again leaving a blessing behind them.

Second only in popularity to *Ganj il-'Arsh* in the Indian Shī'a manuals is the cry to 'Alī.

Call on 'Alī, the manifestor of marvels, thou wilt find him a help to thee in necessities. All care and gloom will be lightened by thy Prophethood, O

Muḥammad, and by thy sanctity, O 'Alī! O 'Alī! O 'Alī![1] *Majmū'u suwarin wa ad'iya*, p. 52.

Plenary Intercession

If for the *Shī'a* world the *imāms* are the intercessors *par excellence*, for the Sunnī world that place is held by a small inner group of saints of the twelfth and thirteenth Christian centuries to whom has been given the office of universal and accepted intercession. These are Aḥmad ar-Rifā'ī, Aḥmad al-Badawī, Ibrāhīm ad-Dasūqī, and 'Abd al-Qādir al-Jīlānī. While the *Shafā'a* of the Prophet is his people's great hope for the life of the world to come, these four are intercessors concerning the life that now is.

The manuals in our collection give only a few *awrād* of the first three, but many details concerning 'Abd al-Qādir al-Jīlānī as Succourer (*al-Ghawth*) and Intercessor. They tell (quoting from Shaikh Ibn al-Qāsim ibn Bakr Aḥmad in *Bahjatu 'l-asrār*) of his heavenly ordination to the universal ministry of intercession:

> And the Truth Most High said to him in the language of mysterious ecstasy, "Verily to-day art thou firmly installed before us and trusted." And he caused him to sit with the spirits of the prophets on a seat between this world and the next, between the Creator and the created, between the visible and the spiritual, between the perceptible and the imperceptible. And he gave him four countenances, one to look towards the earth, one to look towards the other world, one to look towards created beings, and one to look towards the Creator.

The claim to a seat among the spirits of the prophets is remarkable, because entrance to that rank had been regarded as closed since the coming of Muḥammad, and 'Abd al-Qādir could not without legal penalties have claimed it. Was there in his subconscious a resentment at the barrier which (if the saying is genuine) he thus came near to leaping in his ecstatic state? The whole corpus of sayings, writings, acts attributed to him, seems to reveal a character in which deep saintliness and natural ambition strangely worked together. He was perhaps an exemplar of the inward state behind the traditional prayer:

> Lord make me in my own eyes small and in the eyes of mankind great. *Du'ā'un nabawī*.

[1] A Persian manuscript from Lahore translated in *Revue des Études Islamiques*, 1927, p. 251, shows that this cry to 'Alī is one of the guild-prayers of the water-carriers, to be sung on returning from the well.

We quote a typical poem of the Qādiriyya Order which is an invitation to men to come with their cry for help (*istighātha*) to the founder's tomb:

> My tomb is the house of God. He who comes to visit it, hastening thither, will be granted might and exaltation.
>
> My mystery is the mystery of God, current in his creation. Cleave to my side if thou wouldst have my affection.
>
> My command is the command of God: If thou sayest, "Be," it shall be.
> And all things are under God's command; then judge of my power.
> I was seated in the holy vale[1] on Mount Sinai;
> I was exalted in my robe of honour.
> And all men in all lands call me blessed. . . .
> And all the countries of God are truly my kingdom,
> And their Pole-saints under my command and obedience.
>
> *Manẓūma bi 'l-wasīla* (Qādiriyya).

The method of seeking al-Jīlānī's help (*istighātha*) by members of the Order is as follows. After the evening prayers or the prayers of a night vigil, having given the final "peace", the worshipper is told:

> Prostrate yourself again before God after the "peace" and ask for your need. Then raise your head and call down blessing on the Prophet eleven times. Then rise and take eleven steps in the direction of 'Iraq to the right of the *qibla*, and say as you take the first step, "Oh Shaikh Muḥyī 'd-dīn!" (a cry on al-Jīlānī is then given for each footstep, ending up with), "O Lord of Lords 'Abd al-Qādir, Muḥyī 'd-dīn!"[2] Then say, "O little servant of God help me (*aghithnī*) by permission of God. Oh Shaikh of the heavy-laden, help me and grant me supplies to meet my need." (Finally there is a *du'ā'* to be read three times, which returns from the saint to God:) "O God, Thine are all things and through Thee are all things and from Thee are all things and to Thee are all things, and Thou art the All and All of the All."
> *Al-Fuyūḍātu 'r-rabbāniyya*, p. 45.

The visitor approaching the tomb at Baghdad should thus address the saint:

> Peace be to thee O King of the age, O *Imām* of the place, O wielder of the command of the Merciful, O heir of the Book and representative of the

[1] Scene of the revelation of the Burning Bush (*Qur.* 20.12).

[2] Was this slow advance with a cry at each footstep a relic of some far older ritual? It recalls the dragging footsteps of the priests of Baal about the altar (1 Kings 18.26 R.V. marg.) as they cried, "O Baal hear us", and which D. B. Macdonald compared to the gait for encircling the *Ka'ba*.

Apostle of God, O thou whose benefit is heavenly and earthly, O thou to whom all the people of the time are his family. Thou through whose petitioning help comes down, through whose blessing supplication is efficacious. Ibid., p. 194.

But many another saint than these great four is believed to have power and will to help struggling men. Was not the tomb of Ma'rūf al-Karkhī known in the jargon of Baghdad as *tiryāq mujarrab*, "a proved remedy"?

O saints of God, lo I am sick, and before you is medicine and healing.
Then of your favour look on me for treatment, and grant me of your goodness what is needed.
How many a sick one sought you at your door, and left it, sickness gone from him in healing.
How many a chronic sufferer have you helped, bedridden, whom your bounty has sufficed.
You are the door, and God is generous.
He then who comes to you finds grace and health.

Tawassulun bi 'l-awliyā', Muḥammad 'Alī, Muftī 'l-Jazā'ir.

The Spiritual Help of the Saints

These direct petitions to the saints for their help and intercession represent an extreme usage. A less direct way of seeking their mediation is by offering one's own prayers to God "through the reverence due to them". Thus we have Shī'a prayers *bi ḥurmat* the Shī'a imāms, Sunnī prayers *bi ḥurmat* Uwais al-Qaranī, Ḥasan al-Baṣrī, and a whole list of Ṣūfī saints (the regular usage of the 'Ushshāqiyya Order), Sunnī prayers also in the names of all "the people of Badr":

And they are the mediators for all purposes, the key of the doors on high.
ash-Shāfiya li'l-asqām, 'Abd as-Salām ash-Shaṭṭī.

But even these indirect petitions through the saints are not in the main line of Islamic prayer and would be disapproved by many. We must ask, then, what difference is made to the devout worshipper who does not so use their names, by the fact that Islam, the beloved community not limited to earth, includes so many God-devoted saints. Is there indeed a "communion of saints" in Islam?

We have to own that these Muslim prayers show nothing comparable to the fuller sense of communion in the sacramental life of Christianity, in which believers become "one bread, one body", and the "one body" which they become is "the body of Christ".

But if those depths of communion are outside the ken of these prayers we have also gratefully to recognize in them a sense of spiritual kinship between all whose goal it is to worship in spirit and in truth. We have noted that the greeting in the prayer-rite is a kind of rudimentary sketch for a communion of saints, as also the idea that all, in this world and the next, unite in the *taṣliya*.

The goal of the petition by the first and the last being one blessing by God Most High. *al-Ḥirzu 'l-manī'*, as-Suyūṭī, p. 12.

There is further the sense of a share in the prayers of the blessed.

O Lord give us a share in (*ushriknā fī*)[1] the prayer of the righteous, and allot for us an endowment and a portion in their prayer. *Majmū'u tabāraka dhū 'l-'ulā'*, p. 8.

There may be a strong sense of their spiritual presence when their *awrād* are being used. Thus, part of the preparation for reciting the famous *ḥizbu 'l-baḥr* is:

Then let him seek the presence of the spiritual personality of Sīdī ash-shaikh Abū 'l-Ḥasan ash-Shādhilī. *Al-Fuyūḍātu 'r-rabbāniyya.*

One who was setting out to write a commentary on *ad-Durru 'l-fā'iq* of Muṣṭafā al-Bakrī says:

When, without the company of helper or friend, I put out upon that deep sea, to gather its pearls and jewels, the sea-monster of earthly desire was about to swallow me as I was submerged and all but lost in its depths. And I cried for help to the high majestic one of unapproachable majesty, and lo I was washed up on the other shore and a voice cried to me as I was half asleep and half awake, "Adventure as thou wilt and fear not, O so and so." And through this I rejoiced and was glad, cheered and light-hearted, and I began that work relying on the lord (*Muṣṭafā al-Bakrī*) the Ascetic Traveller. *Fatḥu 'l-karīmi 'l-khāliq*, 'Alī al-Makkī.

In reading the Qur'ān too, the thought of all the devout who have brooded over it night and day may lead to spiritual aspiration:

[1] The verb used here is that adopted by some Churches in Arabic lands for Holy Communion which they call *ash-sharikatu 'l-muqaddasa*. This was probably an effort to give more of the idea of communion than is found in the commonly used *munāwala*, which gives the sense of reception into the hand. As a noun for Communion, *sharika* is somewhat external but has deepened with use.

Give us the fair qualities of the righteous.

Make us to stand in the footprints of those who rose up with it (Qur'ān recitation) in the night season and the daylight hours, till we are purified with its (the Qur'ān's) purification, and made to stand in the footprints of those who were enlightened with its light, whose hope failed not, and who were not cut off from the work by the imposture of deceptions. *Du'ā'un 'inda khatmi 'l-Qur'ān*, 'Alī Zain al-'Ābidīn.

The Open Path

When the Muslim worshipper prays:

Make fair our course of conduct that we may behold the people of heaven near as the people of earth. *ad-Durru 'l-fā'iq*, Muṣṭafā al-Bakrī.

the sequel to that vision commonly hoped for is a learning of their secret and a following in the footsteps of the saints. For while the rank of prophethood is closed, the rank of sainthood is open to all who can accept the cost of following it.[1] Even 'Abd al-Qādir al-Jīlānī, with his high doctrine of his own spiritual rank, realized the communion of leader and led, and in his opening prayer before a sermon used to say:

O God set right the *imām* and the community, the shepherd and the flock, and unite their hearts in good things and defend each of them against the evil in the other. *Du'ā'u 'l-istiftāḥ. Awrād 'Abd al-Qādir al-Jīlānī*, p. 4.

So the worshipper can say:

Deliver us from lower companionship and make us the companions of Thy saints. *al-Munājātu 'l-injīliyyatu 'l-wuṣtā. Saḥīfa sajjādiyya*, p. 219.

And make me one of Thy saints for "surely Thy saints, no fear is upon them, neither shall they grieve." (*Qur. 10.64.*) *Prayer for Tuesday, Miftāḥu 'l-janān*, p. 51.

[1] As, in the New Testament, the humblest members of a little Church in a foully wicked city are addressed as not only permitted but "called" to be saints.

16

THE WORSHIP OF THE CREATOR

al-Khāliq

> They meditate on the creation of the heavens and the earth. Not in vain O Lord hast Thou created this! Praise be to Thee. *Qur.* 3.191.

This Qur'ānic text has indeed tuned the worship of the Creator's Muslim people.

The familiar sentence at the opening of the *Imitation*: "If thine heart were right then would every created thing be to thee a book of holy teaching," might be an echo of the words of Fakhr ad-Dīn ar-Rāzī at the end of the twelfth century:

> The heart's invocation of God is that a man meditates on the secrets of the things created by God Most High till each atom of all their atoms becomes like a polished mirror set over against the unseen world, and when the servant of God looks with his mind's eye on created things the rays of his seeing pass from them to the world of majesty. *Lawāmi'u 'l-bayyināt*, p. 29.

The Names of the Creator

Muslim devotions are rich in such names. *Yā Khāliq* they call Him, *yā Bāri'*, *yā Muṣawwir*, *yā Qayyūm*, *yā Fāṭira 's-samāwāti wa 'l-arḍ*, *yā Badī'a 's-samāwāti wa'l-arḍi wa mā bainahumā*, and again and again, *yā man amruhu baina 'l-kāfi wa 'n-nūn*. All these are Qur'ānic echoes with a long history in Muslim thought that leaves its overtones for the worshippers of to-day. (See *Qur.* 29.24, 2.225, 42.11, 2.117, 36.82.)

al-Khāliq, the Creator, "He whose . . . fiat costs no effort."

al-Bāri' (from a root always including the idea of separation, freedom from . . .) "points to his bringing created things into being out of pure nothingness, to his producing them from utter negation". (*Lawāmi'u 'l-bayyināt*, p. 82.)

al-Muṣawwir is the Divine Artist who fashioned us, and who, in the words of Genesis, could look on his creation and see that it was very good. (Synonym of *ṣawwara, ṣāgha*. Compare the Great Artificer of the *Book of Wisdom.*)

Thou hast fashioned us in the darkness by the modality of thy kindness (*luṭf*) and stirred us to the life-breath of the spirit. *al-Munājātu 'l-injīliyyatu 'l-wusṭā*, 'Alī Zain al-'Ābidīn.

The *Muṣawwir* is He who beautified the outward forms of all and illuminated the inmost being of some. *Lawāmi'u 'l-bayyināt*, p. 226.

al-Qayyūm the Necessary Self-Existent, is a name that has also a meaning in regard to the Creation. He is the One who not only set, but *sets* up, for it is set up not once for all by an original fiat, but continuously by an ever-renewed fiat.

He was the cause of the setting up of everything beside Himself. It is established, then, that He is the One absolutely self-existent and the absolute cause of the existence of all beside Him. He then must be the *Qayyūm*, for it is an intensive form of *Qiyām* and this intensity only reaches perfection when nothing beside Himself is necessary to Him and all that is beside Himself is in need of Him. Ibid., loc. cit.

al-Fāṭir (used perpetually, but only in the phrase *Fāṭiru 's-samāwāti wa 'l-arḍ*) from a root meaning to cleave (used for instance of breaking a fast, like the English "breakfast", and so of doing anything for the first time) is the Creator who is the Divine Innovator. Dr Jeffery points out that it was in Ethiopic that this root had its meaning of "create" rather than "cleave" and it may have been a loan word in this sense.

al-Badī' is the Creator who is the Divine Inventor. If *al-Fāṭir* made things for the first time (neos), *al-Badī'* made them new in kind (kainos). To create means "to embody a pre-existing value or ideal in a new material" and *ibdā'* carries with it a sense of the realization of the Divine intention.

Thou, O Badī', art the First who didst initiate the beginning and didst give it existence. *Du'ā'* for Tuesday. *Ṣaḥīfa sajjādiyya*, p. 319.

He whose fiat lies between the Kāf and the Nūn is the Utterer of the Creative word *kun* the utterance that gives a thing place, *makān*, in His scheme of things.

I asked: "O Lord hast Thou locality?" He said to me, "O succour from the Almighty, I am the Localizer (*mukawwin*) of locality (*makān*), Myself unlocalized." *al-Ghawthiyya*, 'Abd al-Qādir al-Jīlānī.

God's light shone forth.
God's word appeared.
God's command wrought its effect.
God's glory was sanctified in transcendence.
By the word of God things came into being (*kuwwinat*).

Ḥizbu 't-tahlīl, Qādiriyya, but widely used.

Is He a Merciful Creator?

Very rarely do the prayers show any questioning concerning the harsher side of nature and the "red streak" in the creation as we know it. This question is, however, tackled by Fakhr ad-Dīn ar-Rāzī in his devotional commentary on the Names of God.

We see that He created beasts of prey and noxious things and gave some of them power over others so that they kill one another and some of them live on others. How then do you prove that He is merciful, when all this is His decree?

(His reply is as follows.)

There are three views as to the Creation.

The first is that of the philosophers who say that there are five logical divisions. A thing may be either absolutely good or absolutely evil or a mixture of good and evil. If the latter its good and evil may be equal, or the good in it may outbalance the evil, or the evil in it may outweigh the good.

If you recognize this division, we can proceed as follows: The three classes, pure evil, or evil prevailing over good, or evil equal to good, do not exist. We are left then with two divisions. The first of them that in which good is unmixed, and there would be no question that wisdom would accept this. The second is the class in which good preponderates over evil but in such a way that it is impossible to dissociate the prevailing good from the modicum of evil, and wisdom involves the acceptance of this also, for to abandon the greater good, because of the lesser evil involved would itself be a great evil.

The case being so, we see that the good is desired for itself while the lesser evil in that greater good is desired for the sake of the latter.

At this point the philosophers tell us that all the evils occurring in the world belong to this last class. And no one should ask, "Why did not the Almighty Creator dissociate that preponderant good from that minimum of evil?" because that is a thing impossible in itself, self-contradictory. No lack in the power of the Creator is involved, for lack of creative power only comes into question as regards the possible, not as regards the impossible and unthinkable in itself. This is the conclusion of the party of the philosophers on the question.

The second view is that of the Mu'tazilites, and is as follows:

Every evil that occurs in this world such as sickness and suffering, is an act of God Most High and He, praised be He and exalted, brought it about either for a considered reason or for the sake of a recompense. If for a considered reason it was that these ills might be His way of calling us, in His mercy, to the performance of our duties and the avoidance of wrong-doing. If for a recompense, God Most High will give to those animals (that suffer) such benefits in the next world that had they known their value they would gladly have endured the suffering to attain them in the future. Thus His action in causing suffering is not unjust and cruel.

The third view is that of the Sunnis. It is that the Merciful (*ar-Raḥīm*) is He who shows mercy and acts graciously, but the fact of His being merciful does not involve His *only* acting mercifully. For He, may He be exalted, is the Merciful, the Generous, the Bountiful, the Friendly, the Pitiful, as regards some of His servants, and the Queller, the Powerful Compeller, the Avenger as regards others.

So He, may He be exalted, is at once the Constrainer (the Clencher of His fist) and the Open-handed, the Harmer and the Helpful, the Exalter and the Humiliator, the Life-giver and the Slayer—each member of these doublets applies to Him. His mercy and His free favours are not due to the deservingness of the deserving or the obedience of the obedient. His quelling is not due to the undeservingness of the undeserving or the transgression of the transgressor. If the distinction between His quelling and His gentleness is the result of distinctions in the deservingness of the objects, whence comes that distinction in deservingness, that distinction between obedience and transgression? These differences do not arise in men equal in their capacity for right doing, but everyone knows that the one man became obedient because God Most High created in his heart the tendency to obedience, while the other became a transgressor because God created in his heart the will to transgression.

Thus it is clear that His mercy is subject to no limits and His despite is subject to no limits. And neither His mercy nor His despite is in any way caused by the action of any created being, but all that falls to the lot of created beings in the way of dispositions or actions or conditions is from the Real One, and is brought into being by His creative fiat. *Lawāmi'u 'l-bayyināt*, pp. 121–3.

The prayers in our books appear to accept this latter view. If they show less sense than the psalmist of old that "His tender mercies are over all His works", their psalm-like praises show an equally robust glorying in His strength and power, even in His harshness. Their nature-praises deal not so much as those of the Bible with the individualized life of beasts and birds and grass and trees, but are at home in great spaces of earth or desert or in the balancing of the clouds, and they show the delight of the dwellers in dry lands in the gushing forth of water.

God's Presence in Creation

A Qur'ān verse constantly quoted in praise is that which says:

Verily in the Creation of the heaven and the earth and the variation of night and day are signs to the possessors of intelligence. *3*.190. Cf. Rom. 1.19,20.

If it is said to thee, "Through what dost thou know Thy Lord?" then say, "Through His signs and His creations, and among His signs are night and day, the sun and the moon." *Shurūṭu 'ṣ-ṣalāt*, M. ibn 'Abd al-Wahhāb, p. 5.

They are signs to His Muslim worshippers, in their powerful order, not only of His originating wisdom and power, but of His immediate, ever-present working upon His world. Another of the Qur'ān texts most constantly quoted in worship shows Him as the worker in the revolving cycle of nature.

"Thou insertest night into day and Thou insertest day into night: and causest the living to issue from the dead and causest the dead to issue from the living." *Qur. 3*.27.

To the makers of these prayers He was Creator in the beginning and He is equally Creator now. He is *Al-Qiwām*, both the raison-d'être and the sustainer of all things. They hold together not by the outworking of cause and effect implanted in them by the first creative fiat, but by His perpetual momentarily renewed creative fiat.

Not an atom moves but by His permission. *Ḥizbu 's-suryāniyya*, 'Abd al-Qādir al-Jīlānī.

O Thou who holdest the heaven from falling on the earth unless with Thy permission. (Another of the most frequent Qur'ānic echoes: from *22*.15.)

Thou who settest the night and the day as two signs, Thou who erasest the sign of the night and settest in its place the sign of the day, perspicuous, that we may seek from Thee Thy favour and Thy good pleasure.

Thou who dost arrange all things in their divisions, Thou who holdest the heavens from falling on the earth unless with Thy permission, and keepest both of them from passing away, for indeed they would have passed away had the holding of them been in any other hand. *Du'ā'* for the 25th day of Ramaḍān. *Ṣaḥīfa sajjādiyya*, p. 446.

Very unusual is the following prayer with a sense not so much of momentary creative acts as of a divine arrangement of cause and effect, of interaction.

I ask Thee by the wisdom which imposed the first ordering of linked causes and the influence of higher things on lower, to make me behold that first ordering of linked causes in such wise that I see in the innermost the outer, and the first intrinsic in the last, and may observe the wisdom of that ordering through beholding its stages, and things that are caused preceded by their causes, so that I shall not be deterred by the outer vision from the vision of the essence of things. *Wird* for Wednesday evening, Qādiriyya.

Examples of Psalm-like Praise of the Creator[1]

O thou who settest in the heavens the signs of the zodiac, and lamps and a light-giving moon

O Thou who appointest the night and the day an ordinance for him who will meditate thereon or desires to be thankful. *Du'ā'* for the 23rd day of Ramaḍān. *Ṣaḥīfa sajjādiyya*, p. 440.

Thou who hast spread the earth as a plain:
Thou who hast set the mountains as stakes:
Thou who hast set the sun as a lamp:
Thou who hast set the moon as a light:
Thou who hast appointed the night as a covering:
Thou who hast appointed the day for livelihood:
Thou who hast appointed sleep for rest:
Thou who hast appointed hell for the requital of stubborn misbelievers.
Ḥirzu 'l-Jawshan.

My God, the morning is Thy morning. The splendour is Thy splendour. The greatness is Thy greatness. The light is Thy light and the brilliance is Thy brilliance. *Da'watu 'ḍ-ḍuhā*, M. Sirru 'l-khatm al-Mirghanī.

O Lord of the clear heavens and the light and the darkness in them:
O Lord of the outspread lands and the creatures and created things in them:
O Lord of the steadfast mountains:
O Lord of the sweeping winds:
O Lord of the airy clouds balanced between the heavens and the earth.
O Lord of the stars by Thee sent on their business and flashing in the air of heaven. *Du'ā'* for 27th of Ramaḍān. *Ṣaḥīfa sajjādiyya*, p. 323.

My Lord, glory and praise to Thee whom place does not conceal nor time change, for that Thou hast set the dawn in the place of Thy choice, and hast

[1] With these compare the nature-praise of Abraham Abulafia, Jewish-Spanish Kabbalist, 1240–91. See Ben Sion's translation of the *Zohar*, p. 26.

caused the breaking of the daybreak and raised up the dayspring, and by Thy greatness hast lighted up the glooms of obscurity; and hast brought out water from the hard barrier of the rocks, sweet and gushing, and hast forced the cleaving water from Thy presses; and hast set the sun a burning lamp, illuminated and illuminating, and hast created for it mansions, and for the moon and the stars their houses. *Du'ā'* for Thursday morning, 'Alī Zain al-'Ābidīn.

God's Knowledge

Like the writer of the Book of Job or of the 139th Psalm, Muslim worshippers are awed by the perfect, all-embracing awareness of the Creator who, in a common phrase of Muslim prayer,

> . . . knows the creeping of the black ant in the dark night[1] and from whom nothing is hid in earth or heaven or in the depth of the sea. *Majmū'atu 'l-wirdi 'l-'āmm*, p. 25, and frequently.

> Thou who knowest the weight of the mountains and the measure of the seas, and the number of the raindrops and the leaves on the trees; and the number of what is hidden by the darkness of night or revealed by the dawning of the day. *al-Wirdu 'sh-shāfī*, Yūsuf an-Nabhānī, p. 88, and frequently.

Like the Psalmist, the Muslim worshipper sometimes exclaims, "Such knowledge is too wonderful for me . . . whither shall I flee from Thy presence?"

> I cannot seek shelter from Thee in night or day, on land or sea, in any hole of earth or heaven, plain or mountain; for neither does the over-spreading night, nor the heaven with its zodiac, nor the sea with its waves, nor the earth with its ravines, nor the mountains with their eminences hide aught from Thee. *Du'ā'* for the 20th of Ramaḍān. *Ṣaḥīfa sajjadiyya*, p. 425.

Benedicite Omnia Opera

These are human praises; but another note is struck by a famous Qur'ān verse frequently quoted in worship: "Everything that is in the heavens and the earth gives praise to God" (*59.1*). If the great worship of God's Muslim people is the *shahāda*, the creation is also, with man, a witness-bearer to His uniqueness:

> My God, there is not a passing wind nor a drop from the clouds, nor a lightning flash nor a thunder-roll nor aught in the Throne and the Seat nor

[1] Sometimes the phrase is, "He hears the footfall of the ant beneath the stone."

a sign in Thy Kingdom which does not pronounce the *shahāda*, bearing witness that Thou art God and there is no God but Thee. *Ḥizbu 's-suryāniyya*, 'Abd al-Qādir al-Jīlānī.

Thou art praised and beloved by all Thy creatures, beasts and things of earth and men. *al-Ḥizbu 's-saifī*.

Christian legends of the beasts that kneel in their stalls on the Holy Night have their counterpart in this description of the Night of Power:

Some of its signs are that a man may see all things prostrating themselves to God Most High. Among these signs for instance, lights shining in all directions, even in the darkest places, dogs silent from barking, salt water becoming sweet for that night, then returning to its saltness. *al-Mukhtārātu 'l-ḥusān fī faḍli wa aḥkami Ramaḍān*, p. 31.

Of the Qur'ānic basis for this praise of the creatures, Professor Margoliouth wrote:

Everything that is in heaven and earth gives praise to Allāh, as also do the birds, spreading their wings; each one knows its prayer and praise.

The mountains were told to repeat the praise of Allāh with King David as well as the birds. If the Qur'ān were revealed to a mountain you would see it humbled and splitting for fear of Allāh. There are stones which fall down for fear of Allāh. The star and tree prostrate themselves. The statement that the mountains received orders to sing Allāh's praises with King David at evening and at dawn does not lend itself easily to metaphorical exegesis. These passages would appear to have been taken literally by those who asserted that trees saluted Muḥammad as Prophet of Allāh, a detail which figures in his biography. *What do they teach?—Muḥammad*. D. S. Margoliouth.

We forget to question whether texts are to be taken literally when we are swept up into the chorus of the praises of the creatures:

Glory to Him whom the mountains praise with what is in them:
Glory to Him whom the trees praise as they put forth their leaves:
Glory to Him whom the date-palms praise at the maturity of their fruits:
Glory to Him whom the winds praise in the ways of the sea. *Ḥizbu Uwais al-Qaranī, Majmū'atu 'l-aḥzāb*, p. 321.

And the heavens and their canopies praise Him, and the earth and its embroideries, and the mountains and their heights, and trees and their branches, and the seas and their monsters, and the stars in their rising, and the rains in their falling, and the wild beasts of the earth in their preying and their dens, and the fulness of the rivers and their ripples, and the sweetness and brackishness of waters, and the blasts of the winds and their roaring, and everything that may be described or heard. *al-Munājātu 'l-injīliyyatu 'l-kubrā*, 'Alī Zayn al-'Ābidīn.

The Creator of Man

But this Creator to whom the chorus of praise arises, is the Creator of *Man*, and here the Muslim worshipper sees a separate order of creation with a vocation (for some at least) to a high destiny. We quote from the meditations that have found their way into the manuals:

God blessed and exalted be He, said, "We have created man in the best fashion" (*Qur.* 95.4) (with the best "*set-up*"). For man was created capable of receiving the knowledge (personal knowledge) of God Most High; the mirror of his heart was prepared for the reception of the mysteries of God, fitted for the irradiation of the beauty of God Most High. . . . And David said, O Lord why didst Thou create man? (al-Khalq).[1] And God, Blessed and Exalted, said, O David I was a hidden treasure and desired to be known, therefore, I created man that I might be known. *Risālatun fī 'l-maqāmāti 's-sab'*, 'Abd al-Qādir al-Jīlānī.

Or again,

Thou hast created man and tested him with good and evil, and sent him forth into this abode that he may know Thee; and hast veiled from him the inner and spiritual by the outward appearance of things seen. Then Thou hast raised the veil, for whom Thou wilt, from the secret of the declaration of Unity, to which indeed all that is, all that Thy fiat has brought to be, all existing things bear witness. *Wirdu 't-tamjīd*, 'Abd al-Qādir al-Jīlānī.

Thy truth, Thy righteousness, Thine excellence, Thy might, Thy free favour have never failed me for a moment since Thou didst send me into the abode of experience and reflection and discursive thought, to see what I should bring with me to the lasting abode and the session of the blessed. I am Thy slave: make me, then, to be Thy freedman. *al-Ḥizbu 's-saifī.*

It is not only in man's original creation that God is his Creator, but all the sustenance, *rizq*, spiritual and material, that comes to him is due to continuous creative fiats:

Thou, the stores of whose sustenance are in the Creative "Fiat". *Munājātu 'l-imāmi 'sh-Shādhilī* in *Majmū'atu 'l-awrād*.

[1] *Al-Khalq* means, of course, the creation. But it is very often used of man, the creature par excellence, and from the context it would seem that the writer here so understood it. Some mystics use *al-khalq* for the common run of mankind as distinguished from *al-qawm*, the mystics.

The worshipper of this Creator feels the goodness of the boon of life and it is noteworthy that in prayer the Name of God constantly associated with His creative activity is *al-Laṭīf*,[1] the Kindly.

> O Thou Kindly before all kindly ones, O Thou Kindly after all kindly ones, and O Thou who wast kind in the creation of the heavens and the earth, I ask Thee, O my Lord, as Thou wast kind to me in the darkness of the (parental) reins, so be kind to me in Thine irreversible decree and Thy decisions of power concerning me. *Wird* for Thursday, Qādiriyya.

He is bound by no laws, but He has His "customs" and they are customs of kindness for His worshippers.

> O Thou on whose generosity and the beauty of Thy customs all petitioners depend. *Ḥizbu 'l-ibtihāl*, 'Abd al-Qādir al-Jīlānī.

THE PRE-CREATION MYSTERY OF MUḤAMMAD

There is hardly any reference in our prayer-books to a mysterious primordial covenant between Allah and the pre-creation *ṣūra* of Adam, called out before the creation of the worlds to establish a relationship with all the sons of Adam ever to be created.[2]

The thought of this Adamic *ṣūra* and covenant has been merged and submerged in another doctrine in which the pre-creation mystery, and the pre-creation relationship with the race that is to be, is all summed up in the spiritual existence of Muḥammad (the *Nūr Muḥammadī*) before all worlds.

The creation stories in our manuals differ, but all agree in this. An easy and popular book has the following:

> (From Ka'b al-Aḥbār.)[3] The first thing that God created was an essential substance (*jawhara*) and from this essential substance He created darkness and

[1] There are several variants of the much-used "Prayer of Yā Laṭīf", some said to have been taught to travellers in the desert by al-Khiḍr, another said to have been the prayer of Jacob when Judah brought him Joseph's coat as a sign that the latter was alive (*Qur.* 12.93). See, on prayers of Yā Laṭīf, *al-Istighāthatu 'l-kubrā*, Yūsuf an-Nabhānī.

[2] Based on *Qur.* 7.171, combined with the story of Satan's refusal to prostrate himself before the primeval form of Adam (2.23, 7.10–13).

[3] Ka'b al-Aḥbar, a famous convert from Judaism, may be responsible for the obvious relationship of this account to Genesis 1 into which the *Nūr Muḥammadī* has been so curiously woven.

from the darkness He created light, and from the light He created the "Muḥammadic Light" nine thousand years before He created the creation (*khalq*); and when God Most High willed to create things (*al-ashyā'*) He created from the Light of our Lord Muḥammad sweet water and set blessing (*baraka*) in it. Then He divided it into ten parts and created from the first part the Throne and commanded it to abide over the water, and from the second part the Pen and commanded it to circumambulate the Throne a thousand years. And the pen saw the name of Muḥammad written on the base of the Throne. . . . And from the third part He created the Tablet, from the fourth part the Sun, from the fifth part the Moon, from the sixth part Paradise, from the seventh part the Fire, from the eighth part the Angels, from the ninth part the Seat and from the tenth part the Prophets. *al-Majmū'atu 'l-mubāraka*, 'Abduh Muḥammad Bābā, p. 42 f.

Aḥmad at-Tījānī gives a more theological account in a *Wird* not permitted to beginners, but yet printed in popular collections:

God! God! God! My God, Thou art God and there is none other god than Thou, high in the isolation of the Presence of Thy Oneness, in which Thou didst will the coming into existence of Thy purposes, and didst produce from Thy perfect light the production of truth and gavest it discursive reason and didst appoint for it a perfect complete form (*ṣūra*) given existence by reason of the source of its existence in the uniqueness of the Presence of Thy Oneness, before the display of bodily forms.

And from it (this *ṣūra*) and in it and by reason of it Thou didst appoint the unfolding of knowledge; and from the influence and holy power (*baraka*) of this greatness (the *ṣūra*) Thou didst appoint the bodily forms (*ashbāḥ*)[1] of all forms (*ṣuwar*), the motionless and the moving, assigning to them the capacity for motion or stillness. And Thou didst set them in the enclosure of Might, since from that (Might) and in it and for it they had come. And the emerging forms shone out with the acceptance of existence, and Thou didst decree for them and in them and from them what suited and was fitting for the variations of their forms.

And Thou didst command them to emerge to fulfil what Thou hadst decreed for them and appointed for them, engraved for them in the Preserved Tablet[2] from which (the Tablet) Thou didst create, by its holy power (*baraka*). And Thou didst decree for them all that Thou didst will in them and through them. And Thou didst set all the all in Thy All, and didst appoint this all from Thy All, and didst appoint this all a handful of the light

[1] *Ashbāḥ*, forms as yet without individualized spirits.

[2] The Preserved Tablet with the writing of predetermined decrees is often in our prayers (and in this one a few sentences lower down) identified with Muḥammad.

of Thy greatness, a spirit for the purposes of which Thou art worthy as regards him and he is worthy as regards Thee. I ask Thee, O God, by the august rank of this greatness to bless and greet the Interpreter of the Tongue of Pre-Eternity, the Preserved Tablet, the Light issuing forth and spread abroad, which no perceiver can grasp and no pursuer can reach. *Yāqūtu 'l-ḥaqā'iq*, Aḥmad at-Tījānī.

So in the worship of the Creator, this second figure emerges, assuming functions of the Divine Logos, or of the Holy Spirit, called by names that else are reserved for God alone, a creature, yet isolated in the pre-creation glory from all other creatures, accorded a position which gives to him so many of the functions of divinity as to come perilously near the dread sin of *shirk*.

It is narrated that God Most High when He created the Throne wrote upon it with light, "There is no god but God, Muḥammad is the Apostle of God!" And when Adam went out from Paradise he saw written on the base of the Throne and on every part of Paradise the name of Muḥammad conjoined with the Name of God Most High. Then he said, "O Lord who is this Muḥammad?" And God Most High said, "Thy child but for whom I should not have created thee." *Ṭahāratu 'l-qulūb*, ad-Dīrīnī, p. 35.

Muḥammad . . . the abode of the divine irradiations, the Throne of the transcendent mysteries, the ocean of knowledge from on high[1] . . . the Sultan of the Kingdom of Thy Unity. *Ṣalātu Muṣṭafā al-Bakrī*, printed in *Bashā'iru 'l-khairāt ma'a 'l-awrād*.

Muḥammad . . . God's kindness.[2] The mystery of the Adamic Creation, Light of Lights,[3] Mystery of Mysteries, Spirit of Spirits. *al-Jawāhiru 'l-mustaẓhira*, M. 'Uthmān al-Mirghanī.

The Person of the Unity, and yet not Person, but Thy light united with Thy Light.[4] *Ṣalātu Muṣṭafā al-Bakrī*.

The Single one in the right of his prophethood absolutely without like or equal. The Unique whose perenniality in the inwardness of hid

[1] *Al-'ilmu 'l-ladunnī*, knowledge direct from God, from *chez* God.

[2] *Laṭīf*, the name of God so often used in connection with His creative activity.

[3] In the Qur'ānic phrase God is *nūrun 'alā nūr* (24.25 "Light Verse"). In our prayer-books he is addressed as *Yā Nūra 'n-nūr*, the phrase here given to Muḥammad and suggesting an echo from the Nicene Creed. The writer has heard the dwellers in one of the poorest alleys in Cairo chanting in a street *dhikr* (*Bayyūmī*), "I saw the Light of the Prophet ere ever there was sun or moon or fire. Glory to Him who formed thee, O Prophet, Light of Light."

[4] The unusual word translated Person is *uqnūm*, as used in Arabic in the Christian creeds of the "Persons" of the Blessed Trinity.

"Muḥammadhood" is transcendently separate from all that is below his rank inward and outward. The Merciful Father, the Patient Lord.[1] Ibid.

The Praise of Creation for Muḥammad

Muslim worshippers, then, hear a second chorus of all creation joining in the ceaseless praise and blessing of this figure. To build up this worship (for what is it but worship?) they make use of all created things something after the fashion of the nature prayers of Richard Jefferies on the South Downs:

By all these I prayed, by the rolling sun bursting through untrodden space, a new ocean of ether every day unveiled. By the fresh and wandering air encompassing the world; by the sea sounding on the shore—the green sea, white-flecked at the margin, and the deep ocean; by the strong earth under me. Then, returning I prayed by the sweet thyme, whose little flowers I brushed with my hand; by the slender grass; by the crumble of dry chalky earth I took up and let fall through my fingers . . . with these I played, as if they were the keys of an instrument, of an organ, with which I swelled forth the notes of my soul, redoubling my own voice by their power. *The Story of my Heart*, Richard Jefferies.

So of the blessing of the Prophet:

O God call down blessing on our lord Muḥammad . . . to the number of the rolling clouds and the sweeping winds, from the Day when Thou didst create the world to the Resurrection Day . . . to the number of the drops that rain from Thy heavens on Thy earth, and that will rain till the Resurrection Day . . . to the number of breezes of the wind and the movements of trees and leaves and field crops, and all that Thou hast created in desert or cultivated land, from the day of Creation till the Resurrection Day. *Dalā'ilu 'l-khairāt*, p. 129.

O Lord call down a blessing on Muḥammad in the cooing of the doves, in the hovering of birds, in the pasturing of cattle, in the excellence of the strong, in the might of the full-grown, in the sleeping of slumberers . . . in the brightening of morning, in the murmur of the winds and in the tramp of cattle, in the girding on of swords and the brandishing of lances and in the health of bodies and spirits.[2] *aṣ-Ṣalātu li 'l-Būṣīrī*.

[1] The collection, in this extract, of phrases constantly used of God is startling! *Al-witr, al-fard, sarmadatuhu, al-mutliqu 'an . . . ar-raḥīm, al-ḥalīm.*

[2] It is said that when al-Būṣīrī was employed on a sleepless night, on the seashore, in making these verses, the Prophet came to him walking on the sea to give him his encouragement. (*Fatḥu 'r-rasūl*, M. 'Uthmān al-Mirghanī, p. 54.)

So all nature is employed to weave a mystic crown, but for whom? Where is he of whom it is reported that he said:

> "Praise me not as the Christians praise 'Īsā. See, I am the servant of God and His Apostle" at-Tirmidhī, *Shamā'ilu 'l-Muṣṭafā*, 2.148.

To read these prayers and then to turn back to the Muḥammad of the Qur'ān and of history is to pass from one climate to another. Has Islam in its very love for its Prophet been untrue to him?

17

ANSWERS TO PRAYER: GOD THE DOER

Ijāba, Qaḍā, Riḍā

As in other religions so in Islam petitions may range from prayers centred on a request to prayers centred on Him to whom request is made, and the thoughts about answers to prayer vary accordingly.

We begin with prayers centred on the request. In these, any manner of plan may be adopted to secure a favourable answer. We have here the religion of the natural man, outside as well as inside Islam, and the plans for securing answers are much the same at this level of religion, the world over. We note some of them:

Prayer at Favourable Places

Chief among these are *'arafat*, the tomb of the Prophet and the tombs of saints. The Mirghaniyya say of their founder's tomb at aṭ-Ṭā'if:

> Sīdī as-Sayyid 'Abdallah al-Mirghanī al-Maḥjūb, owner of the tomb before which all the needs of creation are met.

At Favourable Moments

> It was said to the Apostle of God, "What petition is most heard?" He said: (That of) the last spell of the night, and immediately following the prescribed hours of prayer. *al-Kalimu 'ṭ-ṭayyib*, p. 47.

There is an hour known as *sā'atu 'l-ijāba*, the hour of answering. This is explained as that blessed time when the Friday prayer-rite is in progress:

> The Prophet said that it was the time between the sitting of the *imām* on the pulpit until he makes the final *salām* of the *ṣalāt*. *Adhkār an-Nawawī*, p. 40.

With a very strong sense of the blessedness of the night-vigils goes the following tradition often quoted in the manuals:

Abū Huraira narrated that the Apostle of God said:

Our Lord, blessed and exalted be He, descends every night to the lowest heaven when there remains the last third of the night. And He says, "Who will make petition to Me that I may answer him?" *Ṭahāratu 'l-qulūb*, ad-Dīrīnī. (Frequent in the manuals.)

The manuals are scattered with prayers which are efficacious on various nights, especially Thursday and Friday night, and on the last Friday of Ramaḍān.

The Power of Numbers

We quote a Shī'a tradition. Exact requirements as to numbers abound in Sunnī manuals as well as Shī'a:

Never do forty men assemble together and make petition to God concerning some matter without God's answering them. And if there are not forty, then if four petition God ten times, He answers them. And if there are not four, then if one petitions God forty times, God the Mighty, the All-Powerful, answers him. al-Kulīnī, *Uṣūlu 'l-Kāfī, Bāb*. 4.

Miss E. Mitchell tells of a sort of *novena* of the Shī'a women of Faizabad to obtain some desired answer. They arrange to come together in a *majlis* seven times to say the *namāz* and read the Qur'ān with this special intention. After meeting six times, they delay the seventh meeting till they see if the petition is granted. The seventh *majlis* only takes place if the prayer is answered favourably.

Verbal Forms

This book has already given examples of forms of prayer with special promises attached to their recitation. These are *ad'iyatun mustajāba*, prayers that are answered.

I lay anyone who possesses or knows this *du'ā'* under an obligation and an adjuration to make it known, for it is of importance, of benefit to Muslims, since it is one of the "answered prayers". al-Ḥabīb 'Alī ibn Ḥasan al-'Aṭṭās concerning one of his *ad'iya* in *Khalāṣatu 'l-Maghnam*.

Of the many forms used to ensure answers by far the commonest is the *ṣalātu 'alā 'n-nabī*. Directions for such use abound in the manuals.

Petition is not refused if the *ṣalātu 'alā 'n-nabī* precedes and follows it. *Ṭahāratu 'l-qulūb*, ad-Dīrīnī, p. 258.

ADJURATIONS

God is continually besought in prayer *bi ḥaqq* or *bi ḥurma* (in virtue of, by the reverence due to) some person or thing of holy power—Muḥammad, named saints, the Qur'ān or some sūra or verse of it, the *shahāda* or some other word of known sanctity, and most of all by His own Names, and by "the Greatest Name".

> Through It Thou didst save Noah's ark, and through It Thou didst cause the dead to speak to Jesus son of Mary, and through It Thou didst subdue the Arabs and the non-Arabs to our Prophet Muḥammad, and through It Thou hast answered petitions.... *Ḥizbu 's-suryāniyya*, 'Abd al-Qādir al-Jīlānī.

Except for the solemn use of the powerful Names, these introductions with *bi ḥaqq* and *bi ḥurma* perhaps partake more of the nature of *tawassul* than of adjuration; they point to the worshipper's sense of the need of someone or something more worthy than himself, to secure him a favourable answer. But pure adjuration is not wanting.

It seems entirely incongruous with the development of Muslim thought about God that anyone or anything can have rights over Him. Yet a Qur'ān verse shows Him binding Himself to an obligation. "It is binding upon us to deliver the believers (*ḥaqqan 'alainā*). *10*.103. A tradition of which worshippers have not failed to make use concedes *ḥaqqu 's-sā'ilīn*, the right of petitioners over Him, their right to His goodness or His reply. (Abū Dāwūd *9*.33, at-Tirmidhī *5*.29, Ibn Mājah *58*.3.)

> O God, I adjure Thee by the right of petitioners over Thee, for indeed the petitioner has his right with Thee, that whatever servant or handmaid of the people of land or sea has had his petitions accepted and answered by Thee, Thou wilt give me a share in whatever was right in their petitions, and wilt give them a share in whatever is right in mine. *al-Wirdu 'l-a'ẓam*, 'Alī ibn Sulṭān Muḥammad al-Qārī. (This form of adjuration is not infrequent in the manuals.)

A strong form of pure adjuration, which again raises our astonishment that His Muslim worshippers should venture upon it, is *aqsim 'alaik*.

> I adjure Thee by our lord Muḥammad... that Thou subdue to me mankind with its different divisions and colours....
>
> I adjure Thee O God by these august Names, and their angels, Thy noble

servants, that Thou deal kindly with me and keep me. *Du'ā'u 'l-basmala*, 'Abd al-Qādir al-Jīlānī.

We are reminded of what St Gregory Nazianzen tells us of his sister:

She came, says he, to a religious impudency with God, and to threaten Him that she would never depart from His altar, till she had her petition granted. And God suffers this impudency and more.[1] (Sermon of John Donne.)

Types of Answered Prayer

We have already noted the approach to God by way of the Prophet and the saints. In this connection Muḥammad is called *Bābu kulli ṭālib* or *Ghawthu kulli ṭālibin muḥtāj* (Aḥmad al-Tījānī)—the door, or the help of every needy seeker. We have seen too how the prayers of the prophets in the Qur'ān and God's answers to them are held up before Him as reasons for hoping that He will be as good to-day. Of these the type-case (living on through the ages in both Christianity and Islam as such a type) is Zacharias, because of the improbability of the answer granted.

Hear my cry as Thou didst hear the cry of Thy servant Zacharias! *aṣ-Ṣalawātu 'l-mashīshiyya.*

The other typical case is the prayer of the rain-bringer 'Abbās. This comes under the heading of *tawassul* because the story in its traditional form makes him signally *mujābu 'd-da'wā* through his connection with the Prophet. It is no doubt the daring of the request that makes rain-bringing prayers stand out in memory. 'Abd al-Qādir al-Jīlānī had a pious aunt, famous in his native province for such prayers, and the writer has heard in the Near East of a woman to whom such requests are brought to-day.

The famous story of 'Abbās is thus told for edification in one of our manuals:

Ibn 'Abbās said: A drought befell the people in the days of 'Umar ibn al-Khaṭṭāb, and Ka'b al-Aḥbār[2] said, "O Commander of the Faithful,

[1] Wensinck points out that some of the early fathers of Islam and the Prophet himself are said to have used this type of prayer. Bukhārī, *Jihād*, 88, Muslim 5,223. (*Wensinck, Zauberelemente* in Nöldeke's *Festschrift*.)

[2] It is interesting that the famous Jewish convert to Islam, to whom are due many traditions showing a knowledge of Jewish and Christian books should be connected with this story, for in the rite of the Prayer for Rain, the three religions

when a like misfortune befell Banī Isrā'īl they used to pray for rain through the near kin of their prophets." And 'Umar said, "That would be 'Abbās, the uncle of the Prophet." So he went to him and asked him to pray for rain on behalf of the people. And the people went forth and 'Umar and 'Abbās stood up, and 'Umar said: "O God, these Thy servants and the children of Thy servants and the possession of Thy hands have come to Thee desirous, making petition through (*mutawassilīn bi*) the uncle of Thy Prophet, the Best of Prophets, water us then with a watering over all Thy servants and all the land and drive us not to despair."

Then 'Abbās said: "O God, no calamity falls except through sin, nor is it lifted without repentance. Lo here are our hands outspread to Thee with our sins, and our forelocks with repentance.[1] And the people have turned to me because of my position with regard to Thy Prophet. Then water us with Thy succour and leave us not despairing, most Merciful of the merciful." He (Ibn 'Abbās) said: And the sky was overcast with a great rain that filled the hollows till they were level with the ridges. *Ṭahāratu 'l-qulūb*, ad-Dīrīnī, p. 261.

Qur'ānic Basis for Assurance of Answer

Passing from that element in our manuals which reveals the efforts, common to many religions, to ensure answers to prayer, we ask what they have to show as to the basis for the belief of more spiritual Muslim worshippers that God will answer prayer.

Two promises from the Qur'ān, most precious to those worshippers, are quoted again and again.

have been closer than is their wont. In Islam it developed into a performance of the *ṣalāt*, substituting, "I ask forgiveness of God" for "God is most great", to mark the penitential character either stamped on it by the prayer of al-'Abbās or possibly present in more primitive rites. It was a petition of the whole community including women, children and cattle, made outside the town, after a fast, with poor clothing and cloaks reversed. For close Jewish parallels, see *Mishna Taanith* 2.1,7a,19a. Ash-Shāfi'i's disapproval of the attendance of Jews and Christians at the Muslim *ṣalāt* for rain seems to show that they had taken part in it. In so universal a need, even though not invited to the Muslim *ṣalāt*, Jews and Christians were asked to make their own prayers at the same hour, but not at a later hour for fear of any claim that their prayers had succeeded when others failed.

[1] Our narrative here notes that perhaps a word has fallen out and 'Abbās may have said, "our forelocks humbled before Thee in repentance". The connection of sin and calamity while quite in accordance with Qur'ānic teaching is very Jewish in tone.

(1) Call upon me and I will answer you. (*40.60.*) Two constantly used forms are based on this command with promise:

O God Thou hast commanded us to call on Thee and hast promised that Thou wilt answer. And now we have called on Thee according to Thy command, answer us then, according to Thy promise. *al-Ḥizbu 's-saifi.* (A favourite form of at-Tījānī and very generally used.)

O God this is the petition and from Thee is the answer: this is the effort and on Thee is the reliance. (Aḥmad at-Tījānī has the earliest use in our manuals where it constantly occurs and is referred to the Prophet.)

(2) If My servants ask thee concerning Me, indeed I am near. I answer the cry of the suppliant when he calls me. (*Qur. 2.186*).

None fails who runs to God's door, for He said, He who is the Near One, the Answerer, "If My servants ask thee, etc." *ad-Durru 'l-fā'iq*, Muṣṭafā al-Bakrī, p. 7.

It is said that God Most High says in one of His books:
O son of Adam on thee is the obligation to strive, on Me the obligation to pay in full; on thee the duty of patient endurance, on Me the duty of reward; thy part is to petition, My part is to answer; thy part is to dictate, Mine to write; thy part to call, Mine to answer. . . . *Ṭahāratu 'l-qulūb*, ad-Dīrīnī, p. 94.

So they call in assurance that He answers—an assurance based not only on these Qur'ānic words but on personal experience;

A saying quoted from the Shaikh Abū Yazīd al-Bisṭāmī:
Thy obedience to me, O Lord, is greater than my obedience to Thee. I mean Thy answer to such calls from me as "Forgive me", "Have mercy on me", "Pardon me", "Be not vexed with me", which is greater than my answers to Thee in obeying Thy commands and prohibitions. *Laṭā'ifu 'l-minan*, ash-Sha'rānī, p. 123.

Thou art worthy of my thanks for Thy answer to my call when I lift up my voice to Thee calling, and when I whisper to Thee in desire, and when I call to Thee in humiliation and sincere supplication, and when I look to Thee desirously in hope. For I find Thee sufficient. *Awrādu Aḥmad at-Tījānī*, p. 16.

When No Answer is Apparent

Yet there is the experience of petition that seems unanswered. It is realized that this may be through some failure to comply with the conditions imposed. For other requirements are recognized than those legal conditions, for instance, for the valid performance of the prayer-rite, so earnestly taught to little schoolboys. There must be in petition *ikhlāṣu 'n-nīyya* (see Chapter 3) for He is

> near to him who calls on Him with a nearness that is not spatial, respondent to him who whispers to Him with pure, single-hearted petition. *Majmū'atu 'l-wirdi 'l-'āmm*, p. 24.
>
> Wahb ibn Munabbih said: "I have learnt that Moses passed by a man who stood making petition and lowly supplication at great length. As he watched the man, Moses said, 'O Lord, dost Thou not answer Thy servant?' And God Most High said to Moses (by plenary inspiration), 'O Moses were he to weep till his soul returned (in death) and to raise his hands till they reached the sky, I would not answer him.' And Moses said, 'But why so, O Lord?' He said, 'Because forbidden food is in his belly, forbidden raiment on his back, forbidden goods in his house.'" Ibid., loc. cit.

For prayers that met the conditions and yet seemed to receive no answer there is the theory of a sort of deposit in heaven which will more than compensate for the delay.

> He (M.) said: "No believer makes a petition without its being answered, either swiftly in this world, or delayed till the next."—And the answer will sometimes be exactly what was asked, sometimes it will take another form, sometimes swift, sometimes delayed. *Rabī'u 'l-fu'ād*, 'Abd Allah ash-Sharqāwī, p. 103.
>
> Yazīd ar-Raqqāshī said: When the Resurrection Day comes, God Most High will exhibit to His servant every unanswered petition that he made in this world, and will say, "My servant, on such and such a day thou didst ask me thus, and I withheld thy petition from thee. This reward is thine instead of that petition." And as the donations of reward continue, he will even begin to wish that no prayer of his had been granted! Ibid., p. 101.
>
> O Lord let me never despair of Thine answer even when Thou delayest it. *Du'ā'un fī layāli Ramaḍān, aṣ-Ṣaḥīfatu 's-sajjādiyya*, p. 396.

Reasons Laid Before God for the Expectation of His Answer

> Make us to be, O our Master, as one who petitions his Beloved, and He responds to him and gives him his desire and that which he lacks. *Ḥizbu Fawātiḥi 'l-Baṣā'ir*, 'Abd al-Qādir al-Jīlānī.
>
> My God, I do not think Thou wilt deny me the fulfilment of a need which has been the quest of my life. *Munājāt, aṣ-Ṣaḥīfatu 's-sajjādiyya*, p. 157.

If we are not fit to reach Thy mercy, Thy mercy is fit to reach us! *al-Wirdu 'l-kabīr*, ash-Shādhilī.

My Lord Thou hast commanded us to do kindnesses. How much rather wilt Thou do them than those whom Thou hast so commanded! Thou hast urged (us) to give to them that ask, and Thou Thyself art the Best of those who are asked. *al-Munājātu 'l-injīliyyatu 'l-kubrā*, 'Alī Zain al-'Ābidīn.

Be kind to us with a kindness that befits Thy Majesty and Thy generosity. *Du'ā'u Yā Laṭīf* (Mirghaniyya).

Answers to Prayer and God's Decrees

How are God's promises to answer to be reconciled with belief in *qaḍā'* and *jabr*, in the immutable predetermination of everything by the Almighty, and in *qadar*, the executive decrees, irrevocable and inescapable, by which He carries out His predetermination?

While the prayer-books were not written as theological treatises each worshipper faced with such a question must have his own working method of dealing with it, and these differ in the various prayers.

The Logic of the Heart

There are those who state the case; state that their actions, good and bad, are all determined, and yet illogically go on making petition, though petition can change no decree, impelled by a deeper logic of the heart which makes them sure that One whom they know is attentive to their cry.

O God I did not sin through boldness towards Thee nor through a light estimate of Thee. But Thy Pen caused it to happen and Thy command effected it, and Thy knowledge was aware of it, and there is no might nor power save with Thee, and my apology is before Thee, O Most Merciful of the merciful. *Ḥizbu 't-tawassul*, ash-Shādhilī.

No distress of sin to him whom Thou hast taken care of and kept from sinning. For Thou hast commanded and prohibited, and we have no power to obey or to disobey except through Thee. Through Thy power empower us to obey, and through Thy might and authority avert us from disobeying. *Wirdu 't-tamjīd*, 'Abd al-Qādir al-Jīlānī.

Our God, obedience and disobedience are two ships bearing along Thy servant on the sea of (Thy) will to the shore of safety or the shore of destruction. If he were to attain the shore of safety, happy would he be and near to Thee. He of the shore of destruction is wretched and tortured. Our God,

Thou hast commanded obedience and prohibited disobedience and (yet) the decree for them both has already gone forth. And the servant is under the constraint of Thy authoritative disposal of him, his bridle is in Thy hand and Thou leadest him to whichever of the two (safety or destruction) Thou wilt. His heart is between two of Thy fingers, Thou turnest it as Thou wilt. My God attach our hearts to Thy commandments and avert them from Thy prohibitions. *Ḥizbu 'r-rajā'*, 'Abd al-Qādir al-Jīlānī.

DECREES MAY BE INFLUENCED OR EVEN "TURNED BACK"

Another class of prayer, relying on the Qur'ānic promise that prayer will be answered, assumes that it can affect the Divine decree. Moreover the popular beliefs about the Nights of Power and of Mid-Sha'bān as nights when decrees of life and death are promulgated (irrevocable once made) tend to forget the eternal *qaḍā'*, though a few prayers even venture on asking that what is written may be erased, or to see in *qaḍā'* as in *qadar*, a decree which petition may cause to be made in a favourable form.

Petition turns back what has been decreed and what has not yet been decreed. *Uṣūlu 'l-Kāfī*, al-Kulīnī, *Bāb*. 5.

Nothing turns back the pre-determined decree (*qaḍā'*) except petition. *Rabī'u 'l-fu'ād*, 'Abd Allāh ash-Sharqāwī, p. 100.

Our God, it was Thou who didst move and who again didst still every good or every evil that came into existence. In Thy power is the loosing and binding of all things. In Thy hand and through thine acts of will is the disposal of fates and the predetermination of decrees. And Thou hast caused us to stand at Thy door and we seek the protection of Thy Majesty. We stand at Thy threshold asking for help through Thee, in an authoritative disposal on our behalf that will loose us from evils. *Taḍarru'*, in *Aḥzāb wa awrād Aḥmad at-Tījānī*, p. 104.

The evil which Thou hast decreed and causest me to dread, oh, avert it from me.[1] *ad-Durratu 'l-fardiyya*, Sanūsī, p. 24.

On the night of Mid-Sha'bān God apportions the terms of life and decrees which are near and which far off. And it is said that on the midmost night of Sha'bān He writes the name of him who that year shall be born and him who shall die and him who shall stand on 'Arafat. *Ṭahāratu 'l-qulūb*, ad-Dīrīnī, p. 125.

[1] Compare the Shāfi'ī *qunūt* which does not envisage a change of decree but a warding off of attendant evils. *Aṣrif 'annā sharra mā qaḍaitahu*, Ward off from us the evil of what Thou hast predetermined.

Appoint, among that which Thou dost pre-determine and decree in the great irreversible command of the Night of Power, the irrevocable, immutable predetermination that Thou dost write me down as one of the pilgrims to Thy house and sanctuary (one of those) whose pilgrimage is accounted righteousness, whose effort is thanked, whose sins are forgiven. (Shī'ā prayer for Ramaḍān, *Ṣaḥīfa sajjādiyya*, p. 395.)

A folk belief that decrees may be changed is indicated by the following story told by Syrian peasants.

A hedgehog stopped Moses and asked him to inquire of God on his behalf whether he was to be one of the saved or of the damned (*min al-hālikīn aw min al-mukhallaṣīn*). God's reply was, "one of the damned". Moses was shy at revealing this to the hedgehog and went home by a different road, but the hedgehog followed him, and when he heard God's decree he submitted himself quietly. God was so much pleased with the hedgehog's attitude that He reversed His decision. (Communicated by Miss K. Henrey.)

Petition is Predetermined

A third group finds its solution in the consideration that their petition itself is part of God's predetermination. It is not, therefore, the cause of the answer but part of a chain of events determined by God, in which it is linked by Him with the answer.

The Imām al-Ghazālī has said: If it is asked, "What is the use of petition when predetermination (*qaḍā'*) is irrevocable?" then know that the turning aside of misfortune by means of petition and weeping is a part of the predetermined decree. It is no part of acknowledgment of the doctrine of predetermination to refrain from bearing weapons. *Rabī'u 'l-fu'ād*, 'Abd Allah ash-Sharqāwī, p. 100.

Know that *dhikr* and *du'ā'* do not substitute one decree for another or change divine predetermination. They are only worship joined (by Him) to causes, as the prayer-rite is joined to its hour. And He assigned to them His answering, as He assigned its reward to the prayer-rite. *al-Mafākhiru 'l-'aliyya* (Shādhiliyya), p. 151.

We are told that God does not permit a request till He also permits the answer. *Rabī'u 'l-fu'ād*, loc. cit.

Riḍā

A fourth group finds a solution through the experience of the spiritual life. One of the deepest and most characteristic notes of Muslim sanctity is this word, *riḍā*, deep satisfaction. While any believer may say *raḍaitu bi 'l-islām dīnan*, "I am deeply satisfied with Islam as my religious practice," in its higher reaches *riḍā* is a personal word, a word of mutuality, of complaisance, of mutual satisfaction. It is the state of the soul "God-satisfied, God-satisfying" (for Allāh too has His *riḍā*), a "state of grace" that is the child of faith, and that faith the gift of God.

For a soul so living, the question of answers to prayer is solved by being transcended. Whatever He does becomes acceptable because He does it, and is covered by the deep glow of enduring satisfaction in Him.[1]

Riḍā the child of faith:

O God I ask Thee for faith that shall occupy my heart, and holy certitude, until I know that nothing befalls me except Thou hast written it for me; and make me deeply satisfied with what Thou hast apportioned to me. *Majmū'u 'l-wirdi 'l-'āmm*, p. 13. (This is part of what is said to have been taught by God to Adam, when, cast out of the Garden, he came to the Ka'ba.)

I believe in God's decree (*qadar*), the good and the evil of it both from Him, as His mighty signs and gladdening declarations have taught us. And I trust in Him and surrender all that concerns me to Him, in all that His celestial Pen has written. And I am well-satisfied (*raḍait*) with all that He has written for me and apportioned to me in the two abodes. *Ḥizbun 'azīm, li 'ṭ-ṭarīqati'l-'ashshāqiyya.*

Thou knowest our joy and how and why it comes, so also dost Thou know our sorrow. And Thou hast imposed, in us and from us, the existence of what Thou desirest. We do not ask Thee to divert from us what Thou desirest, but we ask Thee for a steady following on our part of what Thou desirest, through a spirit from Thee (helping us) as Thou didst help Thy Prophets and Apostles and the saints among Thy creatures marked with peculiar grace. Happy is he who knows Thee and is well satisfied with Thy determined decree! Woe to him who knows Thee not, nay woe upon woe to him who acknowledges Thy Soleness but does not accept with satisfaction Thy commands! *al-Ḥizbu 'l-kabīr*, ash-Shādhilī.

Nothing is easy but what Thou makest easy, and Thou makest even sorrow easy. *al-Wirdu 'sh-shāfī*, Yūsuf an-Nabhānī, p. 30.

[1] *Riḍā* has been translated *quietism*, a translation quite unfair to the main stream of teaching and described experience. Every spiritual gift and grace has its temptation, and quietism is that of *riḍā*. It was probably some lack of balance of this kind which gave *riḍā* a bad name in the oasis towns to the south of Algeria, so that the late Miss I. L. Trotter was told that a despised man was called by the epithet *rāḍi(n)*, probably in the sense of weakling, poor-spirited.

Reveal to us the beauty of Thy choice for us, till that which Thou decreest becomes dearer to us than our own choice. *Ḥizbu 'l-Fatḥiyya*, 'Abd al-Qādir al-Jīlānī.

God the Doer

Closely related to this acceptance of God's choice and decree for the worshipper's life is another deep strain in Islamic devotion which sees that in all the experiences of the spiritual life, it was not the human worshipper who was the initiator, but that touches of divine grace (*faiḍ, laṭā'if*) moved him.[1] So he worships God for His prevenient grace, like his Christian brother when he says "We love Him because He first loved us" (1 John 4.19). And looking back at his experiences of worship, the Muslim who ponders sees them with wonder and awe as correspondent to something within God's own activity. God, too, gives thanks; God praises; God, too, calls down blessing; God, too, has His *dhikr*, He bears His part in *munājāt*.

God the Initiator of Worship

To Thee we have come, and it was Thou who didst bring us. *Ṭahāratu 'l-qulūb*, ad-Dīrīnī, p. 265.

And it is said that the beginning of repentance is an awakening from God which falls into the heart. ibid., p. 97.

Give us our request as Thou didst first give us the faith to ask it. *Ḥizbu 'l-baḥr*.

Hadst Thou not willed the attainment of what I seek in my request Thou wouldest not, by an infusion from Thy generosity, have inspired me to ask it. *Rabī'u 'l-fu'ād*, 'Abd Allāh ash-Sharqāwī, p. 100.

He (M.) is the dearest of created beings to God and we only mention him through God's reminder to us, for He is the real Mentioner (*dhākir*). *al-Ḥirzu 'l-manī'*, as-Suyūṭī, p. 5.

If I am able to give thanks it is through the mind that Thou hast given me. If I speak it is through the gracious kindness which Thou didst show me.

[1] If *riḍā* may lose its balance and fall over into quietism, this sense of God as the Doer, sometimes lapses into monism. In our prayers it occasionally trembles on the brink but recovers its balance. A prayer which thus trembles on the brink is the following:

Make me to see Thine activity alone in all that is done, till I see no Doer but Thee, that I may be tranquil under the course of Thy decrees. *Wirdu yawmi 'l-ithnain*, 'Abd al-Qādir al-Jīlānī.

Where is the thanksgiving that I can attribute to myself? The whole business of giving thanks is both to Thee and from Thee. *al-Mukhtārātu 'l-'aliyya fi 'l-ma'āthiri 'sh-Shādhiliyya*, p. 193.

Thanksgiving is from God and to God. *Majmū'u 'l-awrādi 'l-kabīr*, M. 'Uthmān al-Mirghanī, p. 3.

(Our praises) are only forms indicating Thy generosity, forms which Thou Thyself, through the tongue of Thy Prophet, hast granted to us, that in the use of them we may worship Thee according to our power, not according to Thy power. *Ḥizbu 'n-nūr*, ash-Shādhilī.

The Activities of Worship Reflected from the Divine Life

Here is a mystery of grace, believed in by men who are far from monistic thought, and place the sharpest distinction between God and His creation. They see with awe that over against His servants' *dhikr* is God's *dhikr*, and He is the real *dhākir*.

So also with the giving of thanks. That is the duty and the joy of men, but in the glory of His grace it is God who is *shākir*, *shakkūr*, *khairu 'sh-shākirīn*, the Giver of Thanks, the Grateful One, the Best of Thankers.

It is told that a certain man served God Most High twenty years, then lived a disordered life for twenty years. Then he looked in a mirror and saw his beard whitening, and that grieved him and he said, "O Lord if I repent before Thee, wilt Thou receive me?" And he heard a voice say, "O so-and-so, thou didst obey Us and We thanked thee. Then thou didst leave Us and We bore with thee. Now thou hast returned to Us and We have received thee." *Ṭahāratu 'l-qulūb*, p. 95.

Thou dost thank for the slight thanks that are rendered to Thee, Thou dost praise for the little of religious observance rendered in obedience to Thee. . . . And that because Thy habitual usage is generosity, Thy custom to confer benefits, Thy way to pardon. Thou dost thank the man who obeys Thee, for what Thou didst empower him to do. *al-Istiqṣā'u fī 'th-thanā'*, 'Alī Zain al-'Ābidīn. *Ṣaḥīfa sajjādiyya*, p. 23.

In medieval England another worshipping soul had reached a similar vision of the marvel of God's thanks:

God showed me three degrees of bliss that each soul shall have in heaven that wilfully has served God in any degree here in earth.

The first is the worshipful thanking of our Lord God that He shall receive, when he is delivered from pain. This thanks is so high and so worshipful that it seems to him to fill him, though there were no more bliss. For methought that all the pain and turmoil that might be suffered of all living men might not have deserved the thanks that a man shall have that wilfully has served God.

The second is that all the blessed creatures that are in heaven shall see that worshipful thanking of our Lord God; and He makes his service known to all that are in heaven.

The third is, that as new and as pleasing as it is received at that time, right so shall it last without end. *The Shewings of the Lady Julian of Norwich* (about 1373). Edition, Dundas Harford, p. 53.

But it is not only the divine thanks to the sons of men that our worshippers see, but an activity of thanks and praise within the life of God. These prayers indicate a mystery that calls for the doctrine of the Blessed Trinity.

One of the great ones used to say in his converse with God—O God, Thou knowest my inability to set forth my thanksgiving to Thee. Then do Thou thank Thyself on my behalf. al-Kalabādhī, *Ta'arruf, Bāb.* 43. Arberry's edition, p. 71.

The Divine Tasbīḥ

For He is the Praiser from eternity. *Qaṣīdatun istighfāriyya*, M. 'Alamī al-Qudsī.

I am not able to praise Thee as Thou hast praised Thyself. *Du'ā'un nabawī.*

This last is the traditional form that echoes through Muslim praises.

The Divine Ḥamd

The Muslim worshipper constantly asks that he may be enabled to praise with a praise

Like that with which Thou hast praised Thyself. *Du'ā'un nabawī.*

The Divine Shahāda

The Watcher, the Witness-bearer, who bore witness to His own Unity before the witness of his creatures. *Ṭahāratu 'l-qulūb*, ad-Dīrīnī, p. 3.

Muslim worshippers, then, have seen in the life of God Himself the prototype and source of their activities of worship, and for some He is also that *wasīla*, that means of access to Himself so earnestly sought:

Thou art my shelter and my *wasīla*, and to Thee I lift up my gladness and my sorrow. (Ismā'īl al-Jīlānī, in *Al-Fuyūḍātu 'r-rabbāniyya.*)

He is the Way to Himself.

18

THE LAST THINGS

Qabḍu 'r-Rūḥ, A'dhābu 'l-Qabr, al-Fawz 'l-'aẓīm, al-Janna

The Little Death of Sleep

"Sleep is the brother of Death" (Ash-Sha'rānī, *Laṭā'if*, p. 124) for in both God takes the spirit (which may make strange journeys and see rare visions) from the quiet body.

> The spirit when it leaves the body in sleep, if it is in a state of ritual purity, has permission to prostrate itself before God (in His presence) until the man wakes. And if in a state of defilement it leaves the body, it falls far from the presence-chamber and misses that spiritual worship, bodiless like that of the angels. . . . We sleep having made our ablution with water or sand out of fear that our spirits may be seized in a state of defilement.
>
> (The Ṣaḥāba and the Tābi'ūn) said: Our spirits are in the hand of God and we know not if our spirits will be returned to us after our sleep or not. *Khatma* to *al-Hirzu 'l-Manī'*, M. al-Fatḥī, pp. 136, 137.

This thought of the little death of sleep is very present in the prayers of morning and evening. Two forms attributed to the Prophet occur again and again.

> The Prophet said: When one of you wakes, let him say: Thankful praise to God who has returned to me my spirit. *al-Kalimu 'ṭ-ṭayyib*, p. 22. *Adhkāru 'n-Nawawī*, p. 11.
>
> And when he (M.) woke he said: Praise be to God who brought us to life after He had caused us to die, and to Him is our resurrection. *al-Kalimu 'ṭ-ṭayyib*, p. 17, *Adhkāru 'n-Nawawī*, p. 11.

The following prayer uses, for raising up from sleep, the verb *ba'atha* technically used for the resurrection from the dead:

> Praise be to Thee who hast raised me up (*ba'athtanī*) from my lying down, which, hadst Thou wished, Thou couldst have made everlasting. *Miftāḥu 'l-Janān*, p. 51 (Shī'a).

These prayers rouse many a question that the manuals do not answer.

What of dreams? Especially of those *ru'ā 'n-nabī fī 'l-manām*, so detailed in description of clothing, gesture, argument, conversation on the details of earthly life, treated as experience valid for the direction of conduct? Can these be experiences of the spirit only, or is the spirit momentarily returned to the *nafs* to enjoy them? But would not that be waking?

And if "sleep is the brother of death" in the one fundamental respect of the removal of the *rūḥ* (*Qabḍu 'r-rūḥ* is the seizure of the spirit by the angel of death), how far does the analogy extend? What of that which is *not* seized? These prayers seem at one in envisaging a conscious life within the tomb, either enduring *a'dhābu 'l-qabr* (the suffering or chastisement of the grave) or solaced by the opening of *abwābu 'r-raḥma*, doors of mercy that relieve the constriction of the tomb, where the dead is sometimes gladdened by the companionship (can it be called spiritual when the *rūḥ* is absent?) of God or of the Prophet, which turns the tomb into a *rawḍa* (garden). This life, generally regarded as painful, of the *nafs* without the *rūḥ*, is hardly comparable with the rest of sleep.

And what of the separated spirit awaiting reunion at the Resurrection with its body and *nafs*? Are we to think of it (as in the extract printed above, from Muḥammad al-Fatḥī's *Khatma*), as prostrate in worship before God? On this the prayer-manuals throw no light. Folk religion tells of a sort of subterranean waiting-room for spirits. It has been described to the writer in Egypt as "a sort of large well in the valley close to the Mount of Olives" (the traditional site of the Last Judgment). Folk religion, too, has caught the idea of the "green birds" (a description of the souls of the martyrs already in Paradise. Al-Ghazālī, *Tahāfut*, p. 88D). A Berber servant in Egypt told the writer that the spirit of his dead baby was a little green bird clinging to the side of "the well of spirits" as martins press their breasts against the mud-banks beside the Nile.[1]

Let me Die the Death of the Righteous

Death is the King of terrors for Muslims as for other mortals. But for those whose lives are lived with God the terror is at least partially

[1] In the Assyrian myth of Ishtar's descent into the lower world, the dead have wings like birds but are unable to escape. For belief in the soul-bird in Arabia see Doughty, *Arabia Deserta*, ed. 1921, p. 168, and Wellhausen, *Reste Arabischen Heidentums*, 185.

conquered and this in virtue of a death they have already died. Commenting on the saying of al-Junaid, "Those who know God do not die, they are only removed from one abode to another," ash-Sha'rānī says:

> Junaid's meaning was that those who know God are, while still living, as though they had already died (i.e. through the death to self and to the world in *al-fanā'*) so that to say "those who know God" is equivalent to saying "the dead" and how should the action of "dying" be attributed to death itself? *Laṭā'ifu 'l-Minan*, p. 130.

A Shī'a prayer says:

> My Lord how can I despair of Thy good regard for me after my death, when in my life-time Thy treatment of me has been nothing but beautiful? *al-Munājātu 'l-injīliyyatu 'l-kubrā*. (*Ṣaḥīfa sajjādīyya*, p. 197.)
>
> Cause us at the hour of death to repeat the *shahāda* knowing what it is that we say. And be compassionate to us with the compassion of the lover to his loved one. *al-Ḥizbu 'l-kabīr*, Shādhili.
>
> Give us the happy ending that Thou didst give to Thy saints, and make the best of our days the day when we shall meet Thee. *Ṣalawātu 'd-Dardīr.*
>
> Have a good confidence in God that He will generously grant you a good ending, and that He will ease for you the pangs of death and the constriction of the grave.
>
> The Prophet said: "Verily none of you shall die except confident in God Most High." And he went to see a man in his death agony and said to him, "How do you find yourself?" He replied, "I find myself in fear of my sins and in hope of the mercy of my Lord." Then the Prophet said, "These two are never united in the heart of a servant in this world without God giving him what he hoped for and securing him against what he feared." *al-'Aṭiyyatu 'l-haniyya*, 'Alī b. Hasan al-'Attās, p. 145.

The King of Terrors

In general the prayers concerning death are cries for help against terrors, a series of terrors. While the fear of a sinner at meeting his judge is right and natural, a Christianity unworthy of herself is perhaps in part to blame for the terrible gloom of the picture here. For the hermits of the Syrian desert, who were not without influence on the early thought of Islam, seem to have given themselves to a most un-Christian absorption, year after year, in the terrors of death and judgment, with a forgetfulness that a sinner had heard the words "To-day shalt thou be with Me in Paradise" and that for the redeemed "to depart and be with Christ is far better".

Although the manuals do not set out to give an ordered programme of the after-life, something of this may be gathered from the expressions used in worship.

> I bear witness that Thy promise is a verity, and the meeting with Thee is a verity, and Paradise is a verity, and the Fire is a verity and that the Hour is coming without a doubt, and that Thou wilt raise up those in the tombs. (Traditional form constantly added to the *Shahāda* in the manuals.)

I reckon against the two tempters of the tomb "There is no god but God", etc.

„	„	the darkness of the tomb	„	„
„	„	the constriction of the tomb	„	„
„	„	blast of the trumpet	„	„
„	„	the prolonged standing (at the assize) and the sweat from fear and heat	„	„
„	„	the exposure before the All-Powerful	„	„
„	„	the standing before the Generous Forgiving One	„	„
„	„	the questioning on the small and the great (sins)	„	„
„	„	the erection of the scales and the knowledge of the weights	„	„
„	„	the bringing out of the books	„	„
„	„	the waiting for the call when the decrees of destiny are allotted	„	„
„	„	the crossing of the Bridge	„	„
„	„	the arrival in Gehenna	„	„

Majmūʻu 'l-wirdi 'l-ʻāmm, p. 29.

The prayers of the multitude about deliverance from the Fire are innumerable, even though to be a Muslim is often considered a passport to such deliverance. We have already referred (Chapter 13a) to the *duʻā'un nabāwī* most commonly taught as part of the prayer-rite—universally for Turkish children—which ends "Deliver us from the Fire, O Lord." The very popular *Ḥirzu 'l-Jawshan* sold by thousands in the Cairo streets has for refrain eighty-five times, "Help! Help! Save us from the Fire, O Lord."

The Terror of the Tomb

Loneliness and Constriction

The prayers bear witness to the fact that loneliness is for these worshippers a great part of *a'dhābu 'l-qabr*. When the great solidarity of family groups and neighbourhood groups in Arabic lands, and the very general lack of privacy from birth to death, is considered, this fear is the more understandable. Long years ago Imru'l-Qais wrote his famous lines to the dead princess by whose lonely tomb he was buried,

> O neighbour of mine, we are both of us strangers here
> And one stranger to another is ever close and dear.
> (D. B. Macdonald's translation of the lines.)

and the thought of being a stranger in the tomb still haunts Arabic prayers.

> Have mercy on me, laid on my bed, when the hands of my loved ones turn me over. Have mercy on me, laid on the washing table when compassionate neighbours wash my corpse. Have mercy on me, borne along, when my relatives hold the sides of my bier. Have mercy, in that dark house, on my homesickness, my strangeness, my solitude. For whom has the slave to show mercy to him save his Master? *Du'ā'un fī Rajab. Ṣaḥīfa sajjādiyya*, p. 375.
>
> My God it is as though I with my soul (*nafs*) had lain down in her cavity, and the funeral party of the neighbours had departed, and even strangers had wept over her (the soul's) strangeness while compassionate relatives were abundant in tears. . . .
>
> Then Thou wilt say, "My angels, a single one who has been deserted by those near to him, a lonely one who has been rebuffed by the community has come to stay with Me as a near one, has become a guest from afar, in the tomb. . . . Then Thou wilt show forth the fairness of Thy hospitality to me, and wilt be more merciful to me than my family and relatives. *Munājāt*, attributed to 'Alī Zain al-'Ābidīn. *Ṣaḥīfa sajjādiyya*, p. 159.

There is sometimes a pathetic effort to cheat this terror of loneliness by some recommended pious practice. Thus to the reciter of *Bashā'iru 'l-khairāt* it is promised that:

> He who recites it, though but once . . . when his appointed term is come, four angels of mercy will come with it, the first fending off Satan from him, the second inspiring him with the two words of the *shahāda*, the third giving him to drink a chalice from *al-Kawthar*, the fourth bearing in his hands a golden vessel filled with the fruits of Paradise. And God will say to him,

"Receive good news, O servant of God. See there is an abode for thee in Paradise." And he will look and behold it with his eye, ere his spirit goes forth. And he will be brought to his grave secure, rejoicing, happy, and will see in it neither loneliness nor constriction. And forty doors of mercy will be opened to him, and a lantern of light will hang over his head. *Bashā'iru 'l-khairāt*, 'Abd al-Qādir al-Jīlānī, pp. 4, 5.

The last prayer said at the grave before mourners depart is a wholesome medicine for loneliness:

O God, Thou Companion of every lonely one, Thou Present One who art never a stranger, Thou Near One when others are far, be the Companion O God of our loneliness and his loneliness, have mercy on our strangeness and his strangeness, and whiten his page and forgive us and forgive him and forgive the one who stood over his grave to say: *Lā ilāha illā 'llāh Muḥammadun rasūlu 'llāh.* (As generally used in Egypt. There are slight variations in different localities.)

A beautiful Shī'a form is:

O Companion of every stranger be the Companion of my strangeness in the grave. O Second with every solitary one have mercy on my solitude in the grave. *aṣ-Ṣaḥīfatu 's-sajjādiyya*, p. 159.

The Questioning

Whatever be the source of the doctrine of a final test or temptation within the grave (*fitnatu 'l-qabr*) it is an intensely living one.

(From 'Abd Allāh ibn 'Umar.) The Prophet said: The first night that thou descendest into the tomb two angels will descend to thee, one of them called Munkar, the other Nakīr, harsh, rough, and enormous, their eyelashes sweep the dust, flames issue from their mouths. They will perturb and flurry thee and will say, "Who is thy Lord and what is thy religious practice?" What will be thy reply to them? . . . *al-Majmū'atu 'l-mubārakatu fī 'ṣ-ṣalawāti 'l-ma'thūra*, p. 26.

My God, safety, safety, at the questioning of Munkar and Nakīr!

My God, safety, safety, in the loneliness of the tomb and its hardship. *Ḥizbu 'l-maghnā.*

Before the final funeral prayer quoted above, occurs the solemn *talqīn al-mayyit* when the dead is given his instructions for the answering of the questions of the tomb. This is considered of such importance that little Urdu primers for teaching the prayer-rite in Arabic will also include the Arabic of this precious instruction. We quote part of it as so taught:

Thou slave of God son of the bondwoman of God, N. or M. Thou bondwoman of God daughter of Eve, N. or M. Remember the Covenant . . . which is the witness that there is no god but God and that Muḥammad is the Apostle of God . . . and that thou art well satisfied with God as (thy) One Lord and with Islam as (thy) religious practice and with Muḥammad as Apostle and Prophet. This is the first abiding place of the abodes of the other world and the last abiding place of the abodes of this transitory world. . . . Let them not (the two angels) disturb thee, or affright thee, or terrify thee or fill thee with dread, for they are only creatures, a part of God's creation. And when they ask thee, "Who is thy Lord and who is thy Prophet and what is thy *imām*, and thy religion, and thy *qibla*, and thy brethren?" Then say, "God is my Lord and Muḥammad my Prophet, the Qur'ān is my *imām* and the Ka'ba my *qibla*, and all the believers and Muslims are my brethren."[1] In that faith wast thou created, in that faith thou hast lived, in that faith thou hast died, and in that faith thou shalt be raised up if it be God's will. . . . *Majmū'u suwarin wa ad'iya*, Bombay.

There are pathetic devices to cheat the terror of this dread visitation. Thus of the famous *Ḥirzu 'l-Jawshan* it is written:

He who writes this petition (and puts it) in a glass goblet with camphor and musk, and washes it, and sprinkles that water on the shroud of a dead man, God Most High will cause a hundred thousand mercies to descend into the tomb and will lift from that dead man the fear of Munkar and Nakīr. *Ḥirzu 'l-Jawshan*. Preface.

Those who have built their spiritual life on trust in Muḥammad look to him for help at this crisis also:

Make him the one who replies on our behalf in our spiritless bodies. *Ṣalātun nājiya*, Abū 'l-Muwahhib ash-Shādhilī.

And with what passion must the prayers of the believers be offered for their dead in this emergency:

It is reported of the Prophet in *Nuzhatu 'l-Majālis* that he said: Nothing more severe does the dead man pass through than the first night, therefore show mercy to your dead by almsgiving, and he who has not the wherewithal let him pray two *rak'as* . . . and say, "O God I make the intention of this prayer-rite and Thou knowest what I desire. O God send the merit of it to the tomb of N. the son of M." *al-Majmū'atu 'l-mubārakatu fī 'ṣ-ṣalawāti 'l-ma'thūra*, p. 2.

[1] In some forms, "and Abraham, Thy Friend, my Father", is added here.

THE TERROR OF THE RESURRECTION TO JUDGMENT

The Qur'ānic details and the whole tradition show how the certainty and the terror of the great assize had laid hold on Muḥammad and this is reflected in the prayer of his people, which echo both the Qur'ānic phrases and the traditional prayers of the Prophet.

There are two sides to the treatment of the subject in the prayer-books, the first being an echo of the terror in those early prayers, the second a seeking for relief from it in the thought of preferential treatment for the people of Muḥammad.

A constantly used traditional prayer is the brief one:

> O God deliver me from Thy chastisement on the day when Thou wilt raise up Thy servants. *al-Kalimu 'ṭ-ṭayyib*, p. 19 (Muslim).

This is sometimes quoted as what fellow-worshippers heard the Prophet murmur when he was leading them in the prayer-rite, sometimes as what he said three times when "he put his right hand under his head" as he lay down to sleep.

Another much-echoed traditional form, attributed to him when he awoke at night, is:

> O God I take refuge with Thee from the tribulation of this world and the tribulation of the Resurrection Day. *Adhkāru 'n-Nawawī*, p. 11.

The tone of the prayers is true to this tradition.

> I take refuge with Thee from Thy chastisement on the day when Thou shalt raise Thy servants, and I take refuge with Thee from swift punishment and an evil reckoning on the day of the assembly and of requital, for Thou art swift to requite. *Wirdu 'l-musabbaʿāt.*

> Praise to Thee, glorified be Thy Majesty, while I live, and when I die . . . and when I am brought forth to Thee astounded by the awful cry (calling to) the Assembly and when I stand dumbfounded in Thy presence at the publishing of the pages of my past life. And when Thou askest me and my very members are witnesses for Thee against me. . . . *Duʿā'* for the first day of the New Year. *Ṣaḥīfa sajjādiyya*, p. 378.

> Have mercy on me on the day when I come before Thee alone, my gaze turned towards Thee, my deeds tied round my neck, all creatures dissociating themselves from me, yes even my father and my mother and those for whom I toiled and strove. Then if Thou dost not show me mercy who will have mercy upon me? . . . Who will teach my tongue to speak when I am

alone with my deeds and am asked concerning those things that Thou knowest better than I. If I say, "Yes (I did them)", whither can I fly from Thy justice? If I say, "I did them not", Thou wilt say, "I am the witness against thee." Shī'a *Du'ā'* for *Nuṣfu Sha'bān*.

Whiten my face O Lord in the day when Thou dost blacken faces and grant me safety on the day of the tremendous terror. *Mukhtaṣaru ad'iyati Ramaḍān*, and frequently in the manuals.

Hope of Preferential Treatment

The greatest hope of his people lies in the mediation of Muḥammad (see Chapter 1). We give here an example of the treatment of this in popular religion. The tradition, in almost conversational Arabic, is quoted by as-Suyūṭī.

Adam will have a stance given him by God in the place of the Throne. He will be clad in two green robes as though he were a towering palm tree. He will watch which of his children are carried away to Paradise and which to the Fire. He ('Abdallah ibn 'Umar) said: And while Adam is thus occupied, if he sees a man of Muḥammad's community carried away to the Fire, then Adam will call, "O Aḥmad! O Aḥmad!" And he will reply, "Here am I at thy service, O Father of Mortals." Then Adam will say, "They are taking off this man of thy community to the Fire!" And he (Muḥammad) will gird his loins and run after the angels, saying, "O messengers of my Lord, let go!" And they will say, "We are the rough, the violent, who never disobey our Lord's command but do as we are told." And when the Prophet is in despair he will clutch his beard (apparently the beard of the man being carried away) with his left hand, and turning to face the Throne will say, "O Lord didst Thou not promise me not to put me to shame through my community?" And the cry will come from the Throne, "Obey Muḥammad." *al-Ḥirzu 'l-manī'*, p. 78.

Other hopes of safe-conduct through the perils of that day are held out in the performance of good works. Thus of the reciter of al-Jīlānī's *Bashā'iru 'l-khairāt* it is said:

And he will rise on the Resurrection Day, on his right hand an angel who gives him words of cheer, on his left hand an angel who gives him security, two robes of glory covering him and a well-bred steed will be brought for him to ride. *Bashā'iru 'l-khairāt*, p. 5.

Or of those faithful to the Ramaḍān Fast:

Those who fast will come forth from their graves hungry and thirsty, and they will be met with whatever (food) they fancy from Paradise. And

Riḍwān will cry, "O pages and youths, bring dishes of light!" And he will gather them around him more than the stars in number, with fruits and delicious beverages, and welcome the fasting men and women, saying to them, "Eat and drink with health of this loan from your empty days." *al-Mukhtārātu 'l-ḥusān*, Ḥasan 'Alī Sharīf, p. 10.

This is folk-religion for the hungry multitudes. All the Qur'ānic data of the other life admit of (and receive) both a materialistic and a spiritual interpretation. We may take by way of contrast:

Poor soul be persevering in the remembrance of God Most High. For on the Resurrection Day everyone will say, "My soul, my soul", and Paradise will say, "My people, my people", and the Fire will say, "My due, my due", and the worshipper will say, "My Lord, my Lord", and the Lord will say, "My worshipper, My worshipper". *Lawāmi'u 'l-bayyināt*, Fakhr ad-Dīn ar-Rāzī, p. 40.

TERROR OF THE FIRE

In spite of all the passports devised, the final *shahāda*, the right answer for the questioning angels, the *ṣalātu 'alā 'n-nabī* and his final intercession, with many another *vade mecum* mentioned in the course of this book, the terror of Hell-Fire still haunts these prayers. From the data in the prayers, while it would seem impossible for any Muslim to remain in hell, it is clear that some are to go there, despite such comforting traditions as that quoted above from *al-Ḥirzu 'l-manī'*.[1] On emerging and laving their burnt flesh in the Paradise stream, *al-Kawthar*, they will be restored to beauty. The belief as it is held (with no clear Qur'ānic support) comes very near to the doctrine of Purgatory.

Qinā a'dhābi 'n-nār, deliver us from the pains of hell! *Ajirnī mina 'n-nār*, save me from the fire! *Allāhumma ajirnā wa ajir wālidainā mina 'n-nār bi jāhi 'n-nabiyyi 'l-mukhtār*. O God deliver us and our parents from the Fire by virtue of the Chosen Prophet! These are the constant ejaculations of prayer.

[1] Al-Jīlānī, who even dared to see some non-Muslims in Paradise and who had a theory that some in hell were more righteous than some in heaven and content to be there to realize in themselves part of the truth of God (the truth of His quelling and chastising Names), also ventured on a theory that in the end all the burning quality would be taken out of hell itself and its rough angels would come to an end with the fire of their service, and in the place of hell would grow the green tree of *Jarjīr*, "and the best of the colours of Paradise is green". (See *Insān Kāmil*, Bab 38). Our manuals show no trace of these theories.

A type of prayer which recalls the minatory preachings of medieval Christian revivalists, and like those regards the Fire as physical, is found both in Sunnī and Shī'a collections.

(Sunnī)—That Thou wilt forgive this urgent soul, this anxious heat which cannot bear the heat of Thy sun, how then will it bear the heat of Thy Fire? *Wird* for Tuesday, 'Abd al-Qādir al-Jīlānī. *al-Fuyūḍātu 'r-rabbāniyya*, p. 143.

(Shī'a)—I ask Thee to have mercy on this delicate skin, this slender frame which cannot endure the heat of Thy sun. How then will it endure the heat of Thy Fire? And when it cannot bear the voice of Thy thunder how will it bear the voice of Thine anger? *Du'ā'* attributed to 'Alī Zain al-'Ābidīn. *Ṣaḥīfa sajjādiyya*, p. 249.

Common also to both Sunnī and Shī'a is the appeal that the face which so often touched the earth in prostration before God should not be given to the Fire. We give a Shī'a embroidery on this theme:

My God wilt Thou burn with Thy fire my face which used to pray to Thee? My God, wilt Thou burn with fire my eyes which used to weep with fear of Thee? My God, wilt Thou burn with fire my tongue which used to recite the Qur'ān? My God, wilt Thou burn with fire my heart which was loving towards Thee? My God, wilt Thou burn with fire my body which was humbled before Thee? My God, wilt Thou burn with fire my limbs which used to bow and prostrate themselves before Thee? *Munājāt*. Ibid., p. 234.

Poor human nature still hopes for some kind of safe-conduct.

On the Resurrection Day have mercy on us and write for us a quittance from the Fire, a safe-conduct from chastisement. *Mukhtaṣaru ad'iyati Ramaḍān*, p. 26.

The Death of Children

One of the stages or storeys of al-Jīlānī's Paradise is reserved for children and idiots who have retained their first innocence, together with those who by ascesis have regained it. There is such a sense of the security of white innocence that discussion has been raised about the petition made (and attributed to the Prophet's use) at funerals, "O Lord forgive our little ones and our grown persons":

As for the rightness of asking forgiveness for a little one though no guilt is attached to him, it is as our shaikh said (when he was asked concerning their saying in the funeral petition, "O Lord forgive our little ones and our grown persons"): There are various theories, the first of which is that the words refer to the time when the "little one" will be grown up, since, when he is grown up, he will do what needs forgiveness. The second is that the request is effective for his parents or one of them or whoever brings up the child. A third is that it is effective for the child himself and means that his station (in the other world) is to be raised, which would be the effect of praying the prayer for a grown-up who had no sin, as we might suppose to be the case if someone died only just after reaching the age of responsibility or just after making a sincere surrender to Islam. *al-Ḥirzu 'l-manī'*, as-Suyūṭī, p. 8.

The special prayer in use at a child's funeral[1] is:

O God, he is Thy servant and the son of Thy servant. Thou didst create him and sustain him and bring him to death and Thou wilt give him life. O God make him for his parents an anticipation, riches sent on before, a reward which precedes, and through him make heavy the balance (of their good works) and increase their rewards. Let neither us nor them be seduced by temptation after his departure. O God cause him to overtake the believers who preceded him, in the guardianship of Abraham, and give him in exchange (for his earthly home) a better dwelling place and a family better than his family, and keep him sound from the temptation of the tomb and the Fire of Gehenna. (As used in Egypt.)

A very similar form used in India has this variation:

O God, as for this infant who has not attained to intellectual life, against whom the pens have not begun their record, who has not acquired sin and wickedness, Thou didst create him through Thy mercy and didst cause him to die through Thy will, and he is one of Thy righteous servants (*'ibādika 'ṣ-ṣāliḥīn*, a phrase used of the saintly). *Majmū'u suwarin wa ad'iya*, Bombay, p. 162.

Paradise and Its Joys

All the Qur'ānic data about Paradise are taken literally by humble millions, half-starved of earthly pleasures, who see in these pictures a recompense laid up for them, in scenes not unlike those of the Arabian Nights, yet unlike those in having about them a sense of holy Presence,

[1] Of this prayer Professor Guidi notes that in the commentary of ad-Dardīr, *al-Mukhtaṣar*, it is given to Abū Huraira but it is not in the *Mudawwana*, and that elsewhere (as in our manuals, by as-Suyūṭī) it is given to the Prophet. Whoever composed it, it must have helped to comfort many a sore heart. (See *Una Preghiera Musulmana*, I. Guidi, *Islamica* 2, p. 232 ff.)

of *baraka*, an unearthly radiance. Or these Qur'ānic texts may be, and are by spiritual souls, read as parables and hints of spiritual joys that cannot otherwise be set before poor mortals.

This spiritualization of the data has led to their being used of some of the joys of the spirit that begin here and now, though they are of the eternal world, and in the prayers of those who have, in the Christian phrase "tasted the powers of the age to come", it is sometimes hard to tell whether the thoughts of the worshipper are dwelling on present experience or on the life after death. We begin with two examples of the simpler kind:

> No weariness, no remorse, and an easy reckoning for him. And when he passes the Bridge, the fire will say to him, "Fly quickly O freedman of God, for I am forbidden to touch you." And he will enter Paradise with the first. And in Paradise will be given him forty domes of silver, in every dome a castle of gold, in every castle a hundred pavilions of light, in every pavilion a bed of silken brocade, on every bed a slave-girl of the *ḥūr* . . . then will be given him what eye hath not seen, nor ear heard, neither hath entered into the heart of man.[1] *Bashā'iru 'l-khairāt*, 'Abd al-Qādir al-Jīlānī.

> On the raised couches of Paradise O Lord make us to lie down, and from a chalice of white metal O Lord give us to drink, and of the wine of pleasure to the drinkers Lord make us imbibe. With rare brocade and golden embroidery and silken robes, O Lord, enrobe us, and with the large-eyed *ḥūr*, O Lord, marry us.[2] *Du'ā'* at the beginning of Ramaḍān in *Awrādu Aḥmad at-Tījānī*.

If there are beverages and cups which all hope to quaff, there is also more spiritual thought about the chalice of Paradise, or about two chalices. For before entrance to Paradise the laver of purification must

[1] This echo of 1 Cor. 2.9 is constantly reiterated in Muslim prayer. ash-Shādhilī (*adh-dhikru 'l-kabīr*) seems to attribute it to the Prophet.

[2] The Qur'ānic basis for this prayer is *38*.71; *77*.12–17.

The houris and marriage with them may either be taken as a continuation of earthly pleasure for those who have kept the law on earth but have not acquired the taste for more spiritual joys; or they may be taken as a kind of "muse" or "virtue" like the figures that walk about among men in medieval tales (in the stories of Raymond Lull for instance) or in the *Faery Queen*. There are even "damsels" of the Palace Beautiful in the *Pilgrim's Progress*. In Christian literature these figures do not marry men, but this marriage has been explained by Muslims as a parable of union with the spiritual. On the other hand the modern Aḥmadiyya sect explains the houris as the paradisaic form of the present wives of the believers, an idea that is a little hard to reconcile with the Qur'ānic picture.

be passed, the reservoir or tank (*ḥawḍ*), in which, however, the elect do not seem to lave themselves, but from which they are given to drink by Muḥammad who is its cupbearer. This is the communion of Muḥammad with his people. And there is a further experience (based on Qur'ānic hints in 52.10–26 about the *muqarrabūn*) of a chalice for the inner circle, a communion in which some of our prayers have dared to see God as the Cupbearer of a Holy Grail (its sacrificial nature to them unknown); to which Communion God bring them and us!

The Cup of Communion with Muḥammad

May God make him the Intercessor for us all and give us to drink from his pure Reservoir. *Fatḥu 'r-rasūl*, M. 'Uthmān al-Mirghanī, p. 4.

And at his hands give us to drink. Ibid., p. 75.

Thou shalt come to the Reservoir and drink from it a cup, desirable, clear, that enriches thee with fellowship. *Tashṭīru 'l-qaṣīdati 'l-ḥaḍramiyya.*

Muḥammad the cup-bearer from the Reservoir to created beings. *ad-Durru 'l-fā'iq*, Muṣṭafā al-Bakrī, p. 24.

The Divine Communion

The cup-bearer of the (mystic) people is the Lord of Mankind. . . .

Despair not, for the Cup-bearer of the people ever abideth. *Qaṣīdatun fi lailati 'l-qadr*, *Awrād*, Aḥmad at-Tījānī, p. 9.

That Thou wilt give us to drink a draught from the pure beverage of the people of Thy love. *ad-Durru 'l-fā'iq*, Mustafā al-Bakrī.

A thirsty one, and oh what a thirsty one! Ah may he be nourished with the beverage of being drawn near, and given drink from the beverage of love and made to sip the cups of access (*qurb*). *Wirdu 'ṣ-ṣubḥ*, attributed to 'Abd al-Qādir al-Jīlānī; the same words are also attributed to ash-Shādhilī.

The Summum Bonum

He said to me, O help from the Almighty, if men knew what was after death they would take no pleasure in the life of the world below but would say before Me every moment, every instant, O Lord give me death.

Then he said to me, There is no more companionship and pleasure even in Paradise, once I have appeared there, and no more loneliness and burning in hell once I have addressed its people. *al-Ghawthiyya*, 'Abd al-Qādir al-Jīlānī.

APPENDIX

Appendix I

LIST OF MANUALS STUDIED[1]

	TITLE	ASCRIBED AUTHORSHIP	WHERE BOUGHT
		Alif	
1	*Aḥzābu wa awrādu Aḥmad at-Tījānī*	Aḥmad at-Tījānī	Bombay, Cairo, Omdurman, Tunis
2	*Aḥzābun wa awrādun wa ad'iyatun li 'Abd al-Qādir al-Jīlānī*	'Abd al-Qādir al-Jīlānī	Tunis
3	*Adhkāru 'n-Nawawī*	Muḥyī 'd-dīn an-Nawawī	Cairo
4	*Afḍalu 'ṣ-ṣalawāti 'alā sayyidi 's-sādāt*	Yūsuf b. Ismā'īl an-Nabhānī	Damascus
5	*al-Awrādu 'l-usbū'iyya*	Muḥyī 'd-dīn al-'Arabī	Damascus
6	*Awrādun fatḥiyya* (Urdu-Arabic)		Lahore
		Bā'	
7	*Bashā'iru 'l-khairāt*	'Abd al-Qādir al-Jīlānī	Cairo
8	*Burdatu 'l-madīḥi 'l-mubāraka*	Muḥammad al-Būṣīrī	Cairo
9	*al-Barqu 's-saṭi' fi madḥi 'l-ḥabībi 'sh-shafī'*	Muḥammad al-Makkī (Ismā'īliyya)	Cairo El-'Obeid
10	*Ba'ḍu suwarin mina 'l-Qur'ān . . . wa ba'ḍu aḥzābin li sīdī 'Abd al-Qādir*, etc.		Lahore
		Tā'	
11	*Tashṭīrāt li Burdati 'l-imāmi 'l-Būṣīrī*	Aḥmad ash-Sharqāwī and as-Suyūṭī	Tunis

[1] As has been stated, editions are small and ephemeral. Intending purchasers of such books would do well to enquire of 'Īsā 'l-Bābi 'l Ḥalamī & Co., Shāri'a Khan Ja'far, Cairo. Post Office Box 26. They are the largest publishers of such material which they print for export as well as for local use.

	TITLE	ASCRIBED AUTHORSHIP	WHERE BOUGHT
12	*Tafrīḥu 'l-khāṭiri fī manāqibi . . . 'Abd al-Qādir al-Jīlānī*	Translated from Persian by 'Abd al-Qādir al-'Azalī	Aden
		Jīm	
13	*Jāmi'u 'l-uṣūli fī 'l-awliyā'*	Aḥmad al-Kamshakhānī (Naqshabandī)	Cairo
14	*Jāmi'u 'th-thanā'i 'alā 'llāh*	Yūsuf an-Nabhānī	Baghdad
		Ḥā'	
15	*Ḥasanu 'ṣ-ṣanī'i 'l-badī'i fī madḥi 'n-nabiyyi 'sh-shafī'*	Muḥammad b. Ḥusain ash-Shāmī	Cairo
16	*Ḥirzu 'l-Jawshan*, etc. (Numerous copies sold in the streets as charms)	Given by Gabriel to the Prophet	Cairo, Aden
17	*al-Ḥirzu 'l-manī'i fī 'ṣ-ṣalāti 'alā 'l-ḥabībi 'sh-shafī'*	Jalāl ad-Dīn 'Abd ar-Raḥmān as-Suyūṭī	Cairo
18	*al-Ḥizbu 's-saifī* (also bound with the *awrād* of most of the orders)	'Alī ibn Abī Ṭālib	Damascus
		Khā'	
19	*Khulāṣatu 'l-maghnam* (*Ḥaddādiyya 'Aṭṭāsiyya*)	Al-Ḥabīb 'Alī al-'Aṭṭās	Aden, Cairo
		Dal	
20	*ad-Durratu 'l-fardiyya fī bayāni mabnā 't-ṭarīqati 's-sanūsiyya*	Aḥmad b. Muḥammad as-Sanūsī	Bombay
21	*Durūd Tāj* (Urdu-Arabic)	Various	Lahore
22	*ad-Durūsu 'l-bahiyya fī majmali aḥwāli 'n-nabiyyi wa 'l-a'imma.* (Shī'a)	Ḥasan al-Ḥusainī an-Najafī	Sidon

	TITLE	ASCRIBED AUTHORSHIP	WHERE BOUGHT
23	*Du'ā'u khatmi 'l-Qur'āni 'l-'aẓīm*	Anon.	Bombay
24	*Kanzu 'l-'arsh* (In *Indi—Ganju 'l-'arsh*, universal in India)	Anon.	Delhi, Bombay
25	*Du'ā'u Nūr mutarjam* (Shī'ā)	Anon.	Lahore
26	*Dalā'ilu 'l-khairāt* (Universal)	Muḥammad al-Jazūlī	Istanbul, Cairo, Tunis
27	*Dalā'ilu 'l-khairāti ma'a 'l-aḥzāb*	al-Jazūlī, etc.	Cairo
28	*Dalīlu 'l-Ḥajj*	Muḥammad Ḥusain Makhlūf	Cairo
29	*Dīwānun fī madḥi 'n-nabī*	Abū Zaid al-Fāzāzī	Cairo

Rā'

30	*Rabī'u 'l-fu'ādi fī . . . tartībi 'l-awrād*	'Abd Allāh ash-Sharqāwī	Cairo
31	*Rātibu 'l-Ḥaddād* (*Ḥaddādiyya Ghaṭṭāsiyya*)	'Abd Allāh al-Ḥaddād al-'Alawī	Aden
32	*Rātibu 'l-imāmi 'l-Mahdī*	Muḥammad ibn 'Abdallāh	Bombay, Omdurman
33	*Rawḍu 'l-anwāri . . . fī 'ṣ-ṣalāti . . . 'alā 'n-nabiyyi 'l-mukhtār*	Aḥmad ibn Muḥsin al-'Alawī	Cairo
34	*Riyāḍu 'l-Janna* (also called *Kishāfu 'l-kurūb*)	Yūsuf an-Nabhāni	Cairo
35	*Riyāḍu 'ṣ-ṣāliḥīna min kalāmi sayyidi 'l-mursalīn*	Muḥyī 'd-dīn an-Nawawī	Cairo
36	*Riyāḍu 'l-madīḥ*	Ja'far aṣ-Ṣādiq al-Mirghanī	Cairo, Omdurman

Sīn

37	*Safīnatu 'n-najāti 'l-marḍiyya* (Shādhilī hymns)	Zakariyyā ibn Aḥmad	Cairo

	TITLE	ASCRIBED AUTHORSHIP	WHERE BOUGHT
38	*as-Silsilatu 'dh-dhahabiyyatu fī 't-tawassuli bi 's-sādati 'sh-shādhiliyya*	Muḥammad Aḥmad al-Madanī	Cairo
39	*Sūratu 'l-Kahfi wa Ḥizbu yawmi 'l-jum'a*	Al-Jazūlī (from *Dalā'ilu 'l-khairāt*)	Cairo
40	*Sūratu Yā Sīn wa du'ā'uhā*, etc. (Street leaflets sold at time of Nuṣfu Sha'bān)		Cairo
		Shīn	
41	*Sharḥu 'smi 'llāhi 'l-a'ẓam* (tending to magic)	Aḥmad ibn 'Alī al-Būnī	Jerusalem
42	*Shurūṭu 'ṣ-ṣalāt*	Muḥammad b. 'Abd al-Wahhāb	Damascus
43	*ash-Shāfiyatu li 'l-asqām*	al-Quṭbu 'd-Dajānī	Damascus
		Ṣād	
44	*aṣ-Ṣaḥīfatu 'l-khāmisatu 's-sajjādiyya* (Shī'a breviary)	'Alī Zain al-'Ābidīn, etc. (arranged by Muḥsin al-Ḥusainī)	Baghdad, Damascus
45	*Ṣifātu 'l-'Abīd*	'Abd Allāh Maḥmūd Māḍī	Minya (Egypt)
46	*Ṣafā'u 'l-'Āshiqīn*	"Ba'du 'l-'ārifīn" and others	Alexandria
47	*Ṣalawātun mansūbatun li . . . 'Abd al-Qādir al-Jīlānī*	'Abd al-Qādir al-Jīlānī	Aden, Cairo
		Ṭā'	
48	*Ṭahāratu 'l-qulūbi wa 'l-khuḍū'u li 'allāmi 'l-ghuyūb*	'Abd al-'Azīz ad-Dīrīnī	Cairo
49	*aṭ-Ṭā'ilu mina'l-fuyūḍāti wa 'd-dalā'il*	Muḥammad 'Alī al-Qabbānī (Naqshabandī, Qādirī)	Sidon
		'Ain	
50	*al-'Aṭiyyatu 'l-haniyya*	'Ali Ḥasan al-'Aṭṭās (Ḥaddādiyya)	Aden

	TITLE	ASCRIBED AUTHORSHIP	WHERE BOUGHT
51	*al-ʿIqdu 'l-munaẓẓamu ʿalā ḥurūfi 'l-muʿjam* (Mirghaniyya verse)	ʿAbd Allāh al-Maḥjūb al-Mirghanī	Cairo
52	*al-ʿUqūdu 'l-lu'lu'iyya fī aḥwāli 'sh-shādhiliyya*	Muḥammad al-Bashīr as-Sanūsī	Cairo
53	*ʿAhd-nāma mutarjam* Urdu-Arabic	Abū Bakr aṣ-Ṣiddīq (favourite Shīʿa prayer)	Lahore
		Fā'	
54	*al-Fatḥu 'r-rabbāniyyu fīmā yaḥtāju ilaihi 'l-murīdu 't-tījānī* (*Fatḥu 'r-rasūl*, see under 87)	Muḥammad ibn ʿAbd Allāh aṭ-Ṭasfāwī	Damascus
55	*Fatḥu 'l-karīmi 'l-khāliq* (*sharḥu 'ṣ-ṣalawāti 'l-bakriyya*)	ʿAlī al-Makkī	Baghdad
56	*Fatḥu 'l-kanzi 'l-asnā*	Aḥmad an-Najāra ad-Dimyātī	Baghdad
57	*Fī faḍli lailati nuṣfin min shaʿbān*	Abū 'l-Ḥasan aṣ-Ṣiddīqī	Tunis
58	*Fīmā yaḥtāju ilaihi fī 'l-ʿāmm min adʿiyatin wa ṣalātin wa salām*	Ibrāhīm Arwā	Damascus
59	*al-Fuyūḍātu 'r-rabbāniyyatu fī 'l-ma'āthiri wa'l-awrādi 'l-qādiriyya*	Ismāʿīl b. Muḥammad Saʿīd al-Qādirī	Omdurman, Cairo
		Qāf	
60	*Qiṣṣatu 'l-miʿrāji lil-Mirghanī* (with refrains) (also called *al-ʿUqūdu 'l-fā'iqatu 'd-durriya*)	Jaʿfar aṣ-Ṣādiq al-Mirghanī	Omdurman, Cairo
61	*Qaṣīdatun bur'iyya*, etc.	(Shādhilī verse)	Istanbul
		Kāf	
62	*Kashfu 'l-ḥujūbi 'l-musbala*	ʿAbduh al-ʿAbbāsī as-Suwaidī	Damascus

	TITLE	ASCRIBED AUTHORSHIP	WHERE BOUGHT
63	*al-Kalimu 'ṭ-ṭayyibu min adhkāri 'n-nabī*	Taqī ad-Dīn Abū 'l-'Abbās ad-Dimishqī	Damascus
64	*Kawkabu 'ṣ-ṣabāḥi fī madḥi 'l-muṣṭafā zaini 'l-milāh*	(Compiler) Muḥammad b. Ḥusain ash-Shāmī	Alexandria
65	*al-Kawākibu 'd-durriyya* (*takhmīsu 'l-burda*)	Shamsu 'd-Dīn Muḥammad al-Fayyūmī	Cairo

Lām

66	*Lā thānī*	Arabic-Urdu suras and prayers	Lahore
67	*al-Lu'lu' an-nafīsu 'l-mustakhraju min baḥri Sīdī Aḥmad b. Idrīs*	Muḥammad Amīn al-Ḥasanī	Cairo
68	*Lawāmi'u 'l-bayyināt, sharḥu asmā'i 'llāhi ta'ālā wa 'ṣ-ṣifāt*	Fakhru 'd-Dīn ar-Rāzī	Jerusalem

Mīm

69	*Mujalladunu 'btidā'ī*	First Arabic book with instructions in Shī'a prayers	Bombay
70	*Majmū'atu iḥdā 'ashara rasā'il* (Well-known religious verse and prayers)	No compiler's name	Cairo
71	*Majmū'atu 'l-aḥzāb*	Aḥmad Ḍiyā' ad-Dīn	Istanbul
72	*al-Majmū'atu 'l-mubārakatu fī 'ṣ-ṣalawāti 'l-ma'thūra*	'Abduh Muḥammad Bābā	Cairo
73	*Majmū'atu aḥzābin wa awrādin wa rasā'il* (Sanūsī)	Aḥmad b. Idrīs	Cairo
74	*Majmū'atun sharīfatun muḥtawiyyatun 'alā jumlati awrādin* etc.	Aḥmad b. Idrīs	Bombay, Damascus

	TITLE	ASCRIBED AUTHORSHIP	WHERE BOUGHT
75	*Majmūʿatun mubārakatun fī ṣalawātin mabrūratin*, etc.	ʿAlī Ḥasan ad-Dabbāʿ	Aden
76	*Majmūʿatu 'l-wirdi 'l-ʿāmm li jamīʿi ṭawā'ifi 'l-Islām*	Muḥammad al-Fatḥī al-Marrākushī	Cairo
77	*Majmūʿu 'l-awrādi 'l-kabīri li . . . Muṣṭafā al-Bakrī wa li baʿḍi 'l-ʿārifīn* (Khalwatiyya Sammāniyya)	Muṣṭafā al-Bakrī, etc.	Cairo, Omdurman
78	*Majmūʿu 'l-awrādi 'l-kabīru li . . . Muḥammad ʿUthmān al-Mīrghanī* (Mirghaniyya Khalwatiyya)	Muḥammad ʿUthmān al-Mirghanī	Cairo, Bombay, Aden, Omdurman
79	*Majmūʿu 'l-awrādi 'l-kabīru wa 'l-adʿiyati wa 'l-aḥzābi wa 'l-istighfārāt* (very popular collection from various orders)	No compiler's name	Cairo, Omdurman, Jerusalem, Jaffa Omdurman
80	*Majmūʿu awrādin wa ṣalawātin wa aḥzābin li man arāda 'l-wuṣūla ʿalā ṭarīqati . . . Aḥmād ar-Rifāʿī*	Aḥmad ar-Rifāʿī etc.	
81	*Majmūʿu tabāraka dhū 'l-ʿulā*. (Verse and prayers for Ramaḍān)	No compiler's name	Cairo
82	*Majmūʿu ḥirzi 'l-aqsāmi wa munājāti 'l-qur'āni 'l-ʿaẓīm*	Ḥasan al-Baṣrī, etc.	Aden
83	*Majmūʿu 'r-rawātibi 'l-laṭīfa* (Ḥaddādiyya, ʿAṭṭāsiyya)	ʿAbdallāh ibn ʿAlawī al-Ḥaddād, and others of his family	Aden

	TITLE	ASCRIBED AUTHORSHIP	WHERE BOUGHT
84	*Majmū'u suwarin wa ad'iya*	No compiler's name	Delhi
85	*Majmū'u ṣalawāti wa awrādi sīdī Muṣṭafā 'l-Bakrī* (with *Rabī'u 'l-fu'ād* of 'Abd Allāh ash-Sharqāwī)	Muṣṭafā al-Bakrī	Cairo
86	*Majmū'u 'l-qaṣā'idi wa 'l-ad'iya*	Authors various. No compiler named	Algiers
87	*Majmū'un mushtamilun 'alā fatḥi 'r-rasūl*, etc.	Muḥammad 'Uthmān al-Mirghanī	Cairo
88	*Mukhtaṣaru ad'iyati Ramaḍān* (Shī'a)	Collected by Maṭba'atu 'l-'Irfān, Sidon	Tyre
89	*al-Mukhtārātu 'l-ḥuṣnā fi faḍli wa aḥkāmi Ramaḍān* (Sunnī)	Ḥasan 'Alī Sharīf	Damascus
90	*al-Mafākhiru 'l-'aliyyatu fī 'l-ma'āthiri 'sh-shādhiliyya*	Aḥmad ibn Muḥammad ibn 'Ibād ash-Shāfi'ī	Cairo, Omdurman
91	*Miftaḥu 'l-janan* (Persian Pilgrimage Manual)	No compiler's name	Meshed
92	*Manhalu 'ṣ-ṣafā wa 'l-inshirāḥi fī madīḥi 'l-muṣṭafā zaini 'l-malāḥ*	Muḥammad b. Ḥusain ash-Shāmī	Alexandria
93	*Munājātu sayyidinā 'Isā*	Anon	Beirut
94	*Munājātu sayyidinā Mūsā*	Anon	Damascus, Cairo
95	*Munājāt kalima* (Sunnī prayers in Persian)	Anon	Isfahan
96	*Munājātun maqbūla* (Urdu-Arabic prayers. A favourite collection)	No compiler's name	Lahore

	TITLE	ASCRIBED AUTHORSHIP	WHERE BOUGHT
97	*Mawā'izu bālighatun min zabūri sayyidinā Dāwūd*, etc.	Ya'qūb b. 'Abd ar-Raḥmān al-Mukhtār	Damascus
		Nūn	
98	*Nukhbatu 'd-da'awātin wa 'z-ziyārāt*	Shī'a prayers. No compiler's name	Meshed
99	*an-Naṣīḥatu fī 'l-ad'iyati 'ṣ-ṣaḥīḥa*	'Abd al-Ghanī 'l-Maqdasī	Cairo
100	*Namāz Ja'fariyya* Urdu-Arabic	Shī'a prayers. No compiler's name	Lahore
101	*an-Nūru 'l-barrāqu fī madḥi 'n-nabiyyi 'l-miṣdāq* (Mirghaniyya hymns)	Muḥammad 'Uthmān al-Mirghanī	Omdurman
		Wāw	
102	*al-Wirdu 'l-a'ẓam*	'Alī Muḥammad al-Qārī	Cairo
103	*Al-wirdu 'sh-shāfī*	Compiled from famous prayers by Yūsuf b. Ismā'īl an-Nabhānī	Beirut
104	*al-Wirdu 'l-mukarramu fī 'smi 'llāhi 'l-a'ẓam*	Maḥmūd al-'Askarī	Cairo, Damascus
105	*al-Wasā'ilu 'l-mutaqābilatu fī madḥi 'n-nabī*	Abū Zaid Yakhluftan	Damascus, Beirut
106	*Waṣiyyatu 'l-Muṣṭafā li sayyidinā 'Alī*	From traditions	Tunis
107	*al-Wāqi'atu wa du'ā'uhā*	'Abd al-Qādir al-Jīlānī	Cairo, Omdurman
108	*Yāzida sūrat sharīf ma' du'ā'i qanj il 'arsh* (Arabic-Urdu)		Lahore
109	*Ziyārat Nameh* (Persian pilgrimage prayers)	No compiler's name	Meshed

Appendix 2

SINGLE DEVOTIONS
AND VERY BRIEF TRACTATES FROM THE MANUALS

A complete list would demand too much space, but many of the better known are given below, with numbers referring to those given in the list printed above to the manuals in which they occur.

The mention of an order using these devotions does not necessarily imply that they are confined to that order.

Alif

Abyāt li Sīdī Muḥammad Sirr al-Khatm (Three times weekly. Mirghaniyya)	78
al-Aḥzābu 'l-khamsa: Aḥmad ibn Idrīs	74
al-ad'iyatu 'l-ma'thūra	27 margin
al-ad'iyatu 'n-nabawiyya	78, 99
Adhkāru 'ṣ-ṣubḥ (Mīrghaniyya)	78
Ikhtitām 'ushshāqiyya	71
Istighfāru sayyidinā 'l-Khiḍr (Tījāniyya)	1
al-Istighfāru 'l-kabīr: Aḥmad ibn Idrīs	20, 74, 75, 79
Istighfārun ma'thūr	72
al-Istighfāru 'l-manẓūm (Bakriyya)	85
al-āsās (daily: Mirghaniyya)	78
al-Asmā'u 'l-idrīsiyya (Tījāniyya)	1
al-Asmā'u 'l-ḥuṣnā	18, 27, 49, 73, 75
asmā'u 'n-nabī wa du'ā'uha	49
al-Anwāru'l-mutarākima (Ḥizbu 'l-waẓīfa, Mirghaniyya)	78, 87
al-Awrādu 'l-usbū'iyya (Qādiriyya)	59
Awrādu Aḥmad at-Tījānī dubura 'ṣ-ṣalawāt	1
Awrādu 'l-ayyāmi 's-sab'a (Qādiriyya)	2, 27
Awrādu 'ṭ-ṭarīqati 'l-Aḥmadiyya	74, 75

Tā

at-Tajallī 'l-akbar: Aḥmad ibn Idrīs	73
Tadhkīr shahr Ramaḍān	70
Tartīb qirā'ati 'l-Fātiḥa (Qādiriyya)	55
Tashṭīru 'l-qaṣīdati 'l-ḥaḍramiyya. 'Umar ibn Bakr	10

'Ayn

'Aqīdatu 'l-'awāmm (Ḥaddādiyya)	66

Fā'

Fātiḥatu 'l-awrādi kulliha (Sanūsiyya)	20
Fī 'l-istighāthi bi wāsiṭati 'l-ghawthi 'l-a'ẓam	59

Qāf

Qaṣīdatu tawassulin (Tījāniyya)	1
Qaṣīdatu "'alā bābi khair 'l-khāliq" (Tījāniyya)	1
al-Qaṣīdatu 'l-ghawthīyya (Qādiriyya)	59
al-Qaṣīdatu 'l-mubtahija (Mīrghaniyya)	78
,, 'l-munbahija: Muṣṭafā 'l-Bakrī	77, 85
,, 'l-munfarija	27
,, 'l-munfarija li 'bni 'n-Naḥawī (Ḥaddadiyya)	70, 79
,, 'l-mīmīya: Muṣṭafā 'l-Bakrī	77, 79, 85
,, 'n-nādīya: M. Maṭar al-Ḥakkār (Rifā'iyya)	80
,, 'l-hā'iyya	27
Qaṣīdatu 'l-waṣīl: 'Abd al-Qādir al-Jīlānī	59

Kāf

Al-Kibrītu 'l-aḥmar: 'Abd al-Qādir al-Jīlānī	2
Kalimātu 'l-isti'ādha: Muṣṭafā 'l-Bakrī	77, 85
Kaifiyyatu tilāwati Ḥizbi 'l-baḥr (Qādiriyya)	59
,, Ḥizbi 'l-imāmi 'l-Ghazālī ,,	59
,, aṣ-ṣalāti 'alā 'n-nabī	75

Mīm

al-Maḥāmid (Mirghaniyya)	78
al-Maḥāmidu 'th-thamāniyya: Aḥmad ibn Idrīs	20, 73, 74
al-Musabba'ātu 'l-'ashar: al-Khiḍr *or* Dardīr	1, 48, 59, 77
al-Maghnā: 'Uwais al-Qaranī	1, 20, 73, 74
Munjiyātu 'l-'abīd: M. 'Uthman al-Mīrghanī	87
al-Munājātu 'l-injīliyya: 'Alī Zain al-'Ābidīn	44
Munājātun bi āyāti 'l-Qur'ān: 'Uthmān ibn 'Affān	82
Munājātu 'l-'abīd M. 'Uthmān al-Mirghanī	87
Munājātun 'aẓīma ('Ushshāqīyya)	71
al-Munājātu waqta 's-saḥar (Mīrghaniyya)	78
Manhalu 'sh-shifā': 'Umar ibn Bin Bakr	215
al-Manẓūma: Aḥmad ar-Rifā'ī	82
,, ,, (Bakriyya)	77

GENERAL INDEX

The first words of Arabic book- or prayer-titles are given a capital to distinguish them from similar Arabic phrases in the list not standing for titles.

INDEX OF QUR'ĀN VERSES BASIC FOR THESE DEVOTIONS